Building Blocks of the Future: Unveiling the Potential of 2D Materials

Jack

Table of Contents

Chapter 1: Introduction

The evolution of electronics has become the staple thrust of modern scientific innovation: a need for advancing materials engineered for our equally rapidly advancing needs and computing requirements has fueled recent wealth of new materials.[1,2] Essential to this progress is innovation at a fundamental level. The enmeshment between materials science and chemistry has led to some of the most recent sea changes in this direction: the discovery of graphene as a two-dimensional material in 2004[3], for example.

Here, we use the ideals of exotic materials exploration to survey the landscape of transition metals-based structures. Within this landscape, there lies a lush valley promising exotic and enticing properties: the dimensionally reduced catalog of 2D materials. Various exotic properties have been mined from them, including metals and semimetals, variable band-gap semiconductors, insulators,[4–6] superconductivity[7–10], charge density waves[11,12], and magnetism.[13–15] These can be referred to as van der Waals compounds (vdW), which are signified by anisotropy in the intraplanar front and relatively weak vdW boding in the third dimension. We benefit from this scheme, first truly manifested in graphene, by having more control over layer number through various methods of exfoliation. The work presented here relies on mechanical exfoliation by the Scotch tape or "magic tape method."

Due to the isolation of these materials down to the monolayer (1 layer) or few-layers (<10 layers, the lower limit of bulk distinction), we can simultaneously innovate technologically *and* on a more fundamental basis.

1.1 2D Materials

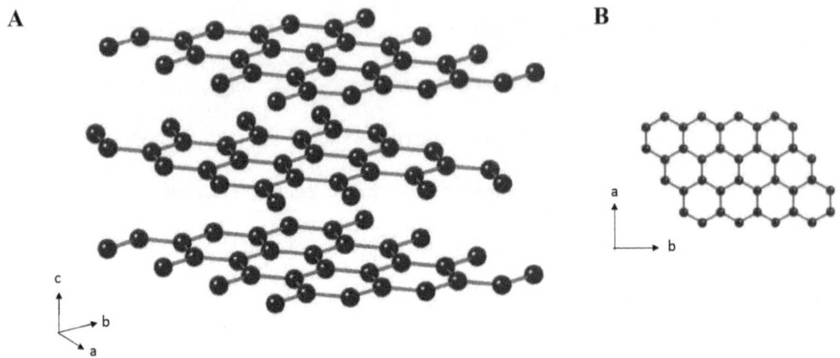

(A) The hierarchical structure of bulk graphite, a layered carbon-based vdW compound. The bonding between layers along the c-direction is weak (van der Waals force) as compared to the relatively stronger intralayer covalent bonds between carbon atoms. (B) A bird's eye view from the top of the hexagonal structure of single layer graphene. Covalent bonding extends along the

Previous to 2004, experimental realization of monolayer/truly 2D states did not occur, partially explained by adherence to the Mermin theorem that predicted stable 2D materials were limited by prohibitively large thermal fluctuations within the crystal lattice[16]. Later garnering a Nobel prize, Geim and Novoselov's 2004 work to isolate and identify large flakes of graphene[5] derived from bulk graphite demonstrated that vdW materials could be exfoliated down to the monolayer and persist; the details of this structure are featured in Figure 1.1[17].

Upon discovery that Mermin's limitations could be overcome, a flurry of research showed that this class of 2D, vdW materials offer vastly different and exotic surface properties to their higher-dimensional counterparts.[4] VdW materials can be identified by their layered, sheet like structure: they are laterally much broader (nm-μm size) with vertical thicknesses in the atomic size regime (down to 1 atomic layer) with the advantage of phenomenally large surface area upon exfoliation.

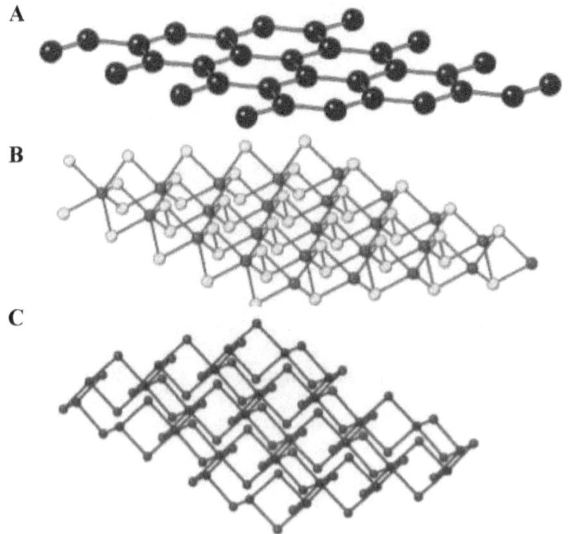

Figure 1. 1: Evolution of 2D vdW materials from graphene to MoS₂ to CrI₃.

(A) Geim and Novoselov's 2004 discovery of graphene paved the way for further exploration in the 2D space, leading to (B) MoS_2 as the paragon of semiconducting vdW systems established in 2010. (C) Finally, in 2017, CrI_3 led the way to show that 2D intrinsic magnetic materials could be experimentally realized.

2D morphological properties manifest in low charge carrier scattering; and tunable optoelectronic functionality based on layer number, charge impurities, defects, temperature, substrate, and localized states. Many of these can be attributed to the strong in-plane covalent coupling and weak interlayer vdW coupling, with electronic band strongly correlated to the thickness of layers.

1.1.1 Magnetic 2D materials

Due to the anisotropic bonding and subsequent weak bonding between layers, vdW are exceedingly ripe for exfoliation down to monolayer limits. We simultaneously see the evolution of layer controlled properties with emergent phenomena. Despite 13 years of materials exploration in this class of materials, no intrinsically magnetic vdW were isolated until 2017 when Xiaodong Xu's group published its ground-breaking results concerning CrI_3[13,18] and Cr_2GeTe_6[19], two insulating intrinsic magnetic vdW systems. Similar to the principal of the Mermin theorem, the Mermin-Wagner amended theorem predicted that intrinsic 2D magnets would are inherently stable due to thermal fluctuations in the long-order magnetic lattice; these become stabilized in the presence of magnetic anisotropy.[20]

Thus far, available magnetic compounds fail to address important practical concerns: low magnetic transition temperatures (61 K in the bulk and 45 K in the monolayer)[13], insulating or metallic bandgaps[13,21,22], or issues with air-sensitivity[23–27]. Growing air stable magnetic compounds with high transition temperatures is vital. Of equal significance is producing magnetic compounds with strong magnetoelectrical coupling that have a high degree of tunability.[28]

With the acceleration of nanofabrication techniques and the 2007 Nobel recognition of giant magnetoresistance[29],the scope of applications for intrinsically magnetic materials has expanded from MRAM*[30] to ultrafast electrical writing and reading[31], bistable relativistic tunneling anisotropic magnetoresistance[32], magnetic cloaking,[33] evidence of radiation hardness, rapidly evolving approaches to optimization,[27,28,31] and perhaps even lossless spin transmission.[34] Advancing the field of spintronics in a meaningful way requires growing and characterizing materials with properties more favorable for applications.

To this end, we searched through the catalogue of vdW materials for a candidate that would provide a high degree of tunability in terms of electronic properties upon electrostatic or chemical doping. [35]A variety of other layered magnetic compounds have drawn interest for their potential to retain magnetic properties down to the monolayer, but the most promising candidate we identified in the Roy group was chromium sulfide bromide (CrSBr), an FeOCl-type bulk antiferromagnet last explored in the early 1990's.[36] It showed high T_N (132 K), high magnetic susceptibility, crystalline anisotropy, and air stability; however, its 2D properties remained unexamined until the exploration described in this book, and forms the bulk of the work presented here.

Although initially dismissed as intellectually stimulating but essentially useless by Louis Néel in his 1970 Nobel lecture,[37] recent literature has proven that AMs offer many advantages and opportunities to manipulate spins in electronics as compared to ferromagnets (FM) or paramagnets (PM). AM materials have potential for superior ultrafast operation (often many orders of magnitudes higher than typical ferromagnetic values)[38], softer conditions[39], THz spin speeds [40] versus gHz speeds,[38] high packing density because of the absence of stray magnetic fields,[30] robustness against external magnetic fields,[41] and require low power due to predicted long spin-diffusion energies[42] to leading FM materials.

1.2 Discussion of Chapter Divisions

The next chapter, Chapter 2, describes the general methods of synthesis and analysis used in the following chapters (Chapters 3-12). The synthetic methods form the basis of the catalogue of my work at Columbia University.

1.2.1 Chromium Sulfur Bromide

The material focused upon in Chapter 3-9, CrSBr, was initially made by Johannes Beck in 1990.[36] He was tremendously helpful in articulating the details of his process through a personal correspondence. We have addressed this in our work by exploring chromium sulfide bromide (CrSBr), a layered compound isostructural to the chromium oxyhalide family,[43] that can be isolated in two-dimensional air-stable sheets. I describe my amended method in Chapter 2, as well as our approach to exfoliation.

Chapters 2-9 will focus on CrSBr, from characterizing the system to eventually integrating it within device frameworks. In Chapter 3, I introduce the material and its chemical characteristics. We explored it in the bulk in order to map out its larger characteristics and giant magnetoresistance. Through transport, scanning tunneling microscopy and spectroscopy, and optical measurements, we find that CrSBr is a semiconductor with an electronic band gap of $\Delta E \sim 1.5$ eV. Through magnetometry, we show that in the bulk, CrSBr is an A-type antiferromagnet with a Néel temperature of 132 K; below this temperature, the system is interplanar antiferromagnetic — alternating layers presenting opposing moments — and intraplanar ferromagnetic. Additional measurements demonstrate the strong coupling between CrSBr's electronic and magnetic properties, showing a large magnetoresistance. We establish the robustness of this material, as air-stable down to two layers — a unique property in contrast to current leading intrinsic 2D magnetics.

Chapter 4 further explores this material's properties into the second dimension, exploring the manifestation of its electronic and magnetic properties down to the monolayer and up to nine layers, the bulk limit. In the first study of its kind on this system, we demonstrate electrostatic and magnetic control of electronic transport by gating to achieve giant negative magnetoresistance in layers 2-9 and finally large positive magnetoresistance in the monolayer. Tunability through electrostatic gating shows the carrier mediated mechanism in which the ferromagnetic coupling of defects is manifested. In combination with SQUID magnetometry, we are able to paint a fuller picture of the ferromagnetic ordering of defects within the CrSBr system, and their impacts on the magnetic behavior we see (further explored in Chapter 6).

In Chapter 5, CrSBr is further probed by SHG; while more traditional techniques have proven useful in studying the higher-level implications of spin behavior, they have not been able to probe magnetic symmetry. In 2013, SHG was shown to be a powerful tool through which to probe symmetry properties of few-layer MoS2 and h-BN from work pioneered at Columbia. Later, SHG was utilized in the CrI3 system to study out of plane moments through examining electric dipole mechanism dominated symmetry. However, CrSBr greatly differs in that its moments are in-plane, calling for SHG that *can* probe the ferromagnetic monolayer: magnetic dipole SHG. We use this methodology to show through an opto-electronic lens that CrSBr are ferromagnetically ordered below 146 K and in the multilayer, these ferromagnetic monolayers are coupled antiferromagnetically. Significantly, the Néel temperature increases with decreasing layer number in stark contrast to other currently available analogous materials.

Continuing on, we explore the role of more nuanced and finer details within the CrSBr system; particularly, the role of bromine-focused defects (Chapter 6) and interlayer electronic coupling (Chapter 7). In Chapter 6, we produce defects first by heating samples to induce mass loss through thermal annealing. This contrived Br weight loss and a dramatic increase in interlayer conductivity — pointing to Br deficiency as the main culprit behind sample-to-sample performance variation. We eliminate structural changes as a contributor, instead showing that polarons and s-d exchange are responsible for the production of positive magnetoresistance in monolayer CrSBr. Additionally, we intentionally introduce Br deficiency into synthesis by producing sub-stoichiometric $CrSCl_xBr_{1-x}$ (x=.17 and .33). By producing an equivalent system with less bromine, we can probe the effect that this produces in coupling, yielding a lower Weiss constant and weaker intralayer ferromagnetic correlations. This work was achieved using PPMS and SQUID magnetometry in concert with electronic transport measurements.

The last chapter to study the intrinsic properties of CrSBr, Chapter 7, examines the role of magneto-excitons within the electronic structure of the system. There is a robust amount of research on 2D materials in which magneto-excitons persist; here, we show that the strongly coupled magneto-electronic properties of CrSBr make it a unique agent of excitonic tuning — an alluring asset. Polarization-resolved optical spectroscopy and PL as seen in differently layer magnitudes with magnetic field sweeps, and RMCD confirmation were used to show that the interlayer magnetic coupling is solely responsible for magneto-excitonic behavior. First, there is a distinct lack of change in behavior seen by PL when sweeping an applied magnetic external field to the FM monolayer; once we reach the bilayer and above, a strong dependence is observed. In effect, we can take advantage of CrSBr's interlayer electronic coupling can be used as a "knob" by which to engineer this semiconductor's excitonic nature through magnetic order switching brought on by applying a magnetic field to different degrees ordained by layer number.

1.2.2 Expansion upon CrSBr

From this point, I make a step into the utilization of CrSBr within externalized systems, straying from study in a more segregated context. In atomically thin vdW materials magnetic proximity effects become dominant, as even short-range effects exceed the thickness of contiguous 2D crystals[44]. Proximity of 2D magnets can break time reversal symmetry in non-magnetic 2D materials, leading to valley polarization in transition metal dichalcogenides, quantum anomalous Hall effect in topological insulators, and other emerging phenomena including multiferroicity and topological superconductivity[2] Obviously, as a compound with great potential as a spintronics font, it is of great importance to make an evolved advance into applications. I sent samples of pristine bulk CrSBr crystals to Talieh S. Ghiasi at the University of Groningen, Netherlands. She used these crystals as an augment to bilayer graphene in a proximity-induced exchange interaction device, with a three-terminal spin-valve measurement architecture in which CrSBr served as the terminals. In this context, graphene's spin transport sensitivity is its greatest asset: we see high sensitivity, spin-polarization of conductivity up to 14% and spin-dependent Seebeck effect in the now magnetic graphene. CrSBr is used to control this aspect through its antiferromagnetic spin-charge coupling/antiferromagnetic nature. It excels here as a way in which to engineer and modulate these aforementioned properties, steering the way to ultra-thin magnetic memory and sensory devices.

In Chapter 9, CrSBr is exposed to strong strain through a unique arrangement engineered by the team at University of Washington. Tuning such material parameters as interlayer separation or stacking order via the application of pressure or strain is an effective method for controlling magnetism in vdW materials[45]. For instance, hydrostatic pressure of 1 GPa significantly affects Curie temperature of $Cr_2Ge_2Te_6$[46], while higher pressures reorient its spins from out-of-plane to in-plane[47]. Furthermore, interlayer exchange coupling depends on layer separation and stacking order which can both be tuned by hydrostatic pressure – as seen in hBN/graphene/CrI$_3$/graphene/hBN heterostructures, pressure induces an AF-to-FM transition in bilayer CrI$_3$[48,49]. Nanoscale structural modifications also induce switching between ferromagnetic and antiferromagnetic ordering, as was in the case of magnetic transition and enhanced magnetization observed in hBN- or graphene-encapsulated CrI$_3$ flakes indented with a diamond scanning probe[50]. Another possibility in controlling magnetism in vdW materials is through strain[45]. A FM phase transition at room temperature is predicted in CrWI$_6$ and CrWGe$_2$Te$_6$ monolayers subjected to an in-plane tensile strain[51], while monolayer chromium trihalides show AF phase transition upon a compressive strain[52]. Tensile strain has traditionally been a harder mode of extrinsic stimulus to apply; for the first time, it is applied in uniaxial, constant, in-situ manner at cryogenic temperature. When CrSBr is exposed to critical strain of ~1.2%, even with zero magnetic field applied, there is a transition from antiferromagnetic to ferromagnetic ordering. Once again, interlayer magnetic exchange is the mechanism through which this change evolves.

1.2.3 Other 2-Dimensional Works

Finally, the last three chapters are a demonstration of my work within the 2D materials field but outside of the realm of CrSBr. My initial interest in this field was sparked by our work on superatomic solids; first, in clusters of the Chevrel class. As my prowess grew into solid state synthesis, my work developed into collaborations on $Mo_6S_3Br_6$, $Re_6Se_8Cl_2$ and eventually $TaFeTe_4$. In Chapter 10 and 11, I focus on the former and in Chapter 12, the latter.

1.2.3.1 2D Chevrel Phases: $Mo_6S_3Br_6$ and $Re_6Se_8Cl_2$

Superatoms, or atomic clusters, are important hierarchical building blocks: the atomic precision with which they can be assembled and their tunable intercluster coupling hold much potential for utilization as a new basis for 2D materials. Chevrel phases are acutely modular: described as $[M_6L_8]L'_6$ (M: transition metal and L,L': chalcogen or halogen bridging ligands); with the appropriate number of ligands per M6 cluster (<14), the isolated units start to form a 1-,2-, or 3-dimensional structure. Through synthetic methods and materials choice, we can use this information to get to

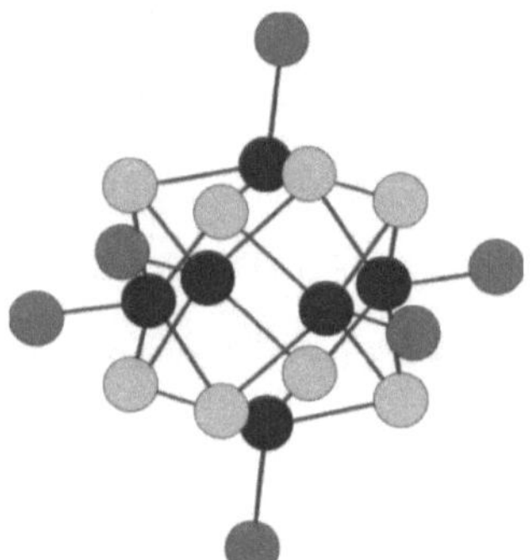

Figure 1. 2: Chevrel octahedron A classic representation of $M_6L_8L'_6$ octahedral Chevrel phase superatomic cluster unit. The colors represent as follows: navy, M; pink, L; green, L'.

compounds in which dimensionality is rationally designed. My work has been focused on two such Chevrel phase 2D semiconductors — $Mo_6S_3Br_6$ and $Re_6Se_8Cl_2$.

Due to synthetic bottlenecks, $Mo_6S_3Br_6$ has remained largely unstudied. In Chapter 10, we reference a new method of synthesis that yields millimeter-sized crystals (described in depth in

Chapter 2) large enough to mechanically exfoliate and subsequently study in both the bulk and few layers. SCXRD and AFM are used to study the structure and post-exfoliation arrangement of $Mo_6S_3Br_6$, which is based on an $[Mo_6]$ octahedral unit surrounded by a sulfur-bromide cage and connected to each other. Through STS and first-principle calculations, we show that $Mo_6S_3Br_6$ is in-plane anisotropic with a direct gap of 1.6 eV. By using polarization-dependent Raman we confirm its strong in-plane anisotropy; by DFT, we show this is due to its pseudo-1D electronic structure. This specific structure is particular use within the 2D regime, as it boosts its directionality, a tuning knob that differentiates it from more quotidian superatomic solids.

Next, in Chapter 10, I cast $Re_6Se_8Cl_2$ in a similar light as $Mo_6S_3Br_6$ as tunable optoelectronic candidates, potentially appliable as light emitters, photodetectors, or solar cells in a similar role as transition metal dichalcogenides due to their electron dynamics and quantum efficiency. $Re_6Se_8Cl_2$ and $Mo_6S_3Br_6$ are both semiconductors with 1.49 eV and 1.65 eV bandgaps respectively. Their applicability rests upon their Auger dynamics — this process is an essential recombination process in which an electron and a hole recombine. Instead of emitting a photon, they release excess energy to a third carrier. These dynamics are probed here by ultrafast terahertz photoconductivity measurements. We show that each material has high local carrier mobilities in the 100 cm2/Vs range; $Mo_6S_3Br_6$ has an Auger lifetime over and order of magnitude faster than the carriers we see in $Re_6Se_8Cl_2$.

1.2.3.2 Weyl Semimetal: $TaFeTe_4$

The final chapter of this work, Chapter 12, explores $TaFeTe_4$ as a Weyl semimetal (in which Weyl nodes are present in the topology). Weyl fermions have been subject of great interest for years, first predicted in 1929; one of the three classes of fermions amongst Dirac and Majorana types, there has been a significant amount of work in an attempt to realize Weyl nodes in practical materials. They were only proven to exist in 2014 through angle-resolved photoemission spectroscopy and realized in 2015 with tantalum arsenide. In an attempt to move this topologically exotic sect into the 2D realm, we have synthesized $TaFeTe_4$. $TaFeTe_4$ is a polytypic system composed of alternating stripes of two TMDCS: $TaTe_2$, a metal, and $FeTe_2$, a semiconductor. Both α-$TaFeTe_4$ and β-$TaFeTe_4$ are synthesized; the latter having been prepared within this work for the first time ever. In concert, these produce strongly anisotropic in plane electronic transport; in the alpha analogue, we see anisotropy up to 250%. We use a combination of SCXRD, AFM, optical spectroscopy to qualify them. Computational methods predict that β-$TaFeTe_4$ is an ideal candidate for a Weyl semimetal as a result of Weyl nodes. Future work will focus on achieving more complete conversion from α-$TaFeTe_4$ to β-$TaFeTe_4$ to be able to fully study this exciting new Weyl opportunity.

1.3 References

1. Duan, X., Wang, C., Pan, A., Yu, R. & Duan, X. Chem Soc Rev Two-dimensional transition metal dichalcogenides as atomically thin semiconductors : opportunities and challenges. *Chem. Soc. Rev.* **44**, 8859–8876 (2015).
2. Gong, C. & Zhang, X. Two-dimensional magnetic crystals and emergent heterostructure devices. *Science (80-.).* **363**, (2019).
3. Novoselov, K. S. *et al.* Electric Field Effect in Atomically Thin Carbon Films. *Science (80-.).* **306**, 666 LP – 669 (2004).
4. Novoselov, K. S., Mishchenko, A., Carvalho, A. & Castro Neto, A. H. 2D materials and van der Waals heterostructures. *Science (80-.).* **353**, aac9439 (2016).
5. Novoselov, K. S. *et al.* Two-dimensional atomic crystals. *Proc. Natl. Acad. Sci.* **102**, 10451–10453 (2005).
6. Geim, A. K. & Grigorieva, I. V. Van der Waals heterostructures. *Nat. 2013 4997459* **499**, 419–425 (2013).
7. Tsen, A. W. *et al.* Nature of the quantum metal in a two-dimensional crystalline superconductor. *Nat. Phys. 2015 123* **12**, 208–212 (2015).
8. Xi, X. *et al.* Ising pairing in superconducting NbSe 2 atomic layers. *Nat. Phys. 2015 122* **12**, 139–143 (2015).
9. Lee, M. *et al.* Study of charge density waves in suspended 2H-TaS2 and 2H-TaSe2 by nanomechanical resonance. *Appl. Phys. Lett.* **118**, 193105 (2021).
10. Benyamini, A. *et al.* Fragility of the dissipationless state in clean two-dimensional

superconductors. *Nat. Phys. 2019 159* **15**, 947–953 (2019).

11. Tsen, A. W. *et al.* Structure and control of charge density waves in two-dimensional 1T-TaS2. *Proc. Natl. Acad. Sci.* **112**, 15054–15059 (2015).

12. Xi, X. *et al.* Strongly enhanced charge-density-wave order in monolayer NbSe 2. *Nat. Nanotechnol. 2015 109* **10**, 765–769 (2015).

13. Huang, B. *et al.* Layer-dependent ferromagnetism in a van der Waals crystal down to the monolayer limit. *Nature* **546**, 270–273 (2017).

14. Jiang, S., Li, L., Wang, Z., Mak, K. F. & Shan, J. Controlling magnetism in 2D CrI 3 by electrostatic doping. *Nat. Nanotechnol.* **13**, 549–553 (2018).

15. Gong, C. *et al.* Discovery of intrinsic ferromagnetism in two-dimensional van der Waals crystals. *Nature* **546**, 265–269 (2017).

16. Mermin, N. D. Crystalline Order in Two Dimensions. *Phys. Rev.* **176**, 250 (1968).

17. Vadlamani, B., An, K., Jagannathan, M. & Chandran, K. S. R. An In-Situ Electrochemical Cell for Neutron Diffraction Studies of Phase Transitions in Small Volume Electrodes of Li-Ion Batteries. *J. Electrochem. Soc.* **161**, A1731 (2014).

18. Huang, B. *et al.* Electrical control of 2D magnetism in bilayer CrI3. *Nat. Nanotechnol.* **13**, 544–548 (2018).

19. Xing, W. *et al.* Electric field effect in multilayer Cr2Ge2Te6 : a ferromagnetic 2D material. *2D Mater.* **4**, 24009 (2017).

20. Wilson, N. P. *et al.* Interlayer Electronic Coupling on Demand in a 2D Magnetic Semiconductor. (2021).

21. Fei, Z. *et al.* Two-dimensional itinerant ferromagnetism in atomically thin Fe3GeTe2. *Nat. Mater.* **17**, 778–782 (2018).

22. Verzhbitskiy, I. A. *et al.* Controlling the magnetic anisotropy in Cr2Ge2Te6 by electrostatic gating. *Nat. Electron.* **3**, 460–465 (2020).

23. Wang, X. *et al.* Raman spectroscopy of atomically thin two-dimensional magnetic iron phosphorus trisulfide (FePS3) crystals. *2D Mater.* **3**, (2016).

24. Lin, M. W. *et al.* Ultrathin nanosheets of CrSiTe3: A semiconducting two-dimensional ferromagnetic material. *J. Mater. Chem. C* **4**, 315–322 (2016).

25. Yi, J. *et al.* Competing antiferromagnetism in a quasi-2D itinerant ferromagnet: Fe3GeTe2. *2D Mater.* **4**, (2017).

26. Deng, Y. *et al.* Gate-tunable room-temperature ferromagnetism in two-dimensional Fe3GeTe2. *Nature* vol. 563 94–99 (2018).

27. Lee, J. U. *et al.* Ising-Type Magnetic Ordering in Atomically Thin FePS3. *Nano Lett.* **16**, 7433–7438 (2016).

28. Jungwirth, T., Marti, X., Wadley, P. & Wunderlich, J. Antiferromagnetic spintronics. *Nat. Nanotechnol.* **11**, 231–241 (2016).

29. Grünberg, P. A. Nobel lecture: From spin waves to giant magnetoresistance and beyond: The 2007 Nobel Prize for Physics was shared by Albert Fert and Peter Grünberg. This paper is the text of the address given in conjunction with the award. *Rev. Mod. Phys.* **80**, 1531–1540 (2008).

30. Baltz, V. *et al.* Antiferromagnetic spintronics. *Rev. Mod. Phys.* **90**, 15005 (2018).

31. Shick, A. B., Khmelevskyi, S., Mryasov, O. N., Wunderlich, J. & Jungwirth, T. Spin-orbit coupling induced anisotropy effects in bimetallic antiferromagnets: A route towards antiferromagnetic spintronics. *Phys. Rev. B - Condens. Matter Mater. Phys.* **81**, 1–4 (2010).

32. Mcguire, T. R. & Potter, R. I. Anisotropic Magnetoresistance in Ferromagnetic 3D Alloys.

IEEE Trans. Magn. **11**, 1018–1038 (1975).

33. Coey, J. M. D. Louis Néel: Retrospective (invited). *J. Appl. Phys.* **93**, 8224–8229 (2003).

34. Serga, A. A., Chumak, A. V. & Hillebrands, B. YIG magnonics. *J. Phys. D. Appl. Phys.* **43**, (2010).

35. Flatté, M., Byers, J. & Lau, W. Spin Dynamics in Semiconductors. in 107–145 (2002). doi:10.1007/978-3-662-05003-3_4.

36. Beck, J. Über Chalkogenidehalide des Chroms. Synthese, Kristallstruktur und Magnetismus von Chromsulfidbromid, CrSBr. *Z. anorg. allg. Chem.* **685**, 157–167 (1990).

37. Néel, L. Magnetism and local molecular field. *Science (80-.).* **174**, 985–992 (1971).

38. Fiebig, M. *et al.* Ultrafast magnetization dynamics of antiferromagnetic compounds. *J. Phys. D. Appl. Phys.* **41**, (2008).

39. Máca, F. *et al.* Room-temperature antiferromagnetism in CuMnAs. *J. Magn. Magn. Mater.* **324**, 1606–1612 (2012).

40. Olejník, K. *et al.* Terahertz electrical writing speed in an antiferromagnetic memory. *Sci. Adv.* **4**, 1–9 (2018).

41. Železný, J., Wadley, P., Olejník, K., Hoffmann, A. & Ohno, H. Spin transport and spin torque in antiferromagnetic devices. *Nat. Phys.* **14**, 220–228 (2018).

42. Lebrun, R. *et al.* Tunable long-distance spin transport in a crystalline antiferromagnetic iron oxide. *Nature* **561**, 222–225 (2018).

43. Christensen, A. N., Johansson, T. & Quézel, S. Preparation and Magnetic Properties of CrOCl. *Acta Chem. Scand.* **28a**, 1171–1174 (1974).

44. Huang, P. *et al.* Recent advances in two-dimensional ferromagnetism: Materials synthesis, physical properties and device applications. *Nanoscale* **12**, 2309–2327 (2020).

45. Huang, B. *et al.* Emergent phenomena and proximity effects in two-dimensional magnets and heterostructures. *Nature Materials* vol. 19 1276–1289 (2020).

46. Sun, Y. *et al.* Effects of hydrostatic pressure on spin-lattice coupling in two-dimensional ferromagnetic Cr2Ge2Te6. *Appl. Phys. Lett.* **112**, 072409 (2018).

47. Lin, Z. *et al.* Pressure-induced spin reorientation transition in layered ferromagnetic insulator Cr2Ge2Te6. *Phys. Rev. Mater.* **2**, 051004 (2018).

48. Song, T. *et al.* Switching 2D magnetic states via pressure tuning of layer stacking. *Nat. Mater.* **18**, 1298–1302 (2019).

49. Li, T. *et al.* Pressure-controlled interlayer magnetism in atomically thin CrI3. *Nat. Mater.* **18**, 1303–1308 (2019).

50. Thiel, L. *et al.* Probing magnetism in 2D materials at the nanoscale with single-spin microscopy. *Science (80-.).* **364**, 973–976 (2019).

51. Huang, C. *et al.* Toward Intrinsic Room-Temperature Ferromagnetism in Two-Dimensional Semiconductors. *J. Am. Chem. Soc.* **140**, 11519–11525 (2018).

52. Webster, L. & Yan, J. A. Strain-tunable magnetic anisotropy in monolayer CrCl3, CrBr3, and CrI3. *Phys. Rev. B* **98**, 144411 (2018).

Chapter 2: General Methods

2.1 Synthetic Methods

The synthetic basis of my work generally follows the "shake and bake" method, in conjunction with chemical vapor transport. This is generally the oldest, simplest, and most common method of solid-state synthesis:[1] mix together reactants and then heat in a furnace. Variations in this method can involve first having to mix/grind together by mortar and pestle, pellet pressing, involving solutions, auto transport, and more complex annealing processes. These steps are oft-required because these reactants require a high level of processing to homogeneously interact, which occurs *in situ* either by liquid- or gas-phase transport (e.g., what we see with chemical vapor transport) or by solid state diffusion. This general technique is deceptively simple; despite its humble nomenclature, long incubation times are required and experimentation to achieve the desired product can be arduous and sometimes fruitless but can yield new, exotic, and exciting compounds.

In my work, I have managed to synthesize, expand upon, and even develop different 2D compounds. The compounds made in this work were made first by combining the reactants in a glovebox under an inert atmosphere with minimal O_2 and H_2O impurities. Next, they were introduced into a quartz tube, attached to a vacuum adapter, and sealed under vacuum once attached to an external in-hood vacuum manifold by acetylene torch.

2.1.1 Chromium Sulfur Halides

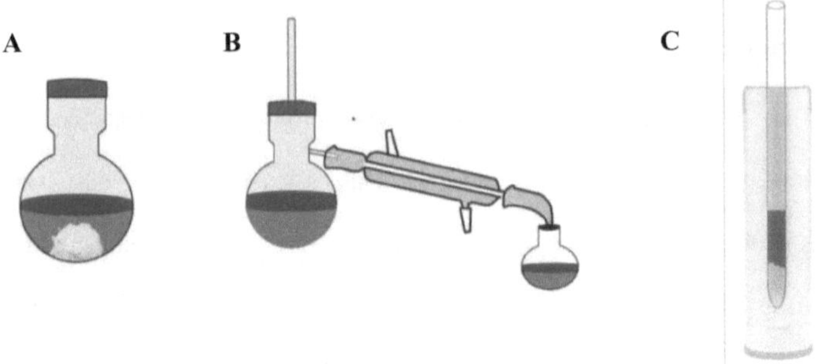

Figure 2. 1 Chromium sulfur bromide synthetic process.
(A) The S_2Br_2 reagent is produced in a pressure vessel. (B) S_2Br_2 is distilled under vacuum at 40 ˚C. (C) The tube is sealed by submerging the bottom under liquid N_2 while attached to a vacuum manifold.

2.1.1.1 CrSBr

CrSBr was originally made by Johannes Beck using chemical vapor transport in a one-zone oven heated from 1023 K to 1223 K using a 7:13 molar ratio of S_2Br_2:Cr.[2] The synthesis described therein was helpful as a beginning point, but required re-tooling in the equipment available at Columbia. By changing the reaction times, ratios, and temperature differential between the hot and cold zones as well as the intermediate zone, I was able to increase CrSBr production in each tube. In the spirit of full discretion, only very recently, a new method has been developed by J. Luxa at the University of Chemistry and Technology Prague with direct combination of the elements in a stoichiometric ratio to eliminate excess S_2Br_2.[3]

CrSBr single crystals were synthesized using a modified chemical vapor transport approach adapted from the original report by Beck[2]. Disulfur dibromide (S_2Br_2) and chromium metal were added together in a 7:13 molar ratio to a fused silica tube approximately 35 cm in length, which was sealed under vacuum and placed in a three-zone tube furnace. The tube was heated in a temperature gradient (1223 to 1123 K) for 120 hours. CrSBr grows as black, shiny flat needles along with $CrBr_3$ and Cr_2S_3 as side products. CrSBr crystals were cleaned first by washing in warm pyridine, water, and acetone, and then by mechanical exfoliation to ensure no impurities remained on the surface.

2.1.1.2 Chloride-substituted $CrSBr_xCl_{1-x}$

The mixed halide analogues were made by substituting in stoichiometric amounts of S_2Cl_2 for S_2Br_2 at ratios of 1:5 and 1:2 to produce $CrSBr_{.83}Cl_{.17}$ and $CrSBr_{.67}Cl_{.33}$ respectively. The ratios of sulfur halides (S2Br2:S2Cl2:Cr) were thus 5.83:1.17:13 and 4.67:2.33:13 for $CrSBr_{.83}Cl_{.17}$ and $CrSBr_{.67}Cl_{.33}$ respectively . The same heating regime was applied as for CrSBr with the 1223 to 1123 K gradient for 120 hours in a 3-zone furnace.

2.1.2 Chevrel phases

2.1.2.1 $Mo_6S_3Br_6$

$Mo_6S_3Br_6$ was prepared in the following procedure, modified from Perrin et al. [4] A stoichiometric mixture of Mo_6Br_{12}[5] (200 mg, 0.13 mmol), S (25 mg, 0.78 mmol), Mo (70 mg, 0.73 mmol) and Nb (6 mg, 0.06 mmol) was ground with a mortar and pestle in an inert atmosphere, pressed into a pellet and sealed in a quartz tube under vacuum. The tube was then heated to 1175 °C in a box furnace with a ramp rate of 1 °C/min, held for 72 hours at the reaction temperature, and finally cooled to room temperature at a ramp of 0.5 °C/min. Millimeter-size crystals of $Mo_6S_3Br_6$ are deposited in the cooler region of the tube.

2.1.2.2 $Re_2Se_8Cl_2$

$Re_2Se_8Cl_2$ was prepared by grinding together Re, Se, and ReCl5 in an inert atmosphere in a molar ratio of 1.7:2.4:0.5. This mixture was then pelletized and deposited in a quartz tube to be sealed under vacuum. Chemical transport was achieved with the included $ReCl_5$; the tube was heated to 1100° C in approximately 18 hours, then maintained at that temperature for 72 hours. After being cooled to room temperature in ambient conditions, the excess $ReCl_5$ that gets deposited on the desired crystals by setting a temperature gradient of 300 to 25° C for approximately three hours, as previously demonstrated.[6]

2.1.3 TaFeTe$_4$

2.1.3.1 Synthesis of α-TaFeTe$_4$

Single crystals of α-TaFeTe$_4$ were prepared by chemical vapor transport. Tantalum, iron, tellurium, and $TeCl_4$ powders were combined in a 1:1:3:0.04 mole ratio, pressed into a pellet, and sealed in a quartz tube (7 mm in diameter and approximately 35 cm in length) under vacuum. The quartz ampule was loaded into a three-zone furnace with a temperature gradient from 700 to 500 °C. After eight days, thin crystals with rectangular or needle-like habits and metallic luster were obtained in the cold end of the tube. The crystals were washed with dry dichloromethane followed by dry hexanes to ensure no impurities remained on the surface of the crystals. For structural determination by single-crystal X-ray diffraction, 400 mg of α-TaFeTe$_4$ was ground, pressed into a pellet, and loaded into a quartz tube with ~20 mg of I_2. The tube was sealed (7 mm in diameter and approximately 20 cm in length) under vacuum and heated in a tube furnace to 950 °C for seven days.

2.1.3.2 Conversion of α-TaFeTe$_4$ to β-TaFeTe$_4$

Crystals of β-TaFeTe$_4$ were prepared by sealing α-TaFeTe$_4$ (unground and unpelletized) in a quartz tube (approximately 20 cm in length) under vacuum. The quartz ampule was loaded into a tube furnace with the cold end of the tube extended outside of the furnace and heated to 450 °C for 1 hour. X-ray diffraction data collected on single crystals before and after thermal annealing was performed by selecting crystals of α-TaFeTe$_4$ that produced high quality single-crystal X-ray diffraction data, which were adhered to a glass slide by static. The glass slide was sealed in a quartz tube (approximately 15 cm in length) under vacuum. The quartz ampule was loaded into a box furnace and heated to 450 °C for 30 minutes.

2.2 Methods of Characterization

2.2.1 Chemical Analysis

2.2.1.1 Simple SCXRD at Columbia

Single crystal x-ray diffraction data were collected on an Agilent SuperNova diffractometer using mirror-monochromated Mo Kα radiation. Each crystal was mounted under oil at room temperature using a MiTeGen MicroMount. Data collection and unit cell determination was performed in CrysAlisPro. Samples were matched against previous crystallographic characterizations[2,7] or internal standards (in the case of CrSBr1-xCLx).

2.2.1.2 Synchotron low temperature single crystal x-ray diffraction –NSF'sChemMatCARS

A single crystal with dimension of 10x20x12 μm^3 was mounted on the tip of a glass fiber. Data were collected at x-ray energy 30 keV (0.41328Å) using Huber 3 circles diffractometer with kappa angle offset 60° and equipped with Pilatus3X 1M (CdTe) detector at temperature of 50 and 15 K. The distance between the detector and crystal was 130 mm. A total of 1440 frames were collected at two θ-angles sitting at 0˚ follow up two different ω-angles: -180 °; kappa: 0 ° and ω-angles:-200˚; kappa: 30˚, respectively. The data were collected while the φ-angle was scanned over the range of 360˚ using shutterless mode. A user-friendly data collection software was used. Pilatus standard CBF frames were converted to Bruker sfrm format. Data integrations were performed with APEX II suite software. The reduction of data was conducted with SAINT v.8.32B and

SADABS v.2013 programs included in the APEX suite. The structure solution and refinement were carried out with SHELX software using the XPREP utility for the space group determination, and the XT and XL programs for the structure solution and refinement, respectively.

2.2.1.3 Energy Dispersive X-Ray Spectroscopy

The chemical composition was confirmed by energy dispersive x-ray spectroscopy using the Zeiss Sigma VP SEM in conjunction with its EDS functionality. Samples were mounted to pucks by attaching them to carbon tape. These samples were then introduced under vacuum into the chamber. Imaging was conducted with SEM to orient the samples, after which the current was increased to get clean spectra.

2.2.1.4 Thermogravimetric analysis

Samples were weighed out on a microbalance before introduction to the TA Instruments Q500 TGA in the Columbia SMCL to ensure they met the minimum weight requirement of 5 mg. Gas was chosen (O_2 or N_2) and the heating regime was as follows: ramp at 3 ˚C per minute to 50 ˚C; temerpature was maintained for 10 minutes at 50˚ C; ramp at 2 ˚C/minute to 100 ˚C; temperature was mainted for 360 miuntes at 100 ˚C; and then ramp at 5 ˚C/minutes to 300 ˚C. Results were then processed by Igor and Microsoft Excel to determine weight loss.

2.2.2 Layer-ID and crystal exfoliation

In the 2D regime, it was necessary to devise a system to reliably identify layer number of CrSBr flakes without performing AFM each time; optical identification was also necessary to establish sample sites for device manufacturing and other 2D-related processes.

CrSBr flakes were exfoliated onto 285 nm or 90 nm SiO_2/Si+ substrates using mechanical exfoliation with Scotch® Magic™ tape[8,9]. For > 1 L devices, SiO_2/Si+ substrates were exposed to a gentle oxygen plasma for 5 minutes to remove adsorbates from the surface and increase flake adhesion[10]. The exfoliation was done under ambient conditions by heating the mother tape for 3 minutes at 100° C, letting it cool to room temperature, then peeling the tape from the substrate as quickly as possible[10]. For 1 L devices, the SiO_2/Si+ substrates were passivated by depositing a thin layer of 1-dodecanol before exfoliation[11]. The exfoliation was done under inert conditions in an N_2 glovebox with < 1 ppm O_2 and < 1 ppm H_2O content. The mother tape was placed onto the SiO_2/Si+ substrates without heating and removed as quickly as possible. CrSBr flake thickness was identified using optical contrast before encapsulation and then confirmed with atomic force microscopy after encapsulation with hexagonal boron nitride (h-BN).

2.2.2.1 AFM

Atomic force microscopy was performed in a Bruker Dimension Icon® using OTESPA-R3 tips in tapping mode. Flake thicknesses were extracted using Gwyddion to measure histograms of the height difference between the substrate and the desired CrSBr flake.

2.2.2.2 Optical Contrast Calbration

To more quickly and reliably identify the thickness of CrSBr flakes, a contrast calibration curve was developed for both 285 nm and 90 nm SiO_2/Si+ substrates. First, a series of images was collected of various CrSBr flakes with varying thicknesses using a Nikon Eclipse LV150N microscope and Nikon DS-Fi3 camera. The images were then shading corrected in which the inhomogeneous illumination of the substrate across a single image was corrected by dividing an optical image of a pristine area of the chip without CrSBr flakes. The contrast of the flakes was then extracted using Gwyddion to measure the difference in RGB color between the substrate and the desired flake. We found that the red color contrast was the most significant, so all reported optical contrasts are with respect to red. The series of extracted contrasts were binned into a histogram and the histrogram was fitted to an N-peak gaussian, where N is the number of expected flake thicknesses. The extracted positions of the gaussian peaks is the average red optical contract for each CrSBr thickness (**Figure C.1** and **C.2**). The thicknesses of the flakes were confirmed with atomic force microscopy (**Figure C.3**).

2.2.2.2.1 > 1 L CrSBr

Raman spectroscopy for CrSBr flakes > 1 L was performed under ambient conditions in a Renishaw InVia™ micro-Raman microscope using a 532 nm wavelength laser. A 50x objective was used with a laser spot size of 2-3 μm . A laser power of 100 μW was used with a grating of 2400 g/mm for all spectra. Varying acquisition times were used depending on the flake thickness (longer times for thinner flakes). For each flake, 10 spectra were acquired and averaged after subtracting a dark background. The dark background was a spectra acquired with no laser excitation and the same acquisition parameters.

2.2.2.2.2 < 1 L CrSBr

Raman spectroscopy for 1 L CrSBr flakes was performed inside an N_2 glovebox with < 5 ppm O_2 and < 0.5 ppm H_2O with a Horiba XploRA™ Raman microscope using a 532 nm wavelength laser. A x100 objective was used with a laser spot size of ~1-2 μm. A laser power of ~20 μW was used with a grating of 2400 g/mm for all spectra. For each flake, 5 spectra were acquired with an acquisition time of 180 s and averaged after subtracting a dark background. The dark background was a spectra acquired with no laser excitation and the same acquisition parameters.

2.2.3 Magnetometry

2.2.3.1 SQUID methods

DC magnetic susceptibility was measured in a Cryogenic R-700 X SQUID magnetometer at Columbia's SMCL. Sample masses were on the order of 1 mg and were prepared in ambient conditions inside of gel capsules which were subsequently punctured to ensure no air would remain in the sample upon evacuation. Temperature and magnetic field were carefully monitored for stability at each data point.

2.2.3.2 PPMS

All vibrating sample magnetometry (VSM) was conducted on a Quantum Design PPMS® DynaCool™ system. A single CrSBr crystal was selected and the surface was exfoliated mechanically to expose a pristine interface. The crystal was attached to a quartz paddle using GE varnish (which was cured at room temperature under ambient conditions for 30 minutes) and oriented with the a-, b-, or c- axis perpendicular to the length of the quartz paddle. The same crystal was used for all axial orientated measurements. The variable temperature scans and field-dependent magnetic susceptibility curves for each axis were measured during the same measurement cycle. The crystal was removed using a 1:1 ethanol/toluene solution, dried in air, then reoriented and reattached using the previously prescribed varnish method. Each full-range variable temperature scan was programmed as follows using the DynaCool™ VSM module: 1) demagnetization of the SC magnet at 300 K by sweeping the field from 20000 Oe to 0 Oe with an oscillatory field ramp, 2) magnetic field set to 1000 Oe using a linear field ramp, 3) cooled to 2 K at 12 K/min, 3) measured susceptibility versus temperature upon warming with a ramp rate of 5 K/min. The field dependent-magnetic susceptibility curves at different temperatures were programmed as follows using the DynaCool™ VSM module: 1) demagnetization of the SC magnet at 300 K by sweeping the field from 20000 Oe to 0 Oe with an oscillatory field ramp, 2) cooled to the desired temperature at 12 K/min, 3) measured magnetization versus field from -50000 Oe to 50000 Oe over 3 cycles (0 to -50000, -50000 to 50000, 50000 to -50000, -50000 to 0). The low-temperature zero-field-cooled and field-cooled variable temperature scans were programmed as follows using the DynaCool™ VSM module: 1) demagnetization of the SC magnet at 300 K by sweeping the field from 20000 Oe to 0 Oe with an oscillatory field ramp, 2) cooled to 2 K at 12 K/min, 3) set the magnetic field to 100 Oe, 4) measure susceptibility versus temperature from 2 K up to 40 K ramping the temperature with a ramp of 1 K/min, 5) measure susceptibility versus temperature from 40 K down to 2 K ramping the temperature with a ramp of 1 K/min, 6) re-measure susceptibility versus temperature again from 2 K down to 40 K ramping the temperature with a ramp of 1 K/min.

2.3 References

(1)   Harvey, D.; Hale, A. J.; Editor, S.; Ernslay, J.; Fay, H.; Fierz-david, B. H. E.; Blangey, L.; Baer, H. H.; Coombes, R. G.; Myhre, P. C.; Nielsen, A. T.; Heaney, F.; Hübener, S.; Farrer, B. T.; Vincent, L.; Busch, M. A.; Atwood, J. L.; Hauptmann, S.; Elements, M.; Elements, M.; Elements, T.; Patnaik, P.; Lange, N. A.; Dean, J. A.; Conant, J. B.; Strauss, G.; Yurkanis Bruice, P.; Wegner, H. a.; Discussion, G.; Bard, A. J.; Faulkner, L. R.; York, N.; @bullet, C.; Brisbane, W.; Toronto, S. E.; Boyd, R. N.; Morrison. Brauer - Handbook of Preparative Inorganic Chemistry - Vol. 1.Pdf. *Synthesis (Stuttg)*. **2001**. https://doi.org/10.1002/jctb.5000501807.

(2)   Beck, J. Über Chalkogenidehalide Des Chroms. Synthese, Kristallstruktur Und Magnetismus von Chromsulfidbromid, CrSBr. *Z. anorg. allg. Chem.* **1990**, *685*, 157–167.

(3)   Klein, J.; Pham, T.; Thomsen, J. D.; Curtis, J. B.; Lorke, M.; Florian, M.; Steinhoff, A.; Wiscons, R. A.; Luxa, J.; Sofer, Z.; Jahnke, F.; Narang, P.; Ross, F. M. Atomistic Spin Textures On-Demand in the van Der Waals Layered Magnet CrSBr. **2021**.

(4)   Perrin, C.; Potel, M.; Sergent, M. Mo6Br6S3: Nouveau Composé Bidimensionnel à Clusters Octaédriques Mo6. *Acta Crystallogr. Sect. C* **1983**, *39* (4), 415–418.

(5)   Koknat, F. W.; Adaway, T. J.; Erzerum, S. I.; Syed, S. Convenient Synthesis of the Hexanuclear Molybdenum(II) Halides Mo6Cl12 and Mo6Br12·2H2O. *inorg. nucl. chem. lett.* **1980**, *16*, 307–310.

(6)   Zhong, X.; Lee, K.; Meggiolaro, D.; Dismukes, A. H.; Choi, B.; Wang, F.; Nuckolls, C.; Paley, D. W.; Batail, P.; De Angelis, F.; Roy, X.; Zhu, X.-Y. Mo6S3Br6: An Anisotropic 2D Superatomic Semiconductor. *Adv. Funct. Mater.* **2019**. https://doi.org/10.1002/adfm.201902951.

(7)   Göser, O.; Paul, W.; Kahle, H. G. Magnetic Properties of CrSBr. *J. Magn. Magn. Mater.* **1990**, *92* (1), 129–136. https://doi.org/10.1016/0304-8853(90)90689-N.

(8)   Novoselov, K. S.; Geim, A. K.; Morozov, S. V; Jiang, D.; Zhang, Y.; Dubonos, S. V; Grigorieva, I. V; Firsov, A. A. Electric Field Effect in Atomically Thin Carbon Films. *Science* **2004**, *306* (5696), 666–669. https://doi.org/10.1126/science.1102896.

(9)   Novoselov, K. S.; Jiang, D.; Schedin, F.; Booth, T. J.; Khotkevich, V. V.; Morozov, S. V.;

Geim, A. K. Two-Dimensional Atomic Crystals. *Proc. Natl. Acad. Sci.* **2005**, *102* (30), 10451–10453. https://doi.org/10.1073/PNAS.0502848102.

(10) Huang, Y.; Sutter, E.; Shi, N. N.; Zheng, J.; Yang, T.; Englund, D.; Gao, H. J.; Sutter, P. Reliable Exfoliation of Large-Area High-Quality Flakes of Graphene and Other Two-Dimensional Materials. *ACS Nano* **2015**, *9* (11), 10612–10620. https://doi.org/10.1021/acsnano.5b04258.

(11) Lee, K.; Dismukes, A. H.; Telford, E. J.; Wiscons, R. A.; Wang, J.; Xu, X.; Nuckolls, C.; Dean, C. R.; Roy, X.; Zhu, X. Magnetic Order and Symmetry in the 2D Semiconductor CrSBr. *Nano Lett.* **2021**, acs.nanolett.1c00219. https://doi.org/10.1021/acs.nanolett.1c00219.

Chapter 3: Layered Antiferromagnetism in the Bulk Regime of CrSBr

3.1 Preface

In this work, we synthesized CrSBr and reveal strong coupling between its magnetic ordering and transport properties. We measured magnetotransport down to 5 K and observed large intrinsic negative magnetoresistance (nMR) of up to ~40%, almost 10 times greater than the magnetoresistance in typical metallic magnetic materials[1-4] (< 5%) and more than twice that of the magnetoresistance values in many dilute magnetic semiconductors (~15%).[5,6] Magnetic measurements on single crystals confirm the previously reported magnetic structure: the emergence of an A-type antiferromagnetic (AF) phase below $T_N = 132 \pm 1$ K consisting of ferromagnetic (FM) layers, with an in-plane magnetic easy axis along the crystallographic b-axis, coupled antiferromagnetically along the c-axis (**Fig. 3.1 A,B**).[7] The magnetic structure of CrSBr, coupled with its easily cleavable layered vdW structure, high magnetic ordering temperature, and strong coupling between magnetism and transport make this compound attractive to advance the fields of magnetic semiconductors, 2D magnetism, and nanospintronics.

3.2 Introduction and Background

Materials that combine bulk magnetic order and semiconducting transport properties have received widespread attention for their ability to control both charge and spin carriers, allowing for complete spin polarization of their conduction electrons.[8] By exploiting the spins of electrons as information carriers, instead of their charge, these materials promise to improve the speed, density, and energy efficiency of electronic devices through single-spin transport.[9–11] This makes magnetic semiconductors particularly attractive for device applications that utilize the electronic tunability, spin-polarized transport, and exotic magneto-optical properties characteristic of magnetic semiconductors such as magnetic tunnel junctions and spin field effect transistors.[11–17] For these reasons, semiconductors with strongly coupled electrical properties and magnetic order offer advantages over magnetic metals and insulators but they are comparatively notably scarce.[18] Thus, synthesizing new materials that intrinsically exhibit both semiconducting behavior and magnetic ordering is imperative from a material design perspective to advancing spin-based technologies.

The recent discovery of two-dimensional (2D) magnets from bulk van der Waals (vdW) materials[19–21] provides an ideal platform to understand and ultimately control 2D magnetism, fueling opportunities for atomically-thin spintronic and magneto-optic devices, valleytronics and on-chip communication.[22–26] In addition, 2D magnets can be used to engineer interfacial phenomena in vdW heterostructures through the proximity effect,[25,27–29] including spin superexchange, anomalous Hall effects, and topological superconductivity. The realization of a 2D magnetic semiconductor would be particularly exciting owing to the possibility of taking the increased electronic tunability and unique magnetotransport and magneto-optical properties of bulk magnetic semiconductors down to the few-layer limit. To date, however, the design of vdW materials, from which 2D magnets can be exfoliated, remains a major synthetic challenge underscored by the inadequacies of currently available materials, including low magnetic transition temperatures (45 K and 25 K for few layer CrI$_3$[19] and Cr$_2$Ge$_2$Te$_6$,[21] respectively), extreme air instability, and poor transport properties. In this context, the vdW material CrSBr is expected to be an important milestone: bulk CrSBr has a high antiferromagnetic ordering temperature ($T_N \sim$ 132 K) with a number of theoretical studies predicting the monolayer to have an even higher ferromagnetic ordering temperature ($T_C \sim$ 150 K), semiconducting transport properties, stability under ambient conditions, and gate-tunable magnetic ordering.[8,30,31] Despite its promise, few experimental probes have been reported.[7]

3.3 Synthesis and Characterization of CrSBr

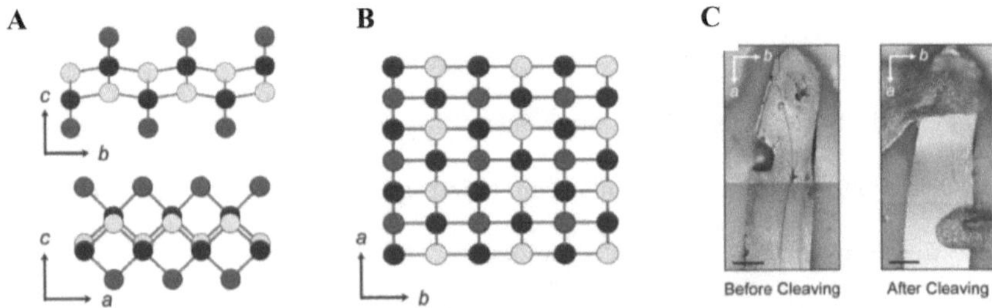

Figure 3. 1 Crystal structure and semiconducting behavior of CrSBr.
(**A, B**) Crystal structure of CrSBr as viewed along the a-axis (**A: top**), b-axis (**A: bottom**), and c-axis (**B**). Cr, S, and Br atoms are false colored to appear blue, yellow, and red, respectively. (**C**) Optical images of a CrSBr single crystal before (left) and after (right) mechanically cleaving with Scotch tape. The scale bars are 100 μm. Orientation of the crystal axes are given in the inset.

We grew CrSBr single crystals as millimeter scale shiny black flat needles using a modified chemical vapor transport approach adapted from the original method reported by Beck.[32] Single crystal x-ray diffraction (SCXRD) crystallography reveals the layered vdW structure of CrSBr (**Fig. 3.1 A,B** and **Table 3.1**). Each layer is made of two buckled planes of CrS sandwiched between Br sheets; the CrSBr layers stack along the c-axis through vdW interactions.[7,32,33] The space group is $Pmmn$ (D_{2h}), which consists of a rectangular structure as viewed along the c-axis (7.96 Å), with a larger interplanar spacing of the b-axis (4.76 Å) than the a-axis (3.50 Å). The crystal symmetry remains unchanged between 15 and 300 K.

Table 3.1 Selected crystallographic data

T (K)	15	50	100	294
Formula	CrSBr	CrSBr	CrSBr	CrSBr
MW	163.87	163.87	163.97	163.97
Space Group	*Pmmn*	*Pmmn*	*Pmmn*	*Pmmn*
a (Å)	4.7457	4.7484	4.7379	4.7631
b (Å)	3.5126	3.5138	3.5043	3.5029
c (Å)	7.9171	7.9271	7.9069	7.963
a (°)	90	90	90	90
b (°)	90	90	90	90
g (°)	90	90	90	90
V (Å³)	131.98	132.26	131.28	132.86
Z	2	2	2	2
ρ_{calc} *(g cm⁻³)*	4.126	4.117	4.148	4.099
l (Å)	0.3936	0.3936	0.71073	0.71073
$2q_{min}, 2q_{max}$	5.542, 51.848	2.846, 60.142	10.032, 58.958	9.974, 52.396
Nref	4347	744	1685	223
R(int), R(s)	0.0312, 0.0233	0.0446, 0.0341	0.0735, 0.0406	0.0624, 0.0837
μ *(mm⁻¹)*	3.762	3.754	19.976	19.738
Data	661	744	219	142
Restraints	0	0	0	0
Parameters	14	14	13	13
R_1 *(obs)*	0.0225	0.0411	0.0674	0.0779
wR_2 *(all)*	0.0787	0.1741	0.1959	0.1861
S	1.334	1.249	1.486	1.101

The chemical composition is confirmed by energy dispersive x-ray spectroscopy (**Fig. B1**). The needle shape of the crystals reflects the in-plane lattice anisotropy, allowing the identification of crystal axes from the morphology and experimentally observed anisotropic Raman peaks (**Fig. B3**). Its compositional stability is confirmed by thermograviemntric analysis (**Fig. B2**). A consequence of the large interlayer spacing and vdW stacking is the propensity of the crystals to cleave parallel to the ab-planes, providing the ability to mechanically exfoliate CrSBr with Scotch tape and expose pristine surfaces (**Fig. 3.1 C**).

3.4 Electrical Transport Measurements

We performed electrical transport measurements on bulk CrSBr crystals ($\sim 500 \times 200 \times 10$ mm^3) as a function of temperature and magnetic field. The devices were fabricated by cleaving the CrSBr crystals to obtain pristine surfaces (**Fig. 3.1 C**), mounting them into a non-conducting DIP socket and making electrical contact with silver paint.

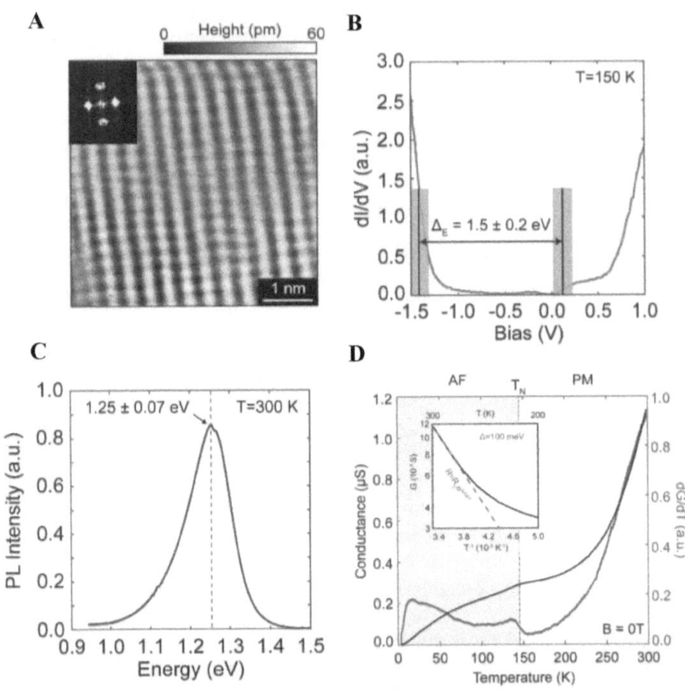

Figure 3. 2 Electronic Transport Properties of Bulk CrSBr
(**A**) Scanning tunneling microscopy image of bulk CrSBr along the c- axis at $T = 150$ K. STM topographical images were obtained in constant current mode ($V_{bias} = 2$V, $I_{tunneling} = 2$ pA). An FFT of the topography is given in the inset. (**B**) dI/dV versus bias, as measured by scanning tunneling spectroscopy. The gap is extracted by fitting a linear segment on both the left and right side of the STS, then taking the mid points of the linear segments (represented by solid black lines) as the gap edges. The extracted electronic bandgap is given in the inset. The grey boxes demarcate the error in determining the gap edges. (**C**) Photoluminescence intensity versus excitation energy at $T = 300$ K. The position of the PL peak is denoted by a black dashed line and given in the inset. (**D**) Conductance (black solid line) and the derivative of conductance (purple solid line) versus temperature at zero magnetic field. The inset plots conductance on a log scale versus inverse temperature. An exponential fit to the data is given by a red dashed line. The extracted transport gap is given in the inset.

Scanning tunneling microscopy (STM) imaging of the exposed surface shows the rectangular lattice with interatomic distances consistent with SCXRD (**Fig. 3.2 A and S4**). The contacts are arranged in a Hall bar geometry, allowing simultaneous measurement of the longitudinal (R_{xx}) and Hall (R_{xy}) resistances (details can be found in the Supporting Information). The crystals display an average sheet resistance (R_S) of 240 ± 60 kΩ at room temperature, where we use the general definition

$$R_S = \frac{\rho_{xx}}{t} = R_{xx}\frac{W}{L} \qquad (1)$$

(where W, L, and t are the channel width, length, and thickness, respectively). The conductance versus temperature (**Fig. 3.2D**) shows a semiconducting response, with conductance decreasing with decreasing temperature. This is consistent with scanning tunneling spectroscopy (STS) measurements (**Fig. 3.2B**) as well as photoluminescence spectroscopy (**Fig. 3.2C**), which identify an electronic gap $\Delta_E = 1.5 \pm 0.2$ eV and a PL peak centered at 1.25 ± 0.07 eV, respectively. The Fermi level is located close to the conduction band edge ($E_C - E_F < 100$ meV) as measured by STM (**Fig. 3.2B**), indicating that the system is electron doped. The measured transport properties also support this claim. At high temperature, the conductance versus temperature is well described by a thermally activated model, $G \propto e^{-(E_C-E_F)/k_BT}$, with $E_C - E_F$ $= 93 \pm 14$ meV (averaged over 4 devices) (**Fig. 3.2D and S6**), in excellent agreement with STS measurements. The sign and magnitude of the room temperature sheet carrier density ($n_{2D} \sim 5$ $\times 10^{13}$ cm^{-2}) as determined from the Hall effect confirm electron doping (**Fig. B5**).

The plot of the conductance versus temperature (**Fig. 3.2D**) displays a sudden change in the slope at $T = 148 \pm 6$ K. We define the transition temperature as the midpoint through the change in slope with the error defined as the width of the transition.

3.5 Magnetic Characterization

3.5.1 Bulk SQUID Measurement

The position of the kink in the conductance and the increase in the slope of conductance versus temperature below the kink are observed in all measured samples (**Fig. B6**). **Fig. 3.3 A**

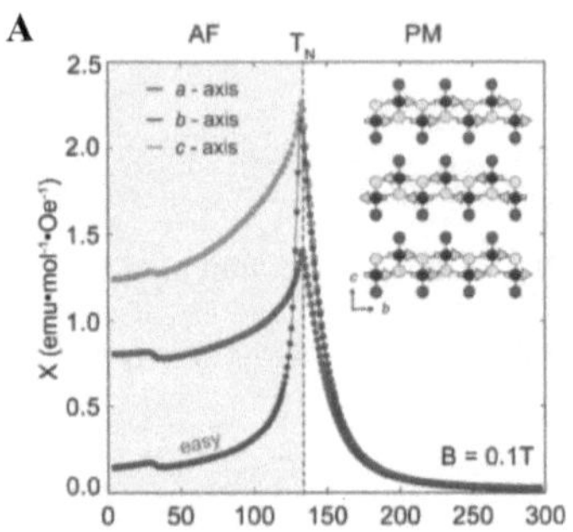

Figure 3. 3 Magnetic Susceptibility versus temperature
(A) Magnetic susceptibility versus temperature along the a-axis (solid red dots), b-axis (solid blue dots), and the c-axis (solid green dots). Inset shows the magnetic ordering of the Cr spins in the AF state. The easy axis (b-axis) is denoted. The data was collected with a magnetic field of 100 mT. The AF and PM phases are denoted with grey and white regions, respectively.

shows the corresponding temperature dependence of the magnetic susceptibility (χ) of CrSBr along each crystallographic axis, as measured by SQUID magnetometry. The sharp cusp at $T = 132 \pm 1$ K identifies the Néel temperature (T_N), signaling that the system transitions to an AF phase[34] below this temperature. T_N is closely matched to the transition in conductance versus temperature, indicating that this kink originates from the onset of the AF phase.[3,35,36] Above T_N, χ follows the Curie-Weiss law ($\chi = \chi_0 + \frac{C}{T - \theta_{CW}}$) (where χ_0 is a temperature independent term including core diamagnetism and the background signal from the sample mount, C is the Curie constant, and θ_{CW} is the Weiss constant), demonstrating bulk paramagnetic (PM) behavior (**Fig. B7**).[34]The extracted Weiss constants are larger than T_N and positive ($\theta_{CW} = 185,$

164 and 184 K for the a-, b-, and c-axes, respectively), signifying strong local FM interactions in the system (**Table 3.2**). We note that in all devices, χ versus T manifests a small kink at $T \sim$ 30 K, the origin of which is unclear at present but will be the subject of future investigation. Along the b-axis, the magnetic phase transition in the χ versus T plot is sharpest and the decrease of the low-temperature χ is more prominent than along the a- or c-axes. Together, these observations indicate that the crystallographic b-axis is the easy magnetic axis. The a- and c-axes are the magnetic intermediate and hard axes, respectively.[7]

Table 3.2 Curie-Weiss fit parameters

Axis	Curie constant ($\chi \bullet$K)	Θ (K)
a	2.00 ± 0.03	185 ± 6
b	3.13 ± 0.03	164 ± 3
c	2.12 ± 0.04	184 ± 6

3.5.2 Magnetotransport and Magnetoresistance Ratio

Fig. 3.4A-C presents the magnetoresistance ratio (defined as $MRR = \frac{R(B)-R(B=0)}{R(B=0)} \times$ 100) versus applied magnetic field (B) along each crystallographic axis as a function of temperature. Above T_N, we observe a small but finite negative magnetoresistance versus B. This is characteristic behavior of a PM state, typically attributed to quenching of spin disorder upon applying an external magnetic field.[3,37] At $T < T_N$, the negative magnetoresistance (nMR) in magnetotransport is strongly enhanced along all crystallographic axes. With increasing B, the nMR is followed by a saturation of the magnetoresistance when the spins are completely aligned with B in the fully polarized (FP) state.[3,35,36]

The field at which the magnetoresistance begins to saturate is denoted as the saturation field (H_S). This behavior can be explained by the fact that the AF phase suppresses interlayer tunneling due to adjacent spins having opposite magnetization. In the FP state all spins are aligned, restoring interlayer tunneling, leading to a decrease in the overall sample resistance.[38–40] In addition, the magnetoresistance curves develop hysteresis along every field direction below T_N which increases in magnitude as temperature decreases (**Fig. B8**), consistent with the formation of magnetic domains. Below $\sim$ 30 K, the magnetotransport shows strong anisotropy with the emergence of a non-monotonic response along the a- and c-axes.

Additionally, at this temperature the initially negative magnetoresistance changes sign and becomes positive with further increasing B, until it saturates at H_S to a constant value when

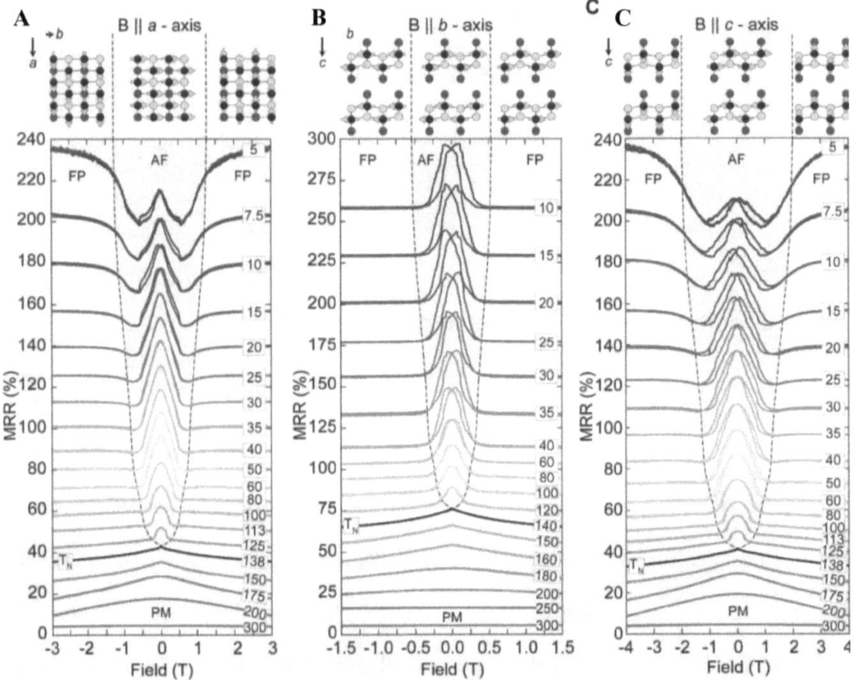

Figure 3. 4 Magnetotransport properties of CrSBr.
Magnetoresistance ratio (defined as $MRR(B) = \frac{R(B)-R(B=0)}{R(B=0)} \times 100$) versus magnetic field at various temperatures with the field oriented along the a-axis (**A**), b-axis (**B**), and c-axis (**C**). Both forward and backward magnetic field scans at each temperature are presented. The curves are offset for clarity. The solid black lines represent curves taken at temperatures near T_N. The AF, FP, and PM phases are labelled, and the phase boundary is denoted by dashed black lines. Schematics showing the orientation of the spins in the AF and FP state are given above each plot.

the FP state is reached. Similar low temperature non-monotonic behaviors observed in other systems[36] have been interpreted to arise from rotating off-axis in-plane domains or secondary magnetic ordering.[36,37,41]

3.5.3 Magnetoelectronic Properties: Spin Behavior in CrSBr bulk as seen through Magnetoelectronic Behavior

To further our understanding of the magnetotransport, we measured the magnetization (M) of CrSBr as a function of the applied magnetic field along each crystal axis via SQUID magnetometry (**Fig. 3.5A-C**). Along the b-axis, M sharply transitions from zero to the saturation magnetization, typical of a first order AF-FP spin-flip transition (**Fig. 3.5B**).[7,34] The M versus B curves along the a- and c-axes (in-plane intermediate and out-of-plane hard magnetic axes, respectively) exhibit a continuous increase of M from zero to the saturation magnetization, indicating that the spins are progressively canting to align with B (**Fig. 3.5A,C**). The sharpness of the AF-FP transition along the b-axis confirms that it is the magnetic easy axis.[7] The saturation magnetic fields determined from the magnetization curves correlate well with Hs extracted from the magnetoresistance data for each field direction. From the combined magnetotransport and magnetization measurements, we conclude that the electrical properties of CrSBr are strongly coupled to the magnetic order; the observed magnetotransport properties are a direct result of the layered antiferromagnetic structure of CrSBr.

Fig. 3.5D,E summarizes the magnetoelectronic properties of CrSBr extracted from magnetotransport measurements. **Fig. 3.5D** presents the temperature dependence of Hs along each field direction. Hs is extracted by plotting the second derivative of MRR ($\frac{d^2}{dB^2}MRR(B)$) versus B and T and extracting contour lines near $\frac{d^2}{dB^2}MRR(B) = 0$ (**Fig. B9**). Hs is largest along the magnetically hard c-axis and smallest along the easy b-axis. At low T, it decreases linearly with increasing temperature and then asymptotically approaches zero as we come close to T_N.

The zero-temperature H_S values (H_{S0}^{a} = 1.17 T, H_{S0}^{b} = 0.58 T, H_{S0}^{c} = 2.00 T) are consistent with

magnetization measurements (**Fig. 3.5A-C**) and the corresponding T_N (~ 140 K) is consistent

with the zero-field conductivity measurements (**Fig. 3.2A**).

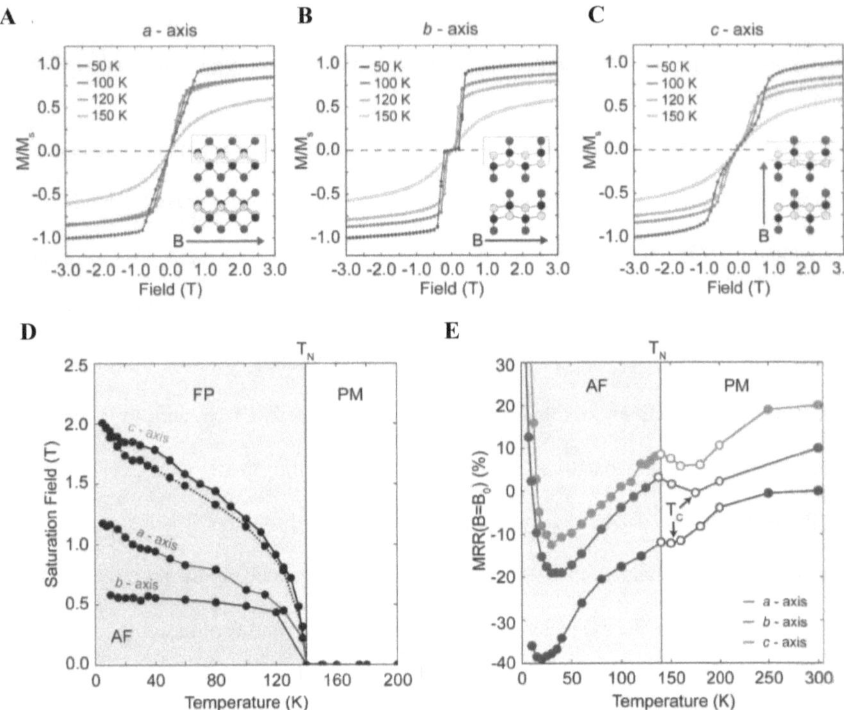

Figure 3. 5 Saturation fields and magnetoresistance ratios versus temperature.
(**A-C**) Magnetization versus magnetic field at various temperatures along the a-axis (**A**), b-axis (**B**), and c-axis (**C**). M is normalized to the saturation magnetization at T = 50 K. Insets of **A-C** show the magnetic field direction relative to the crystal structure. (**D**) Saturation magnetic field versus temperature along the a-axis (red region), b-axis (blue region), and c-axis (green region) as measured by extracting the crossover point from the positive/negative magnetoresistance regime to the saturated regime. (**E**) MRR at a fixed magnetic field $MRR(B{=}B_0) = \frac{R(B=B_0)-R(B=0)}{R(B=0)} \times 100$) versus temperature along the a-axis (red dots), b-axis (blue dots), and c-axis (green dots). Each curve is offset from one other by 20% for clarity. All curves have an MRR = 0% at room temperature. The magnetic fields at which the fixed-field MRR is calculated are B_0 = 3, 2, and 4 T for fields along the a-, b-, and c-axes, respectively. A clear kink in the fixed-field MRR versus temperature above T_N is demarcated along each axis. The open colored circles denote MRR curves versus B that were not saturated at the chosen B_0 value, indicating the MRR may continue to decrease for larger B.

In **Fig. 3.5E**, we plot the fixed-field MRR defined as $MRR(B=B_0) = \frac{R(B=B_0)-R(B=0)}{R(B=0)} \times 100$ (where B_0 = 3, 2, and 4 T for the a-, b-, and c-axes, respectively) along each crystallographic axis. Along all axes, the fixed-field MRR increases significantly below T_N up to a maximum of -29.3%, -39.2%, and -32.7% at a temperature of ~ 30 K for the a-, b-, and c-axes, respectively. Such giant intrinsic fixed-field MRR is nearly 10 times larger than typical magnetic metals[1–4] and double that of many dilute magnetic semiconductors.[5,6] Above T_N, the fixed-field MRR is non-zero and negative, manifesting a local minimum between 150 and 170 K. This temperature range is consistent with the Weiss constants extracted from the magnetic susceptibility data (θ_{CW} = 185, 164 and 184 K for the a-, b-, and c-axes, respectively) (**Table 3.2**) and signals the emergence of a hidden magnetic phase above T_N characterized by ferromagnetically ordered layers, with no long range magnetic order between the layers.[42]

3.6 Discussion of Results

In summary, we demonstrate CrSBr to be a robust antiferromagnetic semiconductor with exceptionally strong coupling between magnetic and electronic properties manifested through the observation of nMR up to ~40%. STM and STS studies combined with PL measurements reveal that CrSBr is a direct gap semiconductor with an electrical gap Δ_E = 1.5 $\pm$ 0.2 eV and a PL peak centered at 1.25 $\pm$ 0.07 eV. Magnetic measurements on single crystals show the emergence of an AF phase consisting of FM layers coupled antiferromagnetically along the stacking direction below T_N = 132 $\pm$ 1 K with a magnetically easy axis parallel to the crystallographic b-axis. In magnetotransport, we observe strong coupling between the magnetic order and the electrical properties through the observation of giant nMR below T_N along all crystallographic axes. The magnetotransport properties of CrSBr, in combination with the ability to easily cleave perpendicular to the stacking axis, establish its unique potential for advancing the fields of 2D magnetism and nanospintronics.

3.7 References

1. Bai, W. *et al.* Intrinsic Negative Magnetoresistance in Van Der Waals FeNbTe $_2$ Single Crystals. *Adv. Mater.* **31**, 1900246 (2019).

2. Morosan, E. *et al.* Sharp switching of the magnetization in Fe1 4 Ta S2. *Phys. Rev. B - Condens. Matter Mater. Phys.* **75**, 104401 (2007).

3. Yang, J. *et al.* Spin-flop transition and magnetic phase diagram in CsCo2Se2 revealed by torque and resistivity measurements. *J. Magn. Magn. Mater.* **474**, 70–75 (2019).

4. Colino, J. *et al.* Spin-flop magnetoresistance in Gd/Co multilayers. *Phys. Rev. B - Condens. Matter Mater. Phys.* **60**, 6678–6684 (1999).

5. Chen, B. *et al.* Li(Zn,Co,Mn)As: A bulk form diluted magnetic semiconductor with Co and Mn co-doping at Zn sites. *AIP Adv.* **6**, 115014 (2016).

6. Sinova, J., Jungwirth, T. & Černe, J. Magneto-transport and magneto-optical properties of ferromagnetic (III,Mn)V semiconductors: A review. *International Journal of Modern Physics B* vol. 18 1083–1118 (2004).

7. Gösser, O., Paul, W. & Kahle, H. Magnetic properties of CrSBr. *J. Magn. Magn. Mater.* **92**, 129–136 (1990).

8. Jiang, Z., Wang, P., Xing, J., Jiang, X. & Zhao, J. Screening and Design of Novel 2D Ferromagnetic Materials with High Curie Temperature above Room Temperature. *ACS Appl. Mater. Interfaces* **10**, 39032–39039 (2018).

9. Hoffmann, A. & Bader, S. D. Opportunities at the frontiers of spintronics. *Phys. Rev. Appl.* **4**, 1–18 (2015).

10. Marrows, C. Addressing an antiferromagnetic memory. *Science (80-.).* **351**, 558 (2016).

11. Hirohata, A. *et al.* Review on spintronics: Principles and device applications. *J. Magn. Magn. Mater.* **509**, 166711 (2020).

12. Mcguire, T. R. & Potter, R. I. Anisotropic Magnetoresistance in Ferromagnetic 3D Alloys. *IEEE Trans. Magn.* **11**, 1018–1038 (1975).

13. Munekata, H. *et al.* Diluted magnetic III-V semiconductors. *Phys. Rev. Lett.* **63**, 1849–1852 (1989).

14. Žutić, I., Fabian, J., Fabian, J. & Das Sarma, S. Spin-polarized transport in inhomogeneous magnetic semiconductors: Theory of magnetic/nonmagnetic p-n junctions. *Phys. Rev. Lett.* **88**, 66603 (2002).

15. Majumdar, S., Das, A. K. & Ray, S. K. Magnetic semiconducting diode of p -Ge1-x Mnx /n-Ge layers on silicon substrate. *Appl. Phys. Lett.* **94**, 122505 (2009).

16. Dierolf, V., Ferguson, I. T. & Zavada, J. M. *Rare Earth and Transition Metal Doping of Semiconductor Materials: Synthesis, Magnetic Properties and Room Temperature Spintronics. Rare Earth and Transition Metal Doping of Semiconductor Materials: Synthesis, Magnetic Properties and Room Temperature Spintronics* (Elsevier Inc., 2016). doi:10.1016/C2014-0-00833-7.

17. Mak, K. F., Xiao, D. & Shan, J. Light–valley interactions in 2D semiconductors. *Nat. Photonics* **12**, 451–460 (2018).

18. Pulizzi, F. Is it really intrinsic ferromagnetism? *Nat. Mater.* **9**, 956–957 (2010).

19. Huang, B. *et al.* Layer-dependent ferromagnetism in a van der Waals crystal down to the monolayer limit. *Nature* **546**, 270–273 (2017).

20. Huang, B. *et al.* Electrical control of 2D magnetism in bilayer CrI3. *Nat. Nanotechnol.* **13**, 544–548 (2018).

21. Gong, C. *et al.* Discovery of intrinsic ferromagnetism in two-dimensional van der Waals crystals. *Nature* **546**, 265–269 (2017).

22. Gibertini, M., Koperski, M., Morpurgo, A. F. & Novoselov, K. S. Magnetic 2D materials and heterostructures. *Nature Nanotechnology* vol. 14 408–419 (2019).

23. Zhang, W., Wong, P. K. J., Zhu, R. & Wee, A. T. S. Van der Waals magnets: Wonder building blocks for two-dimensional spintronics? *InfoMat* **1**, 479–495 (2019).

24. Duong, D. L., Yun, S. J. & Lee, Y. H. Van der Waals Layered Materials: Opportunities and Challenges. *ACS Nano* vol. 11 11803–11830 (2017).

25. Zhong, D. *et al.* Van der Waals engineering of ferromagnetic semiconductor heterostructures for spin and valleytronics. *Sci. Adv.* **3**, e1603113 (2017).

26. Burch, K. S., Mandrus, D. & Park, J. G. Magnetism in two-dimensional van der Waals materials. *Nature* vol. 563 47–52 (2018).

27. Novoselov, K. S., Mishchenko, A., Carvalho, A. & Castro Neto, A. H. 2D materials and van der Waals heterostructures. *Science (80-.).* **353**, aac9439 (2016).

28. Gong, C. & Zhang, X. Two-dimensional magnetic crystals and emergent heterostructure devices. *Science (80-.).* **363**, (2019).

29. Geim, A. K. & Grigorieva, I. V. Van der Waals heterostructures. *Nat. 2013 4997459* **499**, 419–425 (2013).

30. Qi, J., Wang, H. & Qian, X. Electrically Tunable, High Curie Temperature 2D Ferromagnetism in Van der Waals Layered Crystals. *arXiv* 1811.02674 (2018).

31. Guo, Y., Zhang, Y., Yuan, S., Wang, B. & Wang, J. Chromium sulfide halide monolayers: Intrinsic ferromagnetic semiconductors with large spin polarization and high carrier mobility. *Nanoscale* **10**, 18036–18042 (2018).

32. Beck, J. Über Chalkogenidehalide des Chroms. Synthese, Kristallstruktur und Magnetismus von Chromsulfidbromid, CrSBr. *Z. anorg. allg. Chem.* **685**, 157–167 (1990).

33. Miao, N., Xu, B., Zhu, L., Zhou, J. & Sun, Z. 2D Intrinsic Ferromagnets from van der Waals Antiferromagnets. *J. Am. Chem. Soc.* **140**, 2417–2420 (2018).

34. Blundell, S. *Magnetism in Condensed Matter.* (Oxford University Press, 2001).

35. Liu, Y. *et al.* Magnetic reversal in S r4 R u3 O10 nanosheets probed by anisotropic magnetoresistance. *Phys. Rev. B* **98**, 024425 (2018).

36. Kumar, N., Soh, Y., Wang, Y. & Xiong, Y. Magnetotransport as a diagnostic of spin reorientation: Kagome ferromagnet as a case study. *Phys. Rev. B* **100**, 214420 (2019).

37. Pandey, A., Mazumdar, C., Ranganathan, R. & Johnston, D. C. Multiple crossovers between positive and negative magnetoresistance versus field due to fragile spin structure in metallic GdPd3. *Sci. Rep.* **7**, 1–9 (2017).

38. Usami, K. Magnetoresistance in Antiferromagnetic Metals. *J. Phys. Soc. Japan* **45**, 466–475 (1978).

39. Binasch, G., Grünberg, P., Saurenbach, F. & Zinn, W. Enhanced magnetoresistance in layered magnetic structures with antiferromagnetic interlayer exchange. *Phys. Rev. B* **39**, 4828–4830 (1989).

40. Baibich, M. N. *et al.* Giant magnetoresistance of (001)Fe/(001)Cr magnetic superlattices. *Phys. Rev. Lett.* **61**, 2472–2475 (1988).

41. Eden, N., Kopnov, G., Fraenkel, S., Goldstein, M. & Gerber, A. Longitudinal and transverse magnetoresistance in films with tilted out-of-plane magnetic anisotropy. *Phys. Rev. B* **99**, 064432 (2019).

42. Lee, K. *et al.* Giant magnetic-dipole second-harmonic generation reveals symmetry in the ferromagnetic CrSBr monolayer. *Prep.* (2020).

Chapter 4: CrSBr Behavior in the Few Layer Regime

4.1 Preface

Magnetic semiconductors are a powerful platform for understanding, utilizing and tuning the interplay between magnetic order and electronic transport[1–3]. Compared to bulk crystals, two-dimensional magnetic semiconductors have greater tunability, as illustrated by the gate modulation of magnetism in exfoliated CrI_3[4–6] and $Cr_2Ge_2Te_6$[7,8], but their electrically insulating properties limit their utility in devices. Here we report the simultaneous electrostatic and magnetic control of electronic transport in atomically-thin CrSBr, an A-type antiferromagnetic semiconductor[9–13]. Through magnetotransport measurements, we find that spin-flip scattering from the interlayer antiferromagnetic configuration of multilayer flakes results in giant negative magnetoresistance. Conversely, magnetoresistance of the ferromagnetic monolayer CrSBr vanishes below the Curie temperature. A second transition ascribed to the ferromagnetic ordering of magnetic defects manifests in a large positive magnetoresistance in the monolayer and a sudden increase of the bulk magnetic susceptibility.

We demonstrate this magnetoresistance is tunable with an electrostatic gate, revealing that the ferromagnetic coupling of defects is carrier mediated.

4.2 Introduction and Background

Layered A-type antiferromagnets are composed of van der Waals (vdW) sheets with intralayer ferromagnetic (FM) order and interlayer antiferromagnetic (AF) coupling[14]. Upon the application of an external magnetic field, the interlayer AF order can be switched to FM, accompanied by a change in optical and electronic properties[11,13,15-17]. This change of spin structure produces emergent phenomena, including giant tunneling magnetoresistance in vertical vdW spin-filters[15,18,19], giant second harmonic generation (SHG) in the AF state due to the breaking of inversion symmetry by magnetic order[12], and magnetic order-dependent excitonic transitions arising from changes in interlayer hybridization[13]. For applications in spin-based electronics, ideal materials should combine layered magnetism with functional semiconducting transport properties, which would allow for simultaneous control over charge and spin carriers. In studies of bulk magnetic semiconductors, magnetic defects and impurities play a crucial role in determining the magnetic and electronic properties. To further develop 2D magnetic semiconductors, it is thus critical to understand how magnetic order and magnetic defects couple to charge carriers. Transport measurements in currently available 2D magnets, however, are limited to FM metals[20,21] or degenerately-doped FM semiconductors[8], while the role of defects is essentially unexplored.

In bulk single crystals, CrSBr is an extrinsic semiconductor with a direct bandgap of ~1.5 eV and finite conductivity that can be measured down to liquid helium temperatures[11]. We find the transport properties of few-layer CrSBr is dominated by the interlayer AF coupling. When the flakes are polarized with an external magnetic field, their resistances decrease drastically due to differences in interlayer spin-flip scattering between the AF and FM configurations. In monolayer CrSBr, spin-flip scattering arises only from intraplanar FM ordering, which manifests as a peak of negative magnetoresistance near the monolayer Curie temperature (T_C = 146 K[12]), followed by a drop to near zero upon cooling to ~40 K. For all layer numbers, magnetoresistance measurements reveal an unexpected magnetic phase below 40 K, which we identify as carrier-mediated FM ordering of magnetic defects. In monolayer CrSBr we controllably switch between magnetoresistance mechanisms attributed to s-d exchange interactions and bound magnetic polarons by varying the carrier density with an electrostatic gate.

4.3 CrSBr Device and Sample Preparation

Atomically-thin CrSBr flakes are prepared via mechanical exfoliation on Si wafers with a 285 nm thick SiO_2 layer (see **Appendix C** for details)[22,23]. The thickness and crystallographic directions of exfoliated flakes are determined by optical contrast (**Fig. 4.1B** and **Fig. C1-3**), atomic force microscopy (**Fig. 4.1C** and **Fig. C3**), and Raman spectroscopy (**Fig. C4,5**). Mesoscopic transport devices are fabricated using the *via* contact method[24], whereby palladium electrodes embedded in hexagonal boron nitride (h-BN) are transferred onto the desired CrSBr flakes using the dry-polymer-transfer process[25] (**Fig. 4.1D**; see Supplemental for details). We performed electrical transport measurements as a function of temperature (T), magnetic field (B), and electrostatic gate voltage (V_{BG}) on CrSBr flakes ranging in thickness from 1 to 9 layers. Current was sourced along the crystallographic a-axis for all measurements (**Fig. 4.1D**). Owing to the high resistance of the flakes over the entire T range (**Fig. C6,7**), all data reported in the main text were measured in a 2-terminal configuration. Some measurements were repeated in a 4-terminal configuration to confirm the channel resistance dominates the transport properties (**Fig. C8**).

Bilayer CrSBr displays an overall extrinsic semiconducting behavior with conductance (G) decreasing with decreasing T (**Fig. 4.1E**). At T = 136 ± 4 K, there is a sharp kink in the shows a local maximum at the same T due to reduced scattering caused by spin fluctuations as CrSBr becomes antiferromagnetically ordered[26,27]. Thicker flakes display the same kink in dG/dT versus T, signaling the onset of AF order (**Fig. C9**). Within experimental error, the values of T_N measured from transport for flakes ranging in derivative of G versus T (dG/dT), which is attributed to the onset of AF ordering at T_N[11]. G thickness from 2 to 9 layers are unchanged from the bulk value and independent of layer number (**Fig. C9**). In contrast, monolayer CrSBr shows no kink in dG/dT (**Fig. 4.1F**), but displays a local minimum close to the expected monolayer T_C[12]. This is consistent with previous reports that monolayer CrSBr

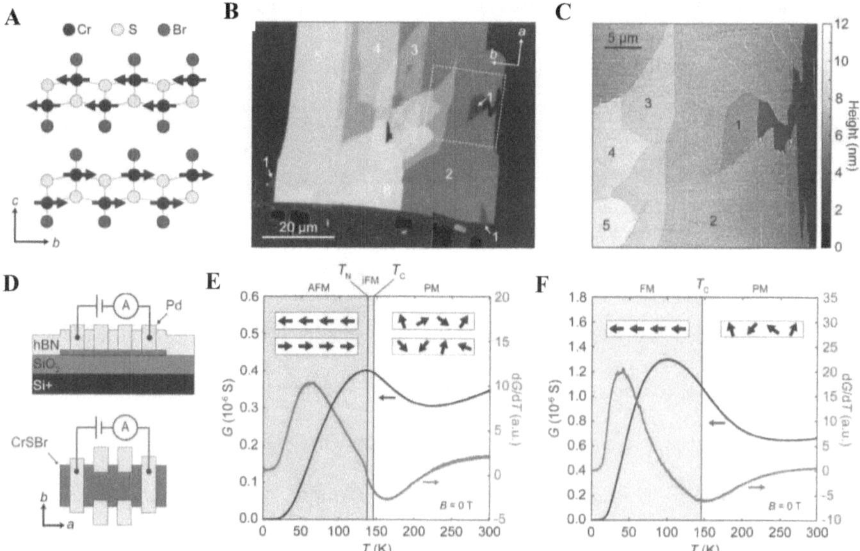

Figure 4. 1 Crystal structure, device fabrication, and transport signatures of CrSBr magnetic ordering.
A) Crystal structure of CrSBr as viewed along the a-axis. Orientation of the Cr spins in the AF state are given by solid blue arrows. Blue, yellow, and red circles correspond to Cr, S, and Br, respectively. **B)** False-colored optical image of an exfoliated CrSBr flake with thicknesses ranging from 1 to 6 layers. The corresponding layer numbers are denoted on the image. The orientation of the crystal axes is given in the upper right inset. C) Atomic force microscopy image of the CrSBr flake shown in (**B**). The region where the image was taken is denoted by a dashed white box in (**B**). The corresponding number of CrSBr layers is labelled on the plot. D) Side-view (top) and top-view (bottom) schematic of the CrSBr device geometry. Color code: h-BN, grey; Pd, yellow; SiO$_2$, dark grey; CrSBr, blue; Si+ substrate, black. The orientation of the crystal axes relative to the electrodes is denoted. **E, F)** Conductance (solid black line) and derivative of the conductance (solid red line) versus T at zero B for bilayer (**E**) and monolayer (**F**) CrSBr. The interlayer AF, intralayer FM (iFM/FM), and PM states are denoted by solid blue, solid green, and white regions, respectively. T_N is defined as the location of the kink in dG/dT. T_C is defined from SHG measurements[12]. Cartoons of the spin orientation in each state are given in the insets. The white rectangles represent single CrSBr sheets, and the blue arrows represent the Cr spins.

only exhibits intraplanar FM ordering[12]. Note that the low-T resistance for both bilayer and monolayer CrSBr is well-described by Efros-Shklovskii variable range hopping, indicating electronic transport is dominated by electron percolation between hopping sites (**Fig. C10**)[28,29].

4.4 CrSBr Magnetoresistance Behavior as a Function of Layer Number

Fig. 4.2A presents the magnetoresistance ratio (*MRR*) versus B and T for bilayer CrSBr. We define $MRR = \frac{R(B)-R(B=0)}{R(B=0)} \times 100$, where in this plot B is oriented along the c-axis. From 300 to ~175 K, the sample is in a PM phase characterized by a broad negative *MRR* (n*MRR*) due to the field-induced suppression of spin-flip scattering between conducting electrons and local magnetic moments[30,31]. The thermal fluctuations which prevent spins from aligning with B diminish with decreasing T, leading to an overall increase in the magnitude of the n*MRR*. Below $T_N = 136$ K, we observe n*MRR* up to a well-defined saturation field (B_{sat}) beyond which the device resistance saturates with increasing B. This manifests as a dome of n*MRR*, the edges of which define B_{sat} (dashed black line in **Fig. 4.2A**). The magnitude of n*MRR* increases with decreasing T as the AF state becomes more ordered, reaching –23.5% at 10 K (**Fig. 4.2B**; see **Fig. C11** for lower T). This giant n*MRR* followed by saturation for $B > B_{sat}$ indicates that carrier scattering between layers is controlled by the interlayer magnetic configuration. In the AF state at zero B, interlayer tunneling is suppressed. As B increases, the spins are gradually canted towards the c-axis, progressively breaking the AF configuration and restoring interlayer tunneling, which results in a decrease of the device resistance. At B_{sat}, the spins are fully polarized (FP), and a further increase of B has little effect on the resistance. Consistent with exhibit the same qualitative *MRR* behavior (see **Fig. C12-15**).

Fig. 4.2C plots the magnetoresistance of the FM CrSBr monolayer versus B and T. Between 300 and 170 K, monolayer CrSBr exhibits the same behavior as multilayer samples; n*MRR* which we attribute to the suppression of spin-flip scattering in the PM state with increasing B, the magnitude of which increases as T decreases. As T is further lowered below

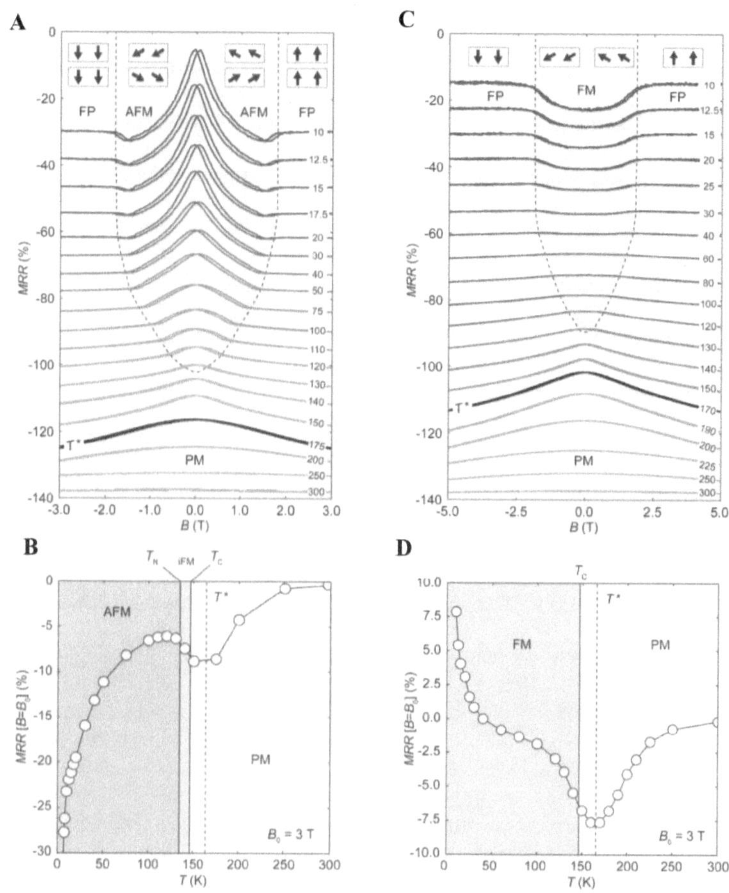

Figure 4. 3 Magnetoresistance measurements of bilayer and monolayer CrSBr.
A, C) *MRR* versus *B* at various *T* with *B* oriented along the *c*-axis for bilayer (**A**) and monolayer
(**C**) CrSBr. Both forward and backward *B* sweeps are presented. The curves are offset for
clarity. The solid black line is the curve taken near T^*, the temperature at which *MRR* has a
local minimum. The corresponding magnetic phases are labeled, and B_{sat} is denoted by a dashed
black line. Insets: schematics showing the orientation of the spins in each state. The white
rectangles represent single CrSBr sheets, and the blue arrows represent the Cr spins. **B, D)** *MRR*
at a fixed *B* parallel to the *c*-axis versus *T* for bilayer (**B**) and monolayer (**D**) CrSBr. The *B* at
which the fixed-field *MRR* is calculated is $B_0 = 3$ T. The interlayer AF, intralayer FM (iFM/FM),
and PM phases are labelled and denoted by blue, green, and white regions, respectively.

170 K, the magnitude of *MRR* decreases and approaches zero by 40 K (**Fig. 4.2D**). This is

expected since the intralayer FM order reduces spin fluctuations at zero *B*, diminishing spin-

this understanding, all CrSBr samples thicker than 1 layer flip scattering. The competition

between these two phenomena leads to a peak in n*MRR* versus *T* at 170 K (black line in **Fig.**

4.2C), which we denote as T^*. This feature is present in all samples (black line in **Fig. 4.2A** for bilayer and bulk[11]), reflecting the onset of intraplanar FM correlations as it closely follows the monolayer T_C measured by SHG and bulk heat capacity[12]. T^* is the same for bilayer and monolayer CrSBr, indicating that this feature is independent of the interlayer AF coupling. The remarkable agreement between transport and previous SHG results demonstrates that magnetotransport is a reliable probe of both FM and AF order in CrSBr. Below 40 K, monolayer CrSBr exhibits a positive *MRR* (p*MRR*) that increases with decreasing T (**Fig. 4.2D**). While this feature is most prominent in monolayer samples, it is also observed in the bilayer CrSBr sample in **Fig. 4.2A** (and in bulk CrSBr[11]) as a small p*MRR* just below B_{sat} (see **Fig. C16** for a detailed analysis).

This low-T p*MRR* response is unexpected for a FM monolayer whose ordering temperature is well above 100 K. To better understand the origin of the p*MRR*, we performed magnetometry on bulk single crystals of CrSBr and complementary field-angle-dependent transport measurements on monolayer CrSBr (**Fig. 4.3**). The bulk magnetic susceptibility (χ) versus T curves (**Fig. 4.3A**) show the expected cusp at 134 ± 2 K associated with the AF transition, followed by a sharp increase of χ onsetting at 35 K (defined as T_D), which is unusual for an A-type antiferromagnet. The crystal structure of CrSBr is unchanged across this transition[11] and we observe an increase in χ for all B directions, which necessarily exempts structural transformation or spin reorientation as the origin of this feature. We also note that the increase in χ below T_D resembles a FM transition. Consistent with this hypothesis, there is a significant difference between the zero-field-cooled and field-cooled traces of χ versus T across T_D (inset of **Fig. 4.3A**). In **Fig. 4.3B**, we plot the magnetization (M) versus B at 2 K. The overall response is dominated by the AF behavior[9,11], characterized by a spin-flip transition at ~0.3 T along the easy b-axis, and gradual canting of spins along the non-easy axes up to B_{sat}. However, if we focus on the low-B region along the easy axis, we observe the emergence of a small sigmoidal hysteresis below T_D, characteristic of FM ordering. The development of an additional FM phase is further evidenced by plotting dM/dB versus B (**Fig. 4.3C**). Above T_D (40 K), dM/dB is constant for all B directions up to ~0.2 T but below T_D (2 K), there is an additional contribution to dM/dB at low B[32].

4.5 Ferromagnetic ordering of magnetic defects in CrSBr

The *MRR* of monolayer CrSBr depends on the direction of B below T_D (**Fig. 4.3E**). The p*MRR* response is characterized by a quadratic dependence at low B followed by a saturation at B_{sat} when B is oriented along the intermediate axis (a-axis) and the hard axis (c-axis). When B is along the easy axis (b-axis), there is negligible *MRR*, indicating that the spins are aligned along the b-axis at zero B. The p*MRR* along the a- and c-axes therefore arises from a canting of the spins from the b-axis towards the respective field directions, supported by the observation that the *MRR* saturation fields closely match the saturation fields in the bulk M versus B curves (**Fig. 4.2B**). The difference in magnitude of p*MRR* between the a- and c-axes is likely due to the anisotropic magnetoresistance (AMR) effect, which produces p*MRR* when the magnetization direction is parallel to the source current direction[33]. For 40 K $< T <$ 100 K, the data is consistent with the AMR effect; *MRR* $>$ 0 for fields parallel to the a-axis and *MRR* ~0 for fields parallel to the c- and b-axes (**Fig. 4.3D**). Below 40 K, the *MRR* along the a- and c-axes increases drastically (**Fig. 4.3 D**). The same anisotropy in *MRR* was previously observed in bulk single-crystal transport measurements, in which p*MRR* features emerge along the a- and c-axes below ~40 K, but its origin was not explained[11].

The coincidence of the FM phase with the onset of p*MRR* is consistent with carrier-mediated FM ordering of magnetic defects[34,35]. In analogous bulk magnetic semiconductor systems, magnetic defects can order collectively as a result of exchange interactions with localized charge carriers[36–38] or with the intrinsic magnetic lattice[39,40]. In CrSBr, the magnetic structure likely consists of the dominant Cr magnetic lattice and a sublattice of coupled defect spins. The magnetometry data indicates that upon cooling below T_N, Cr spins within each layer

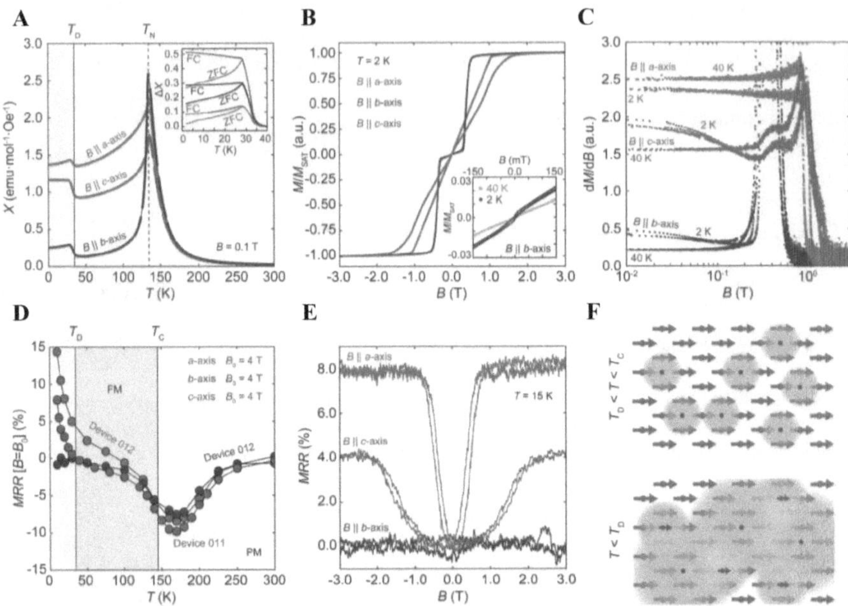

Figure 4. 5 Evidence for ferromagnetic ordering of magnetic defects in CrSBr.
A) Bulk χ versus T for $B = 0.1$ T oriented along the a-axis (red), b-axis (blue), and c-axis (green). Top right inset: plot of the change in zero-field-cooled (ZFC) and field-cooled (FC) susceptibility across T_D with $B = 0.01$ T. **B)** Bulk M versus B at 2 K for B oriented along the a-axis (red), b-axis (blue) and c-axis (green). The lower right inset plots the low-B M versus B for B along the b-axis above (40 K – grey dots) and below (2 K – blue dots) T_D. **C)** dM/dB versus B on a log scale above (40 K) and below (2 K) T_D for B oriented along the a-axis (red), b-axis (blue), and c-axis (green). **D)** MRR at a fixed B versus T for B oriented along the a-axis (red dots), b-axis (blue dots), and c-axis (green dots). The B at which the fixed-field MRR is calculated for each B direction is given in the legend. The FM, PM, and ordered defect phase are labelled by green, white, and grey regions, respectively. **E)** MRR versus B in monolayer CrSBr for B oriented along the a-axis (red), b-axis (blue), and c-axis (green). All curves were taken at 15 K and both forward and backward B sweeps are presented. **F)** Schematic of the spin structure of monolayer CrSBr for $T_D < T < T_C$ (top) and $T < T_D$ (bottom). Cr spins, defect sites, and polarized magnetic defect spins are denoted as blue arrows, black dots, and red arrows, respectively. The yellow clouds represent the localization radius of the carriers.

order ferromagnetically, but the defects remain unpolarized (**Fig. 4.3F: top**). At T_D, the

magnetic defects become polarized and adopt the same FM configuration as the Cr lattice due

to the strong exchange interaction between the Cr spins and magnetic defects (**Fig. 4.3F:**

bottom). The fact that T_D is much lower that T_N strongly suggests that the defect moments (red

arrows in **Fig. 4.3F**) arise from self-trapped electrons near donor sites (known as magnetic polarons) although we cannot entirely exclude the possibility of intrinsic magnetic point defects.

4.6 Electrostatic control of magnetoresistance in monolayer CrSBr

The magnetic defect coupling strength and the corresponding MRR response is predicted to strongly depend upon carrier density, which in our device can be dynamically and reversibly tuned using an electrostatic gate. **Fig. 4.4A** presents the MRR of monolayer CrSBr versus B at different V_{BG}. Starting from 0 V, as we increase V_{BG} (increase electron density), we observe a significant increase in the pMRR response, from 7.6 % up to 16.4 %. Conversely, decreasing V_{BG} (decreasing electron density) decreases the pMRR, and a noticeable region of nMRR emerges below –20 V at low B. At a gate voltage of –60 V, the MRR reaches –0.4 % with regions of nMRR followed by pMRR equal in magnitude when $B < B_{sat}$. **Fig. 4.4B** plots the MRR versus V_{BG} along with the extracted pMRR and nMRR contributions. There is a direct competition between the nMRR and pMRR regimes; increasing the electron density (positive gate bias) yields larger pMRR, while decreasing the electron density (negative gate bias) diminishes the pMRR contribution and induces nMRR. Together, these produce a MRR that depends linearly on V_{BG}. The T dependence of the MRR at different V_{BG} (**Fig. 4.4C** and **Fig. C18**) shows that the slope of MRR versus V_{BG} decreases quickly with increasing T and is negligible above T_D. The sensitivity to doping is further supported by the air-sensitivity of monolayer CrSBr flakes. By exposing a monolayer device to air for a period of three weeks (**Fig. C19**), we were able to change the doping level and the sign and magnitude of the MRR at low T and reproduce the behavior of a second monolayer device with lower intrinsic carrier density (**Fig. C20-23**). The carrier density at which the MRR crosses from pMRR to nMRR increases as T increases and is consistent between multiple samples (inset of **Fig. 4.4C**).

The sensitivity of the MRR to carrier density supports the hypothesis that the magnetotransport properties of CrSBr at low T are governed by the carrier-mediated FM phase.

The existence of two competing magnetoresistance features (p*MRR* and n*MRR*) indicates that

the unique shape of the *MRR* curves results from a competition between multiple mechanisms

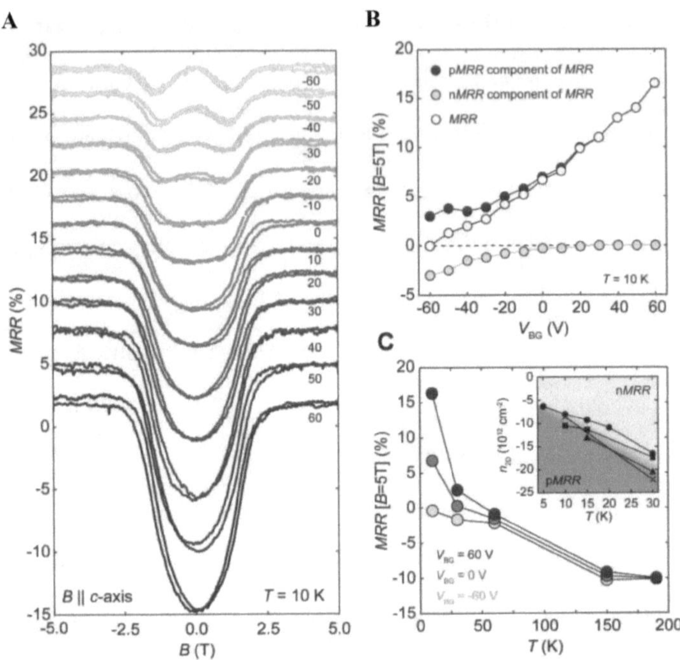

Figure 4. 7 Electrostatic control of magnetoresistance in monolayer CrSBr.
A) Monolayer CrSBr magnetoresistance versus B oriented along the c-axis for various V_{BG}.
Both forward and backward B sweeps at each V_{BG} are presented. The curves are offset for
clarity. **B)** *MRR* at 5 T (grey dots) and the corresponding extracted p*MRR* (blue dots) and n*MRR*
(yellow dots) components versus V_{BG}. **C)** *MRR* at 5 T versus T for V_{BG} = 60 V (blue dots), V_{BG}
= 0 V (pink dots), and V_{BG} = –60 V (yellow dots). A phase diagram depicting the crossover
between p*MRR* (blue region) and n*MRR* (yellow region) versus T and intrinsic carrier density
is given in the inset. Each data marker type corresponds to a different monolayer CrSBr device
(4 in total - black squares, black crosses, black circles, and black triangles).

that dominate within certain carrier density ranges. The n*MRR* component is characteristic of

magnetic polarons[34,35,41–43] and is consistent with our observation that decreasing the carrier

density enhances the n*MRR*[44]. Additionally, the carrier density at which *MRR* crosses from

p*MRR* to n*MRR* (inset of **Fig. 4.4C**) is close to the estimated magnetic defect density (see

Supplemental for calculation), implying that we observe n*MRR* when the carrier density is less

than the magnetic defect density. However, the formation of magnetic polarons is generally not

associated with a large p*MRR*. In dilute magnetic semiconductors, p*MRR* often arises from a field-dependent broadening of the defect density of state due to s-d exchange between magnetic impurities and separate electronic defect states[34,35,42,43,45,46]. This suggests that CrSBr contains both magnetic and non-magnetic defects. Both s-d exchange and magnetic polarons are mechanisms consistent with the emergence of a FM phase and electron transport in the variable range hopping limit[34,35,41,45].

4.7 Discussion of Results

Magnetotransport is typically an indirect probe of magnetism but in CrSBr it reveals in striking detail a rich magnetic structure and its intricate and tunable coupling to charge carriers. For bilayer and thicker flakes, T_N is independent of layer number and giant n*MRR* emerges as the interlayer AF configuration is broken. In monolayer CrSBr, intraplanar FM order gives rise to a peak of n*MRR* close to T_C. This n*MRR* feature is also present in multilayer flakes, signaling the existence of intraplanar FM correlations above T_N. We uncovered a hidden magnetic phase below 40 K ascribed to the FM ordering of magnetic defects. In monolayer CrSBr, this ordered magnetic defect phase dominates the low-T magnetoresistance, which can be linearly tuned using an electrostatic gate. These results highlight the utility of CrSBr as a 2D magnet with giant intrinsic n*MRR*. In the monolayer, the sensitivity of *MRR* to carrier density presents a unique opportunity not only for fabricating tunable spintronic devices, but also for understanding and utilizing defects to engineer tunable properties in vdW magnets.

4.8 References

1.   Matsukura, F., Tokura, Y. & Ohno, H. Control of magnetism by electric fields. *Nat. Publ. Gr.* (2015) doi:10.1038/NNANO.2015.22.
2.   Tanaka, M. Recent progress in ferromagnetic semiconductors and spintronics devices. *Japanese Journal of Applied Physics* vol. 60 010101 (2020).
3.   Li, X. & Yang, J. First-principles design of spintronics materials. *Natl. Sci. Rev.* **3**, 365–381 (2016).
4.   Huang, B. *et al.* Electrical control of 2D magnetism in bilayer CrI3. *Nat. Nanotechnol.* **13**, 544–548 (2018).
5.   Jiang, S., Li, L., Wang, Z., Mak, K. F. & Shan, J. Controlling magnetism in 2D CrI3 by

electrostatic doping. *Nat. Nanotechnol.* **13**, 549–553 (2018).

6. Jiang, S., Shan, J. & Mak, K. F. Electric-field switching of two-dimensional van der Waals magnets. *Nat. Mater.* **17**, 406–410 (2018).

7. Wang, Z. *et al.* Electric-field control of magnetism in a few-layered van der Waals ferromagnetic semiconductor. *Nat. Nanotechnol.* **13**, 554–559 (2018).

8. Verzhbitskiy, I. A. *et al.* Controlling the magnetic anisotropy in Cr2Ge2Te6 by electrostatic gating. *Nat. Electron.* **3**, 460–465 (2020).

9. Göser, O., Paul, W. & Kahle, H. G. Magnetic properties of CrSBr. *J. Magn. Magn. Mater.* **92**, 129–136 (1990).

10. Wang, H., Qi, J. & Qian, X. Electrically tunable high Curie temperature two-dimensional ferromagnetism in van der Waals layered crystals. *Appl. Phys. Lett.* **117**, 083102 (2020).

11. Telford, E. J. *et al.* Layered Antiferromagnetism Induces Large Negative Magnetoresistance in the van der Waals Semiconductor CrSBr. *Adv. Mater.* **32**, (2020).

12. Lee, K. *et al.* Magnetic Order and Symmetry in the 2D Semiconductor CrSBr. *Nano Lett.* acs.nanolett.1c00219 (2021) doi:10.1021/acs.nanolett.1c00219.

13. Wilson, N. P. *et al.* Interlayer Electronic Coupling on Demand in a 2D Magnetic Semiconductor. (2021).

14. Gibertini, M., Koperski, M., Morpurgo, A. F. & Novoselov, K. S. Magnetic 2D materials and heterostructures. *Nat. Nanotechnol.* **14**, 408–419 (2019).

15. Klein, D. R. *et al.* Probing magnetism in 2D van der Waals crystalline insulators via electron tunneling. *Science (80-.).* **360**, 1218–1222 (2018).

16. Deng, Y. *et al.* Quantum anomalous Hall effect in intrinsic magnetic topological insulator MnBi2Te4. *Science (80-.).* **367**, 895–900 (2020).

17. Huang, B. *et al.* Layer-dependent ferromagnetism in a van der Waals crystal down to the monolayer limit. *Nature* **546**, 270–273 (2017).

18. Song, T. *et al.* Giant tunneling magnetoresistance in spin-filter van der waals heterostructures. *Science (80-.).* **360**, 1–6 (2018).

19. Kim, H. H. *et al.* Tailored Tunnel Magnetoresistance Response in Three Ultrathin Chromium Trihalides. *Nano Lett.* **19**, 5739–5745 (2019).

20. Fei, Z. *et al.* Two-dimensional itinerant ferromagnetism in atomically thin Fe3GeTe2. *Nat. Mater.* **17**, 778–782 (2018).

21. Deng, Y. *et al.* Gate-tunable room-temperature ferromagnetism in two-dimensional Fe3GeTe2. *Nature* vol. 563 94–99 (2018).

22. Huang, Y. *et al.* Reliable Exfoliation of Large-Area High-Quality Flakes of Graphene and Other Two-Dimensional Materials. *ACS Nano* **9**, 10612–10620 (2015).

23. Novoselov, K. S. *et al.* Electric Field Effect in Atomically Thin Carbon Films. *Science (80-.).* **306**, 666 LP – 669 (2004).

24. Telford, E. J. *et al.* Via Method for Lithography Free Contact and Preservation of 2D Materials. *Nano Lett.* **18**, 1416–1420 (2018).

25. Wang, L. *et al.* One-dimensional electrical contact to a two-dimensional material. *Science (80-.).* **342**, 614–617 (2013).

26. Alexander, S., Helman, J. S. & Balberg, I. Critical behavior of the electrical resistivity in magnetic systems. *Phys. Rev. B* **13**, (1976).

27. Balberg, I. & Helman, J. S. Critical behavior of the resistivity in magnetic systems. II. below Tc and in the presence of a magnetic field. *Phys. Rev. B* **18**, 303–318 (1978).

28. Shklovskii, B. I. & Efros, A. L. *Electronic Properties of Doped Semiconductors.* vol. 45 (Springer Berlin Heidelberg, 1984).

29. Efros, A. L. & Shklovskii, B. I. Coulomb gap and low temperature conductivity of disordered systems. *J. Phys. C Solid State Phys* **8**, (1975).

30. Brodowska, B. *et al.* Magnetoresistance near the ferromagnetic-paramagnetic phase transition in magnetic semiconductors. *Appl. Phys. Lett.* **93**, 42113 (2008).

31.   Majumdar, P. & Littlewood, P. B. Dependence of magnetoresistivity on charge-carrier density in metallic ferromagnets and doped magnetic semiconductors. *Nature* **395**, 479–481 (1998).

32.   Durst, A. C., Durst, A. C., Bhatt, R. N. & Wolff, P. A. Bound magnetic polaron interactions in insulating doped diluted magnetic semiconductors. *Phys. Rev. B - Condens. Matter Mater. Phys.* **65**, 2352051–23520510 (2002).

33.   Mcguire, T. R. & Potter, R. I. Anisotropic Magnetoresistance in Ferromagnetic 3D Alloys. *IEEE Trans. Magn.* **11**, 1018–1038 (1975).

34.   Jansson, F. *et al.* Large positive magnetoresistance effects in the dilute magnetic semiconductor (Zn,Mn)Se in the regime of electron hopping. *J. Appl. Phys.* **116**, (2014).

35.   Wang, J. *et al.* Giant magnetoresistance in transition-metal-doped ZnO films. *Appl. Phys. Lett.* **88**, 252110 (2006).

36.   Mukherjee, D., Dhakal, T., Srikanth, H., Mukherjee, P. & Witanachchi, S. Evidence for carrier-mediated magnetism in Mn-doped ZnO thin films. *Phys. Rev. B - Condens. Matter Mater. Phys.* **81**, 1–5 (2010).

37.   Coey, J. M. D., Venkatesan, M. & Fitzgerald, C. B. Donor impurity band exchange in dilute ferromagnetic oxides. *Nat. Mater.* **4**, 173–179 (2005).

38.   Kittilstved, K. R., Liu, W. K. & Gamelin, D. R. Electronic structure origins of polarity-dependent high-Tc ferromagnetism in oxide-diluted magnetic semiconductors. *Nat. Mater.* **5**, 291–297 (2006).

39.   Liu, L. & Liu, J. T. C. Theory of the bound magnetic polaron in antiferromagnetic semiconductors. *Phys. Rev. B* **33**, 1797–1803 (1986).

40.   Mauger, A. Magnetic polaron: Theory and experiment. **27**, (1983).

41.   Shon, W., Rhyee, J. S., Jin, Y. & Kim, S. J. Magnetic polaron and unconventional magnetotransport properties of the single-crystalline compound EuBiTe3. *Phys. Rev. B* **100**, 24433 (2019).

42.   Xu, Q. *et al.* Magnetoresistance and anomalous Hall effect in magnetic ZnO films. *J. Appl. Phys.* **101**, 063918 (2007).

43.   Andrearczyk, T. *et al.* Spin-related magnetoresistance of Mn. *Phys. Rev. B* **72**, 121309 (2005).

44.   Bellingeri, E. *et al.* Influence of free charge carrier density on the magnetic behavior of (Zn,Co)O thin film studied by Field Effect modulation of magnetotransport. *Sci. Rep.* **9**, 1–12 (2019).

45.   Xing, G. Z., Yi, J. B., Yan, F., Wu, T. & Li, S. Positive magnetoresistance in ferromagnetic Nd-doped In2O 3 thin films grown by pulse laser deposition. *Appl. Phys. Lett.* **104**, 1–6 (2014).

46.   Yang, Z. *et al.* Electron carrier concentration dependent magnetization and transport properties in ZnO:Co diluted magnetic semiconductor thin films. *J. Appl. Phys.* **104**, (2008).

Chapter 5: Optical Probing of CrSBr with SHG

5.1 Preface

The recent discovery of two-dimensional (2D) magnets[1–3] offers unique opportunities for the experimental exploration of low-dimensional magnetism[4] and the magnetic proximity effects[5,6], and for the development of novel magnetoelectric, magneto-optic and spintronic devices[7,8] . These advancements call for 2D materials with diverse magnetic structures as well as effective probes for their magnetic symmetries, which is key to understanding intralayer magnetic order and interlayer magnetic coupling[9–11]. However, traditional techniques do not probe magnetic symmetry; these examples include magneto-optical Kerr effect[2,3], reflective magnetic circular dichroism and Raman spectroscopy[12–14], anomalous Hall effect[15], tunneling magnetoresistance[16,17], spin-polarized scanning tunneling microscopy[9], and single-spin scanning magnetometry[18]. Here we apply second harmonic generation (SHG), a technique acutely sensitive to symmetry breaking, to probe the magnetic structure of a new 2D magnetic semiconductor, CrSBr. We find that CrSBr monolayers are ferromagnetically ordered below 146 K, an observation enabled by the discovery of a giant magnetic dipole SHG effect in the centrosymmetric 2D structure. In multilayers, the ferromagnetic monolayers are coupled antiferromagnetically, with the Néel temperature notably increasing with decreasing layer number. The magnetic structure of CrSBr, comprising spins co-aligned in-plane with rectangular unit cell, differs markedly from the prototypical 2D hexagonal magnets CrI_3 and

$Cr_2Ge_2Te_6$ with out-of-plane moments. Moreover, our SHG analysis suggests that the order

parameters of the ferromagnetic monolayer and the antiferromagnetic bilayer are the magnetic

dipole and the magnetic toroidal moments, respectively. These findings establish CrSBr as an

exciting 2D magnetic semiconductor and SHG as a powerful tool to probe 2D magnetic

symmetry, opening the door to the exploration of coupling between magnetic order and

excitonic/electronic properties, as well as the magnetic toroidal moment, in a broad range of

applications.

5.2 Introduction and Background

SHG typically originates from the dominant electric dipole (ED) mechanism. ED SHG

is forbidden in centrosymmetric materials, but it becomes nonzero when a magnetic phase

transition breaks both space inversion and time reversal symmetries to produce time-

noninvariant, or c-type, SHG, in contrast to the time-invariant i-type SHG[19–21]. While this

symmetry breaking process was recently demonstrated in c-type SHG from the

antiferromagnetic (AF) CrI_3 bilayer[22], ED SHG cannot probe the ferromagnetic (FM)

monolayer because the inversion symmetry persists across the magnetic phase transition. To

fully characterize magnetic symmetry in centrosymmetric monolayers, we need to detect

higher order contributions, particularly magnetic dipole (MD) SHG[23]. In this work, we

demonstrate this capability by using SHG to probe the layer-dependent magnetic symmetry of

the theoretically predicted 2D magnetic semiconductor CrSBr[24,25]. In the bulk, CrSBr is a

layered van der Waals (vdW) A-type antiferromagnet with a bulk Néel temperature (T_N) of 132

K[26]. Each rectangular layer exhibits in-plane anisotropic FM order and these FM layers couple

antiferromagnetically along the stacking direction[26]. In addition to its unique magnetic

structure and high magnetic ordering temperature, CrSBr offers two additional distinguishing

features compared to other 2D magnets: it is air stable and semiconducting as shown in recent transport measurements[27]. Electronic structure calculations predict that the CrSBr monolayer

hosts a fully spin-polarized conduction band[24,25], opening the door to spintronic and magneto-

opto-electronic applications.

5.3 Preparation and Qualification of CrSBr Flakes for Optical Experimentation

Millimeter-size CrSBr single crystals were grown by chemical vapor transport from Cr

and S_2Br_2[27,28]. Single crystal x-ray diffraction (SCXRD) confirms the layered vdW structure

with orthorhombic *Pmmn* space group and structural anisotropy along all three lattice vectors

(**Fig. 5.1A, Table D1**). CrSBr can be easily exfoliated to produce monolayer flakes with lateral

sizes in the tens of μm range (**Fig. 5.1B,C, Fig. D1**).

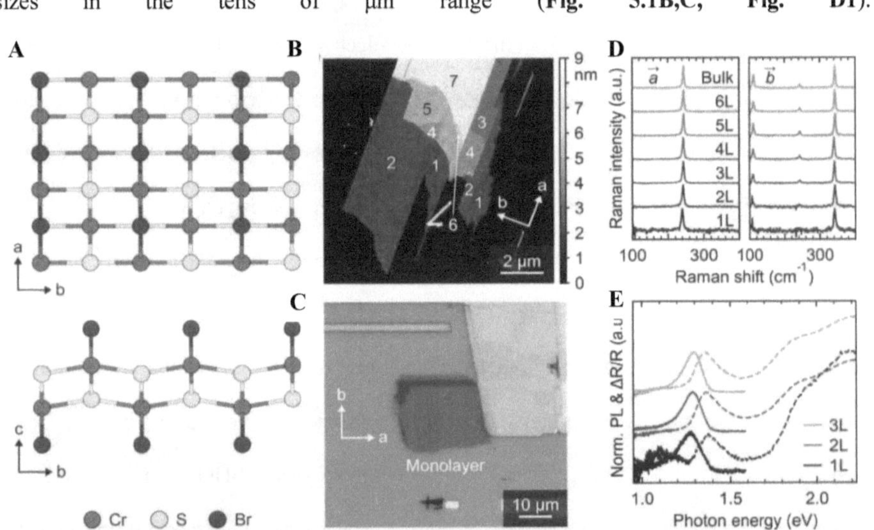

Figure 5. 1 Layer structure and Characterizational spectroscopy of CrSBr
(**A**) Crystal structure of CrSBr viewed along the *c*-axis (top) and *a*-axis (bottom). (**B**) Atomic force microscopy image of an exfoliated flake of varying thicknesses from 1 to 7 layers. (**C**) Optical microscopy image of a CrSBr monolayer on a silicon substrate with 90 nm thermal oxide. (**D**) Layer-dependent Raman spectra (intensity normalized) of samples from one to six layers (1L–6L) and a thin bulk sample on a fused silica substrate with excitation laser polarization along $\vec{a}$ and $\vec{b}$, respectively. (**E**) Normalized photoluminescence (PL, solid) and differential reflectance (dashed) spectra at room temperature from one to three layers (1L–3L) of CrSBr on fused silica. The spectra are offset vertically for clarity.

The thickness of an exfoliated monolayer measured by atomic force microscopy is 0.78 ± 0.03 nm (**Fig. D2**), in excellent agreement with the layer thickness determined from the bulk crystal structure (0.791 nm). The flat needle habit of the CrSBr crystals, a manifestation of the in-plane structural anisotropy, makes identification of the crystallographic directions easy; the long axis coincides with the crystallographic a-axis, as confirmed by SCXRD.

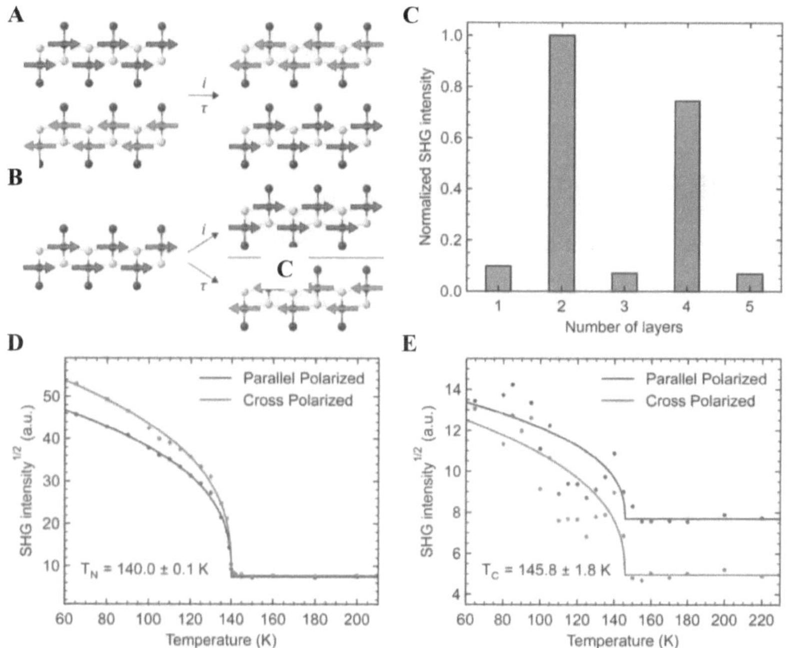

Figure 5. 2 Magnetic symmetries and SHG responses in even and odd numbers of CrSBr layers.
(**A**) AF order in the CrSBr bilayer or other even numbers of layers breaks inversion (i) and time reversal (τ) symmetries and allows ED SHG. (**B**) FM order in the CrSBr monolayer or AF in odd numbers of layers breaks time reversal (τ) but not inversion (i) symmetry and does not allow ED SHG. (**C**) SHG intensity (normalized to that of the bilayer) as a function of the number of layers for the magnetic ordered phases at 4 K. (**D**) Square roots of the average SHG intensity of the bilayer (dots) as a function of temperature in the CrSBr bilayer. The solid curves are fits to $(1-T/T_C)^\beta$ to yield $T_N = 140.0 \pm 0.1$ K and $\beta = 0.36$. (e) Square roots of the average SHG intensities of monolayer CrSBr as a function of temperature. The solid curves are fits to $(1 - T/T_C)^\beta$ with $\beta = 0.36$ to give $T_C = 145.8 \pm 1.8$ K.

Anisotropic peak responses in Raman spectra from bulk down to monolayer confirms that the anisotropic structural morphology persists when the crystals are exfoliated (**Fig. 5.1D,** also **Fig. D3,4)**. **Fig. 5.1E** presents the room temperature photoluminescence (PL) and differential reflectance spectra of CrSBr flakes with 1-3 layer thickness (see **Fig. D5** for PL from bulk crystal). With a PL peak at 1.28-1.29 eV and an absorption peak at 1.36-1.37 eV, the Stokes shifts of ~80 meV are within three times the thermal energy at room temperature, suggesting that PL originates from band-edge emission rather than localized ligand-field luminescence as seen in CrI_3[29]. These results are consistent with CrSBr being a semiconductor as suggested by theoretical calculations[24,25] and demonstrated in bulk transport measurements[27].

5.4 Magnetic Order and Transitions

We probe magnetic order and phase transitions in CrSBr using SHG in parallel and cross-polarization configurations, where fundamental and second harmonic polarizations are parallel and perpendicular to each other, respectively. We choose $hv = 1.55$ eV above the band gap for the resonance enhancement of the SHG signal.

For an even number of CrSBr layers, as illustrated in **Fig. 5.2A** for a bilayer, AF order breaks both inversion (i) and time reversal (τ) symmetry. In contrast, for a monolayer (or an odd number of layers), **Fig. 5.2B**, FM (AF) order breaks time reversal symmetry, but not inversion symmetry. Independent of the number of layers, CrSBr in its paramagnetic (PM) state is centrosymmetric in the mmm (D_{2h}) point group (**Fig. D6**) and thus does not produce SHG intensity in the dominant ED mechanism. Below T_N, the interlayer AF order in the CrSBr bilayer (or other even numbers of layers) breaks spatial inversion and time reversal symmetries (**Fig. 5.2A**) and should exhibit strong nonreciprocal, or time-non-invariant, SHG, as reported for the AF CrI_3 bilayer.[19] In contrast, centrosymmetry is maintained in the magnetically ordered phases of the monolayer or other odd numbers of layers and does not produce SHG in the ED approximation. **Fig. 5.2C** shows the SHG intensity (I_{SHG}) as a function of layer number (1−5) in the magnetically ordered phases at 4 K. SHG intensities from the even numbers of layers are

1 order of magnitude higher than those from the odd numbers, since the ED SHG mechanism

is operative in the former and not the latter.

5.5 SHG in the AF Bilayer

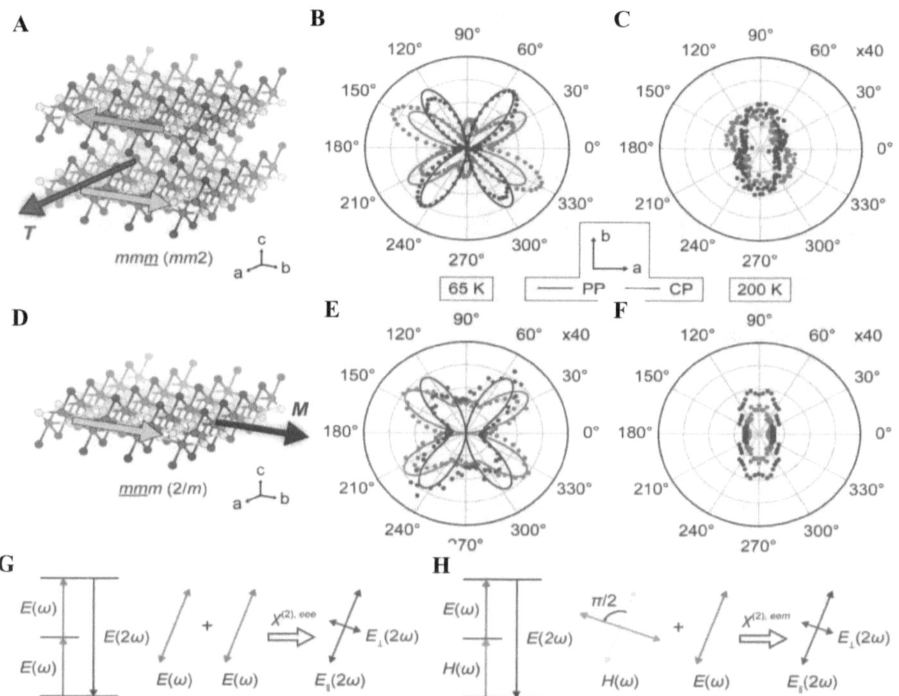

Figure 5. 3 SHG traces of CrSBr
(A) Magnetic symmetry of the AF bilayer, with its magnetic toroidal moment **T** as the order parameter. Polarization-resolved SHG (dots) from the CrSBr bilayer in the AF state at 65 K **(B)** and PM state at 200 K **(C)**. Blue and red colors denote PP and CP excitation and detection configurations, respectively. The solid lines in part b are fits to $|\chi^{(2),ED}|^2$ described by **eq D7**. **(D)** Magnetic symmetry of the FM monolayer, with its net magnetization **M** as the order parameter. Polarization-resolved SHG (dots) from the CrSBr monolayer in the FM state at 65 K **(E)** and PM state at 200 K **(F)**. The solid lines in part e are fits to the magnetic dipole $|\chi^{(2),MD}|^2$ described by **eq D13**. Note that the intensities in parts **C, E,** and **F** are multiplied by a factor of 40, as compared to part **B**. Schematics of the electronic transitions and polarization rules for ED SHG **(G)** and MD SHG **(H)**.

We use $I_{SHG}^{1/2}$ to probe magnetic order as it is proportional to the second-order

susceptibility $|\chi^{(2),ED}|$ in the electric dipole approximation. **Fig. 5.2E** shows the temperature

dependence of $I_{SHG}^{1/2}$ in both parallel and cross-polarizations (PP, CP). Below 140 K, $I_{SHG}^{1/2}$

abruptly increases with decreasing temperature, signaling the loss of centrosymmetry accompanying the PM $\rightarrow$ AF phase transition. The solid curves are fits to $|\chi^{(2),ED}| \propto M(T) = (1 - T/T_N)^{\beta}$,[32] which give $T_N = 140.0 \pm 0.1$ K, higher than the bulk T_N of 132 K. Furthermore, the fits yield $\beta = 0.360 \pm 0.006$, suggesting that the magnetic order of the CrSBr bilayer follows the anisotropic Heisenberg model rather than the Ising ($\beta \approx 0.13$) or the XY model ($\beta \approx 0.23$), and the order is enabled by both single-ion anisotropy and anisotropic exchange interaction.[28,33] There is a weak and constant SHG background signal observed above T_N. The dielectric asymmetry of the sample configuration, with the bottom interfaced to dodecanol passivated fused silica and the top to a vacuum, may break inversion symmetry and lead to weak i-type SHG contribution. In addition, higher-order SHG responses that are independent of the magnetic phase transition may also contribute.[21–23]

5.5.1 SHG in the FM Monolayer

Unexpectedly, for the monolayer where the ED SHG mechanism does not apply, we again observe a rapid rise in $|\chi^{(2)}|$ below a critical temperature, **Fig. 5.2E**, signifying the phase transition from the PM to the FM state. Fits to $(1 - T/T_C)^{\beta}$ yield $T_C = 145.8 \pm 1.8$ K. Note that the SHG background signal above T_C may have the same origin as that in **Fig. 5.2D**. To understand the origin of SHG from the centrosymmetric FM monolayer, we measure and model the polarization dependence of the SHG signals for both the monolayer and bilayer CrSBr. In the AF bilayer, the c-type ED SHG is symmetry-allowed, and the principal axis of rotation is a 2-fold screw axis about the a-axis (**Fig. 5.3A**). Given the mm2 point group of the AF bilayer, we calculate the second-order PP and CP susceptibilities $\chi_{\parallel}^{(2),ED}$ and $\chi_{\perp}^{(2),ED}$ following the procedure detailed in **Tables D2–4**. The resulting fits describing the polarization-dependent SHG intensity (solid lines; **Fig. 5.3B**) agree well with the SHG data measured in the AF phase at 65 K (data point; **Fig. 5.3B**), and the principal axis of rotation determined from the model matches the crystallographic a-axis of the sample. As a comparison, the polarization-dependent SHG signal for the same sample in the PM phase at 200 K is more isotropic and is nearly two orders of magnitude weaker than that from the AF bilayer (**Fig. 5.3C**).

The same cannot be said of SHG from the FM CrSBr monolayer, which stands in stark contrast with the SHG silent FM CrI$_3$ monolayer.[19] When the time reversal operator is considered, the magnetic point group of the FM CrSBr monolayer is _mmm_ (classical subgroup _2/m_), with the principal axis of rotation (2-fold screw axis) along the b-axis (**Fig. 5.3D**). Given that the principal axis of rotation of the AF bilayer is along the a-axis, the ED SHG polarization response of the FM monolayer should be rotated by $\pi/2$ from that of the AF bilayer. Instead, we observe that the AF bilayer and FM monolayer have very similar SHG polar profiles. Thus, the SHG response of the FM CrSBr monolayer does not originate from the ED mechanism, implying that the centrosymmetry is conserved across the magnetic transition, with no sign of an internal canted magnetic structure that could destroy the inversion symmetry (**Fig. D7b**). We must consider SHG arising from higher-order contributions.[24] While the ED SHG mechanism is symmetry-forbidden, the axial tensors χ^{eem} and χ^{mee} governing the magnetic dipole contributions (eqs S8–S14 and associated text) are nonzero with inversion symmetry, making experimentally observable MD SHG a direct probe of the magnetization in the FM monolayer.

The MD susceptibilities $\chi^{(2)}_{\parallel}{}^{,MD}$ and $\chi^{(2)}_{\perp}{}^{,MD}$ calculated for the FM monolayer following the method described in eqs S8–S14 have the same functional forms as $\chi^{(2)}_{\parallel}{}^{,ED}$ and $\chi^{(2)}_{\perp}{}^{,ED}$ for the AF bilayer, and the fits agree very well with the experimental data (**Fig. 5.3E**). As with the bilayer, the SHG spectra in the PM state are not described by the model, confirming that we are probing magnetic symmetry below Tc. Contributions from interface symmetry breaking and the electric quadrupole could be comparable in magnitude to MD SHG, but they remain unchanged with or without time reversal symmetry and may only account for the background SHG signal above Tc. **Fig. 5.3G,H** summarizes the electronic transitions and polarization rules for ED SHG and MD SHG and explains how two different mechanisms can produce the same polar profile. In essence, the change in the principal axis of rotation, from the aaxis in the AF bilayer to the b-axis in the FM monolayer, is compensated by replacing the electric field polarization component of the electromagnetic wave with the perpendicular magnetic field polarization.

The MD SHG signal measured in the centrosymmetric FM CrSBr monolayer is much stronger than expected from the scaling relationship $|\chi^{(2),MD}|/|\chi^{(2),ED}| \sim a/\lambda \sim 10^{-3}$, where a is the unit cell size, and λ is the light wavelength.[21] This scaling law explains why MD SHG has been observed in bulk magnetic solids such as NiO and Cr_2O_3[24,34] but not in 2D materials such as the CrI_3 monolayer.[19] To quantify the surprising MD SHG response of the FM CrSBr monolayer, we compare its magnitude to the SHG responses of the AF CrSBr bilayer, AF CrI_3 bilayer, and MoS_2 monolayer. At 65 K with a 1.55 eV probe, the ED SHG intensity of the AF CrSBr bilayer is ~10 times weaker than that of the MoS_2 monolayer (**Fig. D9**) and comparable to that of the AF CrI_3 bilayer.[19] The MD SHG of the FM CrSBr monolayer is 50 times weaker than the ED SHG of the AF CrSBr bilayer. This translates to $|\chi^{(2),MD}|/|\chi^{(2),ED}| \sim 0.14$, about 2 orders of magnitude higher than that expected from the a/λ scaling.[21] The exact origin for this large MD SHG effect from the FM CrSBr monolayer is not known, but we may speculate on possible origins. There is a well-known mechanism of resonance enhancement,[35] and both $\hbar\omega$ and $2\hbar\omega$ used here are resonant with the above gap optical transitions in CrSBr. Such a resonance effect can lead to a giant enhancement in SHG intensity by up to 3 orders of magnitude when electronic and magnetic transitions are coupled, as reported before for the WSe_2 monolayer.[36] Such electronic–magnetic coupling can be expected in the intrinsic magnetic semiconductor CrSBr.

5.6 Order Parameter of the Magnetic Transitions

Having established the MD SHG and nonreciprocal ED SHG mechanisms for the FM monolayer and AF bilayer, respectively, we address the nature of the order parameter for each magnetic transition. For the FM monolayer, the order parameter is simply the net magnetization along the easy b-axis (**Fig. 5.3D**). For the AF bilayer, the order parameter cannot be the antiferromagnetic vector (i.e., the difference of the net magnetic vector of each layer) because it is noninvariant under symmetry operations of the magnetic order.[32] In agreement with previous studies that have shown SHG as an effective tool[37–39] to probe magnetic toroidal moments, the order parameter for the AF bilayer is likely the magnetic toroidal moment given by

$$\mathbf{T} = \pm \frac{1}{2} d M \hat{a} \qquad (4.1)$$

where d is the distance between two layers, M is net magnetization of each layer, and â is the unit vector along a.[40] Despite that both $\chi^{(2),ED}$ of the AF bilayer and $\chi^{(2),MD}$ of the FM monolayer inherit their values from i-type rank 4 axial tensors of the mmm point group and their paramagnetic phases, they can possess different nonzero elements due to distinct orientations of their order parameters (see the SI for details). The presence of magnetic toroidal moments in the AF CrSBr bilayer offers the enticing possibilities of finding the magnetoelectric effect.[37] We note that the magnetic toroidal moment describes the distribution of spins in space, and the emergence of the toroidal moment as the order parameter of the CrSBr bilayer despite its absence in the bulk likely results from the breaking of translational symmetry along the c-axis. The same principle may be generalizable to the monoclinically stacked AF CrI$_3$ bilayer, those SHG may originate from its nontrivial toroidal magnetic moment.[41]

We turn to the surprising finding that T_N increases with decreasing layer number in CrSBr. In addition to the AF bilayer and FM monolayer (**Fig. 5.2, and Fig.s S10−S12**), we measured SHG from a 6-layer CrSBr flake (**Fig. D13**) and determined its T_N to be 137.9 ± 5.2 K (**Fig. 5.4A**). For a comparison, T_N = 132 K in bulk CrSBr (**Fig. D14**).[28,29] Such an increase in the magnetic phase transition temperature is in stark contrast to observations in other 2D magnets[1–3] and seemingly contradicts conventional understanding, which predicts a decreased stability of the magnetically ordered phase as the materials approaches the 2D limit.[6,42] As a possible explanation for this anomaly, we propose that the interlayer T_C could differ from interlayer T_N; i.e., there is an intermediate magnetic phase (labeled iFM) in which individual layers are ferromagnetically ordered internally, but the interlayer coupling remains

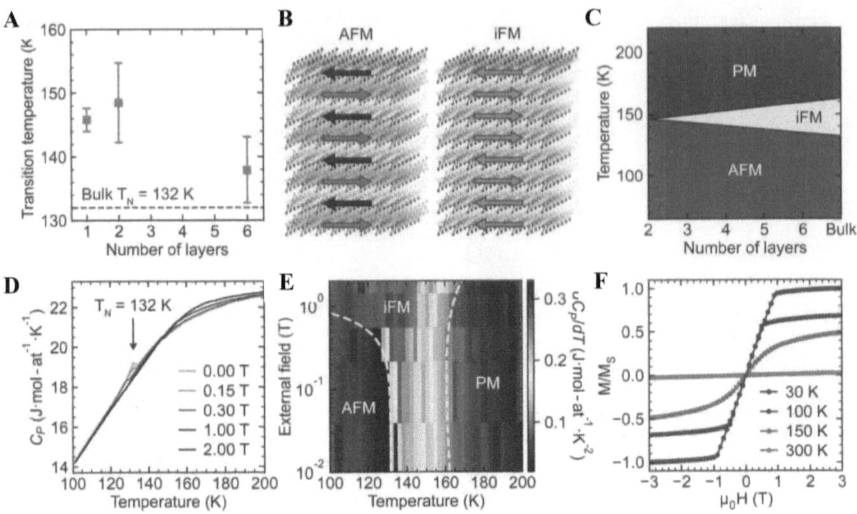

Figure 5. 4 Magnetic transitions of different layers of CrSBr.
(A) Magnetic phase transition temperature as a function of layer number, probed by SHG.
(B) Structures of AF and iFM phases in bulk CrSBr at zero field. (C) Schematic magnetic
phase diagram presented as a function of layer number and temperature. (D) Heat capacity
of bulk CrSBr as a function of temperature at different applied magnetic fields. The curves
show a sharp AF transition at 132 K and a broad feature around 160 K assigned to intralayer
FM ordering. The external field is applied along the c-axis. (E) Magnetic phase diagram of
bulk CrSBr, as determined from C_P measurements. The yellow dashed lines are guides to
the eye to distinguish the different magnetic phases. (F) Magnetization versus applied
magnetic field at T = 30, 100, 150, and 300 K. M is normalized to the saturation
magnetization value at T = 50 K. The magnetic field is applied along the a-axis. Data in part
E are reproduced from ref (29).

paramagnetic. A related spin polarized phase at 17.2 K has been observed for $CrCl_3$, which is

slightly above the bulk AF transition (T_N = 14.1 K).[43–45] The different magnetic phases of CrSBr

and their proposed evolution as a function of layer number and temperature are illustrated in

Fig. 5.4B,C. In bulk, the intralayer Curie temperature (T^{intra}_C) is significantly higher than T_N

because the intralayer superexchange coupling is much stronger than the interlayer super-

super-exchange coupling (**Fig. D15**).[28] Spin waves traveling along the c-direction can disturb

the weak interlayer AF coupling while maintaining the stronger intralayer FM order, resulting

in the iFM phase.

Decreasing the sample thickness confines and suppresses the spin wave excitation along

the c-axis, further stabilizing the AF phase and causing T_N to increase toward T^{intra}_C (**Fig. 5.4C**).

The iFM phase is hidden in the SHG response because the centrosymmetry persists across the PM to iFM phase transition, explaining the apparent increase of T_N with decreasing layer number. Concurrently, Tc^{intra} decreases, following the universal behavior of a spin wave, which destabilizes magnetic order in low-dimensional systems. This issue deserves future experimental (e.g., by neutron scattering, and Lorentz transmission electron microscopy) and theoretical (model Hamiltonian and first-principles) efforts.

Bulk heat capacity (C_P) measurements support this magnetic phase diagram. The temperature dependence of C_P at zero field displays a clear peak at 132 K corresponding to T_N (**Fig. 5.4D**). The curve also shows a broad transition around 160 K (change in the slope) assigned to T^{intra}_C . The features assigned to T_N and T^{intra}_C correspondingly shift to lower and higher temperatures with increasing applied magnetic field, as expected for AF and FM transitions, respectively. The phase diagram presented in Fig. 4e summarizes these results. In agreement with Fig. 4c, we note the decline of T^{intra}_C with decreasing sample thickness, from ~ 160 K in the bulk to ~ 146 K in the monolayer. The iFM phase is also supported by isothermal field-dependent magnetization (M) measurements (**Fig. 5.4F, Fig. D16**). Below T_N (30 and 100 K), the antiferromagnetically coupled spins (along the magnetic easy b-axis) collectively and progressively align with the applied magnetic field (along the a-axis), until fully polarized above the saturation field. In the PM phase (300 K), M increases weakly and linearly with the applied field, never reaching saturation. The same PM behavior would be expected slightly above T_N (150 K), but instead we measure a sigmoidal response eliciting 2D superparamagnetic behavior. At 150 K, the material is in the iFM phase; it does not exhibit 3D long-range magnetic order, but the sigmoidal shape of M indicates that the 2D layers are ferromagnetically ordered internally.

5.7 Discussion of Results

Using second harmonic generation, we have demonstrated the emergence of ferromagnetic order in the 2D semiconductor CrSBr monolayer with a Curie temperature of $T_C = 146 \pm 2$ K. The identification of the FM order is enabled by a large MD SHG effect with $\chi^{(2)}$ 2 orders of magnitude larger than expected. Multilayer CrSBr displays interlayer antiferromagnetic order, and T_N surprisingly increases with decreasing layer number, suggesting the presence of a hidden intralayer FM and interlayer PM phase between T_N and T_C. In addition to magnetic symmetries, SHG analysis suggests the magnetic dipole moment and magnetic toroidal moment as order parameters for the ferromagnetic monolayer and the antiferromagnetic bilayer, respectively. These findings establish the power of SHG in probing magnetic symmetry down to the 2D monolayer limit. Finally, the embodiment of both 2D magnetic and 2D semiconducting properties in a single material opens the door to exciting prospects of controlling one by the other. As the first step toward realizing this exciting potential, our preliminary results confirm that magnetic order in CrSBr is strongly coupled to carriers in magnetotransport measurements showing large negative magnetoresistance.[29] Work is currently underway to understand the microscopic mechanisms of these couplings. Future research may explore the coupling between magnetic order and excitonic/electronic properties, as well as the magnetic toroidal moments, in a broad range of potential applications from coupled magnetic, spin, electronic, and optical processes.

5.8 References

1.   Lee, J.-U.; Lee, S.; Ryoo, J. H.; Kang, S.; Kim, T. Y.; Kim, P.; Park, C.-H.; Park, J.-G.; Cheong, H. Ising-Type Magnetic Ordering in Atomically Thin FePS3. Nano Lett. 2016, 16 (12),7433−7438.
(2) Gong, C.; Li, L.; Li, Z.; Ji, H.; Stern, A.; Xia, Y.; Cao, T.; Bao, W.; Wang, C.; Wang, Y. Discovery of Intrinsic Ferromagnetism in Two-Dimensional van Der Waals Crystals. Nature 2017, 546 (7657), 265−269.

2. Huang, B.; Clark, G.; Navarro-Moratalla, E.; Klein, D. R.; Cheng, R.; Seyler, K. L.; Zhong, D.; Schmidgall, E.; McGuire, M. A.; Cobden, D. H. Layer-Dependent Ferromagnetism in a van Der Waals Crystal down to the Monolayer Limit. Nature 2017, 546 (7657), 270.

3. Mermin, N. D.; Wagner, H. Absence of Ferromagnetism or Antiferromagnetism in One- or Two-Dimensional Isotropic Heisen- berg Models. Phys. Rev. Lett. 1966, 17 (22), 1133.

4. Gong, C.; Zhang, X. Two-Dimensional Magnetic Crystals and Emergent Heterostructure Devices. Science 2019, 363 (6428), No. eaav4450.

5. Gibertini, M.; Koperski, M.; Morpurgo, A. F.; Novoselov, K. S. Magnetic 2D Materials and Heterostructures. Nat. Nanotechnol. 2019, 14 (5), 408–419.

6. Burch, K. S.; Mandrus, D.; Park, J.-G. Magnetism in Two- Dimensional van Der Waals Materials. Nature 2018, 563 (7729), 47– 52.

7. Mak, K. F.; Shan, J.; Ralph, D. C. Probing and Controlling Magnetic States in 2D Layered Magnetic Materials. Nat. Rev. Phys. 2019, 1 (11), 646–661.

8. Chen, W.; Sun, Z.; Wang, Z.; Gu, L.; Xu, X.; Wu, S.; Gao, C. Direct Observation of van Der Waals Stacking–Dependent Interlayer Magnetism. Science 2019, 366 (6468), 983–987.

9. Song, T.; Fei, Z.; Yankowitz, M.; Lin, Z.; Jiang, Q.; Hwangbo, K.; Zhang, Q.; Sun, B.; Taniguchi, T.; Watanabe, K. Switching 2D Magnetic States via Pressure Tuning of Layer Stacking. Nat. Mater. 2019, 18, 1298–1302.

10. McGuire, M. A.; Dixit, H.; Cooper, V. R.; Sales, B. C. Coupling of Crystal Structure and Magnetism in the Layered, Ferromagnetic Insulator CrI3. Chem. Mater. 2015, 27 (2), 612–620.

11. Huang, B.; Cenker, J.; Zhang, X.; Ray, E. L.; Song, T.; Taniguchi, T.; Watanabe, K.; Mcguire, M. A.; Xiao, D.; Xu, X. Tuning Inelastic Light Scattering via Symmetry Control in the Two- Dimensional Magnet CrI3. Nat. Nanotechnol. 2020, 15 (March), 212–217.

12. Jiang, S.; Li, L.; Wang, Z.; Mak, K. F.; Shan, J. Controlling Magnetism in 2D CrI3 by Electrostatic Doping. Nat. Nanotechnol. 2018, 13 (7), 549–553.

13. Huang, B.; Clark, G.; Klein, D. R.; MacNeill, D.; Navarro- Moratalla, E.; Seyler, K. L.; Wilson, N.; McGuire, M. A.; Cobden, D. H.; Xiao, D. Electrical Control of 2D Magnetism in Bilayer CrI3. Nat. Nanotechnol. 2018, 13 (7), 544–548.

14. Liu, S.; Yuan, X.; Zou, Y.; Sheng, Y.; Huang, C.; Zhang, E.; Ling, J.; Liu, Y.; Wang, W.; Zhang, C. Wafer-Scale Two-Dimensional Ferromagnetic Fe3GeTe2 Thin Films Grown by Molecular Beam Epitaxy. npj 2D Mater. Appl. 2017, 1 (1), 1–7.

15. Song, T.; Cai, X.; Tu, M. W.-Y.; Zhang, X.; Huang, B.; Wilson, N. P.; Seyler, K. L.; Zhu, L.; Taniguchi, T.; Watanabe, K. Giant Tunneling Magnetoresistance in Spin-Filter van Der Waals Hetero- structures. Science 2018, 360 (6394), 1214–1218.

16. Klein, D. R.; MacNeill, D.; Lado, J. L.; Soriano, D.; Navarro- Moratalla, E.; Watanabe, K.; Taniguchi, T.; Manni, S.; Canfield, P.; Fernández-Rossier, J. Probing Magnetism in 2D van Der Waals Crystalline Insulators via Electron Tunneling. Science 2018, 360 (6394), 1218–1222.

17. Thiel, L.; Wang, Z.; Tschudin, M. A.; Rohner, D.; Gutiérrez- Lezama, I.; Ubrig, N.; Gibertini, M.; Giannini, E.; Morpurgo, A. F.; Maletinsky, P. Probing Magnetism in 2D Materials at the Nanoscale with Single-Spin Microscopy. Science 2019, 364 (6444), 973–976.

18. Sun, Z.; Yi, Y.; Song, T.; Clark, G.; Huang, B.; Shan, Y.; Wu, S.; Huang, D.; Gao, C.; Chen, Z. Giant Nonreciprocal Second-Harmonic Generation from Antiferromagnetic Bilayer CrI3. Nature 2019, 572 (7770), 497–501.

19. Chu, H.; Roh, C. J.; Island, J. O.; Li, C.; Lee, S.; Chen, J.; Park, J.-G.; Young, A. F.; Lee, J. S.; Hsieh, D. Linear Magnetoelectric Phase in Ultrathin MnPS3 Probed by Optical Second Harmonic Generation. Phys. Rev. Lett. 2020, 124 (2), 27601.

20. Fiebig, M.; Pavlov, V. V.; Pisarev, R. V. Second-Harmonic Generation as a Tool for Studying Electronic and Magnetic Structures of Crystals. J. Opt. Soc. Am. B 2005, 22 (1), 96–118.

21. Kirilyuk, A.; Rasing, T. Magnetization-Induced-Second- Harmonic Generation from Surfaces and Interfaces. J. Opt. Soc. Am. B 2005, 22 (1), 148–167.

22. Němec, P.; Fiebig, M.; Kampfrath, T.; Kimel, A. V. Antiferromagnetic Opto-Spintronics. Nat. Phys. 2018, 14 (3), 229– 241.

23. Fiebig, M.; Fröhlich, D.; Lottermoser, T.; Pavlov, V. V.; Pisarev, R. V.; Weber, H.-J. Second Harmonic Generation in the Centrosymmetric Antiferromagnet NiO. Phys. Rev. Lett. 2001, 87 (13), 137202.

24. Guo, Y.; Zhang, Y.; Yuan, S.; Wang, B.; Wang, J. Chromium Sulfide Halide Monolayers: Intrinsic Ferromagnetic Semiconductors with Large Spin Polarization and High Carrier Mobility. Nanoscale 2018, 10 (37), 18036–18042.

25. Wang, C.; Zhou, X.; Zhou, L.; Tong, N.-H.; Lu, Z.-Y.; Ji, W. A Family of High-Temperature Ferromagnetic Monolayers with Locked Spin-Dichroism-Mobility Anisotropy: MnNX and CrCX (X= Cl, Br, I; C= S, Se, Te). Sci. Bull. 2019, 64 (5), 293–300.

26. Wang, H.; Qi, J.; Qian, X. Electrically Tunable High Curie Temperature Two-Dimensional Ferromagnetism in van Der Waals Layered Crystals. Appl. Phys. Lett. 2020, 117 (8), 83102.

27. Göser, O.; Paul, W.; Kahle, H. G. Magnetic Properties of CrSBr. J. Magn. Magn. Mater. 1990, 92 (1), 129–136.

28. Telford, E. J.; Dismukes, A. H.; Lee, K.; Cheng, M.; Wieteska, A.; Chen, Y.-S.; Xu, X.; Pasupathy, A. N.; Zhu, X.; Dean, C. R.; Roy, X. Layered Antiferromagnetism Induces Large Negative Magneto-

29. resistance in the van Der Waals Semiconductor CrSBr. Adv. Mater. 2020, 32, 2003240.

30. Beck, J. Über Chalkogenidhalogenide Des Chroms Synthese, Kristallstruktur Und Magnetismus von Chromsulfidbromid, CrSBr. Z. Anorg. Allg. Chem. 1990, 585 (1), 157–167.

31. Seyler, K. L.; Zhong, D.; Klein, D. R.; Gao, S.; Zhang, X.; Huang, B.; Navarro-Moratalla, E.; Yang, L.; Cobden, D. H.; McGuire, M. A. Ligand-Field Helical Luminescence in a 2D Ferromagnetic Insulator. Nat. Phys. 2018, 14 (3), 277–281.

32. Sa, D.; Valenti, R.; Gros, C. A Generalized Ginzburg-Landau Approach to Second Harmonic Generation. Eur. Phys. J. B 2000, 14 (2), 301–305.

33. Bramwell, S. T.; Holdsworth, P. C. W. Universality in Two- dimensional Magnetic Systems. J. Appl. Phys. 1993, 73 (10), 6096– 6098.

34. Fiebig, M.; Fröhlich, D.; Krichevtsov, B. B.; Pisarev, R. V. Second Harmonic Generation and Magnetic-Dipole-Electric-Dipole Interference in Antiferromagnetic Cr2O3. Phys. Rev. Lett. 1994, 73 (15), 2127.

35. Yao, K.; Yanev, E.; Chuang, H.-J.; Rosenberger, M. R.; Xu, X.; Darlington, T.; McCreary, K. M.; Hanbicki, A. T.; Watanabe, K.; Taniguchi, T. Continuous Wave Sum Frequency Generation and Imaging of Monolayer and Heterobilayer Two-Dimensional Semi-conductors. ACS Nano 2020, 14 (1), 708–714.

36. Wang, G.; Marie, X.; Gerber, I.; Amand, T.; Lagarde, D.; Bouet, L.; Vidal, M.; Balocchi, A.; Urbaszek, B. Giant Enhancement of the Optical Second-Harmonic Emission of WSe 2 Monolayers by Laser Excitation at Exciton Resonances. Phys. Rev. Lett. 2015, 114 (9), 97403.

37. Spaldin, N. A.; Fiebig, M.; Mostovoy, M. The Toroidal Moment in Condensed-Matter Physics and Its Relation to the Magnetoelectric Effect. J. Phys.: Condens. Matter 2008, 20 (43), 434203.

38. Van Aken, B. B.; Rivera, J.-P.; Schmid, H.; Fiebig, M. Observation of Ferrotoroidic Domains. Nature 2007, 449 (7163), 702–705.

39. Zimmermann, A. S.; Meier, D.; Fiebig, M. Ferroic Nature of Magnetic Toroidal Order. Nat. Commun. 2014, 5 (1), 1–6.
40. Dubovik, V. M.; Tugushev, V. V. Toroid Moments in Electrodynamics and Solid-State Physics. Phys. Rep. 1990, 187 (4), 145–202.
41. Cheong, S.-W. Trompe L'oeil Ferromagnetism. npj Quantum Mater. 2020, 5 (37), 1–8.
42. Zhang, R.; Willis, R. F. Thickness-Dependent Curie Temper- atures of Ultrathin Magnetic Films: Effect of the Range of Spin-Spin Interactions. Phys. Rev. Lett. 2001, 86 (12), 2665.
43. Kuhlow, B. Magnetic Ordering in CrCl3 at the Phase Transition. Phys. status solidi 1982, 72 (1), 161–168.
44. McGuire, M. A.; Clark, G.; Santosh, K. C.; Chance, W. M.; Jellison, G. E., Jr; Cooper, V. R.; Xu, X.; Sales, B. C. Magnetic Behavior and Spin-Lattice Coupling in Cleavable van Der Waals Layered CrCl3 Crystals. Phys. Rev. Mater. 2017, 1 (1), 14001.
45. Cai, X.; Song, T.; Wilson, N. P.; Clark, G.; He, M.; Zhang, X.; Taniguchi, T.; Watanabe, K.; Yao, W.; Xiao, D. Atomically Thin CrCl3: An in-Plane Layered Antiferromagnetic Insulator. Nano Lett. 2019, 19 (6), 3993–3998.

Chapter 6: Polarons and s-d Exchange in CrSBr

6.1 Introduction and Background

The realization of spintronic devices relies on materials with strongly coupled electronic and magnetic properties. [1,2] Magnetic semiconductors, particularly at the two-dimensional (2D) limit, are an ideal platform to study spintronic-related phenomena,[3] including spin-hall effects[4] and giant magnetoresistance,[5,6] due to the field-tunability of both electronic behavior and magnetism.[7,8] Despite this, materials exhibiting both semiconducting transport characteristics and intrinsic magnetic order are rare.[9] One strategy for simultaneously realizing these properties is by introducing magnetic defects into non-magnetic semiconductors. These materials, called dilute magnetic semiconductors (DMSs), manifest strong coupling between magnetic order and transport arising from carrier-mediated exchange interactions. [10] Another route towards accessing these properties is by modifying the electronic structure of intrinsic layered van der Waals (vdW) magnets through defect engineering;[11] however, the role of defects in vdW magnets is relatively underexplored due to the limited number of intrinsic layered magnets and the diversity of exchange mechanisms by which bulk magnetism emerges. Here we identify and investigate the role of charge defects in modifying the magnetic and electronic structures of CrSBr, which shows both an antiferromagnetic transition that is seemingly immune to changes in the charge defect concentration and a ferrimagnetic transition that is sensitive to changes in charge carrier concentration.[12–14]

CrSBr is a layered vdW semiconductor that demonstrates type-A antiferromagnetism below 134 K in which the net magnetic moment for each layer is oriented in-plane, parallel to the *b*-axis (see **Fig. 6.1A**). Recently, it was proposed that the complex low-temperature magnetotransport signatures that emerge below 33 K (**Fig. 6.1B**) are consistent with a hybrid polaron and s-d exchange model (see Ch. 3). The s-d exchange model describes a magnetic state in which localized and spin-polarized charge carriers mediate ferromagnetic coupling between magnetic defects embedded in the nuclear lattice (**Fig. 6.1C**).[15–17] Such a transition results in a ferromagnetic sublattice of coupled magnetic defects within the intrinsic

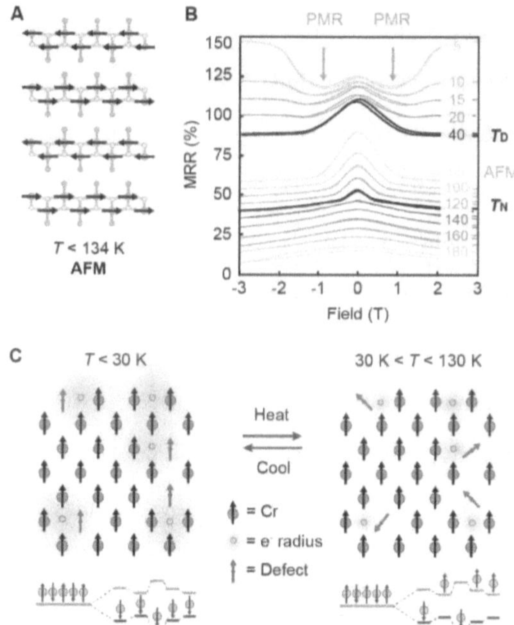

Figure 6. 1 Crystal and magnetic structures of CrSBr.
(**A**) Diagrammatic representation of pristine CrSBr intrinsic magnetic order at temperatures below T_N (134 K). (**B**) Magnetoresistance ratios (MRR) measured as a function of *B*-field strength and temperature (in Kelvin along right axis) with critical points and magnetic orders labeled (MRR $\parallel$ *a*-axis, $B \parallel$ *c*-axis). (**C**) Diagrammatic representation of proposed s-d exchange mechanism in CrSBr at temperatures below 30 K, T_D. The grey spheres represent Cr atoms present in a top-down view of a single layer of CrSBr and the red arrows represent magnetic defects. Green circles represent localized electrons facilitating FM coupling between the magnetic defects through a temperature-dependent coupling radius. Below the magnetic lattice is a representation of the energy splitting of charge defect bands induced by the magnetic lattice.

antiferromagnetic lattice, making this phase ferrimagnetic. Unique to the mechanism proposed for CrSBr compared to the conventional s-d exchange model described for DMSs is the expectation that the magnetic lattice of Cr atoms results in energy splitting of spin-polarized defect bands, leading to exchange splitting even in the absence of an applied magnetic field.

In this work, we demonstrate the strong correlation between magnetotransport features associated with the low-temperature magnetic state ($T < 33$ K) and Br vacancies in the material. We propose that Br deficiency dopes the system with electrons and introduces defect bands that amplify, if not originate, s-d exchange-like coupling, resulting in the low-temperature ferrimagnetic state ($T_D = 33$ K). Importantly, we find that we can amplify the signatures of the ferrimagnetic phase in magnetoresistance (MR) measurements without changing the magnetic susceptibility associated with the coupling of magnetic impurities, leading us to conclude that the charge defects are distinct from the magnetic defects in this system. We further investigate the possibility that the intrinsic magnetic lattice induces energy splitting of spin-polarized charge defect bands by measuring magnetic transition temperatures in the $CrSCl_xBr_{1-x}$ solid solution. In the solid solution, the Weiss constant, in-plane ferromagnetic transition temperature, and low-temperature magnetic transition are thermally suppressed relative to CrSBr. We propose that this results from a decrease in the magnetic exchange splitting energy of spin-polarized defect bands and provides strong evidence that the intrinsic magnetic lattice induces this energy splitting.

6.2 Setting the Baseline: Pristine CrSBr

We observe significant batch-to-batch variation in the low-temperature magnetic and electronic transport behavior of CrSBr: while the antiferromagnetic transition temperature ($T_N = 134$ K) is consistent across samples, the magnitude of the magnetic susceptibility increase (see **Fig. 6.2A**) and MR signatures below 33 K (T_D) vary substantially.[14] We also measure sample-to-sample variation of the in-plane conductivity anisotropy ($\sigma \parallel$ *a*-axis / $\sigma \parallel$ *b*-axis) measured on single crystals of CrSBr; the *a*-axis is more conductive than the *b*-axis, with anisotropies ranging from 15 to 450x between single crystal devices (see **Figures 2B** and **2C**). The in-plane transport anisotropy is particularly intriguing given that electronic structure calculations show the *b*-axis to be more dispersive than the *a*-axis. We observe that more pronounced positive MR (PMR) features emerge at temperatures below the T_D in devices showing higher conductivity anisotropies, suggesting that the PMR features and transport anisotropy are correlated.

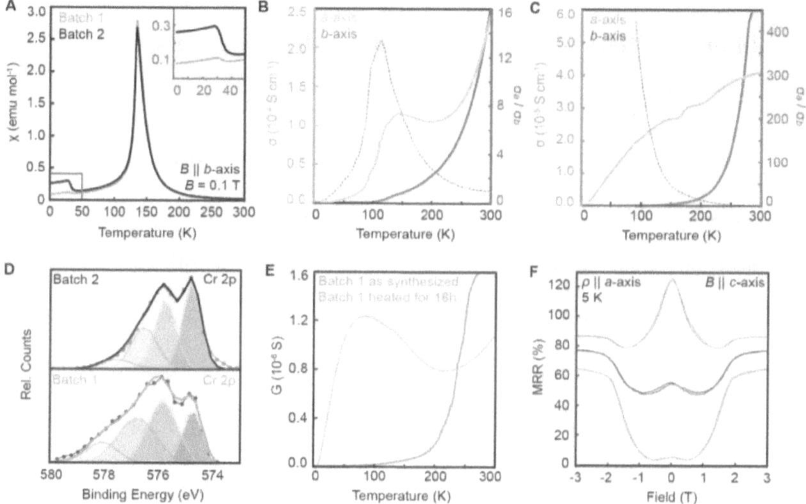

Figure 6. 2 In-plane transport anisotropy in CrSBr.
(**A**) Zero-field-cooled magnetic susceptibility traces collected on single crystals from Batch 1 (purple) and Batch 2 (black) ($B \parallel$ *b*-axis, $B = 0.1$ T). The inset highlights the difference in susceptibility between the two batches below 30 K. The zero-field in-plane conductivity anisotropy between the *a*- and *b*-axes for single crystals from (**B**) Batch 1 and (**C**) Batch 2. (**D**) X-ray photoelectron spectra focused on the Cr 2p region collected on crystals of CrSBr from two different batches, Batch 1 (purple) and Batch 2 (grey), highlighting the decrease in intensity at the peak centered around 577 eV (brown outline) between Batch 1 and Batch 2. (**E**) Zero-field conductance traces for the unheated (light purple) and heated (brown) crystals of CrSBr with the *a*-axis as the source direction. (**F**) MRR traces collected at 5 K for the Batch 1 crystals of CrSBr as synthesized (purple), Batch 2 crystals as synthesized (black), and Batch 1 crystals heated for 18h (brown) with MRR $\parallel$ *a*-axis and $B \parallel$ *c*-axis.

X-ray diffraction (XRD) and energy dispersive X-ray spectroscopy (EDX) measurements performed on CrSBr single crystals with differing magnetic and transport behaviors reveal no significant structural or bulk chemical differences that could account for bbb the difference in performance. X-ray photoelectron spectra (XPS) collected on CrSBr samples did, however, reveal subtle Br deficiency in samples showing higher conductivity anisotropies and PMR features. We observe a decrease in the Cr $2p^{3/2}$ peak intensities that correspond to the Cr-Br bonding environments relative to those that correspond to the Cr-S bonding environments (**Fig. 6.2D**).

6.3 Probing the Effect of Bromine Deficiency by Mass Loss

To further investigate the correlation between Br deficiency and variations in transport behavior, we selected single crystals of CrSBr with stoichiometric Br and cut them to produce several single crystalline fragments derived from the same parent crystal. This was done in order to ensure all of the samples initially had comparable defect densities. Half of the samples were annealed at 100 °C for 18h, which results in a mass loss of ~0.6 wt% in bulk crystals by thermogravimetric analysis (see Appendix E). The other half of the samples were stored at room temperature. A comparison of the XPS Cr 2p spectra for CrSBr samples collected with and without thermal annealing reproduces the difference in peak shape of the XPS spectra for as-synthesized Br-deficient CrSBr samples (**Figure 2D**), suggesting that the 0.6 wt% is loss of Br content (1.2 mol%).

Transport devices prepared from the thermally annealed samples show a dramatic increase in the a-axis conductivity (**Fig. 6.2E**) and amplification of the low temperature PMR features (**Fig. 6.2F**) compared to the unheated samples. Together, these observations point to Br deficiency as the primary contributor to variation in transport performance between as-synthesized CrSBr samples. A recent report on the transport and magnetotransport of CrSBr at the few-layer limit demonstrates that the MR features at below T_D can be tuned by electron doping via electrostatic gating. At low electron doping levels, a negative MR (NMR) response dominates and, as the doping level is increased, the PMR response grows in and finally dominates the MR signature at high electron doping levels. Given that Br deficiency amplifies the PMR features, we propose that Br deficiency dopes CrSBr with electrons and that the defect states occupied by these electrons originate and amplify both the in-plane transport anisotropy and complex low temperature MR signature.

The shape of the MR curve below T_D and its sensitivity to electrostatic gate were used to propose a mechanism for this complex behavior: polarons, which conventionally yield NMR signatures,[18] dominate the MR response at low electron doping levels and s-d exchange, which generally produces a PMR response, dominates at high doping levels. The remainder of this discussion further explores whether these mechanisms appropriately describe the magnetic and electronic behaviors of CrSBr near and below the T_D.

6.4 Mechanisms of Magnetism in low-T CrSBr

6.4.1 Polarons in CrSBr

Previous results strongly suggest the existence of polarons in CrSBr, although it was not shown through direct measurement. We performed a pair distribution function (PDF) analysis of variable-temperature 2D powder XRD images to further investigate this claim. Single-crystal XRD (SCXRD) measurements of CrSBr collected from 5 K to room temperature show that CrSBr does not undergo a commensurate structural change within this temperature range. The variable-temperature PDF traces (**Fig. 6.3A**) reiterate this conclusion, although the lattice constants refined from the PXRD patterns show an onset of negative thermal expansion below ~50 K along all three crystallographic axes consistent with the onset of repulsive polarons (**Fig. 6.3B**). The region of greatest change in PDF traces between temperature sweeps falls within 5 and 7 Å (**Fig. 6.3C**), in which a single broad feature at 350 K sharpens into three distinct peaks upon cooling. The middle of these three peaks is centered at ~5.9 Å, which matches the spacing between Cr atoms along in-plane diagonals measured from the SCXRD structure. We propose that the two peaks centered at 5.4 and 6.3 Å result from clustering and repulsion of Cr atoms along the in-plane Cr diagonals (**Fig. 6.3C inset**). Although direct imaging of this proposed intralayer Cr atom clustering/repulsion is required to further investigate its role in the transport properties of CrSBr, this incommensurate distortion behavior strongly supports the presence of polarons.

6.4.2 s-d exchange

We also investigated the possibility that an s-d exchange-like mechanism produces the PMR signal in CrSBr. s-d exchange is a mechanism by which magnetic defects become ferromagnetically coupled by localized charge carriers occupying spin polarized electronic bands/states. We observe that the magnitude of the PMR response can be increased through Br loss without changing the magnitude of the magnetic susceptibility increase at T_D, indicating CrSBr hosts separate charge defects and magnetic defects, consistent with the s-d exchange model. The increase in the positive MR response would then be interpreted as a direct read-out of the charge defect concentration, while susceptibility increase at T_D corresponds to the magnetic defect concentration.

Conventionally, the onset for s-d exchange occurs in DMSs at temperatures proportional to exchange splitting induced by magnetic defects under an applied magnetic field. In CrSBr, however, the susceptibility and MR features reminiscent of an s-d exchange-like mechanism are present even in the absence of an applied magnetic field. We also observe saturation of the PMR signature at fields comparable to H_S, indicating that the intrinsic magnetic lattice plays a role in the low-temperature magnetic phase. We propose that magnetic defect ordering is directly linked to the magnetization of the intrinsic CrSBr lattice. To investigate this hypothesis, we synthesized the $CrSCl_xBr_{1-x}$ solid solution. Computationally-determined exchange coupling strengths predict weaker coupling in the theoretical CrSCl. For this reason, we predicted that partial substitution of Br for Cl would weaken intralayer exchange coupling, while preserving the relevant magnetic and transport features.

6.5 Sub-stoichiometric CrSBr to weaken Intralayer Exchange Coupling

6.5.1 $CrSBrCl_xBr_{1-x}$: Synthesis and Chemical Analysis

The synthesis of $CrSCl_xBr_{1-x}$ was adapted from the literature; we reacted Cr metal with S_2Br_2 and S_2Cl_2 (2 : 0.67 : 0.33 mol ratio) via chemical vapor transport (see **SI**). EDX spectra of the $CrSCl_xBr_{1-x}$ crystals indicate that the composition of the synthesized crystals reflects the relative stoichiometry between S_2Br_2 and S_2Cl_2 present during crystal growth, $CrSCl_{0.33}Br_{0.67}$ and SCXRD measurements confirm that the average structure of the solid solution matches that of CrSBr (see Appendix E). While the similarity in bonding character between Cl and Br implies substitution of Br atoms for Cl atom in the solid solution, the high propensity to form stacking faults limits single crystal quality and we cannot confirm via SCXRD alone that Cl and Br occupy the same lattice position within the crystal structure. Scanning transmission electron microscopy high-angle annular dark field (STEM-HAADF) images of $CrSCl_{0.33}Br_{0.67}$ flakes show that the flake is structurally homogenous throughout the imaged region and that Cl atoms substitutionally replace Br atoms. The Cl atoms are well distributed throughout the solid solution (**Fig. 6.3D**), only forming patches enriched in Cl atoms smaller than ~10 nm. The STEM-HAADF images are collected with the viewing direction parallel to the stacking axis of the $CrSCl_{0.33}Br_{0.67}$ flake such that there are only two unique lattice sites patterned throughout the image: columns of Cr atoms (low contrast) and columns of S, Cl, and Br atoms (high contrast). Overlayed intensity maps of the fitted Cr and S/Cl/Br atom columns (**Fig. 6.3E**) suggest that regions of the $CrSCl_{0.33}Br_{0.67}$ flake enriched in Cl atoms are also deficient in Cr as

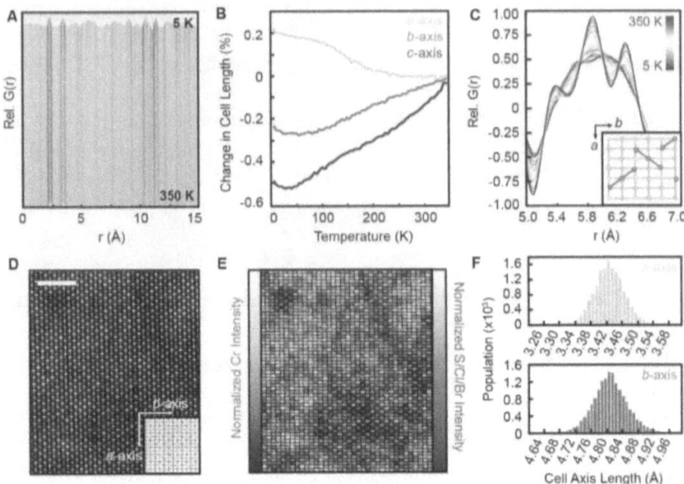

Figure 6. 3 Structural characterization of CrSBr and CrSCl$_{0.33}$Br$_{0.67}$.
(**A**) PDF analysis of CrSBr PXRD patterns between 5 and 350 K in which the probability of atoms interacting at interatomic spacings, G(r), is plotted as a function of the interatomic distance. (**B**) Percent change in the lattice parameters refined from the PDF analysis plotted against the temperature with a vertical dashed black line emphasizing 50 K, the temperature below which the lattice constants all begin expanding with decreasing temperature. (**C**) An expanded region of PDF traces from **Figure 3A**, highlighting the sharpening of the broad single peak into three distinct peaks upon cooling. The inset is our proposed physical interpretation of this sharpening in a top-down view of a CrSBr layer. (**D**) A STEM-HAADF image of a multilayer CrSCl$_{0.33}$Br$_{0.67}$ flake. The scale bar corresponds to 2 nm. (**E**) Overlayed intensity maps of the Cr atom columns (blue) and S/Cl/Br columns (red) fit from the STEM-HAADF image in **Figure 3D**, in which lighter colors correspond to higher intensities and darker colors correspond to lower intensities. (**F**) Lattice parameter distributions for the a- and b-axes of CrSCl$_{0.33}$Br$_{0.67}$ measured from CrSCl$_{0.33}$Br$_{0.67}$ strain maps.

both intensity maps show commensurate decreases in local intensity. Maps of the local strain highlight that the regions showing lower local intensity (higher Cl content and lower Cr content) also show greater strain (see **SI**). We find that the distributions of the a- and b-axis lattice parameters (**Fig. 6.3F**) extracted from the local strain analyses are nearly double those measured for unsubstituted CrSBr. Together, we take these data to conclude that the CrSCl$_{0.33}$Br$_{0.67}$ solid solution is structurally homogenous and isostructural to CrSBr, in which Cl atoms substitutionally replace Br atoms; however, regions enriched in Cl atoms are also locally strained.

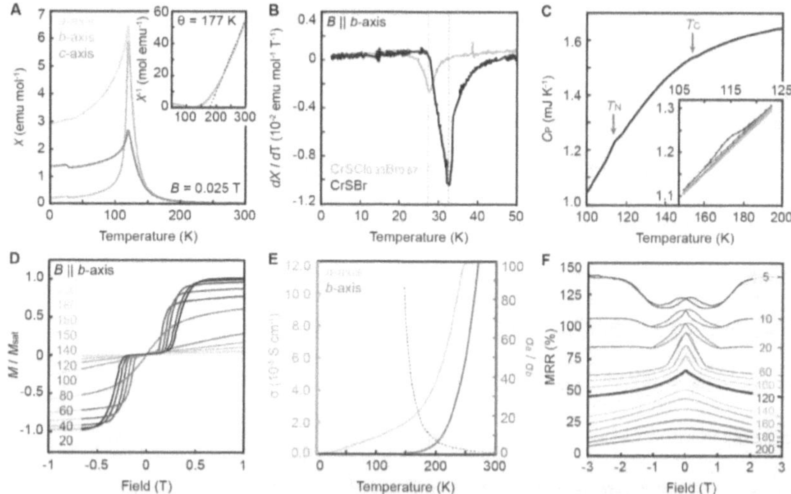

Figure 6. 4 Magnetic and electronic properties of CrSCl$_{0.33}$Br$_{0.67}$.
(A) Zero-field-cooled magnetic susceptibility versus temperature measured on a CrSCl$_{0.33}$Br$_{0.67}$ single crystal with B-field along the a-, b-, and c-axes (B = 0.025 T). The inset shows the Curie-Weiss fit for the magnetic susceptibility measured along the b-axis. (B) Derivatives of the CrSBr (black) and CrSCl$_{0.33}$Br$_{0.67}$ (green) magnetic susceptibilities (B || b-axis, for CrSBr B = 0.1 T and for CrSCl$_{0.33}$Br$_{0.67}$ B = 0.025 T) between 0 and 50 K. Vertical lines are drawn at the derivative minima to highlight the difference in temperature induced by partial Br replacement by Cl. (C) Zero-field heat capacity trace of CrSCl$_{0.33}$Br$_{0.67}$ measured between 100 and 200 K with red arrows highlighting features associated with the approximate T_C (156 K) and T_N (117 K). The inset shows the field dependence of the T_N transition between 0.0 (black) and 1.0 T (light green) in increments of 0.2 T. (D) Magnetization versus magnetic field measured along the b-axis at various temperatures listed (in Kelvin) in the corresponding trace color along the left axis. (E) The zero-field in-plane conductivity (green) and conductivity anisotropy (red) between the a- and b-axes for single crystals of CrSCl$_{0.33}$Br$_{0.67}$. (F) The MRR for the B-field-dependent resistance traces collected along the a-axis of CrSCl$_{0.33}$Br$_{0.67}$ (B || c-axis). Temperatures in Kelvin for the MRR curves are given in the corresponding color along right side of the plot.

6.5.2 CrSBrCl$_{.33}$Br$_{.67}$: Magnetic and Electronic Characterization

Measurements of the CrSCl$_{0.33}$Br$_{0.67}$ magnetic susceptibility along the crystallographic

axes (**Fig. 6.4A**) show that the magnetic structure matches CrSBr, although the intra- and

interlayer exchange coupling is weaker in the solid solution than in CrSBr. CrSCl$_{0.33}$Br$_{0.67}$ has

a T_N of 117 K compared to 134 K for CrSBr, demonstrating the weaker antiferromagnetic

coupling in the solid solution system relative to the stoichiometric CrSBr. A Curie-Weiss fit of

the CrSCl$_{0.33}$Br$_{0.67}$ high temperature susceptibility data (**Fig. 6.4A inset**) yields a Weiss constant of 177 K, lower than that of CrSBr (see Chapter 2, Table 2.2)[19] which suggests weaker intralayer ferromagnetic correlations leading up to the T_N.[20] This is corroborated by measurements of the field- and temperature-dependent heat capacity (**Fig. 6.4C**), which show features at 117 K and 156 K that we attribute to bulk antiferromagnetic ordering and in-plane ferromagnetic coupling, respectively. The weaker antiferromagnetic correlations in the $CrSCl_{0.33}Br_{0.67}$ system is also demonstrated by the decrease in the b-axis saturation field (H_S), which is measured at 0.29 T for $CrSCl_{0.33}Br_{0.67}$ (**Fig. 6.4D**) and 0.60 T for CrSBr at 20 K. The T_D is lower in the solid solution (27 K) compared to CrSBr (33 K), indicating that the exchange splitting energy of spin-polarized bands is decreased[4,21,22] and providing strong evidence that the intrinsic magnetic lattice induces this splitting.[23] The difference in transition temperature corresponds to a ~0.5 meV decrease in the energy splitting between spin polarized bands in the solid solution compared to the unsubstituted CrSBr. Measurement of the $CrSCl_{0.33}Br_{0.67}$ transport behavior shows that the transport anisotropy (**Fig. 6.4E**) and MR signatures below the T_D (**Fig. 6.4F**) are preserved in the solid solution crystal, indicating that the partial halogen exchange and Cr deficiency do not disrupt the formation of charge defect-mediated magnetic sublattice observed in CrSBr.

6.6 Discussion of Results

In this work, CrSBr has been post-synthetically and in-situ modified in order to have methodically produced Br-deficiencies. By altering the composition of this material, we were able to probe the hybrid polaron and s-d exchange mechanism behind its behavior at low temperatures below 33 K. Further study should be performed by increasing stoichiometric alterations to substituting within the chalcogens to more fully explore the role of these substituents within the proposed framework.

6.7 References

1. Huang, B. *et al.* Electrical control of 2D magnetism in bilayer CrI3. *Nat. Nanotechnol.* **13**, 544–548 (2018).
2. Miao, N., Xu, B., Zhu, L., Zhou, J. & Sun, Z. 2D Intrinsic Ferromagnets from van der Waals Antiferromagnets. *J. Am. Chem. Soc.* **140**, 2417–2420 (2018).
3. Železný, J., Wadley, P., Olejník, K., Hoffmann, A. & Ohno, H. Spin transport and spin torque in antiferromagnetic devices. *Nat. Phys.* **14**, 220–228 (2018).
4. Ghiasi, T. S. *et al.* Electrical and thermal generation of spin currents by magnetic bilayer graphene. *Nat. Nanotechnol.* (2021) doi:10.1038/s41565-021-00887-3.
5. Telford, E. J. *et al.* Layered Antiferromagnetism Induces Large Negative Magnetoresistance in the van der Waals Semiconductor CrSBr. *arXiv* (2020).
6. Baibich, M. N. *et al.* Giant magnetoresistance of (001)Fe/(001)Cr magnetic superlattices. *Phys. Rev. Lett.* **61**, 2472–2475 (1988).
7. Wilson, N. P. *et al.* Interlayer Electronic Coupling on Demand in a 2D Magnetic Semiconductor. (2021).
8. Huang, B. *et al.* Emergent phenomena and proximity effects in two-dimensional magnets and heterostructures. *Nature Materials* vol. 19 1276–1289 (2020).
9. Pulizzi, F. Is it really intrinsic ferromagnetism? *Nat. Mater.* **9**, 956–957 (2010).
10. Dietl, T. A ten-year perspective on dilute magnetic semiconductors and oxides. *Nat. Mater.* *2010 912* **9**, 965–974 (2010).
11. Yi, J. B. *et al.* Ferromagnetism in Dilute Magnetic Semiconductors through Defect Engineering: Li-Doped ZnO. *Phys. Rev. Lett.* **104**, 137201 (2010).
12. Beck, J. Über Chalkogenidehalide des Chroms. Synthese, Kristallstruktur und Magnetismus von Chromsulfidbromid, CrSBr. *Z. anorg. allg. Chem.* **685**, 157–167 (1990).
13. Telford, E. J. *et al.* Layered Antiferromagnetism Induces Large Negative Magnetoresistance in the van der Waals Semiconductor CrSBr. *Adv. Mater.* **32**, (2020).
14. Lee, K. *et al.* Magnetic Order and Symmetry in the 2D Semiconductor CrSBr. *Nano Lett.* **21**, 3511–3517 (2021).
15. Mak, K. F. & Shan, J. Photonics and optoelectronics of 2D semiconductor transition metal dichalcogenides. *Nat. Photonics 2016 104* **10**, 216–226 (2016).
16. Soda, T., Matsuura, T. & Nagaoka, Y. s-d Exchange Interaction in a Superconductor. *Prog. Theor. Phys.* **38**, 551–567 (1967).
17. Hitchon, W. N. G., Parker, G. J. & Rebei, A. sd-type Exchange Interactions in Nonhomogeneous Ferromagnets. (2004).
18. Kumar, S. *et al.* Magnetic Polarons and Large Negative Magnetoresistance in GaAs Nanowires Implanted with Mn Ions. *Nano Lett.* **13**, 5079–5084 (2013).
19. Telford, E. J. *et al.* Layered Antiferromagnetism Induces Large Negative Magnetoresistance in the van der Waals Semiconductor CrSBr. *Adv. Mater.* (2020) doi:10.1002/adma.202003240.
20. Rhodes, P. & Wohlfarth, E. P. The effective Curie-Weiss constant of ferromagnetic metals and alloys. *Proc. R. Soc. London. Ser. A. Math. Phys. Sci.* **273**, 247–258 (1963).
21. Wu, Y. *et al.* Large exchange splitting in monolayer graphene magnetized by an antiferromagnet. *Nat. Electron. 2020 310* **3**, 604–611 (2020).
22. Himpsel, F. J., Knapp, J. A. & Eastman, D. E. Experimental energy-band dispersions and exchange splitting for Ni. *Phys. Rev. B* **19**, 2919 (1979).
23. Dalpian, G. M. & Wei, S.-H. Electron-mediated ferromagnetism and negative s−d exchange splitting in semiconductors. *Phys. Rev. B* **73**, 245204 (2006).

Chapter 7: Interlayer Electronic Coupling

7.1 Preface

Two-dimensional (2D) semiconductors host tightly bound excitons that dominate their sub-bandgap optical behavior.[1] When monolayers of the semiconductor are stacked into van der Waals (vdW) structures, interlayer electronic coupling can dramatically alter the excitonic properties. Examples include the change from momentum direct to indirect excitons in transition metal dichalcogenides by increasing the layer thickness from monolayer to multilayers[2,3], and moiré-lattice localized interlayer[4,5], intralayer[6] or layer-hybridized[7] excitons in twisted bilayers. Such 2D excitons may be energetically tuned by the Stark[8,9] or Zeeman[4] effect. Here we demonstrate the switching and tuning of excitons in a 2D layered antiferromagnetic (AFM) semiconductor $CrSBr$[10,11] by interlayer magnetic coupling. Employing photoluminescence and absorption spectroscopy, we observe highly anisotropic excitons in individual ferromagnetic (FM) monolayers with in-plane magnetic order. We found that, while excitons in the monolayer is independent of magnetic order, the exciton properties in bilayer and above can be drastically changed when the magnetic order is switched from layered AFM to the magnetic field-induced FM states. First-principles GW-BSE calculations reveal the Wannier character of these 2D magneto-excitons, whose wavefunction are confined to individual layers due to the anti-aligned spin-orientation in the AFM state and become delocalized across the vdW interface when the spins are aligned in the FM state. Our work uncovers a new approach to engineer excitons in vdW semiconductors by switching their magnetic orders. In return, the strong magneto-excitonic coupling may provide simple optical means for the write-in and read-out of spin information.

7.2 Introduction and Background

In layered antiferromagnets, the intralayer magnetic coupling is ferromagnetic (FM) while the adjacent FM monolayer are antiferromagnetically (AFM) coupled. Such an interlayer AFM order can be switched to FM with an external magnetic field, often accompanying the change of material symmetry. Tuning the spin structures of layered antiferromagnets has thus led to a number of emerging physical phenomena. Examples based on 2D CrI_3 include giant tunneling magneto-resistance via spin filtering effects[15], very large second harmonic generation (SHG) from the AFM state due to magnetic state induced inversion symmetry breaking[16], and tuning inelastic light scattering and spin waves via symmetry controls[17]. In the layered magnet $MnBi_2Te_4$, a topological quantum phase transition occurs when the intrinsic interlayer AFM state is fully polarized to the FM state with an external magnetic field[18,19].

In this work, we report the unique magneto-electronic and magneto-excitonic coupling effects that emerge in CrSBr, a 2D material that combines a direct electronic bandgap with a layered AFM order[20]. The lattice of CrSBr consists of vdW layers made of two buckled planes of CrS terminated by Br atoms (**Fig. 7.1A**). These layers stack along the c-axis to produce an orthorhombic structure with *Pmmn* (D_{2h}) space group. The mechanical exfoliation of CrSBr single crystals produces elongated flakes, a manifestation of the anisotropic structure of the material, which enables the easy identification of the crystallographic axes (see *methods*). The *a*- and *b*-axes correspond to the long and short lateral dimensions of the exfoliated flakes, respectively (**Fig. 7.1B**). Below the bulk Neel temperature ($T_N \sim 132$ K), each CrSBr vdW layer orders ferromagnetically and couples antiferromagnetically to adjacent layers. The structural anisotropy gives rise to in-plane biaxial magnetic anisotropy, with easy and intermediate magnetic axes along the crystallographic *b*- and *a*-axes, respectively, and a hard axis along c[20]. An SHG study confirms that this magnetic structure persist to the FM monolayer and AFM bilayer[11]. Unlike other 2D magnets, the Néel temperature in CrSBr is found to increase with decreasing layer number, from T_N = 132 K in the bulk to T_N = 150 K in the bilayer[11].

7.3 Electronic Structure Landscape of CrSBr

Electronic structure calculation of monolayer CrSBr in its FM ground state within the GW approximation reveals highly anisotropic band structures, with a semiconducting bandgap of ~1.8 eV (**Fig. 7.1C;** , see **Fig. F1a-c** for band structures of two and three layers). The valence band maximum (VBM) is at the Γ point, and there are two nearly degenerate conduction band minima (CBM) at Γ and X points. Our GW calculations are in agreement with previous DFT calculations[21,22], which predicted anisotropic and spin-polarized band structure for the CrSBr monolayer[21,22]. Away from Γ, there is considerable anisotropy of the conduction bands, with significant dispersion along Γ–Y and almost flat bands along Γ–X. These calculations suggest that the interband transition from the VBM to the CBM at the Γ point is dipole-allowed along the *b*-axis, but forbidden along the *a*-axis (see below).

The anisotropic excitonic transition is captured in polarization-resolved optical spectroscopy on exfoliated CrSBr flakes. **Fig. 7.1D** shows the linear polarization-resolved differential reflectance (ΔR/R) spectra of bilayer (2L) CrSBr. The lowest-energy exciton resonance, a sharp peak at ~1.34 eV, exhibits near-perfect linear dichroism with a strong

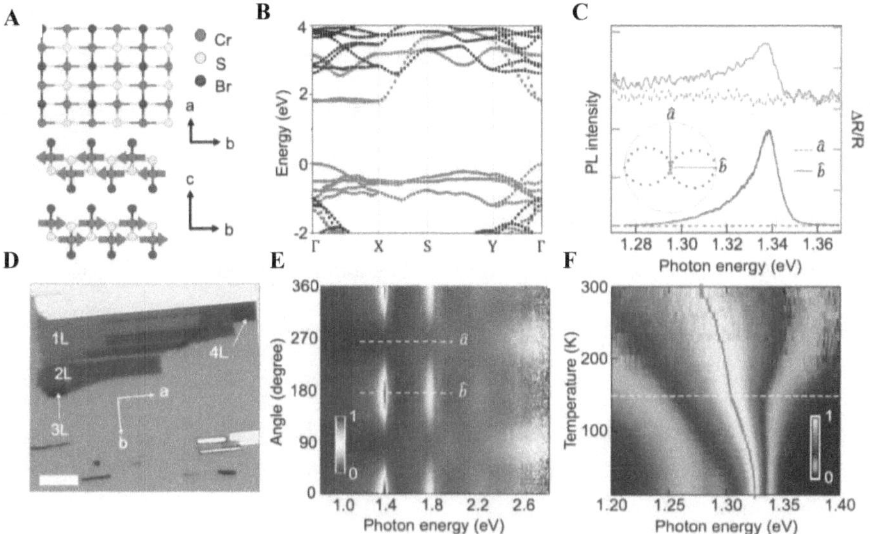

Figure 7. 1 Structure and optical properties of CrSBr.
(A) Crystal and magnetic structures of CrSBr. Top image shows a top-view of a single layer and the bottom image shows a side-view of a bilayer in which the AFM order is represented by the red arrows. (B) Optical microscope image of exfoliated CrSBr. Scale bar is 5 µm. (C) Calculated quasiparticle band structure of monolayer CrSBr. The bands of majority- and minority-spin electrons are shown in red and black, respectively. (D) Polarization resolved differential reflectance spectra of bilayer CrSBr. White dashed lines represent polarization along $\hat{a}$ and $\hat{b}$ axes. (E) Comparison of differential reflectance spectra (blue, right axis) and PL spectra (red, left axis) with polarization along the $\hat{b}$ (solid) and $\hat{a}$ (dashed) axis, respectively, from bilayer CrSBr. The inset shows PL intensity vs. polarization angle. (F) PL spectra from bilayer CrSBr as a function of temperature. The spectrum at each temperature is normalized to its maximum. The green dots are peak positions. The white dashed line shows T_N (for bilayer CrSBr) which coincides with a change in PL peak shape. Measurements in **D** and **E** are carried out at a sample temperature of T = 5 K.

resonant response along the b-axis and no detectable resonance along a. This dichroic response

is also observed for a series of higher energy excitonic resonances (**Fig. F2A**). This behavior

is mirrored in the photoluminescence (PL) spectra. The bright PL emission at 1.34 eV is

observed with near-unity linear polarization (red curves in **Fig. 7.1E**) and this PL polarization

anisotropy is observed for all thicknesses of CrSBr flakes, regardless of magnetic order **(Fig.**

F2B-C). A comparison of the polarization-resolved PL spectra (red) and differential reflectance spectra (blue) underlines the excellent agreement between the position of the excitonic peaks (**Fig. 7.1E**), which is consistent with a direct bandgap transition. Evidence for the exciton-magnetic order coupling is first found in the temperature-dependent PL spectra. For monolayer (1L) CrSBr (**Fig. F3**), the PL spectrum only shows a gradual blueshift of the emission with decreasing temperature as expected for a direct-gap semiconductor. For bilayer CrSBr (**Fig. 7.1F**), the blueshift is accompanied by a change in the peak shape across the magnetic phase transition, as evidenced by a kink at 150 ± 5 K, which closely match the bilayer T_N determined by SHG[11]. The magneto-excitonic coupling becomes even more evident for thicker flakes (**Fig. F3**) as we discuss below.

7.4 PL Probing of Magneto-excitonic Coupling

To gain a deeper understanding of the magneto-excitonic coupling in CrSBr, we measured PL as a function of applied magnetic field (B) at 5 K and establish that the magneto-excitonic coupling originates exclusively from interlayer electronic interaction. For monolayer CrSBr, the PL spectra show no discernible evolution as B is swept along the easy (**Fig. 7.2A**) or intermediate axes from (**Fig. F4a**). The latter establishes that spin canting alone does not affect the excitonic emission. In stark contrast to the monolayer results, the PL response of the bilayer varies dramatically with B. **Fig. 7.2B** presents bilayer PL spectra as B is swept along the easy axis. The PL changes abruptly at $B_c = 0.135$ T and is otherwise constant above and below this transition (**Fig. F4**). Field sweeps along the intermediate and hard axes result in a continuous evolution of the PL responses up to saturation fields B_{sat} of ~0.9 and ~1.6 T, respectively, beyond which the PL spectra become invariant (**Fig. 7.2C,D**). This spin-canting process is corroborated by the reflectance magnetic circular dichroism (RMCD) measurements with B field along the c-axis (**Fig. 7.2F**). The B_{sat} values for bilayer measured by RMCD and magneto-PL are identical (**Fig. 7.2C**). **Fig. 7.2E** compares monolayer and bilayer PL spectra at B field of zero (blue) and above saturation values (red) along the easy axis. While the monolayer spectra are superimposable, the bilayer PL spectra are distinct with their main peak redshifted by ~20 meV at $B \geq 0.135$ T. A similar dependence of the differential reflectance spectra on B is observed for bilayer samples (**Fig. F5**).

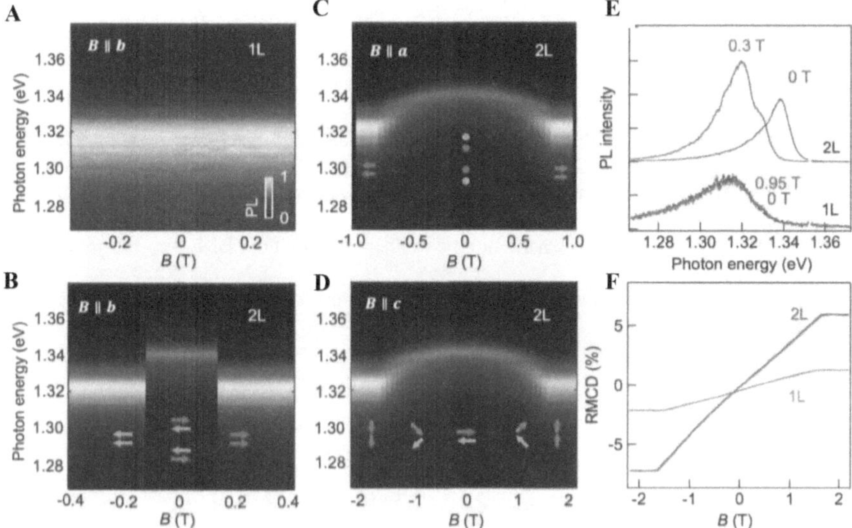

Figure 7. 2 Excitons coupled to magnetic order.
(A) Magnetic field dependence of monolayer PL spectrum with the field oriented along the easy axis. (B,C,D) Magnetic field dependence of bilayer PL spectrum along the easy, intermediate, and hard axes, respectively. (E) Field dependent PL spectra for monolayer (lower) and bilayer (upper, offset for clarity) CrSBr at the indicated magnetic field along the easy axis. Monolayer: 0.0 T (blue) and 0.95 T (red); Bilayer: 0.0 T (blue) and 0.0.3 T (red). (F) RMCD field sweeps of monolayer (blue) and bilayer (red) CrSBr with field along the c axis. The excitation energy is 1.959 eV. The linear RMCD field dependence with abrupt saturation suggests spin canting behavior, characteristic of anisotropic magnetism.

The above results demonstrate that the dramatic change of exciton properties arises from the tuning of interlayer magnetic order. When B is along the easy axis, the abrupt switch in the PL spectra of the bilayer at B_c comes from a spin flip transition (i.e. transition from AFM to FM order), resulting in a sudden transformation of the electronic structure and excitonic states. When B is along the intermediate or hard axes, spin canting produces continuous changes to the interlayer magnetic order, concurrent with the continuous evolution of the electronic

structure and the PL spectra.

7.5 Magnetic Order Dependent Band Structure And Excitonic Transitions

We use first-principles GW-BSE calculations (details in methods) to obtain the quasiparticle

band structures of bilayer CrSBr in the AFM (**Fig. 7.3A**) and FM (**Fig. 7.3B**) states. In the

AFM bilayer, the product symmetry of time reversal and spatial inversion makes the band

structure degenerate in spins. In each Bloch band near CBM and VBM, the spin-up and spin-

down electrons are localized at the top and bottom layer, respectively, since their interlayer

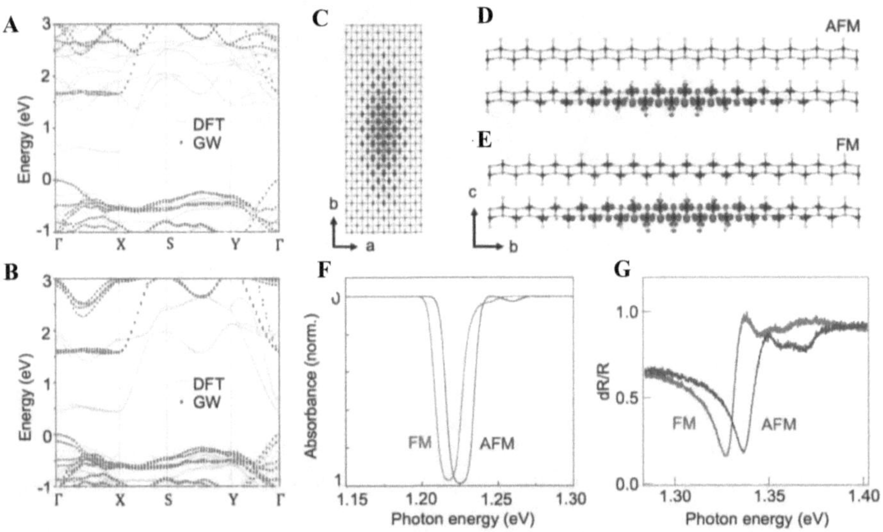

Figure 7. 3 Magnetic order-dependent band structure and excitonic transitions.
(A, B) Band structures of the AFM (A) and FM (B) CrSBr bilayers. Blue line and red dots are
Kohn-Sham band structures calculated using the DFT method and quasiparticle band structures
calculated using the GW method, respectively. In the AFM bilayer, bands are degenerate in spin.
In the FM case, the bands of majority spins are shown (those of minority spins have much larger
gaps).   (C, D, E) Wavefunction amplitude of the lowest-energy exciton. Plots show the
wavefunction amplitude of a bound electron with the hole fixed near a Cr atom (labelled by a black
circle) in the bottom layer. The iso-surfaces represent amplitude set at 5% of its maximum. (C) top
view in the AFM bilayer. Top view in the FM bilayer is very similar. (D) side view in the AFM
bilayer showing that the electron is localized in the same layer as the hole, and (E) side view in the
FM bilayer showing that the electron wavefunction is delocalized in both layers.

hybridization is suppressed by the AFM order of the host lattice. In the FM bilayer, by contrast, the electrons in the two layers can resonantly couple with each other, leading to band splitting of the CBM and VBM and a band gap ~ 0.1 eV smaller than that of the AFM bilayer.

The GW-BSE calculations unveil the nature of the excitonic optical transitions. In the AFM bilayer, the bright excitons in the top and bottom layers are virtually decoupled due to the anti-aligned spins between layers. The lowest energy bright excitons are two-fold degenerate (with energy difference < 0.5 meV), and account for the optical transitions at ~1.34 eV in the experimental spectra. A comparison between the experimentally measured transition energy and the calculated exciton excitation energy (~1.23 eV) shows a ~ 0.1 eV difference, which arises from the error of GW-BSE calculations (details in method). The calculated exciton wavefunction (top view in **Fig. 7.3C**) extends over several unit cells, and is about 2 ~ 3 times more delocalized along the b axis than along the a axis, revealing an anisotropic Wannier character. The sideview of the exciton wavefunction in **Fig. 7.3D** confirms that the electron is localized in the same layer as the hole. In the FM bilayer, by contrast, the excitons can delocalize over both layers due to the interlayer electronic coupling. For the lowest-energy exciton in the FM bilayer, when the hole is fixed in the bottom layer, the electron shows significant spatial delocalization, with the maximum amplitude in the top layer ~ 20 % relative to that of the bottom layer. The calculated optical spectra in both AFM and FM states are shown in **Fig. 7.3F**. By turning on the interlayer hybridization in the FM state, the most significant effect is a red-shift of the optically bright exciton by ~10 meV from that in the AFM state. This calculated red-shift is consistent with the experimental measurements, as shown by the differential reflectance spectra from bilayer CrSBr in the AFM (blue) and field-induced FM (red) states, respectively, **Fig. 7.3H**. The same red-shift is seen in the magnetic field dependent PL spectra in **Fig. 7.2B** and **Fig. 7.2E**.

7.6 Anisotropic Switching Behavior, Controlled through an Applied External Field

The interlayer hybridization also explains the stark difference between the discrete switching behavior of the excitonic transitions when the magnetic field is along the easy axis (**Fig. 7.2B**) and the continuous evolution (**Fig. 7.2C,D**) when it is along the intermediate/hard axis. Due to weak spin-orbit coupling, the wavefunctions near the VBM or CBM of each CrSBr layer can be approximated by the product of the spatial and the spinor parts, with the spatial parts being independent of spin orientation. The interlayer hopping integral t_h is therefore proportional to the inner product of the spinor wavefunctions of adjacent layers, $t_h \propto \langle S_1 | S_2 \rangle = \cos(\theta/2)$, where θ is the angle between the magnetization vectors of the layers. For the spin flip transition, θ jumps from π to 0 at B_c, while for the spin canting behavior, $M = M_{sat} \cos(\theta/2) \propto B$ up to B_{sat}. When B is along the intermediate axis, an approximately quadratic dependence of t_h on B is expected. This is confirmed by our analysis of the PL peak position (**Fig. F6**). Moreover, the interlayer hybridization and the resulting exciton delocalization across the vdW make relaxation into the lowest energy bight exciton more efficient and, thus, more competitive with non-radiative recombination. This explains the abrupt increase in PL intensity across the spin flip transition (**Fig. 7.2B**) and the gradual increase in PL intensity as the spins are progressively canted away from the easy axis (**Fig. 7.2C,D**).

Our interpretation implies that thicker layers should give rise to intermediate excitonic transitions due to transitional magnetic states between the AFM and the fully polarized FM orders. To explore the possibility of identifying these different magnetic states through their PL emissions, we performed PL and differential reflectance measurements as a function of B on 3-layer (3L) and 4-layer (4L) CrSBr flakes. We focus on 4L in **Fig. 7.4** and the 3L data is summarized in **Fig. F7**. The temperature dependence of the PL spectra of 4L CrSBr shows that

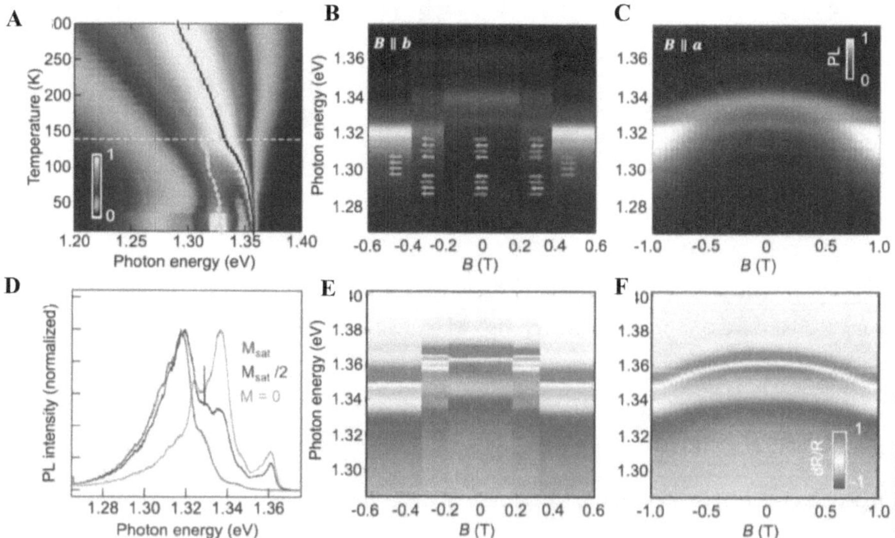

Figure 7. 4 Excitons in 4-layer CrSBr.
(A) Peak normalized PL spectrum of 4L CrSBr as a function of temperature, with the Nèel temperature marked by a white dashed line. Below the transition temperature, a second PL branch emerges. (B) Magneto-PL of 4L CrSBr along the easy axis, with possible magnetic configurations denoted by the red/blue arrows. Layer-flip transitions occur at 0.17 T and 0.33 T. (C, B), Magneto-PL of 4L CrSBr along the intermediate axis. Instrument limitation for in-plane magnetic field of 0.95 T prevents us from reaching B_{sat} along the intermediate axis. (D) Comparison of PL spectra in the three different magnetic configuration of 4L CrSBr. The half-magnetized state resembles a superposition of the AFM and FM configuration. (E,F) Magneto differential reflectance spectra of 4L CrSBr along the easy axis (E) and intermediate axis (F), respectively.

the broad PL peak observed at high temperature splits into two narrower main branches below

$T_N = 139$ K. This splitting is consistent with our understanding: the excitons are delocalized in

the high temperature paramagnetic phase due to interlayer hybridization, and become localized

in individual layers in the AFM phase. We expect the layer-localized excitons to experience

different environments (such as local dielectric screening) depending on the layer they reside,

providing an explanation for the PL peak splitting observed in the AFM phase.

Measuring the PL and differential reflectance spectra as a function of B at 5 K provides

additional insights into the coupling between magnetic order and excitonic transition. When B

is swept along the easy axis, the PL spectra of 4L CrSBr change abruptly at certain critical fields, with no detectable changes between those fields (**Fig. 7.4B** and **Fig. F7**). Unlike the single transition observed for the bilayer, there are two separate transitions at $B_c = 0.17$ and 0.33 T for 4L CrSBr. These two transitions correspond to spin flip transitions of individual layers, as illustrated by the arrows in **Fig. 7.4B**. The PL response when B is along the intermediate axis (**Fig. 7.4C**) mimics that of the bilayer (**Fig. F7** presents PL data when B is along the hard axis). The PL peaks redshift with increasing B and merge into a single broad transition when approaching B_{sat}.

As in bilayer CrSBr, the PL intensity of the 4L flake increases abruptly when the AFM state undergoes layer-by-layer spin flip transitions, or gradually when the spins are gradually canting towards the fully polarized FM state. **Fig. 7.4D** compares intensity normalized PL spectra at zero ($M = 0$), half ($M_{sat}/2$), and fully saturated magnetization (M_{sat}) along the easy axis. The PL spectrum at $M_{sat}/2$ resembles a superposition of those at $M = 0$ and M_{sat}, and can be understood as containing the emission responses from both AFM and FM interfaces. Similar to the PL results, the B dependence of the differential reflectance spectra of 4L CrSBr displays clear optical signatures of intermediate magnetic states, spin flipping transitions when B is along the easy axis (**Fig. 7.4E**) and spin canting behavior when B is along the intermediate axis (Fig. 4f). This agreement between PL and differential reflectance spectra in all magnetic states is a further proof of strong magneto-excitonic coupling in the direct-gap semiconductor.

7.7 Discussion of Results

The results presented here demonstrate an effective approach to control excitons in vdW semiconductors by their magnetic orders. The interlayer hybridization, and thus excitonic transitions, can be used as a "on/off" switch when an external magnetic field is applied to the easy axis of an AFM bilayer or multilayer, or as a "dimmer" when the field is applied to the intermediate or hard axis. Moreover, the magneto-excitonic coupling may enable simple optical means to probe or manipulate spin information, such as the launching or tracking of spin waves. Finally, the possibility of controlling interlayer twist angles in artificially stacked magnetic semiconductor bilayers or multilayers adds rich dimensions to the burgeon field of moiré physics, with the tantalizing prospect of controlling spatially resolved inter-layer hybridization and moiré bands by spin order and external magnetic fields.

7.8 References

1.   Wang, G. *et al.* Colloquium: Excitons in atomically thin transition metal dichalcogenides. *Rev. Mod. Phys.* **90**, 21001 (2018).
2.   Mak, K., Lee, C., Hone, J., Shan, J. & Heinz, T. Atomically Thin MoS2: A New Direct-Gap Semiconductor. *Phys. Rev. Lett.* **105**, 136805 (2010).
3.   Splendiani, A. *et al.* Emerging photoluminescence in monolayer MoS2. *Nano Lett.* **10**, 1271–1275 (2010).
4.   Seyler, K. L. *et al.* Signatures of moiré-trapped valley excitons in MoSe2/WSe2 heterobilayers. *Nature* **567**, 66–70 (2019).
5.   Tran, K. *et al.* Evidence for moiré excitons in van der Waals heterostructures. *Nature* **567**, 71–75 (2019).
6.   Jin, C. *et al.* Observation of moiré excitons in WSe2/WS2 heterostructure superlattices. *Nature* **567**, 76–80 (2019).
7.   Alexeev, E. M. *et al.* Resonantly hybridized excitons in moiré superlattices in van der Waals heterostructures. *Nature* **567**, 81–86 (2019).
8.   Shimazaki, Y. *et al.* Strongly correlated electrons and hybrid excitons in a moiré heterostructure. *Nature* **580**, 472–477 (2020).
9.   Jauregui, L. A. *et al.* Electrical control of interlayer exciton dynamics in atomically thin heterostructures. *Science* **366**, 870–875 (2019).
10.   Telford, E. J. *et al.* Layered Antiferromagnetism Induces Large Negative Magnetoresistance in the van der Waals Semiconductor CrSBr. *Adv. Mater.* **32**, 2003240 (2020).
11.   Lee, K. *et al.* Magnetic Order and Symmetry in the 2D Semiconductor CrSBr. *arXiv Prepr. arXiv2007.10715* (2020).
12.   Lee, J.-U. *et al.* Ising-type magnetic ordering in atomically thin FePS3. *Nano Lett.* **16**, 7433–7438 (2016).
13.   Gong, C. *et al.* Discovery of intrinsic ferromagnetism in two-dimensional van der Waals crystals. *Nature* **546**, 265–269 (2017).
14.   Huang, B. *et al.* Layer-dependent ferromagnetism in a van der Waals crystal down to the monolayer limit. *Nature* **546**, 270–273 (2017).
15.   Song, T. *et al.* Giant tunneling magnetoresistance in spin-filter van der Waals heterostructures. *Science* **360**, 1214–1218 (2018).
16.   Sun, Z. *et al.* Giant nonreciprocal second-harmonic generation from antiferromagnetic

bilayer CrI3. *Nature* **572**, 497–501 (2019).

17. Huang, B. *et al.* Tuning inelastic light scattering via symmetry control in the two-dimensional magnet CrI3. *Nat. Nanotechnol.* **15**, 212–217 (2020).

18. Liu, C. *et al.* Quantum phase transition from axion insulator to Chern insulator in MnBi2Te4. *arXiv Prepr. arXiv1905.00715* (2019).

19. Li, J. *et al.* Magnetically controllable topological quantum phase transitions in the antiferromagnetic topological insulator MnBi 2 Te 4. *Phys. Rev. B* **100**, 121103 (2019).

20. Göser, O., Paul, W. & Kahle, H. G. Magnetic properties of CrSBr. *J. Magn. Magn. Mater.* **92**, 129–136 (1990).

21. Guo, Y., Zhang, Y., Yuan, S., Wang, B. & Wang, J. Chromium sulfide halide monolayers: intrinsic ferromagnetic semiconductors with large spin polarization and high carrier mobility. *Nanoscale* **10**, 18036–18042 (2018).

22. Wang, C. *et al.* A family of high-temperature ferromagnetic monolayers with locked spin-dichroism-mobility anisotropy: MnNX and CrCX (X= Cl, Br, I; C= S, Se, Te). *Sci. Bull.* **64**, 293–300 (2019).

23. Giannozzi, P. *et al.* QUANTUM ESPRESSO: a modular and open-source software project for quantum simulations of materials. *J. Phys. Condens. Matter* **21**, 395502 (2009).

24. Grimme, S. Semiempirical GGA-type density functional constructed with a long-range dispersion correction. *J. Comput. Chem.* **27**, 1787–1799 (2006).

25. Hybertsen, M. S. & Louie, S. G. Electron correlation in semiconductors and insulators: Band gaps and quasiparticle energies. *Phys. Rev. B* **34**, 5390 (1986).

26. Deslippe, J. *et al.* BerkeleyGW: A massively parallel computer package for the calculation of the quasiparticle and optical properties of materials and nanostructures. *Comput. Phys. Commun.* **183**, 1269–1289 (2012).

27. Felipe, H., Qiu, D. Y. & Louie, S. G. Nonuniform sampling schemes of the Brillouin zone for many-electron perturbation-theory calculations in reduced dimensionality. *Phys. Rev. B* **95**, 35109 (2017).

28. Deslippe, J., Samsonidze, G., Jain, M., Cohen, M. L. & Louie, S. G. Coulomb-hole summations and energies for G W calculations with limited number of empty orbitals: A modified static remainder approach. *Phys. Rev. B* **87**, 165124 (2013).

29. Rohlfing, M. & Louie, S. G. Electron-hole excitations and optical spectra from first principles. *Phys. Rev. B* **62**, 4927 (2000).

30. Wu, M., Li, Z., Cao, T. & Louie, S. G. Physical origin of giant excitonic and magneto-optical responses in two-dimensional ferromagnetic insulators. *Nat. Commun.* **10**, 1–8 (2019).

Chapter 8: Electrical and Thermal Generation of Spin Currents by Magnetic Bilayer Graphene

8.1 Preface

Ultra-compact spintronic devices greatly benefit from implementation of 2D materials which provide large spin polarization of charge current together with long-distance transfer of spin information. Here, spin transport measurements in bilayer graphene evidence a strong spin-charge coupling due to a large induced exchange interaction by the proximity of an interlayer antiferromagnet (CrSBr). This results in the direct detection of spin-polarization of conductivity (up to 14%) and spin-dependent Seebeck effect in the magnetic graphene. The efficient electrical and thermal spin-current generation is the most technologically relevant aspect of magnetism in graphene, controlled here by the antiferromagnetic dynamics of CrSBr. The high sensitivity of spin transport in graphene to the magnetization of the outermost layer of the adjacent antiferromagnet, furthermore, enables readout of a single magnetic sub-lattice. The combination of gate-tunable spin-dependent conductivity and Seebeck coefficient with long-distance spin transport in a single 2D material promises ultra-thin magnetic memory and sensory devices based on magnetic graphene.

8.2 Introduction and Background

Memory technology has been revolutionized by the discovery of the giant magnetoresistance[1, 2] and spin transfer torque effects[3, 4], arising from the efficient coupling of charge and spin currents in ferromagnetic materials. The spin-charge coupling is a crucial aspect of magneto-electronic devices, namely spin-valves that consist of two layers of ferromagnetic materials separated by a non-magnetic layer, where altering the relative magnetization orientation of the layers results in a significant change in resistance.[5] Such spin-valves can be designed in the two-dimensional (2D) limit owing to the recent emergence of 2D magnetic materials [6, 7] in the architecture of van der Waals (vdW) heterostructures where exceptional functionalities are achieved by integrating the properties of the individual layers.[8]

Furthermore, most of spintronic applications require the strong spin-charge coupling in the 2D magnetic materials to be accompanied with a long-distance transfer of the spin information. In this regard graphene is a superior choice with its high charge carrier mobility, where the absence of hyperfine interactions and small intrinsic spin-orbit coupling (SOC) allow for a long spin lifetime[9–11]. The proximity of other materials to graphene can efficiently modulate its band structure and induce considerable SOC[12, 13] and exchange interaction[14–18], which are essential for spin generation and manipulation. In particular the proximity effect of 2D magnetic materials would bring the technology of ultra-thin spin-logic devices to the limit where the magnetic behavior of an individual atomic layer directly controls the long-distance information transfer by the spins in the neighboring graphene layer.

The experimental realization of the proximity-induced exchange interaction in graphene has been reported, measuring Shubnikov de-Haas oscillations and Zeeman spin Hall effect [19–21], anomalous Hall effect (AHE)[22, 23] and Hanle precession of injected spins by the induced exchange field (B_{exch})[24–27]. Among them, the latter is the most unambiguous and reliable approach when spin-sensitive Co electrodes are used to directly detect the modulation of the spin signal by the B_{exch}. However, Hanle precession measurements in graphene so far have

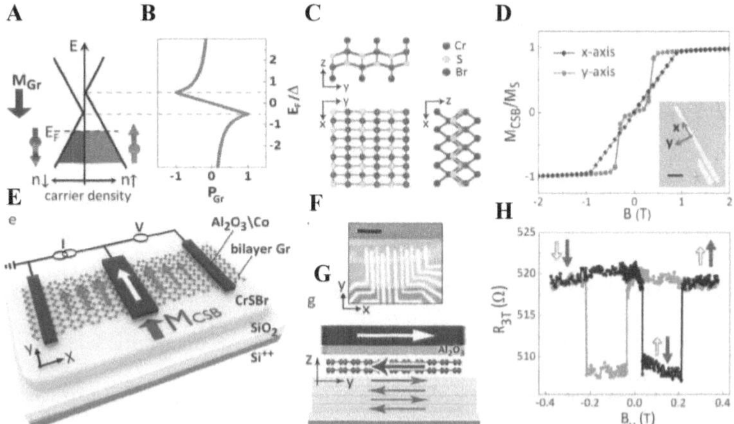

Figure 8. 1 Induced magnetism in bilayer graphene by the proximity of CrSBr.
(A) Spin-dependent density of charge carriers ($n_\uparrow$ and $n_\downarrow$) versus energy of bilayer graphene (Gr) in proximity of CrSBr, with the spin-splitting Δ caused by the exchange interaction. Δ is considered to be constant for the conduction and valence bans. Graphene magnetization (M_{Gr}), shown with black arrow, is assumed to be aligned with spin-down. **(B)** Dependence of spin polarization of graphene conductivity (P_{Gr}) on the position of Fermi energy (E_F), under assumptions of the Drude model (see Supplementary, Sec. 11). **(C)** Side and top views of CrSBr crystal structure. **(D)** Magnetization of a bulk CrSBr single crystal (M_{CSB}) versus external magnetic field (B), measured using SQUID magnetometry at T= 30 K along the x- and y-directions of the crystal. M_{CSB} is normalized to the saturation magnetization (M_s) value taken at B = 3T. The SQUID measurement along the hardest magnetic z-axis is shown in Supplementary Sec. 14. Inset: An optical micrograph of typical CrSBr flakes, exfoliated on SiO_2 substrate (scale bar:5μm). **(E)** Schematics of a three-terminal (3T) spin-valve measurement geometry, showing bilayer graphene/bulk CrSBr heterostructure and ferromagnetic electrodes (Al_2O_3 /Co). The white and purple arrows represent the magnetizations of the Co electrode and CrSBr (top-most layer), respectively. Spin injection by the Co, together with spin current generation by the magnetic graphene result in an accumulation of spin-up electrons (red arrows) under the given alignment of the M_{Co} and M_{CSB}, considering $P_{Gr} > 0$ and $P_{Co} < 0$. **(F)** Optical micrograph of device D1, fabricated with a vdW stack of bilayer graphene and CrSBr ($\sim$ 20 nm) and Al_2O_3 (0.8 nm)/Co (30 nm) electrodes (scale bar:5μm). **(G)** Side view sketch of the spin-valve device, showing a magnetization configuration of M_{Co} (in white), M_{Gr} (in black) and M_{CSB} (in purple). Independent switching of the M_{Co} and M_{CSB} (and so M_{Gr}) under an external magnetic field along y-axis (B_y) leads to **(H)** the unconventional spin-valve measurements in the 3T geometry with the distinct levels of the 3T resistance $R_{3T} = V/I$ (also see Supplementary Sec. 3). The black curve is the R_{3T} measurement starting at $B_y = -0.4$T (trace) and the gray curve is the retrace measurement, starting at $B_y = +0.4$T. The white and purple arrows show the M_{Co} and M_{CSB} magnetization configurations for the trace measurement. The change in R_{3T} versus B_y is proportional to P_{Gr} ($\Delta R_{3T} \propto P_{Gr}$, see Supplementary Sec. 6). The 3T measurement is performed at T = 4.5K, with I = 5μA).

shown rather weak exchange interaction, only leading to an additional precession of the spins around the B_{exch}. Even though all these experimental reports so far have shown the evidence for an induced B_{exch}, active generation of spin currents by graphene both electrically and thermally, as the most technologically relevant aspect of the induced magnetism, has not been addressed yet.

In this work, we detect spin-polarization of conductivity together with the spin-dependent Seebeck effect in bilayer graphene proximity-coupled to 2D inter-layer antiferromagnetic (AFM) CrSBr. The spin transport measurements directly address the conductivity in graphene, showing its strong spin-polarization up to 14% that is as large as in metallic ferromagnets. This is evidenced by the efficient electrical and thermal generation of spin currents by the magnetic graphene, up to the magnetic transition temperature of CrSBr. These observations, together with AHE measurements, promise significant advances in 2D spintronic/spin-caloritronic circuitry. Additionally, they give insight into the magnetic nature of graphene, controlled by the AFM dynamics of CrSBr.

8.3 Spin-Flip Behavior

The strong exchange interaction results in a considerable spin-splitting (Δ) of the graphene band structure. The resulting substantial difference in the density of charge carriers (n) with spin parallel ($\uparrow$) and anti-parallel ($\downarrow$) to the B_{exch} (**Fig. 8.1A**) leads to the spin-dependent conductivity. The spin polarization of conductance in graphene is expected to be efficiently tunable by shifting the position of the Fermi energy with a gate electric field (as proposed in panel b), reaching maxima when the density of one of the carrier types is minimal. Such efficient gate-tunability of spin-polarization of conductivity is the basis for all-electric spin field-effect transistors in spin-logic circuitries.[28] The use of bilayer graphene is particularly encouraged, as it can allow for gate-tunability of the exchange splitting [29–32].

Most of the explored 2D magnetic materials, however, suffer from extreme air-instability and low temperature of magnetic transitions.[33] Here we tackle this obstacle by utilizing the recently explored CrSBr 2D crystal (**Fig. 8.1C**) that is an air-stable vdW semiconductor (bandgap of ~ 1.5eV, see Supplementary Sec. 18 for transport measurements) with an interlayer AFM ordering up to a relatively high Néel temperature of $T_N \approx 132K$[34–37]. Furthermore, the antiferromagnetism promises ultra-fast operations and robustness against external magnetic fields[38] and also is expected to be tunable by a gate electric field [35, 39]. Mechanical cleavage of the CrSBr crystal results in flakes with a specific rectangular geometry that correlates with its in-plane magnetic anisotropy axes (inset of **Fig. 8.1D**). The behavior of CrSBr magnetization (M_{CSB}) measured versus external magnetic field (B), using a superconducting quantum interference device (SQUID) magnetometer (**Fig. 8.1D**), displays a sharp modulation of M_{CSB} when B is applied along the y-axis. This corresponds to the AFM behavior with spin-flip transition (at $B_{M,y} \sim 0.2T$) and defines the y-direction as the in-plane magnetic easy-axis. In contrast, along the x-direction, M_{CSB} increases gradually with a much higher saturation field ($B_{M,x} \sim 1T$). This is a result of the gradual canting of the anti-parallel magnetizations of the CrSBr layers towards the x-direction (the in-plane magnetic hard-axis). When graphene is brought on top of the CrSBr flake, the magnetic behavior of the outermost CrSBr layer gets imprinted in the graphene so that the magnetization of graphene (M_{Gr}) is expected to be collinear to the magnetization of the outermost layer of the CrSBr flake (the alignment of M_{Gr} and M_{CSB} is further discussed in Supplementary, Sec. 13.

8.4 Spin-dependent Conductivity

The presence of spin-dependent conductivity in graphene is directly observed in the spin-valve design shown in **Fig. 8.1E**. Using the three-terminal (3T) geometry, the resistance is measured versus the magnetic field B_y, applied along the easy axes of the Co electrodes and the CrSBr crystal. As shown in panel g, in the spin-valve heterostructure of Co/Al$_2$O$_3$/magnetic graphene, the relative orientation of M_{Gr} with respect to M_{Co}, defines the spin polarization of the injected current and therefore considerably changes the resistance of the contact between graphene and Co (R_{3T}). The abrupt change in resistance (**Fig. 8.1H**), depending on the relative orientation of M_{Gr} and M_{Co} resembles the giant magnetoresistance effect, but with the advantage of long-distance spin transfer in the graphene. This would not happen in a conventional 3T measurement with a non-magnetic graphene, because when the Co magnetization is reversed both spin injection and detection simultaneously change sign, resulting in no magnetoresistance.[40] Therefore, the observation of the 3T spin-valve effect is only possible if the graphene is magnetic, with non-zero spin polarization of conductance P_{Gr}.

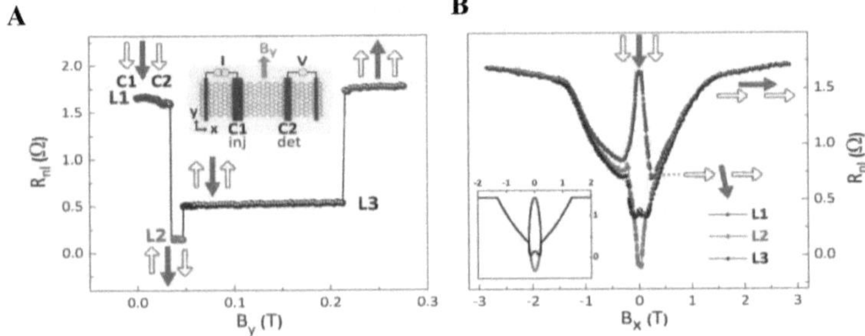

Figure 8. 2 Spin transport in bilayer graphene with spin-polarized conductivity
(A) Non-local spin-valve measurement; 1st harmonic non-local resistance $R_{nl} = V/I$ versus B_y (with $I = 5\mu A$), showing three levels (L1, L2 and L3) corresponding to the different configurations of Co injector/detector magnetization directions (M_{Co}: white arrows) with respect to that of CrSBr (M_{CSB}: purple arrows). Inset: Schematic of the non-local measurement geometry under the applied B_y (green arrow), with C1 and C2 Co electrodes as the spin injector and detector, respectively. For the measurements in the reciprocal geometry and with the other Co detectors see Supplementary Sec. 2 and 15. (B) Modulation of R_{nl} as a function of B_x, measured in Hanle geometry with initial alignment of M_{Co} of the injector and detector and M_{CSB} (corresponding to L1, L2 and L3, defined in panel a). The asymmetry in the Hanle curves could be related to the possible few-degrees misalignment of the magnetization axes of the Co electrodes with respect to that of CrSBr crystal and/or misalignment of B from the x-axis. Inset: Hanle curves calculated by the spin-dependent graphene conductivity model. The best fit to the measured results is provided considering $P_{Gr} \approx 14\%$ and $P_{inj} \approx P_{det} \approx -24\%$ (see Supplementary, Sec. 9). All the measurements are performed at $T = 4.5K$.

The spin-charge current coupling in graphene is further studied by measuring the pure spin current generated by the magnetized graphene in the non-local four-terminal (4T) geometry of **Fig. 8.2A**, where the charge current path can be fully separated from the voltage detection circuit. The non-local resistance ($R_{nl} = V_{nl}/I$) is measured versus B_y. In an equivalent measurement on pristine graphene, one would observe *two* (non-local) resistance levels associated with the parallel and anti-parallel magnetization alignment of the injector and detector Co electrodes[9]. In contrast, here we observe *three* resistance levels that are only possible if the spin transport in graphene depends on the relative orientation of M_{Gr} (or M_{CSB}) with respect to the magnetization of the injector $M_{Co,inj}$ and that of the detector $M_{Co,det}$ electrodes. The spin-valve measurement is performed with initial alignment of all three magnetic elements (injector, detector and CrSBr) at $B_y = -1T$. By increasing the field B_y starting from 0 T, the magnetizations of the injector and the detector electrodes switch to the opposite direction one after the other at $B_y < 50mT$. The third switch (at $B_y = 0.21T$) happens at a value of the field that is too large to be related to the Co electrodes, considering their geometrical anisotropy. However, it corresponds well with switching field of the M_{CSB} along its easy axis (shown in the SQUID magnetometry of **Fig. 8.1D**) which directly confirms the non-zero spin polarization of the graphene conductivity as a result of the proximity-induced magnetism.

The spin polarization in graphene is defined as $P_{Gr} = (\sigma_u - \sigma_d)/(\sigma_u + \sigma_d)$ with σ_u and σ_d as conductivities for spin-up and spin-down channels. Solving the spin-charge coupled diffusive transport equations (Supplementary, Sec. 5), we derive the non-local resistance as:

$$R_{nl} = \frac{\lambda R_{sq}}{2W} e^{-L/\lambda} (P_{inj} - P_{Gr})(P_{det} - P_{Gr}) \qquad (7.1)$$

where P_{inj} and P_{det} are the spin polarizations of the injector and detector contacts and λ, R_{sq}, L and W are the spin relaxation length, square-resistance, length and width of the graphene channel (in between the injector and detector), respectively. The above expression is expanded as:

$$R_{nl} \propto P_{inj} * P_{det} - P_{Gr} * P_{det} - P_{inj} * P_{Gr} + P_{Gr} * P_{Gr} \qquad (7.2)$$

$P_{inj} * P_{det}$ term corresponds to a spin signal injected/detected via ferromagnetic injector/detector contacts. $P_{inj} * P_{Gr}$ is due to the spin injection via ferromagnetic contact, but the non-local signal is detected as a charge voltage that builds up due to the spin-to-charge conversion happening in graphene itself and $P_{Gr} * P_{det}$ corresponds to the reciprocal effect. Finally, $P_{Gr} * P_{Gr}$ is due to

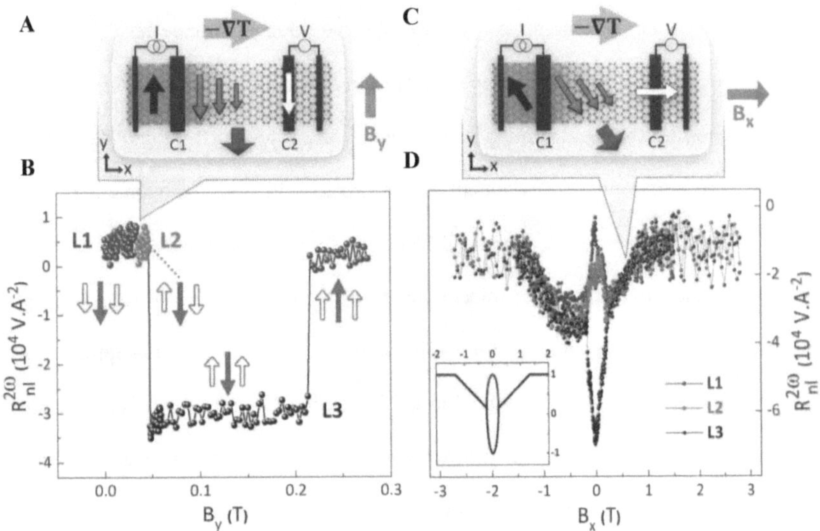

Figure 8. 3 Spin-dependent Seebeck effect (SdSE) in the magnetised bilayer graphene. **(A)** The schematic of the nonlocal measurement geometry shows temperature gradient (∇T) in the graphene channel due to Joule heating at the current source contacts that results in the thermal generation of spin current due to the finite P_{Gr}. The sketch shows the initial alignment of M_{CSB} (purple arrow) and $M_{Co,det}$ (white arrow) with respect to the magnetic field (green arrow), corresponding to L1 or L2. In this case M_{Gr} (black arrow) is pointing up (along y-axis) and there is accumulation of spin-downs (blue arrows) close to the hot region. **(B)** 2nd harmonic non-local spin-valve measurement of $R_{nl}^{2\omega} = V^{2\omega}/I^2$ versus B_y. Different magnetisation configuration of M_{Co} and M_{CSB} are shown, corresponding to L1, L2 and L3. **(C)** The device sketch with the magnetisation configuration of M_{CSB} and $M_{Co,det}$ under the applied $B_x > 0.2$T (saturation field of Co along x-axis), showing gradual tilt of the M_{CSB} and the thermally generated spins towards the B_x. **(D)** Modulation of the $R_{nl}^{2\omega}$ as a function of B_x in the Hanle geometry. Inset: Theoretically calculated Hanle curves for the 2nd harmonic signal, considering the SdSE as the spin generating mechanism (see Appendix G). All the measurements are performed at $T = 4.5$K.

the spin signal that is both generated and detected by graphene itself. The presence of the last term implies that in principle spin polarized contacts are not required in order to observe the charge-spin current coupling. However, it might not be possible to differentiate it from a spurious background under an applied B when only non-magnetic electrodes are used. Here we estimate λ to be about 630nm and obtain the polarizations as $P_{Gr} \approx 14\%$ and $P_{inj} \approx P_{det} \approx -24\%$ (Supplementary, Sec. 4 to 10). Having the P_{Gr}, we roughly estimate the exchange splitting to be $\Delta = 2E_F * P_{Gr} \sim 20$ meV that corresponds to $B_{exch} \sim 170$T, assuming E_F to be the same as in device D3 (see Supplementary, Sec. 11). Note that in an electron-doped device D2 (see Supplementary Sec. 17), we observe an opposite sign for P_{Gr} as compared to the device D1. This is an indication for the possible gate-tunability of the spin polarization of conductivity in graphene, consistent with **Fig. 8.1B**.

The modulation of the spin signal under the magnetic field B_x applied in-plane, perpendicular to the Co and CrSBr easy-axis, further confirms the presence of the very large B_{exch} in the graphene (**Fig. 8.2B**). We label this experiment a Hanle measurement as a generalized term since the effect of the B_{exch} on the spins is similar to that of an external field. In this system the precession is governed by the B_{exch} since its magnitude is much larger than the B_x. The B_x controls the directions of M_{Co} and M_{CSB} (or B_{exch}) by pulling them towards the x-axis with saturation fields of $\vec{B}_{Co} \approx 0.2$ T and $B_{CSB} \approx 1.3$T. The Hanle curves in **Fig. 8.2B** are measured after initial alignment of the M_{Co} and M_{CSB} along the y-axis, setting the magnetization configuration corresponding to L1, L2 or L3 (as labelled in panel a).

The B_x is applied perpendicular to the initial direction of the injected spins. For L1, the R_{nl} has its maximum value at $B_x = 0$T, as the injected spins are aligned with the B_{exch}. Once the B_x pulls the M_{Co} along the x-direction, the strong B_{exch} fully randomizes the component of the injected spins that are perpendicular to it. At $B_x = 0.2$T, the magnetization directions of contacts are saturated along the x-axis while B_{exch} is still mostly pointing along the y-axis.

This yields to only a small projection of the injected spins in the direction of B_{exch}, thus resulting in a considerable decay of R_{nl}. The increase of $B_x > 0.2$T pulls the M_{CSB} further along the x-direction with saturation at 1.3 T. When the M_{CSB} aligns with M_{Co} once again, the R_{nl} retrieves its initial value. The Hanle curves measured for the anti-parallel alignment of M_{CSB} with respect to $M_{Co,inj}$ or $M_{Co,det}$ (corresponding to configurations L2 or L3 in panel a) also show similar behavior, but with the distinct initial value of R_{nl} at $B_x = 0$ T. Overall, the behavior of the spin signal in the Hanle curves is determined by the relative orientation of the M_{Co} and M_{Gr} as the very large B_{exch} allows for the information transfer only by the spins collinear to the M_{Gr}. The inset of **Fig. 8.2B** shows the Hanle curves derived from the analytical expression for the R_{nl} (Supplementary, Sec. 8) which agree well with the experimental results.

8.5 Spin-dependent Seebeck Effect

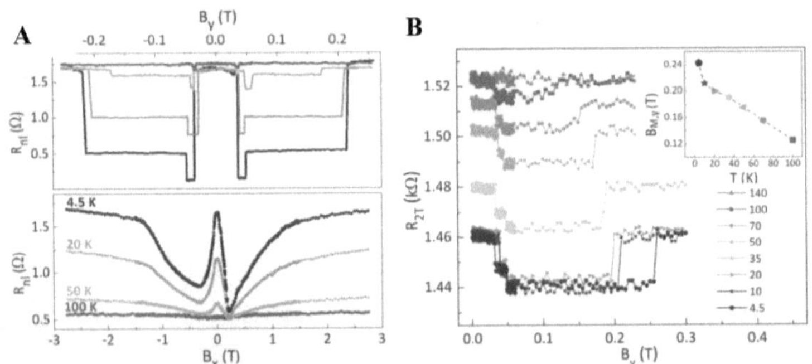

Figure 8. 4 Temperature dependence of the spin signal
(A) The non-local spin-valve and Hanle measurements (with the parallel initial configuration of M_{CSB}, $M_{Co,inj}$ and $M_{Co,det}$) at various temperatures. The measured spin-valve data is shifted along the y-axis for a clearer demonstration (see Supplementary Fig. 7.4, for the R_{nl} shown without the offset). **(B)** Two terminal resistance (R_{2T}) measured between contacts C1 and C2 versus B_y, at various temperatures. Inset: The gradual decay in the switching field of CrSBr along its easy axis ($B_{M,y}$) by the increase in temperature.

The strong induced magnetism in graphene also leads to the first-time observation of spin-dependent Seebeck effect (SdSE)[41,42]. Due to the spin-dependence of the Seebeck coefficient, we can generate spin current by having a thermal gradient in the magnetized graphene channel (**Fig. 8.3A**). We measure the 2nd harmonic signal that is associated with thermal effects due to Joule heating ($\Delta T \propto I^2$). **Fig. 8.3B** shows that the non-local 2nd harmonic resistance ($R_{nl}^{2\omega} = V^{2\omega}/I^2$) abruptly changes with the switch in the detector magnetization direction (at $B_y \sim 50mT$) getting anti-parallel to the CrSBr magnetization. The spin signal retrieves its initial value when M_{CSB} also switches (at $\sim 0.21T$) and gets parallel to $M_{Co,det}$ again. We observe that the switch in the direction of the injector magnetization at $B_y = 35mT$ does not change the $R_{nl}^{2\omega}$. This assures the thermal origin of the measured spin signal that is generated only by the Joule heating of graphene at the injector contact, independent of the injector magnetization. In **Fig. 8.3C** and **D**, we demonstrate the modulation of the SdSE spin signal versus B_x measured for the different magnetization configurations of the injector, detector and CrSBr (defined for L1, L2 and L3 in panel b). The modulation of the $R_{nl}^{2\omega}$ versus B_x is understood considering the collinearity of the thermally injected spins with the magnetization of graphene, consistent with theoretically calculated curves shown in the inset (also see Supplementary, Sec. 12). The similar behavior of the 2nd harmonic L1 and L2 Hanle curves further confirms that $M_{Co,inj}$ has no influence on the detected signal.

8.6 Magnetic Phase Transition

The generation of the spin currents by the magnetized graphene should persist up to the relatively high Néel temperature of CrSBr ($T_N \approx 132$ K). We examine this by the local and non-local spin transport measurements at various temperatures (**Fig. 8.4**). The dependence of the spin signal on temperature reflects the temperature-dependence of the magnetization of CrSBr layers. The spin-valve and Hanle curves, measured non-locally up to $T = 100$ K (panel a) show a significant decay of the spin signal. This is further confirmed by the two-terminal (2T) measurements, plotted in **Fig. 8.4B**. The considerable spin polarization of graphene allows for the detection of large spin signals in the local 2T geometry showing three resistance levels corresponding to the magnetization switch of C1, C2 and CrSBr. Consistent with the non-local measurements, the size of the spin-valve switches decreases with the rise in temperature and fully vanishes (below the noise level) at $T > 100K$. Such a decay is attributed to the randomization of the magnetization of CrSBr and suppression of the induced magnetism in graphene, since the decay is much larger than what is expected from the temperature dependence of Co spin polarization or spin transport in graphene on non-magnetic substrates[11,43]. Moreover, we observe that as the temperature increases, the magnetic field at which M_{CSB} switches along its easy axis ($B_{M,y}$) shifts towards smaller values (shown in the inset), consistent with the temperature-dependence of the SQUID magnetometry of CrSBr.[36]

8.7 Anomalous Hall effect

The induced magnetism in graphene, if accompanied with SOC is expected to result in the emergence of anomalous Hall effect.[44] We assess this by interfacing a thin exfoliated CrSBr bulk flake with a graphene Hall bar (**Fig. 8.5A**) and measuring the transverse voltage (V_{xy}) as a function of the out-of-plane magnetic field (B_z) when longitudinal current is applied. The B_z gradually pulls the M_{CSB} out of the 2D plane leading to the imbalance in density of the out-of-plane spins. The AHE introduces sizable non-linearity in the B-dependence of the transverse resistance R_{xy}. The subtraction of the ordinary Hall effect (linear in B) provides us with the solitary contribution of the AHE (R_{AHE}) that fully saturates at $B_z \sim 4T$, shown for various gate voltages in **Fig. 8.5B**. The strength of the AHE depends on the position of the Fermi-energy in the band structure of the magnetized graphene. **Fig. 8.5C** shows an increase in the extracted non-linearity of Hall voltage as the Fermi-energy approaches the charge neutrality point and preserves sign for both electrons and holes. Note that the possible presence of the electron-hole puddles can contribute to the non-linearity of the Hall voltage when the Fermi energy is close to the charge neutrality point in a non-homogeneous graphene channel.[45] The observation of

the AHE not only confirms the induced magnetism but also indicates enhanced SOC in the

graphene that allows for the emergence of additional spin-to-charge conversion mechanisms

(e.g. spin Hall or Rashba-Edelstein effect).[46]

8.8 Discussion of Results

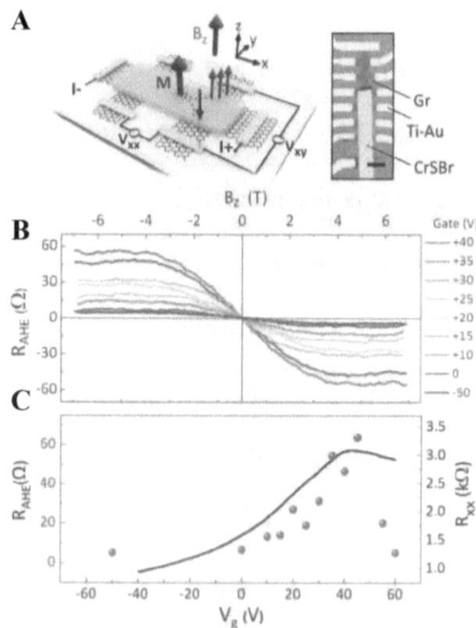

**Figure 8. 5 Anomalous Hall effect (AHE) in a bilayer graphene-CrSBr vdW
heterostructure**
(A) A schematic and an optical micrograph of device D3, consisting of a bilayer graphene Hall
bar on SiO_2, partially covered with a CrSBr flake (thickness $\approx$ 50 nm) with Ti (5 nm)/Au (100
nm) electrodes. Scale bar: 5 μm. The red and blue arrows represent the out-of-plane spins. (B)
The non-linear anti-symmetric component of the $R_{xy} = V_{xy}/I$ as a function of an out-of-plane
magnetic field (B_z), attributed to the AHE (R_{AHE}), measured at different back-gate voltages (also
see Supplementary Sec. 19). (C) Left axis: The magnitude of the AHE signal (defined as an
average of the maximum and minimum values of the R_{AHE} at $B_z > +4$T and < -4T) at the various
V_g, shown by the red dots. Right axis: Longitudinal resistance of graphene (R_{xx}) versus back-
gate voltage (V_g), shown by the black line. The measurements are performed at $T = 30$K.

These findings present the air-stable graphene/CrSBr vdW heterostructure as an exceptional

platform for addressing a broad range of spin-dependent phenomena[5,11] and quantum effects in magneto-electronic devices[47,48] since the magnetism, spin-orbit coupling and a long spin lifetime are brought together in a single 2D lattice.

The direct measurement of the strong spin-polarized conductance in graphene in the proximity of an antiferromagnet ensures its applications for the prospective 2D memory technology with ultra-fast operation and long-distance transfer of spin information. In magnetic tunnel junctions, for instance, the generated spin currents by the magnetic graphene can be used to induce spin-transfer torque in 2D magnetic random-access memories[49, 50]. Moreover, graphene with the high sensitivity of charge and spin transport to the magnetization of the outermost layer of the neighboring 2D AFM CrSBr, provides a tool for studying the behavior of a single magnetic sub-lattice that is also promising for magnetic sensory systems.

The electrical and thermal generation of spin currents by the magnetized graphene grants the design of spin-logic devices (e.g., spin-valves) without the need for magnetic injector/detector electrodes. This, together with the possibility for the efficient modulation of the spin-polarization of conductivity by electric fields via local (top-)gates allow for all-electric graphene-based spin-logic devices. These realizations, if accompanied with the large-scale growth of the vdW heterostructures and the development of the 2D magnets with magnetic phase transition above room temperature would lead to substantial advances in the 2D spintronics and spin-caloritronics technology.

8.9 References

1. Baibich, M. N. et al. Giant magnetoresistance of (001) Fe/(001) Cr magnetic superlattices. *Physical review letters* **61**, 2472 (1988).
2. Binasch, G., Grünberg, P., Saurenbach, F. & Zinn, W. Enhanced magnetoresistance in layered magnetic structures with antiferromagnetic interlayer exchange. *Physical review B* **39**, 4828 (1989).
3. Slonczewski, J. C. et al. Current-driven excitation of magnetic multilayers. *Journal of Magnetism and Magnetic Materials* **159**, L1 (1996).
4. Myers, E., Ralph, D., Katine, J., Louie, R. & Buhrman, R. Current-induced switching of domains in magnetic multilayer devices. *Science* **285**, 867–870 (1999).
5. Zutíc, I., Fabian, J. & Sarma, S. D. Spintronics: Fundamentals and applications. *Reviews of modern physics* **76**, 323 (2004).

6. Gong, C. et al. Discovery of intrinsic ferromagnetism in two-dimensional van der waals crystals. *Nature* **546**, 265–269 (2017).

7. Gong, C. & Zhang, X. Two-dimensional magnetic crystals and emergent heterostructure devices. *Science* **363**, eaav4450 (2019).

8. Geim, A. K. & Grigorieva, I. V. Van der Waals heterostructures. *Nature* **499**, 419–425 (2013).

9. Tombros, N., Jozsa, C., Popinciuc, M., Jonkman, H. T. & Van Wees, B. J. Electronic spin transport and spin precession in single graphene layers at room temperature. *Nature* **448**, 571–574 (2007).

10. Abergel, D., Apalkov, V., Berashevich, J., Ziegler, K. & Chakraborty, T. Properties of graphene: a theoretical perspective. *Advances in Physics* **59**, 261–482 (2010).

11. Han, W., Kawakami, R. K., Gmitra, M. & Fabian, J. Graphene spintronics. *Nat Nano* **9**, 794–807 (2014). Review.

12. Gmitra, M. & Fabian, J. Graphene on transition-metal dichalcogenides: A platform for proximity spin-orbit physics and optospintronics. *Phys. Rev. B* **92**, 155403 (2015).

13. Garcia, J. H., Vila, M., Cummings, A. W. & Roche, S. Spin transport in graphene/transition metal dichalcogenide heterostructures. *Chemical Society Reviews* **47**, 3359–3379 (2018).

14. Haugen, H., Huertas-Hernando, D. & Brataas, A. Spin transport in proximity-induced ferromagnetic graphene. *Physical Review B* **77**, 115406 (2008).

15. Yang, H.-X. et al. Proximity effects induced in graphene by magnetic insulators: First-principles calculations on spin filtering and exchange-splitting gaps. *Physical review letters* **110**, 046603 (2013).

16. Zollner, K., Gmitra, M., Frank, T. & Fabian, J. Theory of proximity-induced exchange coupling in graphene on hbn/(co, ni). *Physical Review B* **94**, 155441 (2016).

17. Asshoff, P. et al. Magnetoresistance of vertical co-graphene-nife junctions controlled by charge transfer and proximityinduced spin splitting in graphene. *2D Materials* **4**, 031004 (2017).

18. Behera, S. K., Bora, M., Chowdhury, S. S. P. & Deb, P. Proximity effects in graphene and ferromagnetic crbr 3 van der waals heterostructures. *Physical Chemistry Chemical Physics* **21**, 25788–25796 (2019).

19. Wei, P. et al. Strong interfacial exchange field in the graphene/eus heterostructure. *Nature materials* **15**, 711–716 (2016).

20. Wu, Y.-F. et al. Magnetic proximity effect in graphene coupled to a bife o 3 nanoplate. *Physical Review B* **95**, 195426 (2017).

21. Tang, C., Zhang, Z., Lai, S., Tan, Q. & Gao, W.-b. Magnetic proximity effect in graphene/crbr3 van der waals heterostructures. *Advanced Materials* 1908498 (2020).

22. Wang, Z., Tang, C., Sachs, R., Barlas, Y. & Shi, J. Proximity-induced ferromagnetism in graphene revealed by the anomalous hall effect. *Physical review letters* **114**, 016603 (2015).

23. Tang, C. et al. Approaching quantum anomalous hall effect in proximity-coupled yig/graphene/h-bn sandwich structure. *APL Materials* **6**, 026401 (2018).

24. Leutenantsmeyer, J. C., Kaverzin, A. A., Wojtaszek, M. & Van Wees, B. J. Proximity induced room temperature ferromagnetism in graphene probed with spin currents. *2D Materials* **4**, 014001 (2016).

25. Singh, S. et al. Strong modulation of spin currents in bilayer graphene by static and fluctuating proximity exchange fields. *Physical review letters* **118**, 187201 (2017).

26. Karpiak, B. et al. Magnetic proximity in a van der waals heterostructure of magnetic insulator and graphene. *2D Materials* **7**, 015026 (2019).

27. Cummings, A. W. Probing magnetism via spin dynamics in graphene/2d-ferromagnet heterostructures. *Journal of Physics: Materials* **2**, 045007 (2019).

28. Behin-Aein, B., Datta, D., Salahuddin, S. & Datta, S. Proposal for an all-spin logic device with built-in memory. *Nature nanotechnology* **5**, 266–270 (2010).

29. Michetti, P., Recher, P. & Iannaccone, G. Electric field control of spin rotation in bilayer graphene. *Nano letters* **10**, 4463–4469 (2010).

30. Michetti, P. & Recher, P. Spintronics devices from bilayer graphene in contact to ferromagnetic insulators. *Physical Review B* **84**, 125438 (2011).

31. Zollner, K., Gmitra, M. & Fabian, J. Electrically tunable exchange splitting in bilayer graphene on monolayer cr2x2te6 with x= ge, si, and sn. *New Journal of Physics* **20**, 073007 (2018).

32. Cardoso, C., Soriano, D., Garc´ıa-Mart´ınez, N. & Ferna´ndez-Rossier, J. Van der waals spin valves. *Physical Review Letters* **121**, 067701 (2018).

33. Gibertini, M., Koperski, M., Morpurgo, A. & Novoselov, K. Magnetic 2d materials and heterostructures. *Nature nanotechnology* **14**, 408–419 (2019).

34. Göser, O., Paul, W. & Kahle, H. Magnetic properties of crsbr. *Journal of magnetism and magnetic materials* **92**, 129–136 (1990).

35. Wang, H., Qi, J. & Qian, X. Electrically tunable high curie temperature two-dimensional ferromagnetism in van der waals layered crystals. *Applied Physics Letters* **117**, 083102 (2020).

36. Telford, E. J. et al. Layered antiferromagnetism induces large negative magnetoresistance in the van der waals semiconductor crsbr. *Advanced Materials* **32**, 2003240 (2020).

37. Lee, K. et al. Magnetic order and symmetry in the 2d semiconductor crsbr. *arXiv preprint arXiv:2007.10715* (2020).

38. Jungwirth, T., Marti, X., Wadley, P. & Wunderlich, J. Antiferromagnetic spintronics. *Nature nanotechnology* **11**, 231 (2016).

39. Jiang, S., Shan, J. & Mak, K. F. Electric-field switching of two-dimensional van der waals magnets. *Nature materials* **17**, 406–410 (2018).

40. Dash, S. P., Sharma, S., Patel, R. S., de Jong, M. P. & Jansen, R. Electrical creation of spin polarization in silicon at room temperature. *Nature* **462**, 491–494 (2009).

41. Uchida, K. et al. Observation of the spin seebeck effect. *Nature* **455**, 778–781 (2008).

42. Rameshti, B. Z. & Moghaddam, A. G. Spin-dependent seebeck effect and spin caloritronics in magnetic graphene. *Physical Review B* **91**, 155407 (2015).

43. Villamor, E., Isasa, M., Hueso, L. E. & Casanova, F. Temperature dependence of spin polarization in ferromagnetic metals using lateral spin valves. *Physical Review B* **88**, 184411 (2013).

44. Nagaosa, N., Sinova, J., Onoda, S., MacDonald, A. H. & Ong, N. P. Anomalous hall effect. *Reviews of modern physics* **82**, 1539 (2010).

45. Song, G., Ranjbar, M. & Kiehl, R. A. Operation of graphene magnetic field sensors near the charge neutrality point. *Communications Physics* **2**, 1–8 (2019).

46. Mendes, J. et al. Spin-current to charge-current conversion and magnetoresistance in a hybrid structure of graphene and yttrium iron garnet. *Physical review letters* **115**, 226601 (2015).

47. Zhang, Y., Tan, Y.-W., Stormer, H. L. & Kim, P. Experimental observation of the quantum hall effect and berry's phase in graphene. *nature* **438**, 201–204 (2005).

48. Tse, W.-K., Qiao, Z., Yao, Y., MacDonald, A. H. & Niu, Q. Quantum anomalous hall effect in single-layer and bilayer graphene. *Physical Review B* **83**, 155447 (2011).

49. Zhou, B., Chen, X., Wang, H., Ding, K.-H. & Zhou, G. Magnetotransport and current-induced spin transfer torque in a ferromagnetically contacted graphene. *Journal of Physics: Condensed Matter* **22**, 445302 (2010).

50. Chappert, C., Fert, A. & Van Dau, F. N. The emergence of spin electronics in data storage. 147–157 (World Scientific, 2010).

51. Novoselov, K. et al. Two-dimensional atomic crystals. *Proceedings of the National Academy of Sciences of the United States of America* **102**, 10451–10453 (2005).
52. Li, H. et al. Rapid and reliable thickness identification of two-dimensional nanosheets using optical microscopy. *ACS nano* **7**, 10344–10353 (2013).
53. Zomer, P. J., Guimar˜aes, M. H. D., Brant, J. C., Tombros, N. & van Wees, B. J. Fast pick up technique for high quality heterostructures of bilayer graphene and hexagonal boron nitride. *Applied Physics Letters* **105**, 013101 (2014).
54. Beck, J. Uber chalkogenidhalogenide des chroms synthese, kristallstruktur und magnetismus von chromsulfidbromid, crsbr." *Zeitschrift fu¨r anorganische und allgemeine Chemie* **585**, 157–167 (1990).

Chapter 9: Strain Application to CrSBr

9.1 Preface

Stretching a crystal leads to changes in its material parameters, such as lattice constants, shape, crystal symmetries etc., which can fundamentally affect its physical properties. For instance, even small changes in bond geometry can completely change the spin interactions, and thus magnetic behavior of a material. Due to their atomically thin nature, 2D van der Waals (vdW) crystals possess extraordinary mechanical durability[1,2] and sensitivity to external tuning knobs[3-5], making them ideal candidates for exploring the interplay of strain and magnetism in the 2D limit. Despite theoretical predictions of strain-induced magnetic phase transitions[6-8] and experimental demonstrations of strain tuning of magnetic properties such as ordering temperature[9,10], coercive fields[10], and Néel vectors[11] in several systems, reversible strain switching of the magnetic ground state has remained a challenge. One obstacle is that the predicted phase transitions often require high strains, while experiments on vdW magnets to date have failed to exceed 1% strain with continuous in-situ tunability at low temperature. Here, we report a strain-induced magnetic phase transition at zero magnetic field in the A-type layered magnetic semiconductor CrSBr. This is achieved by designing a strain device which can apply continuous, in-situ uniaxial tensile strain approaching several percent at cryogenic temperatures. Using this apparatus, we realize continuous and drastic tuning of magnetic properties and a reversible antiferromagnetic (AFM) to ferromagnetic (FM) phase transition which occurs at a critical strain of ~ 1.2%. First-principles calculations reveals that the tuning of in-plane lattice constant of CrSBr strongly modifies the interlayer magnetic exchange interaction, which changes sign at the critical strain. Our work creates new opportunities for harnessing the strain control of magnetism and other electronic states in low dimensional materials and heterostructures.

9.2 Introduction and Background

Controllable phase transitions between electronic states with distinct symmetries are at the heart of condensed matter physics. For instance, switching the sign of spin-spin exchange interactions in magnets can lead to antiferromagnetic (AFM) and ferromagnetic (FM) phase transitions, which is of fundamental importance for both condensed matter and statistical physics as well as spintronic applications. The recent discovery of atomically thin van der Waals (vdW) magnets provides a new platform for the manipulation of magnetic properties with versatile controls, such as electrical and nano-mechanical means. In particular, for the latter, hydrostatic pressure has been used to switch AFM to FM states in the A-type antiferromagnet CrI_3 at zero magnetic field[12,13]. However, the pressure-induced magnetic state switching in CrI_3 is non-reversible; it originates from a rearrangement of the layer stacking from monoclinic to rhombohedral. In addition, only discrete hydrostatic pressure can be applied due to the limitation of the pressure cells. It would thus be highly desirable to develop both a continuously tunable knob and a material system for achieving reversable magnetic phase transitions.

Tensile strain is a proven method for tuning the fundamental properties of three-dimensional bulk quantum materials. Examples include the strain control of magnetic[14], superconducting[15,16], nematic[17], and topological phases[18] by directly modifying the lattice constant and symmetry of a given crystal. For vdW magnets, several recent works have highlighted the tantalizing opportunities for strain controlling magnetism at the nanoscale. These results include the enhancement of coercive field and Curie temperature in thin Fe_3GeTe_2[10], tuning of Néel temperature in $FePS_3$ resonators[9], and control of the orientation of the Néel vector in $MnPSe_3$[11]. In addition, many theoretical studies have predicted that magnetic phase transitions in certain materials can be achieved under a large strain[6-8,19]. However, the experimental realization of a reversable AFM to FM phase transition by continuous strain tuning remains a challenge. One difficulty lies in the lack of cryo-strain devices which can apply large (over 1%) and *in-situ* tunable strain on 2D materials.

In this work, we design a novel cryo-strain device capable of applying large strains to 2D materials and develop an approach to calibrate the applied strain in-situ. Using this new capability, we realized drastic and continuous tuning of the magnetic properties, such as magnetic anisotropy and interlayer exchange interactions, and an AFM to FM phase transition of a vdW magnet in a reversable fashion. The magnet we found to have a large strain response is CrSBr, which is a recently discovered A-type antiferromagnetic semiconductor with an in-plane easy axis[19,20]. Recent studies of CrSBr have revealed a strong connection between magnetic order and transport properties in bulk single crystals[21], and a unique coupling between excitons and the magnetic order in atomically thin flakes, where the alignment of the spins in constituent layers controls the interlayer hybridization of the exciton wavefunctions[22]. In addition to the observed coupling of charge and spin, theoretical investigations have predicted that the magnetic order of monolayer CrSBr is switchable through tensile strain[19].

9.3 Application of Strain

9.3.1 Apparatus

We begin by introducing our cryogenic strain apparatus and techniques. We used two

different approaches that are based on a piezoelectric strain cell (**Fig. 9.1A**) which has

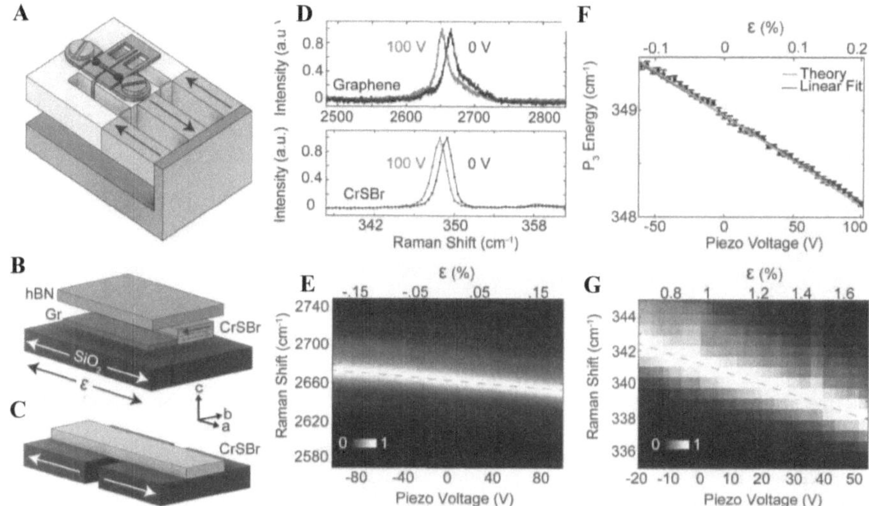

Figure 9. 1 Cryo-strain devices, tuning of Raman modes, and strain calibration
(A) Schematic of the strain cell based on three parallel piezostacks glued to a titanium backing and flexure. Strain is then applied to van der Waals materials placed on a SiO2/Si substrate which is fixed on top of the strain device (see Appendix H). (B) Diagram of a hBN/CrSBr/graphene strain gauge heterostructure deposited on a Si/SiO2 pillar. When the pillar is strained, the strain is transferred to the heterostructure on top. In our experiments, the strain is aligned with the a crystal axis of the CrSBr, which is orthogonal to the easy (b) axis. The red and blue arrows CrSBr depict the AFM interlayer coupling which produces an A-type layered AFM structure. (C) Schematic of a thin CrSBr sample suspended over a micron-scale gap of a SiO2/Si substrate. (D) Raman spectra of the graphene 2D peak (top) and CrSBr Raman mode centered around 349 cm^{-1} (bottom) with 0 (black) and 100 (red) volts applied to the strain cell. (E) Full strain dependence of the graphene 2D peak. The grey line represents a linear fit of the peak position as a function of piezo voltage determined by Lorentzian fits. Compared to previous report Raman shift rates of graphene, the strain values are then calculated. (F) CrSBr Raman peak extracted from Lorentzian fits as a function of piezo voltage and strain along with linear fits to the data (blue line) and the first-principles calculated Raman shift rate (green line, shifted vertically to ~ 349 cm^{-1} at V = 0). Error bars represent the uncertainty of the Lorentzian fit. (F) Raman spectrum as a function of piezo voltage and strain for a suspended bulk CrSBr sample. The strain values are determined using the measured CrSBr Raman shift rate, presented in panel (F), and an unstrained reference spectrum taken far off the gap.

previously been used to apply uniaxial strain to bulk crystals[16,18,23]. The first one is a strain gauge device, consisting of 2D materials deposited on a 50 μm thick silicon pillar which is attached to the strain cell. The heterostructure is formed by a hexagonal boron nitride layer (~20 nm) stacked on top of both a thin (~ 30 nm) CrSBr and graphene flake (**Fig. 9.1B** top). The CrSBr a-axis, which is orthogonal to the magnetic easy axis b, is aligned to the strained axis of the silicon pillar. The decision to align the strain axis with the a axis will be explained later. Finite element analysis modelling using parameters similar to our experiment (see Appendix G) indicate the surface of the pillar has a highly uniform strain profile on the length scale of the sample (Fig. G1).

9.3.2 Calibration

We use the Raman modes of both graphene and silicon to calibrate the strain applied to the CrSBr. **Fig. 9.1C** shows the Raman spectra of the graphene 2D mode and CrSBr phonon mode[24] centered at ~ 349 cm^{-1} (henceforth labeled as P_3) with 0 V and 100 V applied to the piezo stacks. Both peaks undergo a detectable redshift with increasing tensile strain. Full strain-dependent Raman measurements of the graphene (**Fig. 9.1D**) and CrSBr (**Fig. 9.1E**) show a highly linear strain response which enables us to accurately calibrate our system. Using values obtained from previous experiments on graphene[25], we determine that the cell applies ~ .0019 %/V to the heterostructure (see Appendix G). This calibration is further confirmed by an independent estimation based on the measured silicon Raman mode as a function of piezo voltage (Fig. G2)[26]. Based on this calibration, we find that the P_3 mode in CrSBr redshifts at a rate of ~ 4.2 cm^{-1}/%. The measured redshift rate of P_3 is in good agreement with first-principles calculations which predict a redshift of ~ 4.4 cm^{-1}/% (green line in **Fig. 9.1E**). Furthermore, the measured strain shift rates of the two other main Raman modes in this sample are in good agreement with the predicted rates (Fig. G3). From the calibration, we obtain that the silicon pillar technique can apply about ~0.4% strain in this voltage range.

To achieve larger strain, our second approach is based on a cleaved silicon substrate, which produces microscopic gaps for suspending the sample over (**Fig. 9.1B** bottom). Since the applied strain is equal to the fractional change in length, the small gap enables the application of much larger strains than the relatively long silicon pillar. Due to the anisotropic crystal structure, exfoliated thin CrSBr flakes tend to exhibit a rectangular structure with a long edge of ~ 100 μm along the a-axis and a short edge of ~ 10μm along the easy b-axis for a typical flake. This type of structure is desirable for suspending the sample over the gap with the a-axis perpendicular to the gap (**Fig. 9.1B** bottom). Since the suspended region of the sample is much smaller than its total length, the sample is anchored to the substrate well enough to sustain large strains without sliding. Additionally, since the end of the sample is far from the gap, it provides a convenient unstrained reference which we can use to understand the effects and magnitude of the applied strain. **Fig. 9.1F** shows the Raman spectra of a suspended CrSBr sample as a function of piezo voltage. Using the above determined shift rate of 4.2 cm^{-1}/% of the P_3 mode and a zero-strain peak energy of 345 cm^{-1} taken far off the gap, we find that we can apply strains ranging from ~ 0.6% up to 1.7% with negligible slippage in this particular device. This range of applied strain is typical for the samples we measured. This technique thus enables the application of significantly larger strains at cryogenic temperatures than both the thin silicon pillar technique and previous experiments which rely on bendable substrates[10,25].

9.4 The Effects of High Strain on Magnetic Order of Few-layer CrSBr

After strain calibration, we proceed to present the effects of high strains on the magnetic order of thin CrSBr samples. A recent study[22] revealed rich excitonic features in both the photoluminescence (PL) and optical absorption spectra of CrSBr. Although not all spectral features are well understood, the work established that the properties of excitons in thin CrSBr flakes are sensitive to the interlayer magnetic order. This enables us to probe the interlayer magnetic coupling through the exciton PL spectrum. The data presented in the rest of this paper were taken from a ~ 20 nm CrSBr flake (**Fig. 9.2B** inset) (see Fig. G4 for additional sample details).

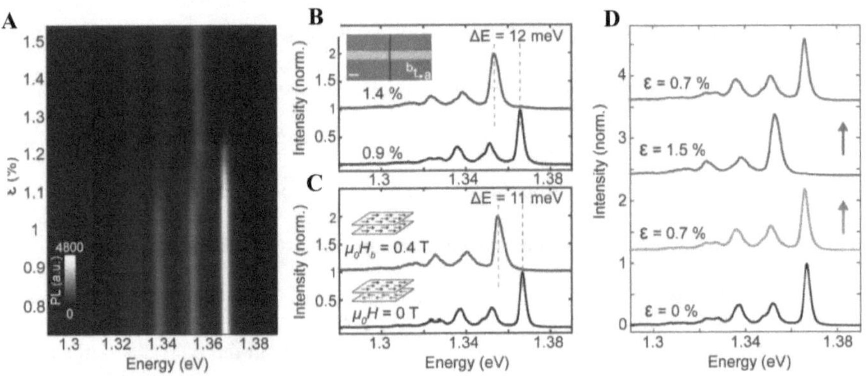

Figure 9. 2 Reversable strain induced antiferromagnetic (AFM) to ferromagnetic (FM) phase transition in CrSBr

(A) Strain dependent photoluminescence spectrum of a 20 nm CrSBr flake with the strain applied along the a axis. The strain is swept up from a starting value of ~ 0.7 %. (B) Photoluminescence spectra at 0.9 % (black) and 1.4 % strain (blue). Inset: optical micrograph of the sample. Scale bar: 30 μm. (C) Photoluminescence spectra at 0 T (black) and 0.4 T magnetic field applied along the b (easy) axis. Insets depict the zero field A-type AFM and high field FM states. (D) Select photoluminescence spectra as the strain is swept up and then down. The arrows indicate the progression of the applied strain: the strain is ramped up from 0.7% (bottom) to 1.5% (middle) and then back down to 0.7% (top).

Fig. 9.2A shows the PL intensity plot as a function of applied strain and photon energy in the absence of magnetic field. Several discrete exciton PL features are observed, at similar energies to the ones reported in Ref [22]. These peaks remain nearly unchanged as the strain increases from 0.7% to about 1.1%. This observation agrees with strain dependent band gaps from first-principles calculations. As shown in Fig. G5, a tensile strain < 1% only results in a continuous change of < 5 meV of the band gap in the AFM phase. Remarkably, as the strain further increases, the intensity of these peaks reduces, while a new set of peaks emerge. Above

~1.3%, the new features dominate the spectrum, which does not show appreciable changes as

the strain further increases. **Fig. 9.2B** plots the PL spectra at two selected strains, 0.9% (black)

and 1.4% (blue), which correspond to before and after the abrupt, strain-induced changes to

the PL, respectively. The spectra reveal a clear ~12 meV red shift of the peaks between the

high and low strain states, while the number of peaks does not change, i.e. the PL pattern

remains the same. We have measured several samples and have observed similar jumps in the

PL spectrum (see Fig. G6).

To understand the observation, we compare the strain dependent PL spectra with unstrained

ones in different magnetic states. The black curve in **Fig. 9.2C** corresponds to the PL spectrum

of the A-type AFM ground state of unstrained CrSBr at zero magnetic field. The bottom inset

illustrates the spin configuration. Each monolayer has ferromagnetic intralayer ordering with

spins aligned along the easy axis, while the interlayer coupling is antiferromagnetic. The blue

spectrum is the PL of CrSBr with a magnetic field of 0.4 T applied along the magnetic easy

axis (*b* axis). Since the applied magnetic field is larger than the coercive field of about 0.22T

(see below), all the spins are aligned resulting in a field-induced FM state (top inset). There is

an abrupt red shift of about 11 meV in the spectra between the AFM to the FM states while the

PL pattern remains the same. These magnetic state dependent PL spectra are remarkably

similar to the above strain dependent exciton PL spectra. The slight discrepancy (~ 1 meV) in

the energy difference between the AFM and FM spectra arises from a small additional redshift

of the 1.4% high strain spectra. This comparison thus implies a strain-induced AFM to FM

phase transition with the spins aligned along the easy *b*-axis.

The strain-induced phase transition is reversable and repeatable. **Fig. 9.2D** illustrates the

PL spectra at selected strains as the piezo voltage is continuously swept up and then back down.

The black curve at the bottom is the taken at a spot far away from the gap, corresponding to

zero strain. As strain increases to the intermediate regime, e.g. 0.7%, the spectrum barely

changes, consistent with the minor redshift observed in **Fig. 9.2A** and the band structure

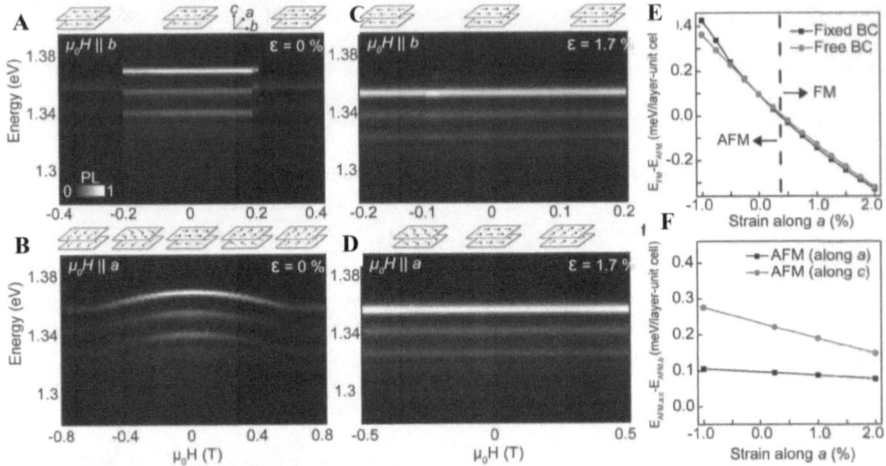

Figure 9. 3 Magnetic field dependent PL before and after the strain induced magnetic phase transition.
a-b, Magnetic field dependent photoluminescence measurements of unstrained CrSBr with the field applied along the easy axis (b crystal axis) (a) and intermediate hard axis (a crystal axis) (b). Diagrams on top of each panel depicts the evolution of the magnetic states. c-d, Magneto-PL measurements along the b axis (c) and a axis (d) with a strain of 1.7% applied. Cartoons of the ferromagnetic interlayer magnetic coupling are shown above the intensity plots. e, DFT-LSDA scalar relativistic calculation of the energy of FM and AFM interlayer coupling as a function of strain applied along the a axis with lattice constants in b and c kept constant (black) and free to relax (red). The calculations show a strain induced AFM to FM phase transition, denoted by the dashed black line. f, DFT-LSDA fully relativistic calculation of the energy difference between AFM phases with spin along either a (black) or c (red), versus spin along b as strain is applied in a axis with lattice parameters in b and c kept constant. The calculation shows the easy axis is along b with strain applied a axis, consistent with the experiments.

calculations. At 1.5%, an abrupt change in the PL is observed, corresponding to the strain-

induced FM state. As the strain sweeps back down to 0.7% (top blue curve), the exciton PL

spectrum returns to the one corresponding to the AFM state. We note that there is a hysteresis

between the strain sweeping directions around the critical strain for the magnetic phase

transition (Fig. G7), which is larger than the piezo hysteresis.

To further investigate the strain-induced switching of the PL spectrum, we applied magnetic fields along all three magnetic axes to the strained and unstrained areas of the sample. **Fig. 9.3A** shows magneto-PL measurements of the unstrained region with the field applied along the easy axis (b-axis). The PL is invariant until a critical field $H_c \sim 0.22$ T is reached, at which point the sample undergoes a spin-flip transition to the field-induced FM state (see insets for the corresponding magnetic states). On the other hand, when the field is applied along the intermediate axis (a-axis) (**Fig. 9.3B**), a continuous red shift of all of the main exciton lines is observed as the spins within each layer cant until they eventually align at the saturating field $H_s \sim 0.68$ T. Regardless of the direction of the applied field, the PL spectrum remains invariant when the magnetic field is increased above the saturating field. Similar canting effects are observed for a magnetic field applied along the had (c) axis with a saturating field of $H_s = 1.6$ T (Fig. G8). The observed field dependence is consistent with previously reported magneto-PL measurements on atomically thin CrSBr samples[22].

In the high strain state, the sample has a completely different field dependence. **Fig. 9.3C** shows magneto-PL measurements with the field applied along the b axis of the CrSBr flake at 1.7% strain. In stark contrast to the unstrained case, no detectable difference is observed between the high positive field and zero field spectra (Fig. G9). As the magnetic field sweeps from positive to negative, the PL remains invariant except at the coercive field near -0.09T, which corresponds to the switching of the ferromagnetic states with the spins pointing in opposite directions along the b-$axis$ (inset). This coercive field is more than two times smaller than the one corresponding to the AFM to FM transition at zero strain, providing additional evidence that the interlayer magnetic coupling is significantly modified by the applied strain.

For a small range of applied fields near the coercive field (about -0.09T), the PL intensity suddenly increases, and an additional high energy peak appears. This observation implies the formation of vertical domains near the switching of the magnetic state, which leads to AF interfaces and thus large PL intensity and additional high energy peaks. The change of the PL spectrum at the coercive field is hysteretic when the magnetic field is swept up and down (Fig. G9). As the field is further increased, the spin orientation of the ferromagnetic state is fully switched, and the PL goes back to being indistinguishable from the spectra at other magnetic fields. Applying fields along the other axes reveals further differences from the unstrained sample. For instance, no detectable shift is observed in the main exciton lines when the field is swept along the a-axis (**Fig. 9.3D**).

In thin CrSBr samples, the main magnetic field effect on the exciton PL originates from a dependence of the interlayer electronic hybridization on the interlayer magnetic coupling: the angle between spins in different layers controls the degree to which the wavefunctions between adjacent layers hybridize[22]. In the AFM state, the interlayer hybridization is suppressed due to anti-aligned spin states in the adjacent layers. In the ferromagnetic state, the interlayer hybridization would always be maximized, except at the coercive field where domains may contain layers with antiparallel orientations. This explains the lack of PL field dependence in the high strain ferromagnetic phase when the field is swept along the a-axis, and the abrupt hysteretic changes when the field is applied along the b-axis, which is the magnetic easy axis.

The experimental signatures of the magnetic phase transition are further corroborated by DFT calculations. **Fig. 9.3E** shows the calculated energy difference Δ between the interlayer FM and AFM states as a function of strain. The sign switching from positive to negative as strain increases reveals a strain-induced AFM to FM transition. We found that the calculated Δ shows little difference between open- and fixed-boundary conditions (i.e., if b and c axes are either free to relax or kept fixed). Also, calculations with fixed in-plane lattice constants but different interlayer distances show that CrSBr remains in the A-type AFM phase. These results suggest that the sign switching of the interlayer magnetic exchange interaction is not a result of changes to the interlayer spacing caused by the Poisson effect. In addition, CrSBr has only one stable stacking structure. Combined with the demonstrated reversable tunability, we rule out switching of the layer stacking arrangement as the cause of AFM-FM phase transition (Fig. G10). Rather, the transition originates from the modulation of interlayer magnetic exchange interaction by changing the in-plane lattice constant, which affects the geometry of the exchange pathway between Cr atoms in adjacent layers. This modulation leads to switching of the interlayer magnetic exchange interaction from AFM to FM type at the critical strain, while the magnetic easy axis remains along the b axis (**Fig. 9.3F**).

9.5 Strain Changes Spin Behavior in CrSBr in an applied Magnetic Field

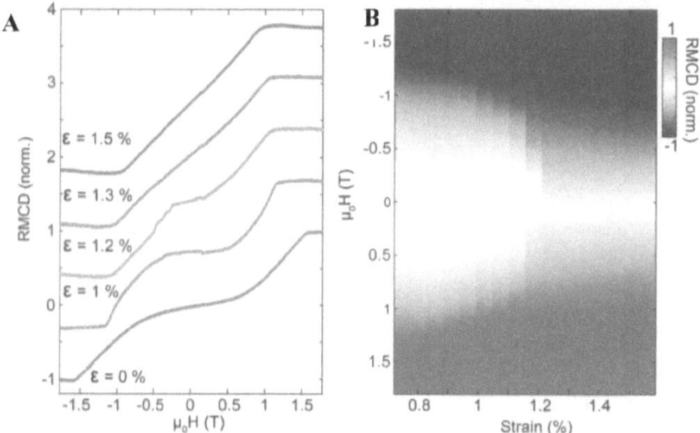

Figure 9. 4 Strain tuning of out-of-plane spin canting process
(A) Magnetic field dependent polar reflective magnetic circular dichroism (RMCD) measurements as the out-of-plane magnetic field is swept down at select strains. The RMCD sweeps are normalized at each strain value. Near the critical strain, the discrete jumps in the RMCD vs magnetic field imply domain effects (see 1.2% curve). (B) Color plot of the RMCD sweeps as a function of the applied strain.

We also found that strain leads to dramatic changes in the spin canting process with an applied out-of-plane magnetic field. **Fig. 9.4A** shows normalized polar reflective magnetic circular dichroism (RMCD) measurements at selected strains. Polar RMCD is a sensitive probe of the out-of-plane magnetization. At zero strain, RMCD shows a highly nonlinear dependence with increasing magnetic field, consistent with SQUID measurements on the bulk crystal[21]. This non-linear behavior suggests the out-of-plane spin canting behavior in thin bulk CrSBr cannot be explained by a classical Heisenberg model with quadratic anisotropic exchange or single ion anisotropy, because these terms should yield a linear dependence of magnetization with out-of-plane B field. Rather, a higher order magnetic anisotropy term, e.g. originated from biaxial anisotropies, is needed to account for the observation. As strain increases to drive the AFM to FM transition, the RMCD switches from the nonlinear behavior to linear spin canting, implying strain tuning of high-order magnetic anisotropy. The full dependence of RMCD on strain is presented in the color plot in **Fig. 9.4B**. Notably, the application of intermediate strain leads to a large reduction in the saturating magnetic field, from 1.6T in the unstrained case to about 0.9T at 1.6% strain. These results demonstrate that both the saturating field and spin canting process can be controlled through strain.

9.6 Discussion of Results

In summary, we have presented new techniques for exploring the effects of uniaxial strain in 2D materials and heterostructures at cryogenic temperatures with in-situ tunability. The first approach, which is based on straining a silicon substrate, is compatible with all standard heterostructure fabrication procedures, offering a universal platform for studying the effects of moderate uniaxial strain in a wide variety of systems including 2D moiré materials. On the other hand, the second approach relies upon opening a micron scale gap, enabling the application of high strains to suspended samples. Using these techniques, we realized a reversable strain-induced AFM to FM transition in the layered A-type antiferromagnetic semiconductor CrSBr, which enables the control of interlayer hybridization and exciton wavefunction due to the strong magneto-excitonic coupling. Consequently, these results could enable new ultrathin devices which leverage the unique coupling of lattice, spin, and charge, such as strain-actuated magneto-resistive switches or magnetic tunnel junctions which operate

without an applied magnetic field. In addition, strain gradients are inevitable in these devices,

e.g. near the edge of the gap, which may introduce rich spin-textures. Beyond van der Waals

magnets, we envision that these strain platforms can be used to realize dynamic control of

structural, electronic and optical properties in many other 2D materials, heterostructures, and

moire superlattices.

9.7 References

1. Huang, B. *et al.* Emergent phenomena and proximity effects in two-dimensional magnets and heterostructures. *Nature Materials* **19**, 1276-1289, doi:10.1038/s41563-020-0791-8 (2020).
2. Gong, C. & Zhang, X. Two-dimensional magnetic crystals and emergent heterostructure devices. *Science* **363**, eaav4450, doi:10.1126/science.aav4450 (2019).
3. Du, L. *et al.* Engineering symmetry breaking in 2D layered materials. *Nature Reviews Physics* **3**, 193-206, doi:10.1038/s42254-020-00276-0 (2021).
4. Wu, Z., Yu, J. & Yuan, S. Strain-tunable magnetic and electronic properties of monolayer CrI3. *Physical Chemistry Chemical Physics* **21**, 7750-7755, doi:10.1039/c8cp07067a (2019).
5. Zhang, J.-M., Nie, Y.-Z., Wang, X.-G., Xia, Q.-L. & Guo, G.-H. Strain modulation of magnetic properties of monolayer and bilayer FePS3 antiferromagnet. *Journal of Magnetism and Magnetic Materials* **525**, 167687, doi:10.1016/j.jmmm.2020.167687 (2021).
6. Pizzochero, M. & Yazyev, O. V. Inducing Magnetic Phase Transitions in Monolayer CrI3 via Lattice Deformations. *The Journal of Physical Chemistry C* **124**, 7585-7590, doi:10.1021/acs.jpcc.0c01873 (2020).
7. Šiškins, M. *et al.* Magnetic and electronic phase transitions probed by nanomechanical resonators. *Nature Communications* **11**, doi:10.1038/s41467-020-16430-2 (2020).
8. Wang, Y. *et al.* Strain-Sensitive Magnetization Reversal of a van der Waals Magnet. *Advanced Materials* **32**, 2004533, doi:https://doi.org/10.1002/adma.202004533 (2020).
9. Ni, Z. *et al.* Imaging the N\'eel vector switching in the monolayer antiferromagnet MnPSe3 with strain-controlled Ising order. (2021).
10. Li, T. *et al.* Pressure-controlled interlayer magnetism in atomically thin CrI3. *Nature Materials* **18**, 1303-1308, doi:10.1038/s41563-019-0506-1 (2019).
11. Song, T. *et al.* Switching 2D magnetic states via pressure tuning of layer stacking. *Nature Materials* **18**, 1298-1302, doi:10.1038/s41563-019-0505-2 (2019).
12. Cherifi, R. O. *et al.* Electric-field control of magnetic order above room temperature. *Nature Materials* **13**, 345-351, doi:10.1038/nmat3870 (2014).
13. Chu, J.-H. *et al.* In-Plane Resistivity Anisotropy in an Underdoped Iron Arsenide Superconductor. *Science* **329**, 824-826, doi:10.1126/science.1190482 (2010).
14. Hicks, C. W. *et al.* Strong Increase of Tc of Sr2RuO4 Under Both Tensile and Compressive Strain. *Science* **344**, 283-285, doi:10.1126/science.1248292 (2014).

15. Chu, J.-H., Kuo, H.-H., Analytis, J. G. & Fisher, I. R. Divergent Nematic Susceptibility in an Iron Arsenide Superconductor. *Science* **337**, 710-712, doi:10.1126/science.1221713 (2012).
16. Mutch, J. *et al.* Evidence for a strain-tuned topological phase transition in $ZrTe_5$. *Science Advances* **5**, eaav9771, doi:10.1126/sciadv.aav9771 (2019).
17. Xu, B. *et al.* Switching of the magnetic anisotropy via strain in two dimensional multiferroic materials: CrSX (X = Cl, Br, I). *Applied Physics Letters* **116**, 052403, doi:10.1063/1.5140644 (2020).
18. Jiang, Z., Wang, P., Xing, J., Jiang, X. & Zhao, J. Screening and Design of Novel 2D Ferromagnetic Materials with High Curie Temperature above Room Temperature. *ACS Applied Materials & Interfaces* **10**, 39032-39039, doi:10.1021/acsami.8b14037 (2018).
19. Telford, E. J. *et al.* Layered Antiferromagnetism Induces Large Negative Magnetoresistance in the van der Waals Semiconductor CrSBr. *Advanced Materials* **32**, 2003240, doi:10.1002/adma.202003240 (2020).
20. Wilson, N. P. *et al.* Interlayer Electronic Coupling on Demand in a 2D Magnetic Semiconductor. (2021).
21. Hicks, C. W., Barber, M. E., Edkins, S. D., Brodsky, D. O. & Mackenzie, A. P. Piezoelectric-based apparatus for strain tuning. *Review of Scientific Instruments* **85**, 065003, doi:10.1063/1.4881611 (2014).
22. Lee, K. *et al.* Magnetic Order and Symmetry in the 2D Semiconductor CrSBr. (2020).
23. Wang, L. *et al.* In Situ Strain Tuning in hBN-Encapsulated Graphene Electronic Devices. *Nano Letters* **19**, 4097-4102, doi:10.1021/acs.nanolett.9b01491 (2019).
24. Ureña, F., Olsen, S. H. & Raskin, J.-P. Raman measurements of uniaxial strain in silicon nanostructures. *Journal of Applied Physics* **114**, 144507, doi:10.1063/1.4824291 (2013).
25. Hopcroft, M. A., Nix, W. D. & Kenny, T. W. What is the Young's Modulus of Silicon? *Journal of Microelectromechanical Systems* **19**, 229-238, doi:10.1109/jmems.2009.2039697 (2010).
26. Paolo Giannozzi, S. B., Nicola Bonini, Matteo Calandra, Roberto Car, Carlo Cavazzoni, Davide Ceresoli, Guido L Chiarotti, Matteo Cococcioni, Ismaila Dabo, Andrea Dal Corso, Stefano de Gironcoli, Stefano Fabris, Guido Fratesi, Ralph Gebauer, Uwe Gerstmann, Christos Gougoussis, Anton Kokalj, Michele Lazzeri, Layla Martin-Samos, Nicola Marzari, Francesco Mauri, Riccardo Mazzarello, Stefano Paolini, Alfredo Pasquarello, Lorenzo Paulatto, Carlo Sbraccia, Sandro Scandolo, Gabriele Sclauzero, Ari P Seitsonen, Alexander Smogunov, Paolo Umari, Renata M Wentzcovitch. Quantum ESPRESSO: a modular and open-source software project for quantum simulations of materials. *Journal of Physics: Condensed Matter* **21** (2009).
27. Grimme, S. Semiempirical GGA-type density functional constructed with a long-range dispersion correction. *Journal of Computational Chemistry* **27**, 1787-1799, doi:10.1002/jcc.20495 (2006).

Chapter 10: $Mo_6S_3Br_6$

10.1 Preface

Two-dimensional (2D) van der Waals materials with in-plane anisotropy are of great interest for directional transport of charge and energy, as exemplified by recent studies on black phosphorus and α-MO$_3$. Here we report a layered van der Waals semiconductor with in-plane anisotropy built upon the superatomic units of $Mo_6S_3Br_6$. This material possesses robust 2D character with a direct gap of 1.64 eV, as determined by scanning tunneling spectroscopy and first-principle calculations. Polarization dependent Raman spectroscopy measurement and DFT calculation reveal strong in-plane anisotropy. These results suggest an effective strategy to explore anisotropic 2D electronic and optoelectronic properties from superatomic building blocks with multi-functionality, emergent properties, and hierarchical control.

10.2 Introduction and Background

Two-dimensional (2D) van der Waals materials with in-plane anisotropy are of interest for directional transport of charge and energy. One prominent example is black phosphorus, which has been shown to host highly anisotropic excitons and theoretically predicted to exhibit elliptic and hyperbolic dispersions for plasmon polaritons.[1-3] Likewise, in-plane anisotropy in α-MoO$_3$

has been demonstrated to yield ultra-low-loss phonon polaritons.[4] Besides, in rhenium dichalcogenides,[5] the in-plane anisotropy[6] can be used to fabricate unique photodetectors and filed-effect transistors.[7] When compared to traditional 2D atomic solids, however, the structural diversity combined with in-plane anisotropy is limited, which has restricted their use.

Beyond atomic solids, there is a growing interest in designing 2D materials from complex, hierarchical, and tunable building blocks,[8] as exemplified by colloidal nanoparticle 2D superlattices.[9–11] The use of zero-dimensional building blocks formed by atomic clusters, known as superatoms, is particularly attractive and advantageous due to their atomic precision, as well as the tunability of inter-cluster coupling.[12–14] Their assembly into strongly coupled hierarchical lattices has been shown to produce unique emergent material properties. For instance, three-dimensional cluster-assembled solids such as Chevrel phases[15] and endohedral gallide cluster phases[16] are well-known for their superconducting behaviors. In view of this, 2D structures with in-plane anisotropy promise unique physical properties and functions. However, there are very few examples of layered cluster-based structures[17–19] that can be exfoliated, and the existing ones typically have isotropic in-plane structures (e.g., Re$_6$Se$_8$Cl$_2$).[20–22]

Here, we investigate Mo$_6$S$_3$Br$_6$, a superatomic van der Waals material with strong in-plane anisotropy derived from the Chevrel phase in which [Mo$_6$] octahedral cluster subunits are covalently linked into layers.[19,23] Each [Mo$_6$] octahedron is tilted, enclosed in a cube of S and Br, and connected to two neighboring clusters along the c-axis via a shared S atom located at the apical positions as well as via an additional two bridging Br atoms (**Fig. 10.1A**). The resulting corner-sharing one-dimensional chains of clusters are linked into layers in the bc-plane by means of two inter-chain Mo–S linkages along the b-axis. The clusters form in such a way that the S atoms are inside the layers and the Br atoms are at the surface, establishing the van der Waals planes. The weak van der Waals contacts between the layers along the a-axis and strong in-plane bonding give this material a robust 2D character with stronger coupling along the c-axis.

Mo$_6$S$_3$Br$_6$ was discovered in 1983 by Perrin and coworkers,[23] but its bulk physical properties are essentially unknown, and it has never been investigated as a mono- or few-layer material. One obstacle to such studies is that Mo$_6$S$_3$Br$_6$ is typically obtained as small crystals (tens of micrometers), precluding mechanical exfoliation. In this work, we report a new synthetic approach to grow millimeter-size single crystals of Mo$_6$S$_3$Br$_6$ that can be mechanically exfoliated. We focus on freshly cleaved surfaces of bulk crystals in all experiments based on scanning tunneling microscopy/spectroscopy (STM/STS) and polarization dependent Raman spectroscopy combined with first-principles calculations. We demonstrate the strong in-plane anisotropic electronic structure. DFT calculations support the pseudo-1D electronic structure of this material and reveal a direct bandgap with the valence band maximum (VBM) and the conduction band minimum (CBM) located at the S (0, 1/2, 0) point in momentum space. The electronic bandgap determined by STS is 1.64 eV, with the Fermi level (E_F) located 0.21 eV above the VBM, indicating p-type doping.

10.3 Synthesis and Chemical Characterization of Mo$_6$S$_3$Br$_6$

We synthesize microcrystalline Mo$_6$S$_3$Br$_6$ by heating a stoichiometric mixture of Mo$_6$Br$_{12}$, Mo and S to 1175 °C in a fused silica tube sealed under vacuum. Remarkably, millimeter-size crystals (shown in the inset of **Fig. 10.1b**) are obtained when a mixture of Mo and Nb (in a molar ratio of 92.5:7.5) is used instead of the pure Mo metal. In addition to microcrystalline Mo$_6$S$_3$Br$_6$ powder and macroscopic crystals, the tube contains a few crystals of NbBr$_5$, which form *in situ* and presumably acts as a chemical vapor transport agent that allow large Mo$_6$S$_3$Br$_6$ crystals to grow. The flattened needle morphology of these crystals indicates different growth rates along the b- and c-axes, consistent with the anisotropic in-plane structure (inset **Fig.**

10.1B). The structure of the $Mo_6S_3Br_6$ crystals was determined by single-crystal x-ray diffraction (SC-XRD). In agreement with previous reports, the structure is orthorhombic (space group: *Cmcm*), with lattice parameters a = 17.27 Å, b = 6.58 Å, c = 11.90 Å at 297 K and *c*-axis corresponds to the elongated direction of the crystal (**Fig. I1**). Variable temperature SC-XRD measurements between 100 and 297 K shows monotonic increase of the lattice due to thermal expansion, with no structural phase transitions (**Fig. I2**). The composition of $Mo_6S_3Br_6$ crystals was confirmed by energy dispersive x-ray spectroscopy (**EDX, Table I2**) and x-ray photoelectron spectroscopy (**Fig. I3**).

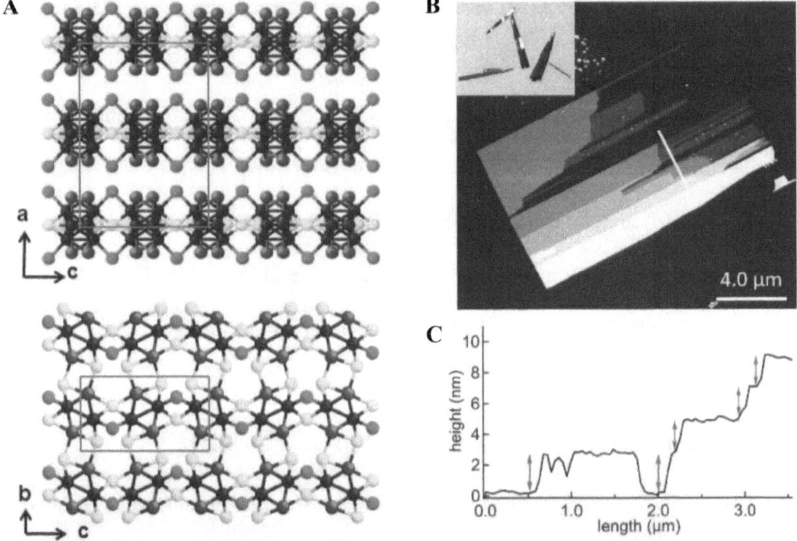

Figure 10. 1 Crystal structure and AFM height analysis of Mo6S3Br6
(**A**) Crystal structure of $Mo_6S_3Br_6$. Side view (top) of the *ac*-plane and top view (bottom) of the *bc*-plane. Unit cells are marked by the red boxes. One directional chain is along *c*-axis. Color code: Mo, blue; S, yellow; Br, brown (inner-cluster) and pink (inter-cluster bridging). (**B**) AFM image on an exfoliated $Mo_6S_3Br_6$ flake on a SiO_2/Si substrate. Top inset: optical image (~3 mm x 2 mm) of the macroscopic $Mo_6S_3Br_6$ crystals. (**C**) The height profile along the white line in b). The thickness of the first layer and the sequential layers is marked by red and blue arrows, respectively.

10.4 Mechanical Exfoliation of Mo₆S₃Br₆

To demonstrate the feasibility of $Mo_6S_3Br_6$ as a practical 2D material, we first mechanically

exfoliated macroscopic crystals using the Scotch tap method[24] and determined the thicknesses

of the resulting rectangular flakes by atomic force microscopy (AFM) under ambient

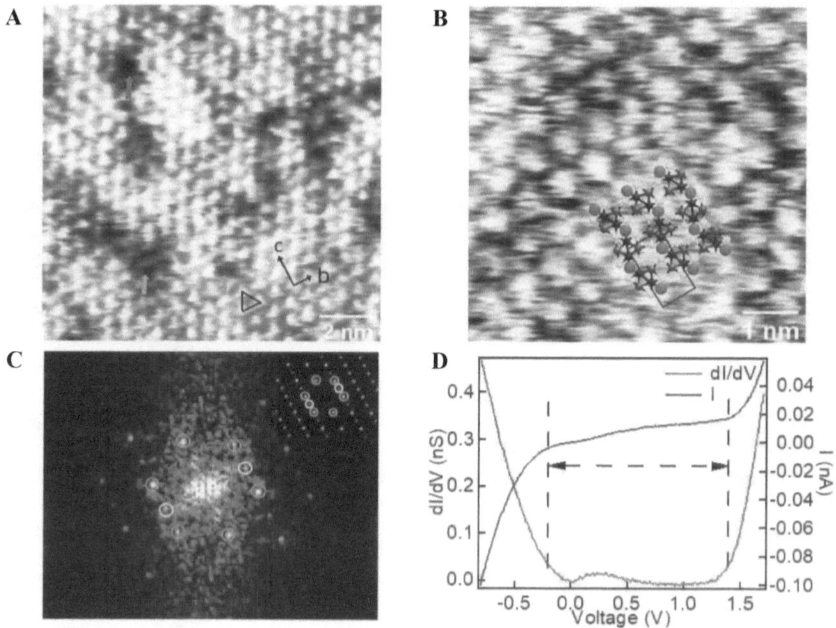

Figure 10. 2 STM and STS analysis of Mo6SBr6 exfoliated layer(s)
High-resolution STM image of $Mo_6S_3Br_6$ at 298 K (12 x 12 nm, U = 1.6 V, I = 60 pA). *c*- and *b*-
axes are marked by the black arrows. Several types of defects are identified by the blue arrows.
(B) Zoom in STM image with overlaid atomic structures. The unit cell is marked by the
rectangular box. **(C)** Fast Fourier transform (FFT) of (a). Inset is the simulated FFT of the top
layer of Br atoms. **(D)** STS spectrum with I-V curve in blue and the dI/dV-V curve in red. The
VBM and CBM are marked by the black dashed lines, giving a bandgap of 1.64 ± 0.05 eV.

conditions. The thinnest flakes obtained using this approach are bilayers (**Fig. 10.1B**) with

thickness of ~ 2.5 nm (marked by red arrows in **Fig. 10.1C**) and sequential steps along the line

profile are 2.1 nm on average (marked by blue arrows in **Fig. 10.1C**), close to the height of two

monolayers based on the SC-XRD data (~1.8 nm). The apparent difference between the height measured by AFM and the SC-XRD data is mainly due to the AFM tip - surface interactions,[22,25,26] which overestimate the step height. Based on these exfoliation results, we explore the in-plane structural and electronic anisotropy of the material by conducting all measurements on freshly cleaved surfaces of bulk $Mo_6S_3Br_6$.

We carried out real-space imaging of the (100) surface structure of $Mo_6S_3Br_6$ using STM. The high-resolution STM image in **Fig. 10.2A** features the bright spots arranged in a triangular pattern with periodicity of 6.5 Å, 6.6 Å, and 7.0 Å. These bright spots correspond to the positions of the inter-cluster bridging Br atoms, which are protruding from the plane of the layer (represented as pink spheres in **Fig. 10.1A** and **Fig. 10.2B**). The Br atoms located at the vertex of the $[Mo_6S_4Br_4]$ clusters are topographically lower than the bridging Br atoms, and thus are not clearly resolved in the STM (represented as brown spheres in **Fig. 10.1A** and **Fig. 10.2B**). A Fourier transform (FFT) of the image (**Fig. 10.2C**) identifies the pseudo six-fold symmetry of the bridging Br atoms. Two more points (identified as yellow circles in **Fig. 10.2C**) indicates a periodicity of 5.9 Å along one direction, in excellent agreement with the c lattice parameter determined from SC-XRD ($c/2$ ~5.97 Å). By comparing the simulated FFT calculated from the bridging Br atom lattice (inset in **Fig. 10.2C**) with the experimental data, we determine the b [010] and c [001] directions (represented as black arrows in **Fig. 10.2A** and as a box in **Fig. 10.2C**). In addition to the crystal surface structure, we identify several types of defects in **Fig. 10.2A**, including missing Br atoms or incomplete clusters. More details are included in the Support Information (**Fig. I4**).

10.5 Electronic Structure

10.5.1 Experimentally Determined through STS

We determine the single-particle electronic structure by current-voltage (I-V) measurement in STS. **Fig. 10.2D** displays I-V (blue) and dI/dV-V (red) curves. Each I-V or dI/dV-V curve is an average of over 80 curves under the same tunneling conditions at multiple positions on the surface. The VBM is located at –0.20 V ± 0.03 V and the CBM at 1.44 ± 0.03 eV. These give the electronic bandgap $E_G = E_{CBM} - E_{VBM} = 1.64 \pm 0.05$ eV; this value comes from the average measurements in multiple areas on three samples. The positions of the band edges relative to E_F indicates p-doping. A weak and broad mid-gap feature near E_F is attributed to surface defects. Despite the direct bandgap characteristic (see below), we found that photoluminescence emission from the bandgap transition in the current sample is negligibly, likely due to the defect mediated nonradiative recombination. Further experiments are necessary to improve the quality of the crystals.

10.5.2 DFT Band Structure

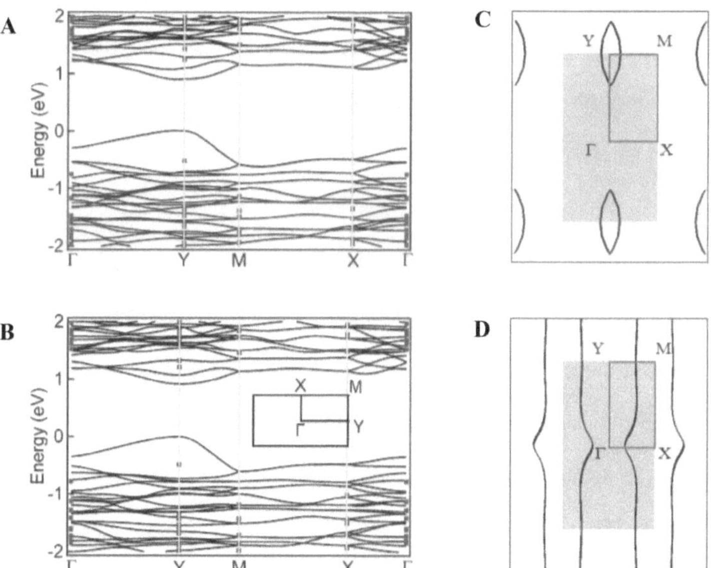

Figure 10. 3 DFT Band Structure
(A,B) Calculated DFT band structure by using PBE functional (solid black line) and HSE06 functional (blue dots). Inset is the 2D Brillouin zone projected on (100) plane. **(A)** is for the 3D bulk and **(B)** is the 2D monolayer. **(C)** Fermi surface of an intrinsic 2D monolayer. **(D)** Fermi surface of p-doped 2D monolayer with doping level of 0.5 holes/cluster.

To support our experimental observations, we performed DFT calculations of the electronic band structure of Mo$_6$S$_3$Br$_6$ using the Perdew-Burke-Ernzherof (PBE) functional[27] and refined the calculation with the Heyd-Scuseria-Ernzerhof (HSE06) functional.[28] **Fig. 10.3A** displays the PBE bulk electronic band structure (black curves) and HSE06 refinements (blue dots) at selected high-symmetry points in the Brillouin zone. A direct bandgap of 0.90 eV is derived from PBE functional, which typically underestimates bandgaps. The HSE06 band structure, which generally overestimates bandgaps, indicates a direct bandgap of 1.69 eV, slightly above the value determined by STS. Both VBM and CBM locate at Y (0, 0.5, 0) point in momentum space. To understand the properties of Mo$_6$S$_3$Br$_6$ in the 2D limit, we performed similar calculations on the 2D monolayer, as shown **Fig. 10.3B**. The electronic band structure of monolayer Mo$_6$S$_3$Br$_6$ is nearly identical to that of the bulk, indicating weak inter-layer electronic interactions. The direct band gaps calculated from PBE and HSE06 functional have the same values at Y (0, 0.5, 0) point as those of the bulk.

Strong anisotropy appears in the band structure along the principal direction Γ-Y (0, 0.5, 0) compared to Y-M (0.5, 0.5, 0). The electronic structure produces two free electron-like bands with starkly different effective masses for electrons and holes, respectively. Similar band structures have been observed in other anisotropic 2D materials, e.g. black phosphorus.[1,29] The strong in-plane anisotropy is also reflected in the Fermi surface of 2D Mo$_6$S$_3$Br$_6$, both in the intrinsic and doped states. **Fig. 10.3C** displays the Fermi surface for an intrinsic 2D monolayer. By increasing the doping level to 0.5 hole per cluster, the band along the Γ−Y direction generates pseudo-1D electronic chains (**Fig. 10.3D**), revealing highly anisotropic electronic properties.

10.5.3 Experimental confirmation with Raman Spectroscopy

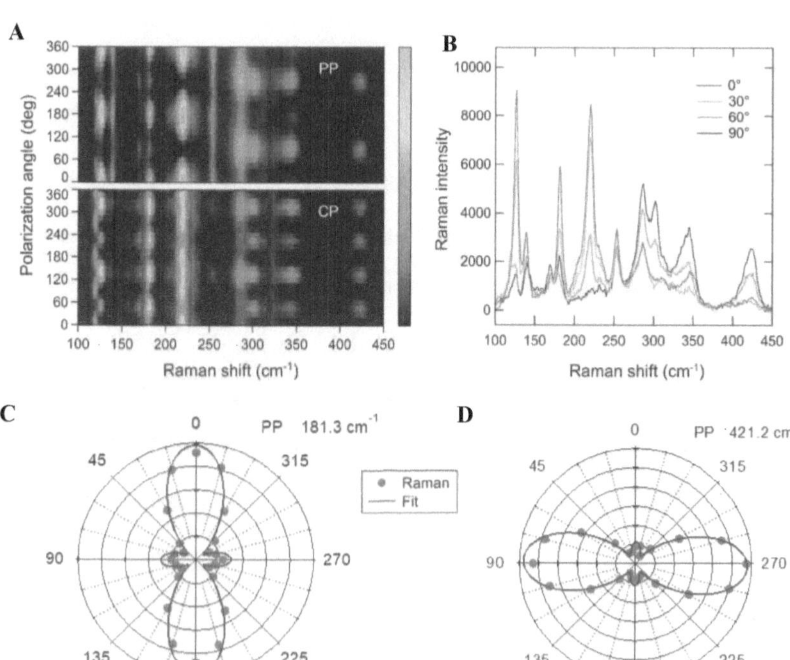

Figure 10. 4 SHG spectra
Image plots of polarization dependent Raman for parallel polarization (PP) (top) and cross polarization (CP) (bottom). 0° angle denotes the c-axis of the crystal. **(B)** Representative parallel-polarized Raman spectra at 0°, 30°, 60°, 90°. **(C)** Polar plot of parallel polarized Raman intensity of A$_g$ mode at 181.3 cm^{-1}, showing preferential scattering along the c-axis. **(D)** Polar plot of parallel polarized Raman intensity of A$_g$ mode at 421.2 cm^{-1}, showing strong response along the b-axis.

The anisotropic properties of Mo$_6$S$_3$Br$_6$ are confirmed experimentally in polarization dependent Raman spectroscopy.[6,30–34] **Fig. 10.4A** shows Raman spectra for parallel polarization (PP, top) and cross polarization (CP, bottom) configurations. Spectra were taken in a backscattering geometry, where the incident and scattered light are both perpendicular to the sample. The polarization angle is defined as the angle between the incident polarization and the crystal c-axis. Each Raman active mode has either two- or four- fold symmetry governed by the crystal symmetry. Since Mo$_6$S$_3$Br$_6$ has an orthorhombic structure with space group

Cmcm, there are 45 Raman active modes (13A$_g$ + 11 B$_g$ + 9 B$_{2g}$ +12 B$_{3g}$),[35] among which 25 modes (13A$_g$ + 12 B$_{3g}$) are detectable in the backscattering geometry. Raman selection rules dictate that the A$_g$ mode has two-fold symmetry for PP and four-fold symmetry for CP, while B$_{3g}$ mode has four-fold symmetry in either PP or CP configurations (details in the Support Information). **Fig. 10.4B** presents parallel-polarized Raman spectra at 0 °, 30 °, 60 °, 90 °: 15 of the 25 Raman modes are resolved and assigned to A$_g$ or B$_{3g}$ mode based on DFT calculations (Table I3). The nonresonant Raman spectrum obtained from DFT calculations is shown in **Fig. I5** as a reference.

To highlight the variations of each peak as a function of angle, **Fig. 10.4C-D** show polar plots of two A$_g$ modes (181.3 cm^{-1} and 421.1 cm^{-1}) in PP configuration. The Raman intensity of the 181.3 cm^{-1} A$_g$ mode along the *c*-axis is higher than that along the *b*-axis, while the intensity along the *b*-axis shows a secondary maximum instead of a minimum, indicating a complex Raman tensor, as seen in other 2D materials.[36–38]

We performed quantitative analysis of the phonon anisotropy by extracting Raman tensors for A$_g$ and B$_{3g}$ modes from the polarization dependent Raman spectra in parallel and cross polarized configurations. The Raman intensity can be expressed as

$$I \propto |e_i R e_s|^2 \qquad (10.1)$$

where e_i and e_s are the incident and scattered light vectors and **R** is the Raman tensor for a specific phonon mode.[39,40] For incident light perpendicular to the sample (i.e. parallel to the *a*-axis), the incident light vector $e_i = (0, sin\theta, cos\theta)$ and the scattered light vector $e_s = (0, sin\theta, cos\theta)$ for PP configuration and $e_s = (0, -cos\theta, sin\theta)$ for CP configuration. The Raman tensors of A$_g$ and B$_{3g}$ are given by:

$$\overleftrightarrow{R}_{A_g} = \begin{bmatrix} a & 0 & 0 \\ 0 & b & 0 \\ 0 & 0 & c \end{bmatrix}, \quad \overleftrightarrow{R}_{B_{3g}} = \begin{bmatrix} 0 & 0 & 0 \\ 0 & 0 & f \\ 0 & f & 0 \end{bmatrix} \qquad (10.2)$$

where a, b, c, and f are complex Raman tensor elements.

The imaginary parts in the Raman tensor elements can be attributed to photon absorption[32,33,36,41] with excitation photon energy above the band gap and birefringence effects[42] along b- and c- axes of the crystals. We obtain the tensor elements of each mode by fitting both parallel and cross polarized Raman spectra simultaneously (details in Appendix I). The fits, included in the polar plots in **Fig. 10.4C,D** as blue solid lines demonstrate an excellent agreement between experiment and theory. More polar plots of Raman active modes are presented in **Fig. I6**.

The strong in-plane anisotropy of $Mo_6S_3Br_6$ is also reflected in the separation of the A_g modes in the PP configuration (**Fig. 10.4A**): the maximum peak intensity of each A_g mode $<$ 270 cm^{-1} is at 0 ° or 180 ° while that $>$ 270 cm^{-1} is at 90 ° or 270 ° (Table I4). This anisotropy is evident when we compare the polar plots of A_g modes 181.3 cm^{-1} and 421.2 cm^{-1} shown in **Fig. 10.4C,D.** . This could be understood by taking nuclear motions of each mode into account. Raman active phonons below 270 cm^{-1} involves twisting modes of Mo_6 cluster units. Since in those modes two adjacent Mo_6 units on the c-axis rotate in opposite direction, the phonons modulate Mo-S bonds of shared μ_6-S bridge. This results in strong perturbation of electronically-coupled 1D chains of corner-sharing clusters, agreeing with the discussions mentioned above. Phonons above 270 cm^{-1} consist of stretching modes of Mo-S bonds. Such vibrations exhibit the strongest effect along the b-axis of the crystal, where [Mo_6] cluster subunits are connected by two Mo-S linkages. The additional sulfur atom on the b-axis allows stretching mode phonons to heavily modulate polarizability in that direction, explaining preferential Raman response in b-direction for high-frequency A_g modes. While there exists Mo-S stretching A_g mode in c-direction, its Raman cross-section is significantly smaller and not experimentally resolved.

10.6 Discussion of Results

In summary, we have demonstrated that the layered van der Waals cluster solid Mo$_6$S$_3$Br$_6$ is a novel 2D semiconductor with strong in-plane anisotropy. This anisotropy is anticipated to produce directional transport of charge and energy, such as carriers, excitons and polaritons. Moreover, in contrast to most conventional 2D atomic solids, the presence of labile Br atoms at the surface of each 2D Mo$_6$S$_3$Br$_6$ layer may allow the tuning of anisotropic properties by functionalizing their surface via halogen substitution.[22] The unique hierarchical structure of Mo$_6$S$_3$Br$_6$ opens the door to new and exciting optoelectronic devices that combine multifunctionality with in-plane anisotropy.

10.7 References

1. Xia, F., Wang, H. & Jia, Y. Rediscovering black phosphorus as an anisotropic layered material for optoelectronics and electronics. *Nat. Commun.* **5**, 4458 (2014).
2. Wang, X., Jones, A., Seyler, K., Tran, V. & Jia, Y. Highly anisotropic and robust excitons in monolayer black phosphorus. *Nat. Nanotechnol.* **10**, 517–521 (2015).
3. Low, T. *et al.* Plasmons and screening in monolayer and multilayer black phosphorus. *Phys. Rev. Lett.* **113**, 106802 (2014).
4. Ma, W. *et al.* In-plane anisotropic and ultra-low-loss polaritons in a natural van der Waals crystal. *Nature* **562**, 557–562 (2018).
5. Wildervanck, J. C. & Jellinek, F. The dichalcogenides of technetium and rhenium. *J. Less Common Met.* **24**, 73–81 (1971).
6. Wolverson, D., Crampin, S., Kazemi, A. S., Ilie, A. & Bending, S. J. Raman spectra of monolayer, few-layer, and bulk ReSe2: An anisotropic layered semiconductor. *ACS Nano* **8**, 11154–11164 (2014).
7. Hafeez, M., Gan, L., Bhatti, A. S. & Zhai, T. Rhenium dichalcogenides (ReX 2, X= S or Se): an emerging class of TMDs family. *Mater. Chem. Front.* **1**, 1917–1932 (2017).
8. Jariwala, D., Marks, T. J. & Hersam, M. C. Mixed-dimensional van der Waals heterostructures. *Nat. Mater.* **16**, 170–181 (2016).
9. Andres, R. P. *et al.* Self-assembly of a two-dimensional superlattice of molecularly linked metal clusters. *Science* **273**, 1690–1693 (1996).
10. Medeiros-Ribeiro, G., Ohlberg, D. A. A., Williams, R. S. & Heath, J. R. Rehybridization of electronic structure in compressed two-dimensional quantum dot superlattices. *Phys. Rev. B* **59**, 1633 (1999).
11. Boneschanscher, M. P. *et al.* Long-range orientation and atomic attachment of nanocrystals in 2D honeycomb superlattices. *Science* **344**, 1377–1380 (2014).
12. Claridge, S. A. *et al.* Cluster-Assembled Materials. *ACS Nano* **3**, 244–255 (2009).
13. Tulsky, E. G. & Long, J. R. Dimensional reduction: A practical formalism for manipulating solid structures. *Chem. Mater.* **13**, 1149–1166 (2001).

14. Roy, X. *et al.* Nanoscale Atoms in Solid-State Chemistry. *Science (80-.).* **341**, 157–160 (2013).

15. Peña, O. Chevrel phases: Past, present and future. *Phys. C Supercond. its Appl.* **514**, 95–112 (2015).

16. Xie, W. *et al.* Endohedral gallide cluster superconductors and superconductivity in ReGa5. *Proc. Natl. Acad. Sci. U. S. A.* **112**, E7048-54 (2015).

17. Perrin, A. & Perrin, C. Low-dimensional frameworks in solid state chemistry of Mo6 and Re6 cluster chalcohalides. *Eur. J. Inorg. Chem.* 3848–3856 (2011) doi:10.1002/ejic.201100400.

18. Chevrel, R. & Sergent, M. From three-dimensional to one-dimensional cluster Mo6 chalcogenides. *Cryst. Chem. Prop. Mater. with Quasi-One-Dimensional Struct.* 315–373 (1986).

19. Fedorov, V., Mishchenko, A. & Fedin, V. Cluster Transition Metal Chalcogenide Halides. *Russ. Chem. Rev.* **54**, 408–423 (1985).

20. Leduc, L., Perrin, A. & Sergent, M. Structure du dichlorure et octaséléniure d'hexarhénium, Re6Se8Cl2: composé bidimensionnel à clusters octaédriques Re6. *Acta Crystallogr. Sect. C Cystal Struct. Commun.* **39**, 1503–1506 (1983).

21. Zhong, X. *et al.* A Superatomic Two-Dimensional Semiconductor. *Nano Lett.* **18**, 1483–1488 (2018).

22. Choi, B. *et al.* Two-Dimensional Hierarchical Semiconductor with Addressable Surfaces. *J. Am. Chem. Soc.* **140**, 9369–9373 (2018).

23. Perrin, C., Potel, M. & Sergent, M. Mo6Br6S3: nouveau composé bidimensionnel à clusters octaédriques Mo6. *Acta Crystallogr. Sect. C* **39**, 415–418 (1983).

24. Novoselov, K. S. *et al.* Two-dimensional atomic crystals. *Proc. Natl. Acad. Sci.* **102**, 10451–10453 (2005).

25. Eda, G. *et al.* Photoluminescence from chemically exfoliated MoS2. *Nano Lett.* **11**, 5111–6 (2011).

26. Stapleton, A. J., Shearer, C. J., Gibson, C. T., Slattery, A. D. & Shapter, J. G. Accurate thickness measurement of graphene. *Nanotechnology* **27**, 125704 (2016).

27. Perdew, J. P., Burke, K. & Ernzerhof, M. Generalized Gradient Approximation Made Simple. *Phys. Rev. Lett.* **77**, 3865–3868 (1996).

28. Heyd, J., Scuseria, G. E. & Ernzerhof, M. Hybrid functionals based on a screened Coulomb potential. *J. Chem. Phys.* **118**, 8207–8215 (2003).

29. Kiraly, B., Hauptmann, N., Rudenko, A. N., Katsnelson, M. I. & Khajetoorians, A. A. Probing Single Vacancies in Black Phosphorus at the Atomic Level. *Nano Lett.* **17**, 3607–3612 (2017).

30. Xu, X. *et al.* In-Plane Anisotropies of Polarized Raman Response and Electrical Conductivity in Layered Tin Selenide. *ACS Appl. Mater. Interfaces* **9**, 12601–12607 (2017).

31. Wu, J. *et al.* Identifying the Crystalline Orientation of Black Phosphorus by Using Angle-Resolved Polarized Raman Spectroscopy. *Angew. Chemie - Int. Ed.* **54**, 2366–2369 (2015).

32. Huang, S. *et al.* In-Plane Optical Anisotropy of Layered Gallium Telluride. *ACS Nano* **10**, 8964–8972 (2016).

33. Song, Q. *et al.* The In-Plane Anisotropy of WTe2 Investigated by Angle-Dependent and Polarized Raman Spectroscopy. *Sci. Rep.* **6**, 1–9 (2016).

34. Liu, Y. *et al.* Raman Signatures of Broken Inversion Symmetry and In-Plane Anisotropy in Type-II Weyl Semimetal Candidate. **1706402**, 1–9 (2018).

35. Kroumova, E. *et al.* Bilbao Crystallographic Server : Useful Databases and Tools for Phase-Transition Studies. *Phase Transitions* **76**, 155–170 (2003).

36. Ribeiro, H. B. *et al.* Unusual angular dependence of the Raman response in black

phosphorus. *ACS Nano* **9**, 4270–4276 (2015).

37. Li, M. *et al.* Revealing anisotropy and thickness dependence of Raman spectra for SnS flakes. *RSC Adv.* **7**, 48759–48765 (2017).

38. Li, L. *et al.* Strong In-Plane Anisotropies of Optical and Electrical Response in Layered Dimetal Chalcogenide. *ACS Nano* **11**, 10264–10272 (2017).

39. Smets, A., Jäger, K., Isabella, O., Van Swaaij, R. & Zeman, M. *Basic semiconductor physics. Solar Energy: The physics and engineering of photovoltaic conversion, technologies and systems* (2016).

40. Establishment, R. R. & Malvern, G. Theory of the first-order Raman effect in crystals. *Proc. R. Soc. London. Ser. A. Math. Phys. Sci.* **275**, 212–232 (1963).

41. Ling, X. *et al.* Anisotropic Electron-Photon and Electron-Phonon Interactions in Black Phosphorus. *Nano Lett.* **16**, 2260–2267 (2016).

42. Mao, N. *et al.* Birefringence-Directed Raman Selection Rules in 2D Black Phosphorus Crystals. *Small* **12**, 2627–2633 (2016).

Chapter 11: Auger dynamics in $Mo_6S_3Br_6$ and $Re_6Se_8Cl_2$

11.1 Preface

Superatom solids are promising for optoelectronic applications, owing to their tunable structural and electronic properties. Yet, the electronic properties of these materials leave much to be explored. Here, we report the scattering times of free charge carriers and their Auger dynamics in two representative two-dimensional (2D) superatomic semiconductors, $Re_6Se_8Cl_2$ and $Mo_6S_3Br_6$, studied using ultrafast terahertz photoconductivity measurements. The response of the free charge carriers reveals carrier scattering times of $\sim$ 24 fs and $\sim$ 44 fs, respectively, for $Re_6Se_8Cl_2$ and $Mo_6S_3Br_6$, implying high local carrier mobilities in the $\sim$100 cm^2/Vs range.

The fast Auger recombination dynamics are characterized by a cubic dependence of the rate constant on carrier density in $Re_6Se_8Cl_2$ and a quadratic dependence in $Mo_6S_3Br_6$. The Auger lifetimes of $Mo_6S_3Br_6$ (0.5 ps) are over an order of magnitude faster than those (20 ps) of $Re_6Se_8Cl_2$. These results highlight the variability of the optoelectronic properties of different superatom solids.

11.2 Introduction and Background

The fundamental building blocks in superatom solids are not atoms, but molecular clusters[1,2]. Superatom solids have great potential for new materials design, given the possibility to control the chemical composition, and thereby the geometric and electronic structures. Among such solids, transition metal chalcogenide halides have attracted particular interest,

following the discovery of superconductivity in the Chevrel phase[3] and unusual magnetic properties[4] of some members of this material family. These transition metal chalcogenide halide clusters share the common structure formula $[M_6L_8]L'_6$, where M is a transition metal forming an octahedron, L, L' are halogen- or chalcogenide- ligands bridging with other clusters (Fig 1a). The characteristic dimensionality of the material depends on the number of bridging ligands between clusters. With the decrease of the number of ligands per M_6 cluster from 14, the isolated $[M_6L_8]L'_6$ complexes start to form 1, 2, or 3-dimensionally extended structure, by sharing L' or L site atoms with neighboring clusters. For example, $Mo_6S_3Br_6$ and $Re_6Se_8Cl_2$ with 9 and 10 ligands per cluster, form 2D layered structures (Fig 1). The possibility to tune the cluster properties and their interactions in superatom solids allows for great variation in properties, such as superconductors[5,6], semiconductors (e.g., $Mo_6S_3Br_6$ and $Re_6Se_8Cl_2$)[7,8], and insulators (e.g., $PbMo_6Cl_{14}$ or $Re_6Se_4Cl_{10}$)[9], to name a few.

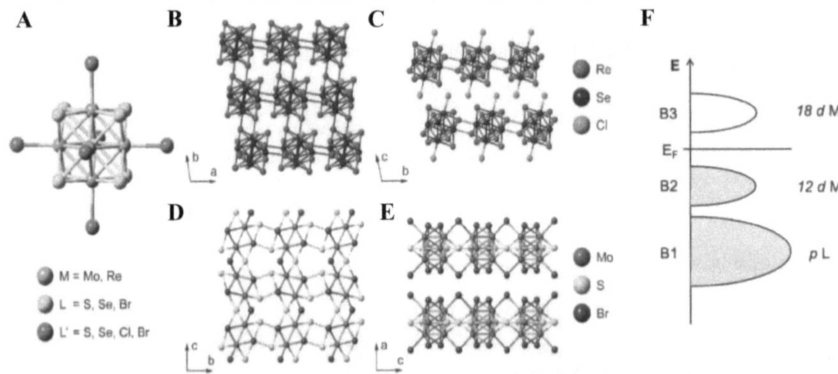

Figure 11. 1
(A) The common structure formula $M_6L_8L_6$', where M is a transition metal forming an octahedron, L, L' are halogen- or chalcogenide- ligands bridging with other clusters. (B,C) Crystal structure of $Re_6Se_8Cl_2$. Top view of a single layer (ab and bc plane). (D,E) Crystal structure of $Mo_6S_3Br_6$. Top view of a single layer (bc and ac plane). (F) The schematic of the simplified three-band model.

Interestingly, it has been shown that a single simplified band structure model can describe the electronic structure of this variety of superatom materials with different metal-ligand combinations. In this so-called three-band model[9], the valence orbitals, the lowest-energy, filled B1 band is composed almost exclusively of p L ligand orbital, and the d metal orbitals (d M) are split into two bands in M_6 clusters: the B2 band made of 12 d M levels and the B3 band of 18 d M levels (**Fig. 11.1F**) [9]. As the Fermi level lies in the B2 band or between the two metallic bands, the number of electrons in the metallic cluster determines the electronic properties. The gap between the two metallic bands is sensitive to the ligand configuration, consistent with ligand field theory. Clearly, understanding the variety of electronic and magnetic properties derived from the common simplified band structure could provide insights into further applications of this type of materials.

Here, we investigate ultrafast charge carrier dynamics in $Re_6Se_8Cl_2$ and $Mo_6S_3Br_6$ single crystals, both 2D semiconductors[10] and representatives of transition metal chalcogenide halides, using time-resolved optical-pump terahertz-probe spectroscopy. In both materials, the B2 d M band is filled with 24 electrons (i.e., completely full), which means both materials are semiconductors[10]. The band gaps of $Re_6Se_8Cl_2$ and $Mo_6S_3Br_6$ are known to be 1.49[7] and 1.65 eV[8], respectively, with potential applicability of these materials as light emitters, photodetectors, and solar cells, analogously to the 2D transition metal dichalcogenides[11–13]. The electron dynamics and quantum efficiency of such devices are determined by carrier recombination processes[14]. In particular, for applications of light-emitting diode (LED) and lasers, the devices usually suffer from the reduction of the quantum efficiency at high current densities[15,16]. For improving the device efficiency, an important recombination mechanism to understand and control is the Auger process, where an electron and a hole recombine by transferring the released excess energy to a third carrier, rather than emitting a photon.

11.3 THz Photo Injection-Spectroscopy

In order to investigate the recombination processes, we photo-inject charge carriers with a femtosecond pulses with a photon energy close to (1.55 eV) and above (3.10 eV) the band gap of the material, and monitor the subsequent charge carrier dynamics by ultrafast Terahertz (THz) spectroscopy. The differential transmittance of THz pulses before and after photo-excitation directly reflects the photoconductivity of the sample. Moreover, by scanning the time delay of THz pulses relative to the excitation pulses, the time evolution of the photoconductivity can be recorded. The experimental data analyzed based on a rate equation of the carrier density relaxation reveals a dominant 3rd order process in $Re_6Se_8Cl_2$ and a limiting 2nd order Auger process in $Mo_6S_3Br_6$ with orders of magnitude shorter lifetime.

The transport properties of these photo-injected charge carriers are observed from the photoinduced change in THz transmittance at a specific pump time delay. The transient frequency-dependent complex photoconductivity ($\tilde{\sigma}(\omega)$), or, equivalently, the complex index of refraction of the samples, is extracted numerically[17,18]. The Fourier transforms of the transmitted THz waveforms with ($\tilde{E}_p(\omega)$) and without ($\tilde{E}_{np}(\omega)$) the photo-excitation are compared with incident THz waveforms ($\tilde{E}_0(\omega)$) by taking into account the Fresnel transmission and reflection coefficients, the propagation factors, and a Fabry-Perot term describing multiple reflections within the sample. The sample consists of exfoliated single crystals with lateral dimensions of ~100 μm and thicknesses of 20-100 μm, deposited on a polymer substrate. The optical penetration depth for 800 and 400 nm light is ~140 and 50 nm, respectively. In processing the data, we assume that the sample is a homogeneous dielectric slab of thickness d and has a complex refractive index.[17,19–22]

11.4 Free Charge Carrier Generation by Excitation

For layered semiconductors such as $Re_6Se_8Cl_2$ and $Mo_6S_3Br_6$, one might expect both materials to have strong exciton binding energy even in the bulk state, similar to bulk transition metal dichalcogenides exhibiting quasi-two-dimensional character.[23] However, the primary photo-product in this early time window is not excitonic, as we non-resonantly photo-excite carriers into continuum directly and the lowest excitation density of $4.5 \times 10^{18} cm^{-3}$ is comparable to the Mott density ($6.7 \times 10^{18} cm^{-3}$) of $Re_6Se_8Cl_2$. We thus generate free charge carriers as the major photoproducts by excitation above the Mott density, as evidence in **Fig. 11.2**. We note that the Mott density is estimated from the dielectric constant $\varepsilon_r^* \sim 10.5$ (at 1.5 eV) and the exciton binding energy of ~100 meV[7].

Fig. 11.2 shows the extracted real and imaginary parts of the complex conductivity, $Re[\tilde{\sigma}]$ and $Im[\tilde{\sigma}]$, in the 0.5-1.5 THz region, at $t = 10$ ps after the excitation pulse, in $Re_6Se_8Cl_2$ (a) and $Mo_6S_3Br_6$ (b), respectively, at 84 K. Both spectra display a substantial $Re[\tilde{\sigma}]$, showing significant contribution from free carriers – for excitons only an imaginary response would be expected at these low frequencies.[24]

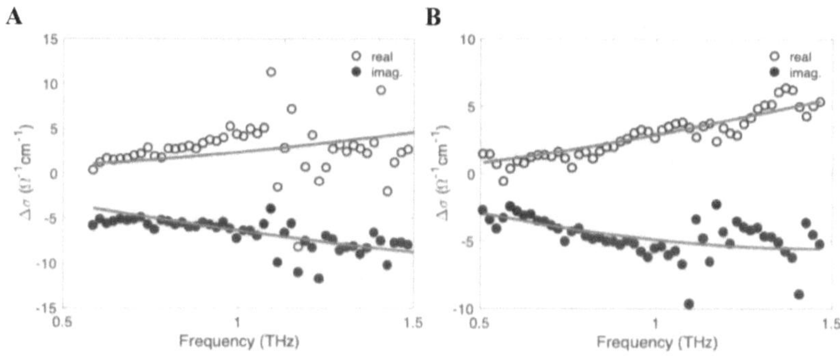

Figure 11. 2 Complex photoconductivity spectra of $Re_2Se_8Cl_2$
(A) and $Mo_6S_3Br_6$ **(B)** obtained at the time delay of t = 10 ps after 800 nm excitation at 84 K. Red lines show the results of the Drude-Smith model, with charge carrier scattering times of 24 fs and 44 fs, respectively.

The free carrier response persists over our experimental time window up to 55 ps in $Re_6Se_8Cl_2$ (**Fig. J1**). The negative sign of the imaginary components in both materials is typical for charge mobility under confinement, which can be well described by the Drude-Smith (DS) model (Fig 2). In this generalized form of the Drude model, suppression of the conductivity by preferential backward scattering of electrons (as a result of the electron reflecting from surface or grain boundaries or defects or Coulombic force) is taken into account[25] as follows:

$$\tilde{\sigma}(\omega) = \frac{Ne^2\tau}{m^*(1-i\tau\omega)}\left(1 + \sum_{n=1}^{\infty}\frac{c_n}{(1-i\tau\omega)^n}\right) \tag{2}$$

where N is the carrier density, τ is the scattering time, m^* is the effective mass, and $-1 < c_n < 0$ is the persistence of velocity of each scattering event, i.e., the fraction of the electron's original velocity that is retained after the nth collision. It is a coefficient that reflects the memory or persistence of the charge carrier velocity. For $c_n = 0$, the velocity is completely randomized at each scattering event, while for $c_n = -1$, scattering preferentially occurs in the back-direction.

The red solid lines in **Fig. 11.2** are the result of applying this DS model with the carrier effective mass, $1/m^* = 1/m_e^* + 1/m_h^*$, where the effective electron and hole masses are $m_e^* = 1.15\, m_e$ and $m_h^* = 0.66\, m_e$[7]. We assume unity photon-to-free-charge conversion efficiency. The scattering/relaxation time of $Re_6Se_8Cl_2$ and $Mo_6S_3Br_6$ yielded using DS model are 24 ± 2 fs with c = -0.991 ± 0.007, and 44 ± 1fs with c = -1 ± 0.007, respectively while the corresponding averaged infrared mobilities are $46.6 \pm 0.4\ cm^2/V \cdot s$ and $116.8 \pm 2.7\ cm^2/V \cdot s$, respectively. We note that the effective mass has only been reported for $Re_6Se_8Cl_2$; we use the same value for $Mo_6S_3Br_6$. Such range of mobility values is comparable to those of state-of-the-art/conventional inorganic semiconductors (e.g. metal oxides: 20 - 50 cm^2/Vs, polycrystalline silicon: > 100 cm^2/Vs)[26–29] and hybrid organic-inorganic semiconductors (e.g. methylammonium lead iodide perovskites: 30 - 150 cm^2/Vs [30]).

The relaxation dynamics of the charge carriers appear as the temporal evolution of the differential THz transmittance after the photo-excitation. **Fig. 11.3** shows the measured average dynamics, $\Delta E(\tau, t_{peak})$, in $Re_6Se_8Cl_2$ as a function of delay time (τ) after the excitation pulse, at the peak of the THz pulse ($t = t_{peak}$). The signal is proportional to the product of the carrier density $N(\tau)$ and the mobility $\mu(\tau)$[31]. At around $0 < \tau < 1$ ps, we find a pulse-duration-limited rise of the signal, along with an oscillation which reflects the pump-induced generation of

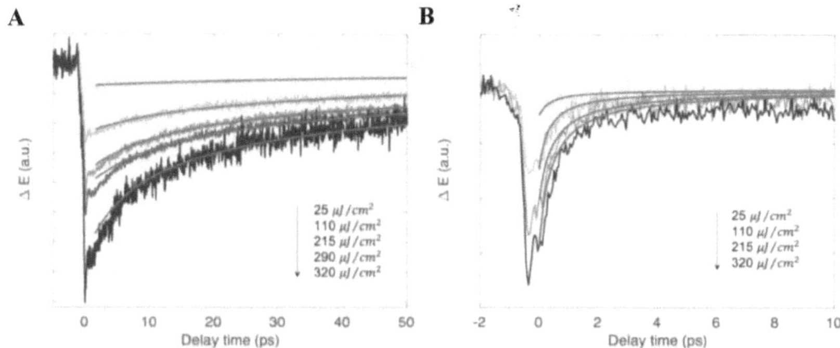

Figure 11. 3 One-dimensional pump scans acquired from $Re_6Se_8Cl_2$
(A) and $Mo_6S_3Br_6$ (B) for 800 nm excitation with different pump-fluences. The red curves are the fitted model of cubic (A) and quadratic (B) dependences on the charge density.

pulsed THz radiation. (**Fig. J4**). The spectra of the emitted THz pulses after excitation of 800

nm and 400 nm are identical as shown in **Fig. J4.** Following the oscillation, the decrease of the

signal suggests the recombination of photo-excited charge carriers. The recombination

dynamics depend markedly on the carrier density. Apparently, the generated charge carriers

eventually undergo relaxation processes via one and/or more particles. These processes are

described by the following rate equation:

$$\frac{dN(\tau)}{d\tau} = -k_3 N(\tau)^3 - k_2 N(\tau)^2 - k_1 N(\tau) \tag{3}$$

where $N(\tau)$ is the free charge carrier density and k_i is the decay constant of ith-order

process. Since the measured THz differential transmission signal (Fig. 3) is proportional to the

photoinduced conductivity, which is directly proportional to N, fitting the above rate equation

to the transients results in the extraction of the decay constants k_3, k_2, and k_1. This model is

used to fit the excess carrier relaxation dynamics as shown in Fig 4. The use of Equation 3

reveals that the third-order process is dominant in $Re_6Se_8Cl_2$, whereas including only the

second-order term in Eq 3 suffices to describe the relaxation dynamics in $Mo_6S_3Br_6$ at the

excitation fluences used here ($25 \sim 320$ $\mu J/cm^2$ for 800 nm pump, and $2 \sim 34$ $\mu J/cm^2$ for 400

nm pump, **Fig. 11.3** and **Fig. J2**).

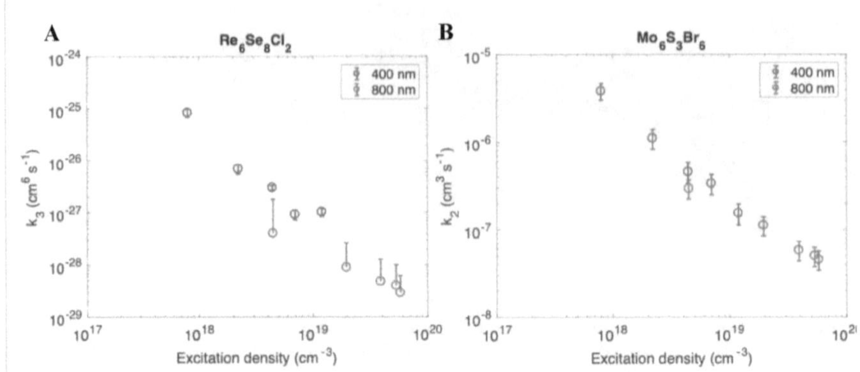

Figure 11. 4 The third-order rate constant of Re₆Se₈Cl₂
(A) and the second-order rate constant of Mo₆S₃Br₆ **(B)** extracted from the data shown in Fig. J 10.3 using the relaxation model of equation (3), as a function of injected photocarrier density upon 400 nm (blue) and 800 nm (red) excitation. The error bars represent the 95% confidence intervals of the fitting parameters.

The third-order dependence of the relaxation rate on carrier density is generally interpreted as the signature of Auger recombination. In Auger recombination, the energy transfer can occur either directly under the energy-momentum conservation or assisted by phonons. The cubic Auger recombination rate constants of bulk Re₆Se₈Cl₂ are presented in **Fig. 11.4a** as a function of the excitation density. Due to the high mobility and small penetration depth, we fit the model (Eq 3) using data up to 8 ps, for which the contribution from the carrier diffusion is negligible.[32] The Auger rate constants decrease monotonically over the excitation density range from 8×10^{17} to $6 \times 10^{19} cm^{-3}$. This phenomenon is known to stem from phase-space filling effects [33]: At low charge densities, the Auger recombination rate has a cubic charge density dependence, owing to the fact that the carrier distribution can be approximated by a Maxwell-Boltzmann distribution. In contrast, at higher densities, where the electron occupation follows the Fermi-Dirac distribution with the limiting value of 1, the cubic dependence of the Auger rate on the carrier density is reduced to quadratic[33]. Thus the carrier density dependence of the rate constant is empirically described by: $k_3(N) = \frac{k_3^0}{1+(N/N_0)^b}$, where k_3^0 is the Auger coefficient at the charge density for $N \ll N_0$; N_0 is the characteristic charge density for the onset of the phase-space filling effect, and b is a dimensionless exponent[34], usually indicating the degree of degeneracy. The effective lifetime ($T = N/(dN/d\tau)$) for $Re_6Se_8Cl_2$ after both 800 and 400 nm excitation is obtained to be ~ 20 ps regardless of the excitation density (**Fig. J3**). The reported Auger lifetimes for InN, one of the leading materials for LED and lasers[35,36], vary from 20 ~ 2000 ps in the 10^{18}~$10^{19} cm^{-3}$ density range[37–40]

In $Mo_6S_3Br_6$, the relaxation dynamics display a quadratic dependence on the carrier density and the rate constant also decreases with the carrier density (**Fig. 11.4b**), similarly to $Re_6Se_8Cl_2$. The second-order relaxation process indicates either a rate-limiting Auger process or radiative bimolecular recombination. The rate-limiting Auger process could be caused by high levels of doping or defects so that the Auger rate has the linear[41] or quadratic[14] dependence on the carrier density already at low photo-injected carrier density. With increasing photo-injected carrier density, phase-space filling effects lead to the monotonic decrease of the Auger rate constant, similarly to the case of $Re_6Se_8Cl_2$. (**Fig. 11.4**)[33]. The contribution of the radiative recombination seems to be negligible, given the sub-picosecond lifetime in $Mo_6S_3Br_6$. Radiative recombination occurs with typical lifetimes of hundreds of picoseconds to a few nanoseconds in semiconductors of reduced dimensionality, such as transition metal dichalcogenides(TMDs)[42], 2D quantum wells[43], and 1D quantum wires[44]. On the other hand, the nonradiative recombination or capture times by defects in TMDs are reported to be in the subpicosecond to a few picoseconds range.[45] Since we observe free charge carriers as the major photo-products, we rule out the notable contribution from the exciton-exciton annihilation process. Excitation of $Mo_6S_3Br_6$ by 400 and 800 nm pulses gives a constant effective lifetime of ~ 0.5 ps, orders of magnitude shorter compared to $Re_6Se_8Cl_2$, which also supports high level of dopant/defect density.

11.5 Discussion of Results

In summary, we have compared the ultrafast carrier dynamics of two representative $Re_6Se_8Cl_2$ and $Mo_6S_3Br_6$ 2D semiconductors of hexanuclear halide chalcogenide cluster family. In both $Re_6Se_8Cl_2$ and $Mo_6S_3Br_6$, the charge carriers exhibit high mobility, comparable to conventional inorganic semiconductors, and chemical difference plays an insignificant role. In contrast, the chemical differences between the two materials strongly affect the Auger-assisted relaxation dynamics, illustrating the prospects of engineering superatomic solid semiconductors to suppress non-radiative losses.

11.6 References

1.   Roy, X. *et al.* Nanoscale Atoms in Solic State Chemistry. *Science* **341**, 157–160 (2013).
2.   Pinkard, A., Champsaur, A. M. & Roy, X. Molecular Clusters: Nanoscale Building Blocks for Solid-State Materials. *Acc. Chem. Res.* **51**, 919–929 (2018).
3.   Chevrel, R., Gougeon, P., Potel, M. & Sergent, M. Ternary molybdenum chalcogenides: A route to new extended clusters. *J. Solid State Chem.* **57**, 25–33 (1985).
4.   Maple, M. B., Fischer, Ø. & Braun, H. F. *Superconductivity in Ternary Compounds II: Superconductivity and Megnetism*. (Springer-Verlag, 1982).
5.   Chen, J., Millis, A. J. & Reichman, D. R. Intermolecular coupling and superconductivity in ${\mathrm{PbMo}}_{6}{\mathrm{S}}_{8}$ and other Chevrel phase compounds. *Phys. Rev. Mater.* **2**, 114801 (2018).
6.   Telford, E. J. *et al.* Doping-induced superconductivity in the van der Waals superatomic crystal Re$_6$Se$_8$Cl$_2$. *arXiv e-prints* arXiv:1906.10785 (2019).
7.   Zhong, X. *et al.* A Superatomic Two-Dimensional Semiconductor. *Nano Lett.* **18**, 1483–1488 (2018).
8.   Zhong, X. *et al.* Mo6S3Br6: An Anisotropic 2D Superatomic Semiconductor. *Adv. Funct. Mater.* (2019) doi:10.1002/adfm.201902951.
9.   Certain, D. & Lissillour, R. The three-band model. A pattern for the electronic structure of M6L8L'6 cluster compounds. *Zeitschrift für Phys. D Atoms, Mol. Clust.* **3**, 411–420 (1986).
10.   Fedorov, V. E., Mishchenko, A. V & Fedin, V. P. Russian Chemical Reviews Related content Cluster Transition Metal Chalcogenide Halides. *Transl. from Uspekhi Khimii* **54**, 694–719 (1985).
11.   Wang, Q. H., Kalantar-Zadeh, K., Kis, A., Coleman, J. N. & Strano, M. S. Electronics and optoelectronics of two-dimensional transition metal dichalcogenides. *Nat. Nanotechnol.* **7**, 699 (2012).
12.   Ross, J. S. *et al.* Electrically tunable excitonic light-emitting diodes based on monolayer WSe2 p–n junctions. *Nat. Nanotechnol.* **9**, 268–272 (2014).
13.   Baugher, B. W. H., Churchill, H. O. H., Yang, Y. & Jarillo-Herrero, P. Optoelectronic devices based on electrically tunable p–n diodes in a monolayer dichalcogenide. *Nat.*

Nanotechnol. **9**, 262–267 (2014).

14. Chlouba, T. *et al.* Interplay of bimolecular and Auger recombination in photoexcited carrier dynamics in silicon nanocrystal/silicon dioxide superlattices. *Sci. Rep.* **8**, 1–7 (2018).

15. Piprek, J. Efficiency droop in nitride-based light-emitting diodes. *Phys. status solidi* **207**, 2217–2225 (2010).

16. Verzellesi, G. *et al.* Efficiency droop in InGaN/GaN blue light-emitting diodes: Physical mechanisms and remedies. *J. Appl. Phys.* **114**, 71101 (2013).

17. Duvillaret, L., Garet, F. & Coutaz, J.-L. L. A reliable method for extraction of material parameters in terahertz time-domain spectroscopy. *IEEE J. Sel. Top. Quantum Electron.* **2**, 739–746 (1996).

18. Bernier, M., Garet, F. & Coutaz, J. L. Precise determination of the refractive index of samples showing low transmission bands by THz time-domain spectroscopy. *IEEE Trans. Terahertz Sci. Technol.* **3**, 295–301 (2013).

19. Zhou, Q. L., Shi, Y., Jin, B. & Zhang, C. Ultrafast carrier dynamics and terahertz conductivity of photoexcited GaAs under electric field. *Appl. Phys. Lett.* **93**, (2008).

20. Walther, M. *et al.* Terahertz conductivity of thin gold films at the metal-insulator percolation transition. *Phys. Rev. B* **76**, 125408 (2007).

21. Prasankumar, R. P. *et al.* Carrier dynamics in self-assembled ErAs nanoislands embedded in GaAs measured by optical-pump terahertz-probe spectroscopy. *Appl. Phys. Lett.* **86**, 201107 (2005).

22. Lloyd-Hughes, J. & Jeon, T. I. A review of the terahertz conductivity of bulk and nano-materials. *J. Infrared, Millimeter, Terahertz Waves* **33**, 871–925 (2012).

23. Saigal, N., Sugunakar, V. & Ghosh, S. Exciton binding energy in bulk MoS2: A reassessment. *Appl. Phys. Lett.* **108**, (2016).

24. Ulbricht, R., Hendry, E., Shan, J., Heinz, T. F. & Bonn, M. Carrier dynamics in semiconductors studied with time-resolved Terahertz spectroscopy. *Rev. Mod. Phys.* **83**, 543–586 (2011).

25. Smith, N. V. Classical generalization of the Drude formula for the optical conductivity. *Phys. Rev. B - Condens. Matter Mater. Phys.* **64**, (2001).

26. Schweicher, G., Olivier, Y., Lemaur, V. & Henri Geerts, Y. What Currently Limits Charge Carrier Mobility in Crystals of Molecular Semiconductors? *Isr. J. Chem.* **54**, 595 (2014).

27. Rivnay, J. *et al.* Large modulation of carrier transport by grain-boundary molecular packing and microstructure in organic thin films. *Nat. Mater.* **8**, 952 (2009).

28. Podzorov, V., Menard, E., Rogers, J. A. & Gershenson, M. E. Hall Effect in the Accumulation Layers on the Surface of Organic Semiconductors. *Phys. Rev. Lett.* **95**, 226601 (2005).

29. Blülle, B., Häusermann, R. & Batlogg, B. Approaching the Trap-Free Limit in Organic Single-Crystal Field-Effect Transistors. *Phys. Rev. Appl.* **1**, 34006 (2014).

30. Milot, R. L., Eperon, G. E., Snaith, H. J., Johnston, M. B. & Herz, L. M. Temperature-Dependent Charge-Carrier Dynamics in CH3NH3PbI3 Perovskite Thin Films. *Adv. Funct. Mater.* **25**, 6218–6227 (2015).

31. Cunningham, P. & Hayden, L. Carrier Dynamics Resulting from Above and Below Gap Excitation of P3HT and P3HT/PCBM Investigated by Optical-Pump Terahertz-Probe Spectroscopy†. *J. Phys. Chem. C* **112**, 7928–7935 (2008).

32. Mics, Z., D'Angio, A., Jensen, S. A., Bonn, M. & Turchinovich, D. Density-dependent electron scattering in photoexcited GaAs in strongly diffusive regime. *Appl. Phys. Lett.* **102**, (2013).

33. Hader, J., Moloney, J. V. & Koch, S. W. Supression of carrier recombination in

semiconductor lasers by phase-space filling. *Appl. Phys. Lett.* **87**, 1–3 (2005).

34. Kioupakis, E., Yan, Q., Steiauf, D. & Van De Walle, C. G. Temperature and carrier-density dependence of Auger and radiative recombination in nitride optoelectronic devices. *New J. Phys.* **15**, (2013).

35. McAllister, A., Bayerl, D. & Kioupakis, E. Radiative and Auger recombination processes in indium nitride. *Appl. Phys. Lett.* **112**, 1–6 (2018).

36. Humphreys, C. J. Solid-State Lighting. *MRS Bull.* **33**, 459–470 (2008).

37. Tsai, T.-R., Chang, C.-F. & Gwo, S. Ultrafast hot electron relaxation time anomaly in InN epitaxial films. *Appl. Phys. Lett.* **90**, 252111 (2007).

38. Jang, D.-J., Lin, G.-T., Hsiao, C.-L., Tu, L. W. & Lee, M.-E. Auger recombination in InN thin films. *Appl. Phys. Lett.* **92**, 42101 (2008).

39. Cho, Y. *et al.* Auger recombination as the dominant nonradiative recombination channel in InN. *Phys. Rev. B* **87**, 155203 (2013).

40. Chen, F., Cartwright, A. N., Lu, H. & Schaff, W. J. Temperature dependence of carrier lifetimes in InN. *Phys. status solidi* **202**, 768–772 (2005).

41. Williams, K. W., Monahan, N. R., Evans, T. J. S. & Zhu, X. Y. Direct Time-Domain View of Auger Recombination in a Semiconductor. *Phys. Rev. Lett.* **118**, 1–5 (2017).

42. Wang, H. *et al.* Radiative lifetimes of excitons and trions in monolayers of the metal dichalcogenide MoS_2. *Phys. Rev. B* **93**, 45407 (2016).

43. Hangleiter, A. Recombination of correlated electron-hole pairs in two-dimensional semiconductors. *Phys. Rev. B* **48**, 9146–9149 (1993).

44. Bellessa, J. *et al.* Quantum-size effects on radiative lifetimes and relaxation of excitons in semiconductor nanostructures. *Phys. Rev. B* **58**, 9933–9940 (1998).

45. Wang, H. *et al.* Fast exciton annihilation by capture of electrons or holes by defects via Auger scattering in monolayer metal dichalcogenides. *Phys. Rev. B - Condens. Matter Mater. Phys.* **91**, 17–19 (2015).

Chapter 12: TaFeTe$_4$

12.1 Preface

Layered van der Waals (vdW) materials belonging to the MM'Te$_4$ structure class have recently received intense attention due to their ability to host exotic electronic transport phenomena, such as in-plane transport anisotropy, Weyl nodes, and superconductivity. Here we report two new vdW materials with strongly anisotropic in-plane structures featuring stripes of metallic TaTe$_2$ and semiconducting FeTe$_2$, α-TaFeTe$_4$ and β-TaFeTe$_4$. We find that the structure of α-TaFeTe$_4$ produces strongly anisotropic in-plane electronic transport (anisotropy ratio of up to 250%), outcompeting all other vdW metals, and demonstrate that it can be mechanically exfoliated to the two-dimensional (2D) limit. We also explore the possibility that broken inversion symmetry in β-TaFeTe$_4$ produces Weyl points in the electronic band structure. Eight Weyl nodes slightly below the Fermi energy are computationally identified for β-TaFeTe$_4$, indicating they may contribute to transport behavior in this polytype. These findings identify the TaFeTe$_4$ poly-types as an ideal platform for investigation of 2D transport anisotropy and chiral charge transport as a result of broken symmetry.

12.2 Introduction and Background

Materials with broken symmetry in their electronic band structures demonstrate unique transport phenomena that can be leveraged to realize multifunctional next-generation technologies. Here, we introduce two new van der Waals (vdW) polytypes, α-TaFeTe$_4$ and β-TaFeTe$_4$, with structures composed of alternating TaTe$_2$ (a metal) and FeTe$_2$ (a semiconductor) stripes, leading to the strongest in-plane electronic transport anisotropy experimentally realized for a 2D metal. Layered vdW materials displaying in-plane anisotropy are of fundamental and technological interest due to their ability to directionally transport charge,[1-8] spin,[9] and/or energy,[10-12] while offering the exciting opportunity to translate these properties to the two-dimensional (2D) limit. Within this class of anisotropic vdW compounds, a select few transition metal dichalcogenides (TMDs) that combine in-plane anisotropy with broken centrosymmetry have emerged as key materials in the area of Weyl physics.[13-22] These materials have crystal structures with broken inversion symmetry at special positions in their electronic band structures (i.e., chiral points of contact between non-degenerate bands),[23] known as Weyl nodes, producing exotic transport properties such as negative magnetoresistance, anomalous Hall effect, chiral magnetic effect, and nonlocal transport.[24] In addition, Weyl materials are exciting candidates to realize ideas of astronomical and high-energy physics within solid-state materials.[25,26]

One of the key challenges to realizing these promises is to design new vdW materials with Weyl nodes at well-defined positions near the Fermi energy. In this context, the MM'Te$_4$ structure type is an ideal platform to study Weyl physics because its symmetry intrinsically leads to the emergence of Weyl nodes with energies that can be tuned by changing the composition of the material.[20,27] That said, only very few MM'Te$_4$ compounds are known, namely TaIrTe$_4$ and NbIrTe$_4$.[20,28,29] Here we show that both TaFeTe$_4$ polytypes have in-plane structures identical to the MM'Te$_4$ family but their interlayer symmetries differ: β-TaFeTe$_4$

shows bulk noncentrosymmetry, resulting in 8 Weyl nodes less than 50 meV below the Fermi

energy, while α-TaFeTe₄ is centrosymmetric, producing an entirely new vdW structure type.

12.3 Synthesis, Characterization, and Structure of TaFeTe₄ crystals

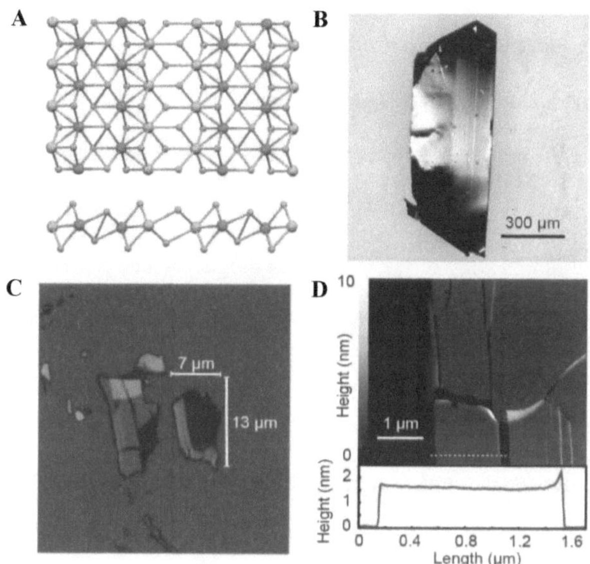

Figure 12. 1: Structure of TaFeTe4 and Exfoliated Flakes

(A) Top- and side-views of the crystal structure of α-TaFeTe₄. Color code: red, Fe; blue, Ta; gold, Te. (B) Optical microscope image of a α-TaFeTe₄ single crystal. (C) Optical microscope image of an exfoliated α-TaFeTe₄ flake on a Si/SiO₂ substrate. (D) AFM image of an exfoliated α-TaFeTe₄ flake and height profile along a line cut (dashed white line) of the exfoliated α-TaFeTe₄ flake.

Single crystals of α-TaFeTe₄ are prepared using a two-step approach. Tantalum, iron,

and tellurium in a 1:1:4 ratio are pressed into a pellet, with TeCl₄ (4 mol. % with respect to Ta)

added to the pellet as a transport agent. The pellet is loaded in a quartz tube, which is sealed

under vacuum and heated in a three-zone tube furnace in a temperature gradient of 700-500 °C

for 8 days (Supporting Information, SI, for synthetic details). Large flaky crystals with metallic

luster grow at the cold end of the tube. These crystals have significant stacking faults, as

determined by single crystal X-ray diffraction (SCXRD) and, to improve their quality, the material is recrystallized at 950 °C for 7 days with iodine as a transport agent. The crystal structure of α-TaFeTe4, determined at 85, 95 and 295 K, solves in the I2/m space group. The compound adopts a layered structure in which isolated zigzag chains of alternating Ta and Fe atoms form a plane capped above and below by Te atoms, resembling parallel stripes of TaTe2 and FeTe2 (**Fig. 12.1A**). Distinct from the MM'Te4 structure type, which hosts broken inversion symmetry along the stacking axis, α-TaFeTe4 shares the same intraplanar structure as the MM'Te4 class but the stacking pattern retains inversion symmetry.

Owing to its layered structure, α-TaFeTe4 can be mechanically exfoliated to produce 2D flakes.32,33 The morphology of the α-TaFeTe4 single crystals can be used to identify the different crystallographic directions. The ab plane and the out-of-plane direction are easily identified as the flat surface and thin direction of the crystal, respectively. Parallel grooves on the surface of the crystals (**Fig. 12.1B** and **1C**) can be used to determine the in-plane orientations: grooves on the surface of the crystal run parallel to the FeTe2 and TaTe2 stripes, while the a-axis is perpendicular to them. Atomic force microscopy (AFM) of exfoliated α-TaFeTe4 flakes reveals a flat surface, while height profiles indicate that flakes as thin as bilayers can be produced (**Fig. 12.1D**).

12.4 Electrical Anisotropy

The anisotropic structure of α-TaFeTe4, built from alternating stripes of metallic TaTe2 and semiconducting FeTe2, suggests that charge transport along the stripes should be more efficient than across them.

12.4.1 First-Principal Calculation of the Electronic and Physical Band Structure

To investigate this prediction, first-principles calculations[34] were performed using density functional theory (DFT) with the PBE functional[35] and ultrasoft pseudopotentials and a 5 x 20 x 2 sampling of the Brillouin zone. A full four-component treatment of relativistic

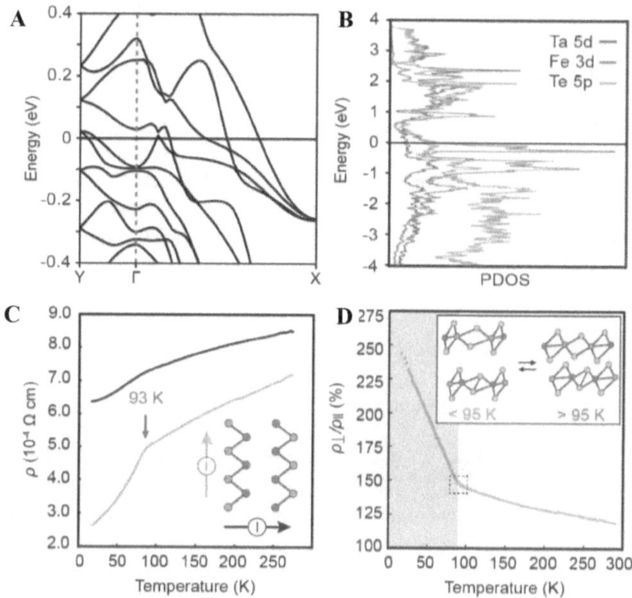

Figure 12. 2 Electronic band structure and transport anisotropy of TaFeTe4
(A) Electronic band structure diagram (with SOC) and (B) projected density of states (PDOS) diagram for α-TaFeTe$_4$ at room temperature. (C) ρ-T curves for transport along the stripes (light purple) and perpendicular to the stripes (dark blue) as shown in the inset. (D) Transport anisotropy curve calculated as $\rho_\perp/\rho_\parallel$. The inset is a schematic of the structural change that results from interlayer charge transfer.

effects was performed in order to include spin-orbit coupling (SOC). Analysis of the electronic band structure parallel (Γ-X) and perpendicular (Γ-Y) to the stripes reveals metallic character with extensive band crossing and large dispersion along Γ-X and indirect semimetallic character with smaller dispersion along Γ-Y (**Fig. 12.2A**). This finding supports the prediction that higher conductivity should be observed parallel to the stripes rather than perpendicular to them and suggests that the difference in conductivity is likely due to a difference in the bandwidth and the density of states along the two directions. Preliminary transport calculations carried out using BoltzTraP[36] also predict a transport anisotropy in agreement with these observations (**S11**). The Fe 3d orbitals have a high projected density of states near the Fermi energy, indicating that they primarily contribute to the transport behavior (**Fig. 12.2B**).

12.4.2 Physical Measurement of the Electronic and Physical Band Structure

To experimentally measure the α-TaFeTe$_4$ electrical anisotropy, we fabricated single crystal electrical devices and measured the electrical resistivity (ρ) as a function of temperature using a four-terminal method. The resistivity was measured parallel ($\rho_\parallel$) and perpendicular ($\rho_\perp$) to the TaTe$_2$ and FeTe$_2$ stripes from 15 to 295 K (**Fig. 12.2C**). For both directions, ρ is on the order of 10^{-4} Ω cm and decreases with decreasing temperature, indicative of (semi)metallic behavior. Across the whole temperature range, $\rho_\parallel$ is lower than $\rho_\perp$, which is consistent with the electronic band structure. At room temperature the anisotropy ratio $\rho_\perp/\rho_\parallel$ is 120%. At ~95 K, there is a clear kink in the ρ vs. T curve, which is much more pronounced in the direction parallel to the stripes, resulting in a dramatic increase in $\rho_\perp/\rho_\parallel$. At 15 K, the transport anisotropy ratio $\rho_\perp/\rho_\parallel$ reaches 250%, which is significantly larger than TaIrTe$_4$ (200% at 10 K).[5]

The transport curve feature at ~95 K is particularly intriguing and unique to this compound within the MM'Te$_4$ family, as TaIrTe$_4$ and NbIrTe$_4$ do not show similar transitions. Upon cooling below 95 K, we observe structural signatures of charge transfer from the Ta-Fe chain to Te atoms in the adjacent layer: the overall symmetry of the crystal is unchanged but the stacking axis lengthens upon cooling below 95 K (see **Fig. 12.2D inset**). While changes in the degree of charge transfer have not been observed for other single member of the MM'Te$_4$ family, each member demonstrates different degrees of charge transfer, which have been correlated with changes in interplanar spacing.[28] Based on these correlations, the charge transfer event that takes place upon cooling TaFeTe$_4$ removes electrons from antibonding orbitals in the Ta-Fe chain,[28] which increases coupling along the Ta-Fe metal chains upon cooling. This interpretation agrees with the increase in conductivity observed primarily along the $\rho_\parallel$ direction. Consistent with this assignment, we find that the temperature dependence of the α-TaFeTe$_4$ heat capacity shows a peak associated with the same transition (**Fig. K9**), with no hysteretic behavior, suggesting a first order transition. Additionally, we find that the transition is not associated with any changes in the magnetic properties of the materials, as determined by SQUID magnetometry (**Fig. K7**). These findings highlight the sensitivity of the in-plane transport in α-TaFeTe₄ to modification of the interlayer spacing and identifies this material as an excellent candidate for future investigations of pressure-dependent transport anisotropy.

12.5 Investigation of Non-Centrosymmetric Features in TaFeTe₄

12.5.1 Weyl Nodes in the ß-TaFeTe4 analogue

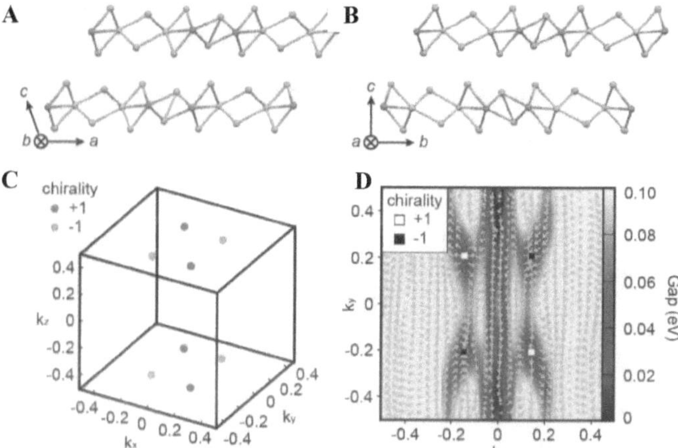

Figure 12. 3 Stacking patterns of both TaFeTe4 polytypes and respective Weyl nodes (**A**) α-TaFeTe₄ and (**B**) β-TaFeTe₄. Color code as in Figure 11.1. (**C**) Location and chirality of Weyl nodes within the Brillouin zone of β-TaFeTe₄. (**D**) Energy gap between neighboring bands hosting Weyl nodes (black and white squares) around the Fermi energy at $k_z = 0.45$ where the blue arrows indicate the Berry curvature.

While the centrosymmetry of α-TaFeTe₄ precludes the presence of Weyl nodes in its electronic structure, we used DFT to explore the possibility of Weyl nodes in a hypothetical noncentrosymmetric compound, β-TaFeTe₄, obtained by altering the Te canting direction of every other layer in α-TaFeTe₄ (**Fig. 12.3A** and **3B**). A tight-binding Hamiltonian was constructed using the Wannier90[37] and Wannier_Tools[38] packages to investigate the Weyl node positions, chiralities, and Berry curvature for β-TaFeTe₄. The topological character of the band structure is described by the Berry curvature, which is an effective magnetic field in momentum space. The Weyl nodes are identified as isolated points of degeneracy between neighboring bands and behave as monopoles, i.e., sinks and sources of the Berry curvature. Due to the complex electronic structure arising from the Fe 3d orbitals near the Fermi energy, numerous possible Weyl nodes were detected; however, one of the more interesting sets of eight Weyl nodes is located at $k = (\pm0.14, \pm0.20, \pm0.43)$ (**Fig. 12.3C**) and 49 meV below the Fermi energy, suggesting they may contribute to transport and/or be observable with angle-resolved photoemission spectroscopy. **Fig. 12.3D** shows the four Weyl nodes (black and white squares) and the Berry curvature (blue arrows) in the $k_z = 0.43$ plane, superimposed on the energy gap between the neighboring bands near the Fermi energy. Notably, DFT calculations performed on unit cells of α- and β-TaFeTe$_4$ reveal that β-TaFeTe$_4$ is only 4.1 kcal mol^{-1} higher in energy than α-TaFeTe$_4$, suggesting that β-TaFeTe$_4$ may be accessible experimentally under higher temperature or irreversible reaction conditions.

12.5.2 Preparation of the Weyl-Node Active Analogue

To investigate whether the β-TaFeTe$_4$ phase can be prepared, we sealed crystals of α-TaFeTe$_4$ in a quartz tube under vacuum and heated the tube to 450 °C for 30 min, quenched it in air, and used SCXRD to assess the single crystal transformation. Remarkably, under these conditions a majority of α-TaFeTe$_4$ converts to β-TaFeTe$_4$, despite the transformation being enthalpically unfavorable: after annealing, we observe two types of stacking in the crystals with 2/3 of the crystal volume corresponding to β-TaFeTe$_4$ and 1/3 to α-TaFeTe$_4$ (see **S2**). Based on the difference in lattice enthalpy between the two phases, only a small fraction α-TaFeTe$_4$ is expected to convert to β-TaFeTe$_4$ at 450 °C, indicating that entropy plays a significant role in stabilizing the β-TaFeTe$_4$ phase. Future work will focus on achieving more complete phase conversion to β-TaFeTe$_4$ in order to investigate chiral and magnetotransport phenomena that may arise in β-TaFeTe$_4$ as a result of the Weyl nodes.

12.6 Discussion of Results

In summary, we have discovered two ternary exfoliatable vdW TMD polytypes with the composition TaFeTe$_4$, one of which (β) shows the prerequisite symmetry elements to be a type-II Weyl semimetal. This is further supported by electronic band structure calculations that predict at least four pairs of Weyl nodes in the Brillouin zone only 49 meV below the Fermi energy of β-TaFeTe$_4$. Transport measurements carried out on single crystals of α-TaFeTe$_4$ indicate that this material displays metallic conductivity with remarkable 250% in-plane electronic anisotropy. The sensitivity of TaFeTe$_4$ transport to interlayer charge transfer offers the unique opportunity to investigate the interplay of the transport anisotropy with the band structure. Such investigations will undoubtedly contribute to our fundamental understanding of transport anisotropy in 2D materials.

12.7 References

1. Liu, J.; Chen, Y.; Tang, P.; Xu, C.; Zhao, C.; Zhang, H.; Wen, S. Generation and evolution of mode-locked noise-like square-wave pulses in a large-anomalous-dispersion Er-doped ring fiber laser. *Opt. Express* **2015**, *23*, 6418–6427.
2. Nam, G. H.; He, Q.; Wang, X.; Yu, Y.; Chen, J.; Zhang, K.; Yang, Z.; Hu, D.; Lai, Z.; Li, B.; Xiong, Q.; Zhang, Q.; Gu, L.; Zhang, H. In-Plane Anisotropic Properties of 1T'-MoS$_2$ Layers. *Adv. Mater.* **2019**, *31*, e1807764.
3. Lai, J.; Liu, X.; Ma, J.; Wang, Q.; Zhang, K.; Ren, X.; Liu, Y.; Gu, Q.; Zhuo, X.; Lu, W.; Wu, Y.; Li, Y.; Feng, J.; Zhou, S.; Chen, J. H.; Sun, D. Anisotropic Broadband Photoresponse of Layered Type-II Weyl Semimetal MoTe$_2$. *Adv. Mater.* **2018**, *30*, e1707152.
4. Zhou, W.; Chen, J.; Gao, H.; Hu, T.; Ruan, S.; Stroppa, A.; Ren, W. Anomalous and Polarization-Sensitive Photoresponse of T$_d$-WTe$_2$ from Visible to Infrared Light. *Adv. Mater.* **2019**, *31*, e1804629.
5. Liu, Y.; Gu, Q.; Peng, Y.; Qi, S.; Zhang, N.; Zhang, Y.; Ma, X.; Zhu, R.; Tong, L.; Feng, J.; Liu, Z.; Chen, J. H. Raman Signatures of Broken Inversion Symmetry and In-Plane Anisotropy in Type-II Weyl Semimetal Candidate TaIrTe$_4$. *Adv. Mater.* **2018**, *30*, e1706402.

6. Li, L.; Gong, P.; Wang, W.; Deng, B.; Pi, L.; Yu, J.; Zhou, X.; Shi, X.; Li, H.; Zhai, T. Strong In-Plane Anisotropies of Optical and Electrical Response in Layered Dimetal Chalcogenide. *ACS Nano* **2017**, *11*, 10264-10272.

7. Li, L.; Wang, W.; Gong, P.; Zhu, X.; Deng, B.; Shi, X.; Gao, G.; Li, H.; Zhai, T. 2D GeP: An Unexploited Low-Symmetry Semiconductor with Strong In-Plane Anisotropy. *Adv. Mater.* **2018**, *30*, e1706771.

8. Qiu, G.; Wang, Y.; Nie, Y.; Zheng, Y.; Cho, K.; Wu, W.; Ye, P. D. Quantum Transport and Band Structure Evolution under High Magnetic Field in Few-Layer Tellurene. *Nano Lett.* **2018**, *18*, 5760-5767.

9. Shi, G.; Kioupakis, E. Anisotropic Spin Transport and Strong Visible-Light Absorbance in Few-Layer SnSe and GeSe. *Nano Lett.* **2015**, *10*, 6926-6931.

10. Askarpour, V.; Maassen, J. Unusual thermoelectric anisotropy in quasi-two-dimensional rhombohedral GeTe. *Phys. Rev. B* **2019**, *100*, 075201.

11. Liu, H.; Choe, H. S.; Chen, Y.; Suh, J.; Ko, C.; Tongay, S.; Wu, J. Variable range hopping electric and thermoelectric transport in anisotropic black phosphorus. *Appl. Phys. Leett.* **2017**, *111*, 102101.

12. Zhao, S.; Dong, B.; Wang, H.; Wang, H.; Zhang, Y.; Han, Z. V.; Zhang, H. In-plane anisotropic electronics based on low-symmetry 2D materials: progress and prospects. *Nanoscale Adv.* **2020**, *2*, 109-139.

13. Yan, B.; Felser, C. Topological Materials: Weyl Semimetals. *Annu. Rev. Condens. Matter Phys.* **2017**, *8*, 337-354.

14. Khim, S.; Koepernik, K.; Efremov, D. V.; Klotz, J.; Förster, T.; Wosnitza, J.; Sturza, M. I.; Wurmehl, S.; Hess, C.; van den Brink, J.; Büchner, B. Magnetotransport and de Haas-van Alphen measurements in the type-II Weyl semimetal TaIrTe$_4$. *Phys. Rev. B* **2016**, *94*, 165145.

15. Belopolski, I.; Sanchez, D. S.; Ishida, Y.; Pan, X.; Yu, P.; Xu, S.-Y.; Chang, G.; Chang, T.-R.; Zheng, H.; Alidoust, N.; Bian, G.; Neupane, M.; Huang, S.-M.; Lee, C.-C.; Song, Y.; Bu, H.; Wang, G.; Li, S.; Eda, G.; Jeng, H.-T.; Kondo, T.; Lin, H.; Liu, Z.; Song, F.; Shin, S.; Hasan, M. Z. Discovery of a new type of topological Weyl fermion semimetal state in Mo$_x$W$_{1-x}$Te$_2$. *Nat. Commun.* **2016**, *7*, 13643.

16. Guo, P.-J.; Lu, X.-Q.; Ji, W.; Liu, K.; Lu, Z.-Y. Quantum spin Hall effect in monolayer and bilayer TaIrTe$_4$. **2019**, arXiv:1910.14307v1. e-Print archive. https://arxiv.org/pdf/1910.14307.pdf.

17. Zhou, X.; Liu, Q.; Wu, Q.; Nummy, T.; Li, H.; Griffith, J.; Parham, S.; Waugh, J.; Emmanouilidou, E.; Shen, B.; Yazyev, O. V.; Ni, N.; Dessau, D. Coexistence of tunable Weyl points and topological nodal lines in ternary transition-metal telluride TaIrTe$_4$. *Phys. Rev. B* **2018**, *97*, 241102.

18. Cai, S.; Emmanuouilidou, E.; Guo, J.; Li, X.; Li, Y.; Yang, K.; Li, A.; Wu, Q.; Ni, N.; Sun, L. Observation of superconductivity in the pressurized Weyl semimetal candidate TaIrTe4. *Phys. Rev. B* **2019**, *99*, 020503.

19. Belopolski, I.; Yu, P.; Sanchez, D. S.; Ishida, Y.; Chang, T.-R.; Zhang, S. S.; Xu, S.-Y.; Zheng, H.; Chang, G.; Bian, G.; Jeng, H.-T.; Kondo, T.; Lin, H.; Liu, Z.; Chin, S.; Hasan, M. Z. Signatures of a time-reversal symmetric Weyl semimetal with only four Weyl points. *Nat. Commun.* **2017**, *8*, 942.

20. Liu, J.; Wang, H.; Fang, C.; Fu, L.; Qian, X. van der Waals Stacking-Induced Topological Transition in Layered Ternary Transition Metal Chalcogenides. *Nano Lett.* **2017**, *17*, 467-475.

21. Koepernik, K.; Kasinathan, D.; Efremov, D. V.; Khim, S.; Borisenko, S.; Büchner, B.; van den Brink, J. TaIrTe$_4$: A ternary type-II Weyl semimetal. *Phys. Rev. B* **2016**, *93*, 201101.

22. Dong, X.; Wang, M.; Yan, D.; Peng, X.; Li, J.; Xiao, W.; Wang, Q.; Han, J.; Ma, J.; Shi, Y.; Yao, Y. Observation of Topological Edge States at the Step Edges on the Surface of Type-II Weyl Semimetal TaIrTe₄. *ACS Nano* **2019**, *13*, 9571-9577.

23. Burkov, A. A. Weyl Semimetals. *Annu. Rev. Condens. Matter Phys.* **2018**, *9*, 359-378.

24. Hosur, P.; Qi, x. Recent developments in transport phenomena in Weyl semimetals. *C. R. Phys.* **2013**, *14*, 857-870.

25. Gooth, J.; Niemann, A. C.; Meng, T.; Grushin, A. G.; Landsteiner, K.; Gotsmann, B.; Menges, F.; Schmidt, M.; Shekhar, C.; Süß, V.; Hühne, R.; Rellinghaus, B.; Felser, C.; Yan, B.; Nielsch, K. Experimental signatures of the mixed axial-gravitational anomaly in the Weyl semimetal NbP. *Nature* **2017**, *547*, 324-327.

26. Gooth, J.; Bradlyn, B.; Honnali, S.; Schindler, C.; Kumar, N.; Noky, J.; Qi, Y.; Shekhar, C.; Sun, Y.; Wang, Z.; Bernevig, B. A.; Felser, C. Axionic charge-density wave in the Weyl semimetal (TaSe₄)₂I. *Nature* **2019**, *575*, 315-319.

27. Koepernik, K. Kasinathan, D.; Efremov, D. V.; Khim, S.; Borisenko, S.; Büchner, S.; van den Brink, J. TaIrTe₄ a ternary Type-II Weyl semi-metal. **2016**, arXiv:1603.04323v3. e-Print archive. https://arxiv.org/pdf/1603.04323.pdf.

28. Mar, A.; Jobic, S.; Ibers, J. A. Metal-Metal vs Tellurium-Tellurium Bonding in WTe₂ and Ternary Variants TaIrTe₄ and NbIrTe₄. *J. Am. Chem. Soc.* **1992**, *114*, 8963-8971.

29. Mar, A.; Ibers, J. A. Synthesis and Physical Properties of The New Layered Ternary Tellurides *M*IrTe₄ (*M* = Nb, Ta) and the Structure of NbIrTe₄. *J. Solid State Chem.* **1992**, *97*, 366-376.

30. Pertlik, F. Strukturverfeinerung der synthetischen Verbindung FeTe₂ (Frohbergit). *Anzeiger der Oesterreichischen Akademie der Wissenschaften, Mathematisch-Naturwissenschaftliche Klasse* **1986**, *123*, 123-125.

31. Rahman, A.; Zhang, D.; Rehman, M. U.; Zhang, M.; Wang, X.; Dai, R.; Wang, Z.; Tao, X.; Zhang, Z. Multiple magnetic phase transitions, electrical and optical properties of FeTe₂ single crystals. *J. Phys.: Condens. Matter* **2020**, *32*, 035808.

32. Novoselov, K. S.; Geim, A. K.; Morozov, S. V.; Jiang, D.; Zhang, Y.; Dubonos, S. V.; Grigorieva, I. V.; Firsov, A. A. Electric Field Effect in Atomically Thin Carbon Films. *Science* **2004**, *306*, 666-669.

33. Yi, M.; Chen, Z. A review on mechanical exfoliation for scalable production of graphene. *J. Mater. Chem. A* **2015**, *3*, 11700-11715.

34. Giannozzi, P.; Baroni, S.; Bonini, N.; Calandra, M.; Car, R.; Cavazzoni, C.; Ceresoli, D.; Chiarotti, G. L.; Cococcioni, M.; Dabo, I.; Dal Corso, A.; de Gironcoli, S.; Fabris, S.; Fratesi, G.; Gebauer, R.; Gerstmann, U.; Gougoussis, C.; Kokalj, A.; Lazzeri, M.; Martin-Samos, L.; Marzari, N.; Mauri, F.; Mazzarello, R.; Paolini, S.; Pasquarello, A.; Paulatto, L.; Sbracci, C.; Scandolo, S.; Sclauzero, G.; Seitsonen, A. P.; Smogunov, A.; Umari, P.; Wentzcovitch, R. M. QUANTUM ESPREESSO: a modular and open-source software project for quantum simulations of materials. *J. Phys. Condens. Matter.* **2009**, *21*, 395502.

35. Perdew, J. P.; Burke, K.; Ernzerhof, M. Generalized Gradient Approximation Made Simple. *Phys. Rev. Lett.* **1996**, *77*, 3865-3868.

36. Madsen, G. K. H; Singh, D. J. BoltzTraP. A code for calculating band structure dependent quantities. *Comut. Phys. Commun.* **2006**, *175*, 67-71.

37. Mostofi, A. A.; Yate, J. R.; Pizzi, G.; Lee, Y.-S.; Souza, I.; Vanderbilt, D.; Mazari, N. An updated version of wannier90: A tool for obtaining maximally-localised Wannier functions. *Comput. Phys. Commun.* **2014**, *185*, 2309-2310.

38. Wu, Q.; Zhang, S.; Song, H.-F.; Troyer, M.; Soluyanov, A. A. WannierTools: An open-source software package for novel topological materials. *Comput. Phys. Commun.* **2018**, *224*, 405-416.

Appendix A: Abbreviations and Variables

2D	Two-dimensional
AF	Antiferromagnetic
AMR	Anisotropic magnetoresistance
B	Magnetic Field
Bsat	Saturation field
CP	Cross Polarization
CP	Heat capacity
EC	Conduction band
ED	Electric dipole
EDS	Energy-dispersive X-Ray Spectroscopy
EF	Fermi level
FM	Ferromagnetic
FP	Fully polarized
Hs	saturation field
I	Inversion
iFM	Intermediate magnetic Phase
M	Magnetization
M	magnetization
MD	Magnetic dipole
MRR	Magnetoresistance Ratio
nMR	Negative Magnetoresistance
nMRR	Negative magnetoresistance ratio
PL	Photoluminescence
PM	Paramagnetic
pMRR	Positive magnetoresistance ratio
PP	Parallel Polarization
$\theta_{X\Omega}$	Weiss constant
Rs	Average sheet resistance
Rxx	Longitudinal resistance
Rxy	Hall resistance
SCXRD	Single crystal X-ray Diffraction
SEM	Scanning Electronic Microscopy
SHG	Second Harmonic Generation
SQUID	Superconducting Quantum Interference device
STM	Scanning tunneling microscopy
STS	scanning tunneling spectroscopy
T	Temperature

Tau	Time reversal
TC	Curie Temperature
TGA	Thermogravimetric Analysis
TN	Néel Temperature
VBG	Electrostatic gate voltage
vdW	Van der Waals
χ	Magnetic susceptibility

Appendix B: Additional Data for Chapter 3

B.1.1 Transport Device fabrication

Exfoliated CrSBr crystals were bonded to a 16-pin DIP socket using low temperature non-conducting epoxy (Loctite EA 1C). Direct electrical connections to the sample were made by hand with silver paint (Dupont 4929N) and 25 μm diameter 99.99% gold wire.

B.1.2 Transport measurements

Longitudinal resistance was measured in a two-terminal configuration using an SRS830 lock-in amplifier to source voltage and measure current using a 17.777 Hz reference frequency. Hall measurements were performed in a four-terminal configuration using SRS830 lock-in amplifiers to source voltage, measure current, and measure the Hall voltage using a 17.777 Hz reference frequency. Variable temperatures between 1.6 K and 300 K and magnetic fields between -9 T and 9 T were achieved in a Janis pumped-^{4}He cryostat. Sample temperature equilibrium was checked by monitoring sample resistivity for stability over time at a fixed temperature. Hysteresis in the superconducting magnet due to trapped fields was measured by identifying the zero-field shift from the forward and backward field scans measured in the non-magnetic state (at $T = 300$ K). This hysteresis was accounted for in all presented magnetoresistance measurements. All transport measurements were repeated for multiple samples.

B.1.3 Spectroscopy

B.1.3.1 Scanning Tunneling Microscopy

Scanning tunneling microscopy (STM) was performed on freshly cleaved bulk CrSBr crystals using our home-made variable temperature STM at T = 150 K in an ultrahigh vacuum chamber (base pressure < 4.0×10^{-10} torr). STM topographical images were obtained in constant current mode (V_{bias} = 2V, $I_{tunneling}$ = 2 pA) with electrochemically etched tungsten tips. To avoid tip artifacts, each STM tip was calibrated on a clean Au (111) surface before all measurements. All tips were verified to be atomically sharp. We obtained the differential conductance (dI/dV) spectra with a lock-in amplifier while keeping the tip fixed above the surface with the feedback loop off.

B.1.3.2 Photoluminescence spectroscopy

Photoluminescence spectroscopy was performed with a 633 nm HeNe laser with Princeton Instruments SpectraPro HRS-300 spectrograph and PyLoN-IR camera. Samples were mounted in a gas-tight cell with a UVFS window and a nitrogen atmosphere. CrSBr crystals were cleaned by cleaving their surfaces using Scotch tape before the measurements. Measurements were performed in a microscopic setup and an on-sample power was maintained at 200 μW.

B.1.3.3 Raman spectroscopy

Raman spectra were acquired in a Renishaw inVia micro-Raman microscope using a 532 nm wavelength laser. A 50x objective was used with a laser spot size of ~2 - 3 μm and a laser power of 200 μW. Spectra were acquired for 30 seconds with a grating of 2400 gr mm^{-1}. 10 spectra were acquired and averaged after removing noise from cosmic background radiation and the detector.

B.1.4 Chemical and structural analysis

B.1.4.1 Scanning electron microscopy and energy dispersive x-ray spectroscopy

Scanning electron micrographs were collected on a Zeiss Sigma VP scanning electron microscope (SEM). Energy dispersive x-ray spectroscopy (EDX) of the CrSBr crystals was performed with a Bruker XFlash 6 | 30 attachment. Spectra were collected with a beam energy of 15 kV. Elemental compositions and atomic percentages were estimated by integrating under the characteristic spectrum peaks for each element using Bruker ESPRIT 2 software.

B.1.4.2 Single crystal x-ray diffraction - Columbia

See Chapter 2 for more details.

B.1.4.3 Synchrotron low temperature single crystal x-ray diffraction – NSF'sChemMatCARS

See Chapter 2 for more details.

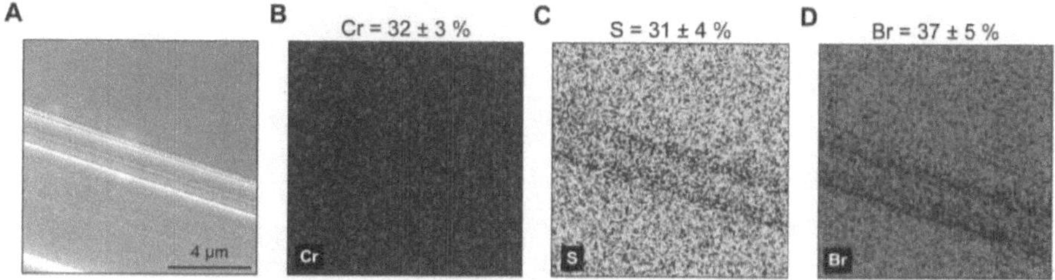

Figure B1. Chemical composition of CrSBr. **(A)** SEM image of bulk CrSBr as grown after cleaning. **(B-D)** Corresponding EDX chemical maps for Cr **(B)**, S **(C)**, and Br **(D)**. Extracted chemical percentages are given above the EDX maps.

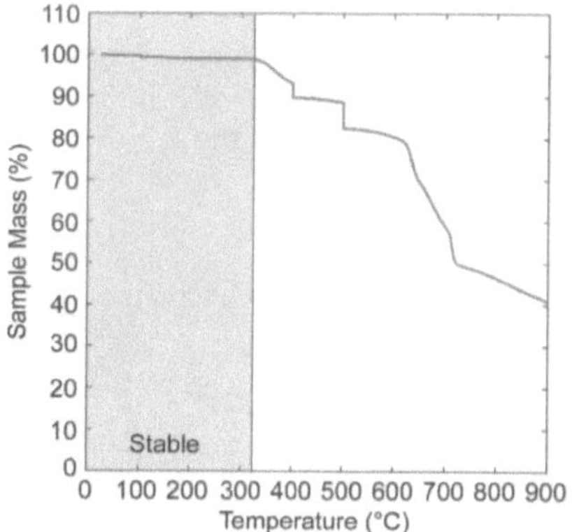

Figure B2. Thermogravimetric analysis of CrSBr. Percentage mass of CrSBr crystals versus temperature in a N_2 atmosphere. Grey region denotes the temperature range over which the crystals are stable.

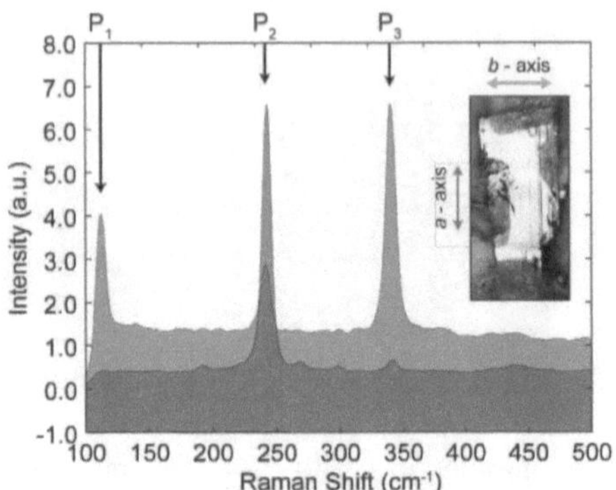

Figure B3. Assignment of crystal axes through optical imaging and Raman spectroscopy. Raman signal intensity versus wave number for light polarized parallel to the b-axis (grey curve) and a-axis (blue curve). Inset: optical image of a bulk transport device with the light polarization marked relative to the physical crystal axes. Three distinct Raman modes (P_1, P_2, and P_3) are denoted. P_1 and P_3 are only observed with a laser polarization aligned parallel to the b-axis, which we use to confirm the orientation of the crystals before mounting into the cryostat.

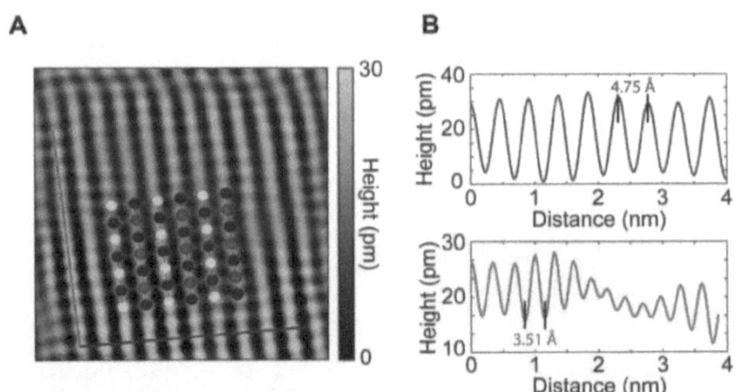

Figure B4. Atomic structure of CrSBr. (A) STM topography of bulk CrSBr as viewed along the c-axis. The crystal structure is overlaid to emphasize the lattice structure. **(B)** Line cuts of **(A)** along the blue (**B:top**) and red (**B:bottom**) lines shown in **(A)**. The extracted lattice parameters are given in the insets of **B:top** and **B:bottom**.

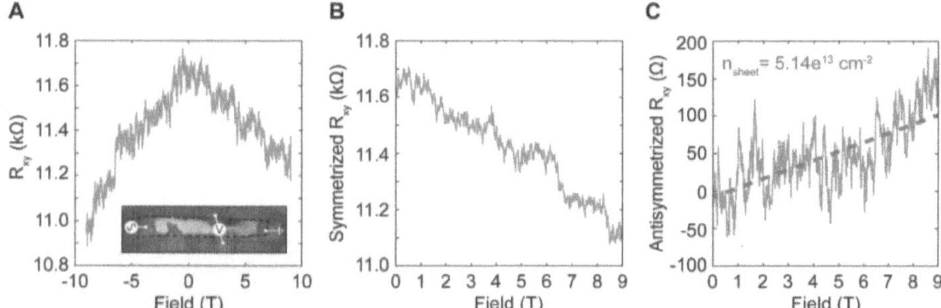

Figure B5. CrSBr electronic carrier density at 300 K. (A) Raw Hall ($R_{xy} = \frac{V_{xy}}{I}$) resistance versus magnetic field. Inset shows an image of a transport device with the measurement schematic overlaid. (B) Symmetrized Hall resistance versus magnetic field $R_{xy-sym} = \frac{R_{xy}(+B) + R_{xy}(-B)}{2}$. (C) Anti-symmetrized Hall resistance versus magnetic field $R_{xy-asym} = \frac{R_{xy}(+B) - R_{xy}(-B)}{2}$. A linear fit is shown as a dashed red line. The extracted carrier density per sheet is given in the inset.

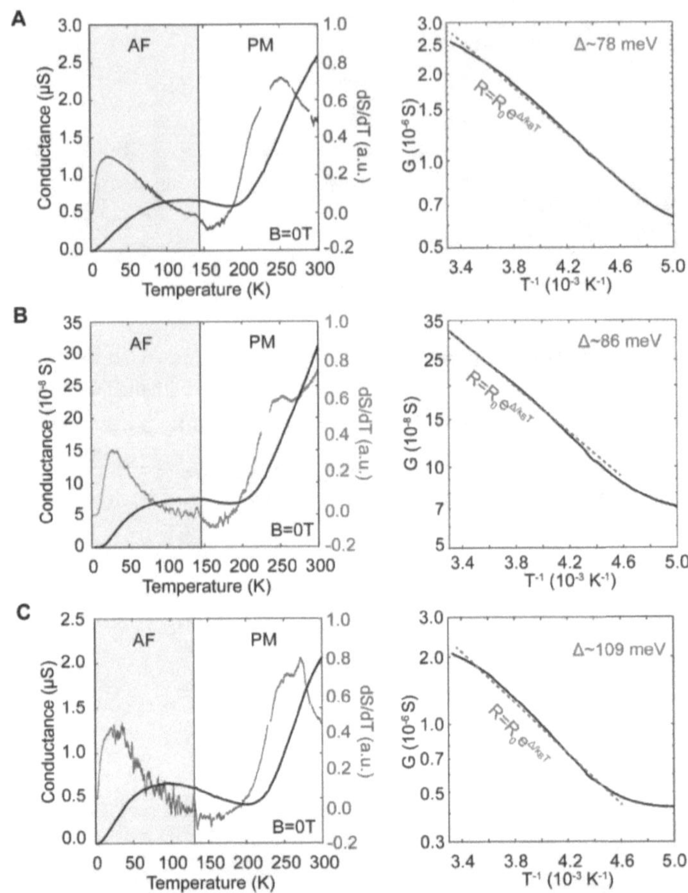

Figure B6. Repeatability of zero-field transport behavior. (A-C: Left) Conductance (left axis) and the derivative of conductance (right axis) versus temperature for 3 additional devices. The AF and PM phases are denoted with grey and white regions, respectively. Extracted Néel temperatures are 147±7 K, 148±8 K, 133±5 K for (**A**), (**B**), and (**C**) respectively. (**A-C: Right**) Conductance on a log scale versus inverse temperature. Linear fits to a thermal activation model are given by red dashed lines. The extracted transport gaps are given in the inset.

172

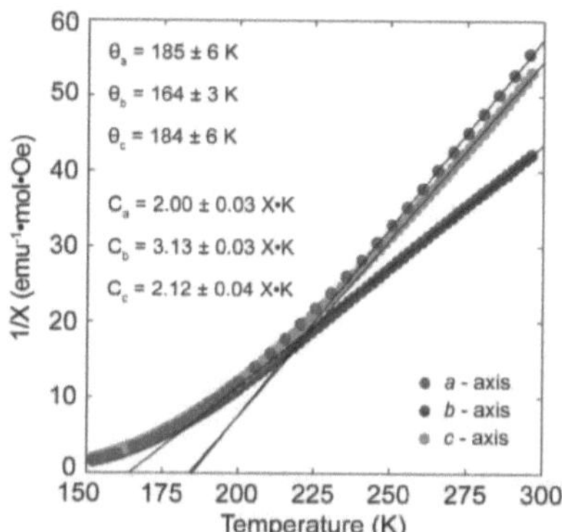

Figure B7. Curie-Weiss fitting of the magnetic susceptibility. Inverse magnetic susceptibility versus temperature along the a-axis (red dots), b-axis (blue dots), and c-axis (green dots). Linear fits to the paramagnetic regime are given by solid black lines. Extracted Curie and Weiss constants are given in the inset.

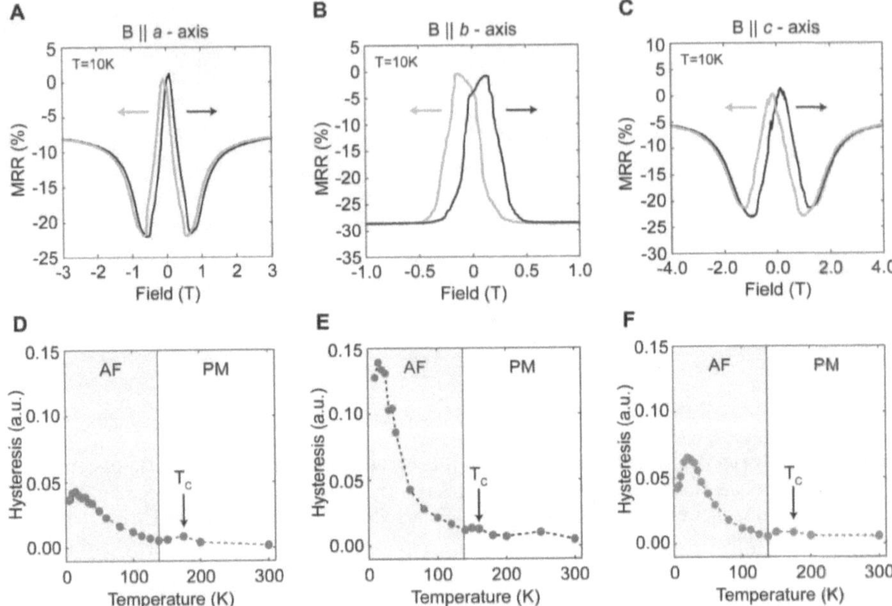

Figure B8: Hysteresis and magnetic ordering above the Néel temperature. (A-C) Magnetoresistance ratio versus magnetic field at 10 K with the field oriented along the *a*-axis (**A**), *b*-axis (**B**), and *c*-axis (**C**). Both forward (solid black line) and backward (solid grey line) magnetic field scans are presented. (**D-F**) Hysteresis in magnetoresistance, defined as the integrated absolute difference between the magnetoresistance ratio measured while sweeping the magnetic field forward minus the magnetoresistance ratio measured while sweeping the magnetic field backward ($H = \int |MRR(B_\rightarrow) - MRR(B_\leftarrow)|\, dB$), versus temperature with the magnetic field oriented along the *a*-axis (**D**), *b*-axis (**E**), and the *c*-axis (**F**). Magnetic phases as identified by the SQUID measurements are overlaid.

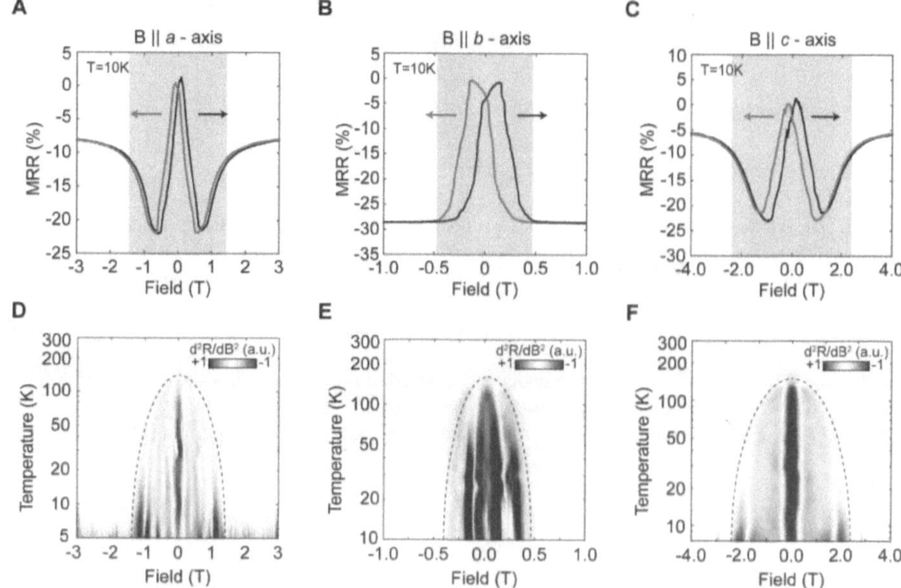

Figure B9: Extracting saturation magnetic fields versus temperature. (A-C) Magnetoresistance ratio versus magnetic field at 10 K with the field oriented along the *a*-axis (**A**), *b*-axis (**B**), and *c*-axis (**C**). Both forward (solid black line) and backward (solid grey line) magnetic field scans are presented. (**D-F**) Second derivative of the magnetoresistance ratio versus magnetic field and temperature with the field oriented along the *a*-axis (**D**), *b*-axis (**E**), and *c*-axis (**F**). The corresponding blue and red features are labeled in **A-C**. Only the forward field scans are presented in **D-F**. In **D-F**, a dashed black line is plotted as a guide to the eye tracking the saturation field versus temperature.

Appendix C: Additional Data for Chapter 4

C.1 General Methods

C.1.1 Exfoliation and Flake Identification

CrSBr flakes were exfoliated onto 285 nm or 90 nm SiO_2/Si+ substrates using mechanical exfoliation with Scotch® Magic™ tape[1,2]. For > 1 L devices, SiO_2/Si+ substrates were exposed to a gentle oxygen plasma for 5 minutes to remove adsorbates from the surface and increase flake adhesion[3]. The exfoliation was done under ambient conditions by heating the mother tape for 3 minutes at 100° C, letting it cool to room temperature, then peeling the tape from the substrate as quickly as possible[3]. For 1 L devices, the SiO_2/Si+ substrates were passivated by depositing a thin layer of 1-dodecanol before exfoliation[4]. The exfoliation was done under inert conditions in an N_2 glovebox with < 1 ppm O_2 and < 1 ppm H_2O content. The mother tape was placed onto the SiO_2/Si+ substrates without heating and removed as quickly as possible. CrSBr flake thickness was identified using optical contrast before encapsulation and then confirmed with atomic force microscopy after encapsulation with hexagonal boron nitride (h-BN).

C.1.2 Optical Contrast Calbration

To more quickly and reliably identify the thickness of CrSBr flakes, a contrast calibration curve was developed for both 285 nm and 90 nm SiO_2/Si+ substrates. First, a series of images was collected of various CrSBr flakes with varying thicknesses using a Nikon Eclipse LV150N microscope and Nikon DS-Fi3 camera. The images were then shading corrected in which the inhomogeneous illumination of the substrate across a single image was corrected by dividing an optical image of a pristine area of the chip without CrSBr flakes. The contrast of the flakes was then extracted using Gwyddion to measure the difference in RGB color between the substrate and the desired flake. We found that the red color contrast was the most significant, so all reported optical contrasts are with respect to red. The series of extracted contrasts were binned into a histogram and the histrogram was fitted to an N-peak gaussian, where N is the number of expected flake thicknesses. The extracted positions of the gaussian peaks is the average red optical contract for each CrSBr thickness (**Figure C.1** and **C.2**). The thicknesses of the flakes were confirmed with atomic force microscopy (**Figure C.3**).

C.1.3 Atomic Force Microscopy

Atomic force microscopy was performed in a Bruker Dimension Icon® using OTESPA-R3 tips in tapping mode. Flake thicknesses were extracted using Gwyddion to measure histograms of the height difference between the substrate and the desired CrSBr flake.

C.1.4 Raman Spectroscopy

C.1.4.1 > 1 L CrSBr

Raman spectroscopy for CrSBr flakes > 1 L was performed under ambient conditions in a Renishaw InVia™ micro-Raman microscope using a 532 nm wavelength laser. A 50x objective was used with a laser spot size of 2-3 μm . A laser power of 100 μW was used with a grating of 2400 g/mm for all spectra. Varying acquisition times were used depending on the flake thickness (longer times for thinner flakes). For each flake, 10 spectra were acquired and averaged after subtracting a dark background. The dark background was a spectra acquired with no laser excitation and the same acquisition parameters.

C.1.4.2 < 1 L CrSBr

Raman spectroscopy for 1 L CrSBr flakes was performed inside an N_2 glovebox with < 5 ppm O_2 and < 0.5 ppm H_2O with a Horiba XploRA™ Raman microscope using a 532 nm wavelength laser. A x100 objective was used with a laser spot size of ~1-2 μm. A laser power of ~20 μW was used with a grating of 2400 g/mm for all spectra. For each flake, 5 spectra were acquired with an acquisition time of 180 s and averaged after subtracting a dark background. The dark background was a spectra acquired with no laser excitation and the same acquisition parameters.

C.1.5 Transport Methods

C.1.5.1 Device Fabrication

Transport devices were fabricated from CrSBr flakes using the via contact technique[5] in which h-BN with embedded palladium electrodes was placed onto the desired CrSBr flake using the dry-polymer-transfer technique[6]. For > 1 L CrSBr flakes, the transfer process was performed under ambient conditions. For monolayer CrSBr flakes, the transfer process was performed under inert conditions in an N_2 glovebox with < 5 ppm O_2 and < 0.5 ppm H_2O. Bonding pads were then designed and deposited using conventional electron beam lithography and deposition techniques. All devices were diced by hand and bonded to a 16-pin DIP socket for measurement in cryogenic systems. Between fabrication steps, 1 L devices were stored in the N_2 glovebox to avoid sample degredation.

C.1.5.2 Electrical Transport Measurements

Longitudinal resistance was measured in a 2-terminal configuration using an SRS830 lock-in amplifier to source voltage and measure current using a 17.777 Hz reference frequency. Four-terminal longitudinal and Hall measurements were performed in a four-terminal configuration using SRS830 lock-in amplifiers to source voltage, measure current, and measure the Hall voltage using a 17.777 Hz reference frequency. Due to the morphology of the exfoliated crystals, the current and longitudinal resistances were measured parallel to the a-axis and the Hall resistance was measured parallel to the b-axis. Variable temperatures between 1.6 K and 300 K and magnetic fields between -9 T and 9 T were achieved in a Janis pumped ^{4}He cryostat. Sample temperature equilibrium was checked by monitoring sample resistivity for stability over time at a fixed temperature. Hysteresis in the superconducting magnet due to trapped fields was measured by identifying the zero-field shift from the forward and backward field scans measured in the non-magnetic state (at $T = 300$ K). This hysteresis was accounted for in all presented magnetoresistance measurements. For measurements without electrostatic gating, the silicon back gate was kept grounded using a grounding cap. For gate-dependent measurements, a Keithley 2400 was used to output voltages between -60 V and 60 V on the silicon back gate. A protection resistor of 100 kOhm was placed in series between the gate and the voltage source.

The transmission line measurements (TLMs) were performed at room temperature by sourcing voltage and measuring current with a Keithley 2400. A voltage excitation of 0.5 V was used to ensure measurements were performed in the linear IV regime.

C.1.6 Magnetometry Methods

C.1.6.1 Vibrating Sample Magnetometry

All vibrating sample magnetometry (VSM) was conducted on a Quantum Design PPMS®

DynaCool™ system. A single CrSBr crystal was selected and the surface was exfoliated

mechanically to expose a pristine interface. The crystal was attached to a quartz paddle using GE

varnish (which was cured at room temperature under ambient conditions for 30 minutes) and

oriented with the a-, b-, or c- axis perpendicular to the length of the quartz paddle. The same crystal

was used for all axial orientated measurements. The variable temperature scans and field-

dependent magnetic susceptibility curves for each axis were measured during the same

measurement cycle. The crystal was removed using a 1:1 ethanol/toluene solution, dried in air,

then reoriented and reattached using the previously prescribed varnish method. Each full-range

variable temperature scan was programmed as follows using the DynaCool™ VSM module: 1)

demagnetization of the SC magnet at 300 K by sweeping the field from 20000 Oe to 0 Oe with an

oscillatory field ramp, 2) magnetic field set to 1000 Oe using a linear field ramp, 3) cooled to 2 K

at 12 K/min, 3) measured susceptibility versus temperature upon warming with a ramp rate of 5

K/min. The field dependent-magnetic susceptibility curves at different temperatures were

programmed as follows using the DynaCool™ VSM module: 1) demagnetization of the SC magnet

at 300 K by sweeping the field from 20000 Oe to 0 Oe with an oscillatory field ramp, 2) cooled to

the desired temperature at 12 K/min, 3) measured magnetization versus field from -50000 Oe to

50000 Oe over 3 cycles (0 to -50000, -50000 to 50000, 50000 to -50000, -50000 to 0). The low-

temperature zero-field-cooled and field-cooled variable temperature scans were programmed as

follows using the DynaCool™ VSM module: 1) demagnetization of the SC magnet at 300 K by

sweeping the field from 20000 Oe to 0 Oe with an oscillatory field ramp, 2) cooled to 2 K at 12

K/min, 3) set the magnetic field to 100 Oe, 4) measure susceptibility versus temperature from 2 K

up to 40 K ramping the temperature with a ramp of 1 K/min, 5) measure susceptibility versus temperature from 40 K down to 2 K ramping the temperature with a ramp of 1 K/min, 6) re-measure susceptibility versus temperature again from 2 K down to 40 K ramping the temperature with a ramp of 1 K/min.

The density of magnetic impurities was estimated by converting the absolute change in susceptibility (in units of emu/mol/Oe) across T_D assuming all impurities undergo ferromagnetic ordering and have a spin of ½:

$$n_D = \frac{\Delta\chi * B}{\mu_B} * \frac{N_M}{V}$$

Where $\Delta\chi$ is the change in susceptibility, μ_B is the Bohr magneton (in CGS units), B is the applied magnetic field, V is the crystal volume, and N_M is the number of moles of CrSBr. The estimated defect density is $\sim10^{13}$ cm^{-2}.

C.1.7 Calculating Carrier Density from Gate Dependence

The carrier density at low temperatures was estimated using the gate-dependence of the sample conductivity. Assuming the conductivity varies linearly with carrier density, we use the capacitor model to estimate the intrinsic doping density.

$$\sigma \propto n$$

$$n = n_D + \frac{\epsilon_0 \epsilon_R}{d} V_G$$

Where n_D is the intrinsic doping density, ε_0 is the vacuum permitivity, ε_r is the relative permitivity of the dielectric (3.9 for SiO$_2$), d is the thickness of the dielectric, and V_G is the value of the back gate in volts. Assuming the density is the only term that varies with gate voltage in the expression for conductance, an expression for the density can be derived from the derivative of conductance versus gate.

$$\frac{d\sigma}{dV_{\mathrm{G}}} \cdot \frac{1}{\sigma(V_{\mathrm{G}})} = \frac{dn}{dV_{\mathrm{G}}} \cdot \frac{1}{n(V_{\mathrm{G}})}$$

Using the expression for density versus gate, we can derive an expression for the intrinsic doping density.

$$n_{\mathrm{D}} = \frac{1}{e} \cdot \left[\frac{1}{\frac{d\sigma}{dV_{\mathrm{G}}} \cdot \frac{1}{\sigma(V_{\mathrm{G}})}} - V_{\mathrm{G}} \right] \cdot \frac{\epsilon_0 \epsilon_{\mathrm{r}}}{d}$$

Here, e is the electron charge, $d\sigma/dV_{\mathrm{G}}$ is the measured slope of the conductance versus back-gate voltage curve, and $\sigma(V_{\mathrm{G}})$ is the conductance at a given back-gate voltage. For the estimated density in **Figure C.22**, V_{G} was set to 0.

C.1.8 Details of Oxidation Dependent Measurement

The controlled oxidation of an encapsulated CrSBr device was performed by storing the sample under ambient conditions and performing a TLM at regular intervals. For the device in **Figure S19**, the measurements were performed at room temperature by sourcing voltage and measuring current with a Keithley 2400. A voltage excitation of 0.5 V was used to ensure measurements were performed in the linear IV regime. The contact resistance and sample resistivity were extracted by fitting the curves of 2-terminal resistance versus channel length to a

line following the TLM model.

$$R = \frac{\rho L}{A} + 2R_C$$

Where R is the measured 2-terminal device resistance, L is the channel length, A is the cross

sectional channel area, ρ is the sample resistivity, and R_C is the contact resistance. The contact

resistance is multiplied by two since the measurements are 2-terminal measurements between two

contacts. In this model, ρ/A is simply the slope of the 2-terminal resistance versus channel length

and the intercept is twice the contact resistance.

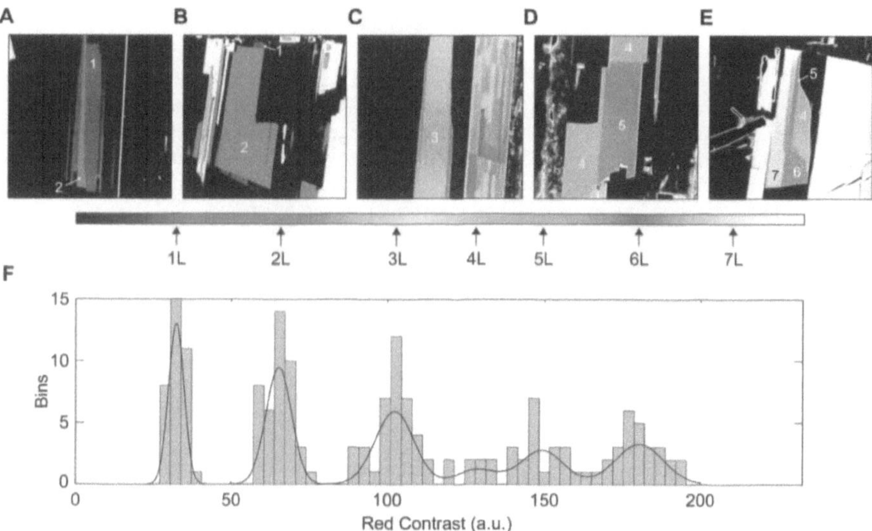

Figure C1: CrSBr optical contrast calibration on 285 nm SiO₂. **A-E)** False-colored optical images of various CrSBr flakes ranging in thickness from 1 to 7 layers exfoliated onto 285 nm SiO₂. The corresponding layer numbers are labelled on each image. **F)** Histogram of the optical contrast for all cataloged CrSBr flakes < 7 L. The solid black line is a 6 peak Gaussian fit to the data. The color bar above the histogram is a conversion from numerical contrast value to false color in (**A-E**). The colors corresponding to each layer number are denoted by arrows.

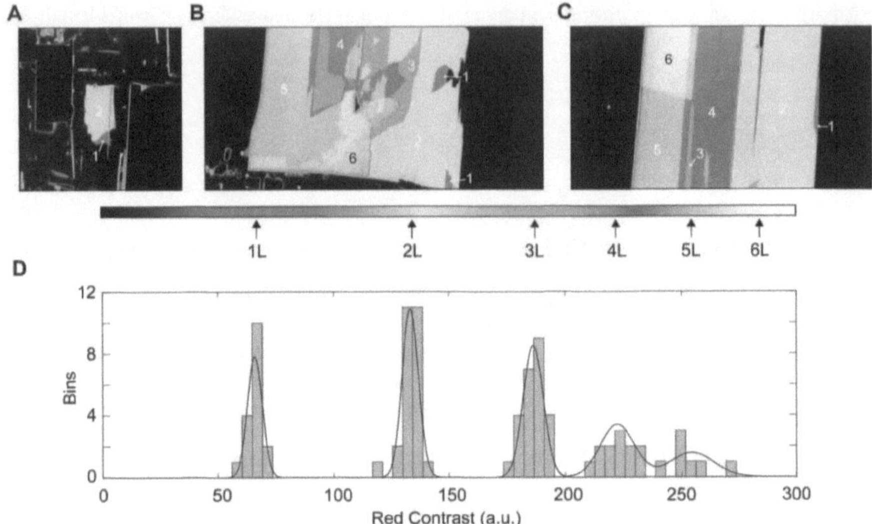

Figure C2: CrSBr optical contrast calibration on 90 nm SiO$_2$. A-C) False-colored optical images of various CrSBr flakes ranging in thickness from 1 to 6 layers exfoliated onto 90 nm SiO$_2$. The corresponding layer numbers are labelled on each image. **D)** Histogram of the optical contrast for all cataloged CrSBr flakes < 6 L. The solid black line is a 5 peak Gaussian fit to the data. The color bar above the histogram is a conversion from numerical contrast value to false color in (**A-C**). The colors corresponding to each layer number are denoted by arrows.

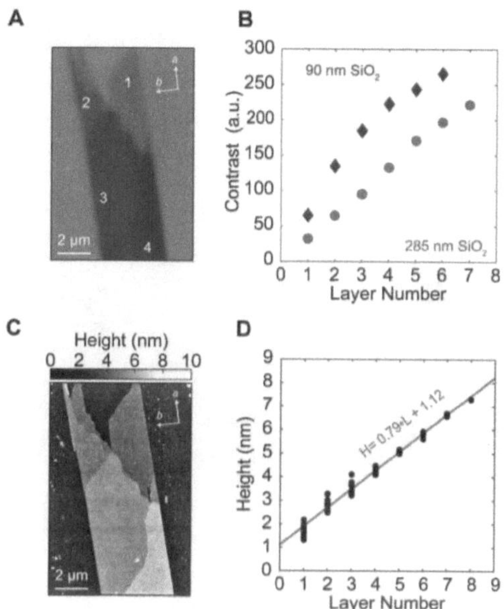

Figure C3: CrSBr thickness versus layer number correlated to optical contrast. A) Optical image of a CrSBr flake exfoliated onto 90 nm SiO_2. The thickness ranges from 1 to 4 layers with the corresponding layer numbers marked on the image. The orientation of the crystal axes is given in the inset. **B)** Optical contrast versus layer number for CrSBr exfoliated on 285 nm SiO_2 (red dots) and 90 nm SiO_2 (blue diamonds). **C)** Atomic force microscopy topography of the flake in **(A)**. **D)** CrSBr flake thickness versus layer number measured through atomic force microscopy. A linear fit to the data is given by a solid green line with the corresponding fit parameters given in the inset.

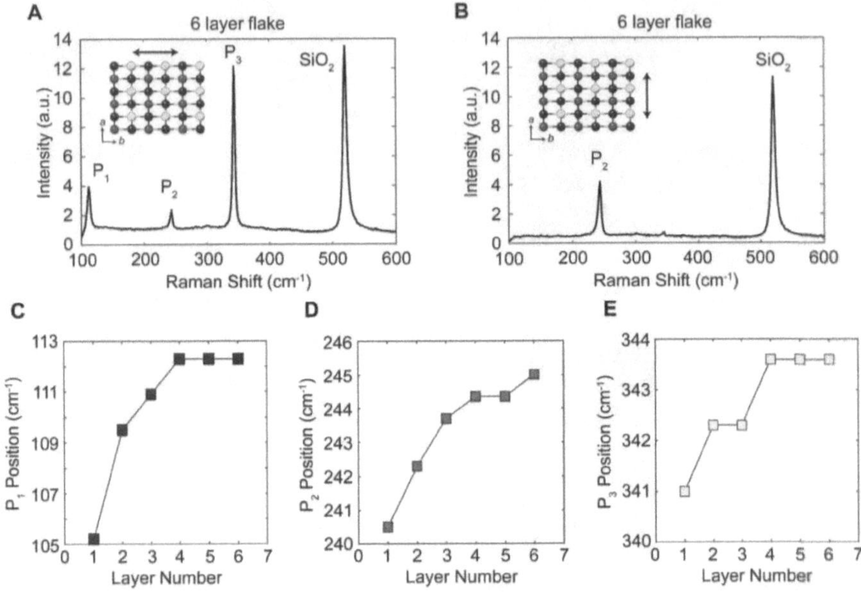

Figure C4: Layer dependence of CrSBr Raman spectra. A, B) Raman intensity versus wavenumber for a 6-layer CrSBr flake with incident light polarized parallel to the *b*-axis (**A**) and the *a*-axis (**B**). The Raman peaks from CrSBr and the SiO_2 substrate are labelled. **C-E)** Extracted peak positions versus CrSBr thickness for P_1 (**C**), P_2 (**D**), and P_3 (**E**). The peaks are denoted in (**A**) and (**B**).

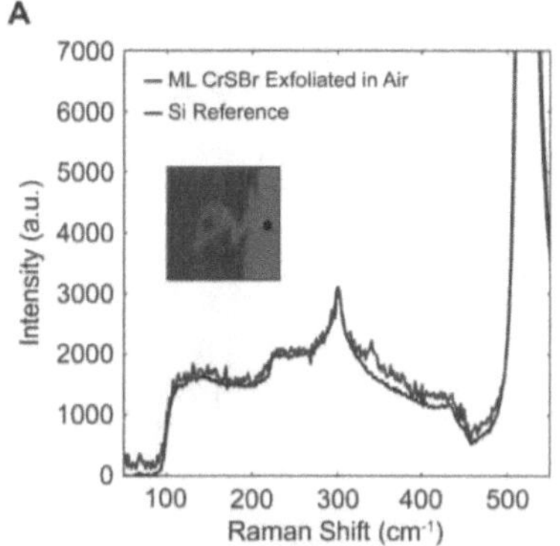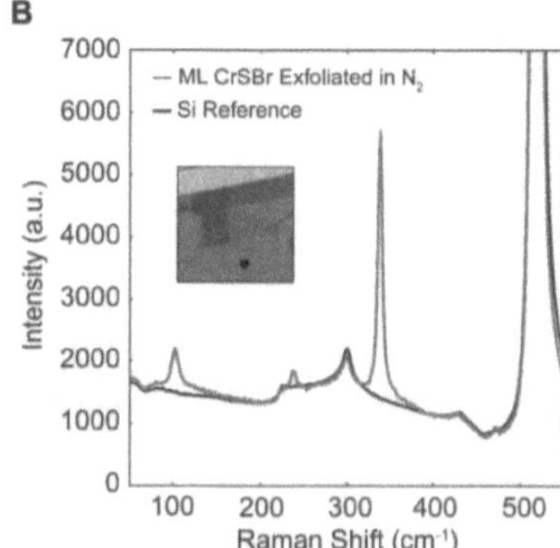

Figure C5: Raman spectra of pristine and oxidized monolayer CrSBr. A) Raman intensity versus wavenumber for a monolayer CrSBr flake exfoliated in air (solid blue line) and the SiO₂ substrate (solid black line). An optical image of the flake is given in the inset. The positions where the Raman spectra were acquired are labelled by a blue (monolayer CrSBr) and black (SiO₂ substrate) dot. **B)** Raman intensity versus wavenumber for a monolayer CrSBr flake exfoliated inside a N₂ glovebox (solid red line) and the SiO₂ substrate (solid black line). An optical image of the flake is given in the inset. The positions where the Raman spectra were acquired are labelled by a red (monolayer CrSBr) and black (SiO₂ substrate) dot.

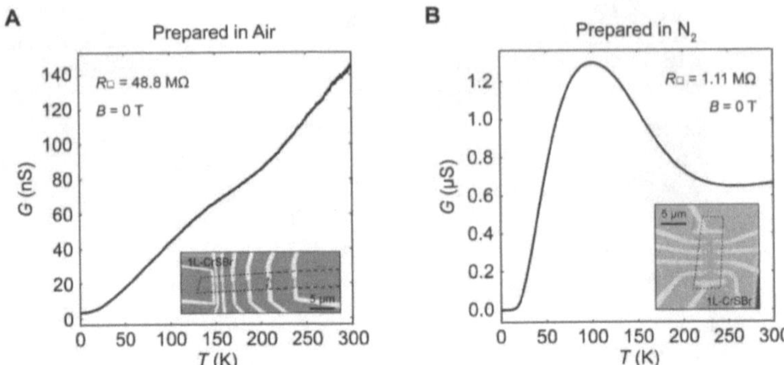

Figure C6: Transport properties of pristine and oxidized monolayer CrSBr. A) Conductance versus temperature for a monolayer CrSBr flake exfoliated and encapsulated under ambient conditions. The room temperature sheet resistivity and an optical image of the device is given in the inset. **B)** Conductance versus temperature for the monolayer CrSBr flake presented in the main text. It was exfoliated and encapsulated inside a N$_2$ glovebox on a passivated substrate. The room temperature sheet resistivity and an optical image of the device is given in the inset.

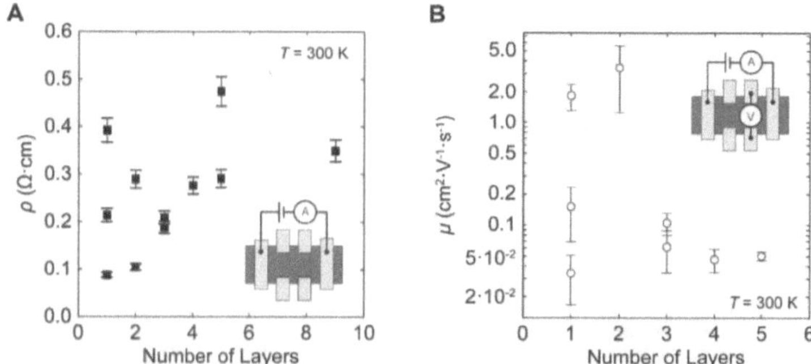

Figure C7: Layer dependence of CrSBr resistivity and mobility at room temperature. A) Resistivity of CrSBr flakes versus layer number. The resistivity was estimated by measuring the 2-probe sample resistance across the longest channel length to minimize the size of the contact resistance relative to the channel resistance. The contact resistance to CrSBr was extracted from a TLM measurement for the 5 L and 1 L devices and confirmed to be a negligible percentage of the measured 2-probe resistances (assuming the contact resistance for 1 L CrSBr is an upper bound on the contact resistance for > 1 layers). The error bar denotes the estimated contribution of the contact resistance to the calculated resistivity. The physical dimensions of the flakes were measured with atomic force microscopy. A schematic of the measurement setup is given in the inset. **B)** Calculated sample mobility of CrSBr flakes versus layer number. The mobility was calculated using $\mu = \frac{\sigma}{ne}$. The density was determined from the Hall effect. The large error bars in the 2 L and 1 L samples are due to uncertainties in the Hall measurement from high sample resistance and relatively low sample mobility.

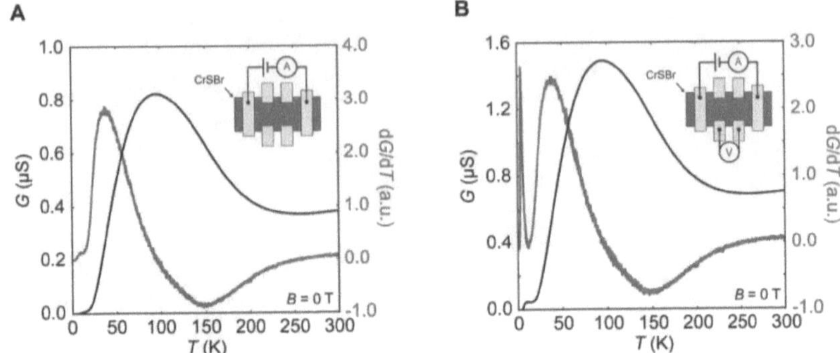

Figure C8: Comparison of 2-probe and 4-probe zero-field conductance versus temperature. **A, B)** Conductance (solid black line) and derivative of the conductance (solid red line) versus temperature at zero magnetic field for a monolayer CrSBr device measured in a 2-terminal configuration (**A**) and a 4-terminal configuration (**B**). Schematics of the measurement geometries are given in the insets.

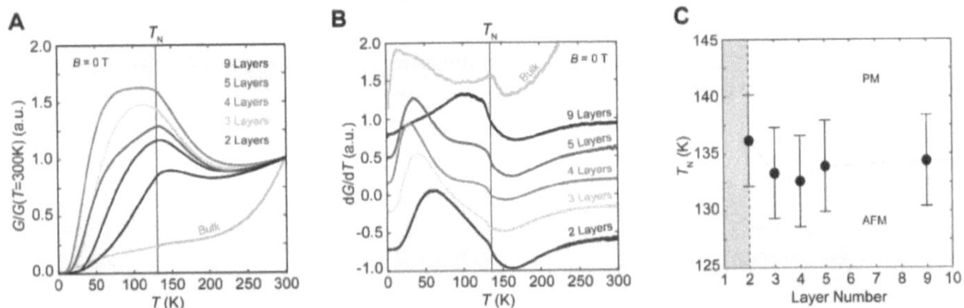

Figure C9: Layer dependence of CrSBr zero-field conductance versus temperature. A) Conductance versus temperature for 2 (solid blue line), 3 (solid yellow line), 4 (solid green line), 5 (solid red line), and 9 (solid black line) layers of CrSBr. The bulk data[7] is given as the solid grey line for reference. **B)** Derivative of conductance versus temperature for 2 (solid blue line), 3 (solid yellow line), 4 (solid green line), 5 (solid red line), and 9 (solid black line) layers of CrSBr. The bulk data[7] is given as the solid grey line for reference. Each curve is offset from one another for clarity. **C)** Néel temperature versus CrSBr flake thickness. Light grey and white regions correspond to antiferromagnetic and paramagnetic regions, respectively. The dark grey region denotes the ferromagnetic phase observed in the monolayer.

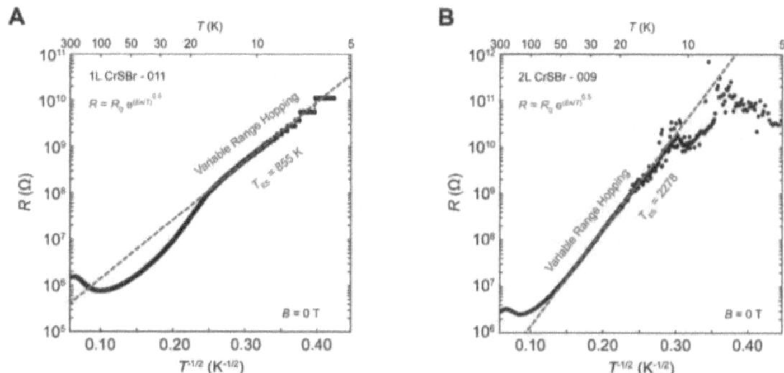

Figure C10: Analysis of low-temperature resistance behavior in CrSBr. A, B) Resistance on a log scale versus inverse square root of temperature at zero magnetic field for the monolayer (**A**) and bilayer (**B**) CrSBr presented in the main text. A fit to a variable range hopping model is given by the solid red line. The extracted Efros-Shklovskii temperature is given in the inset. In both plots, a few absolute temperature values are denoted on the top of each plot.

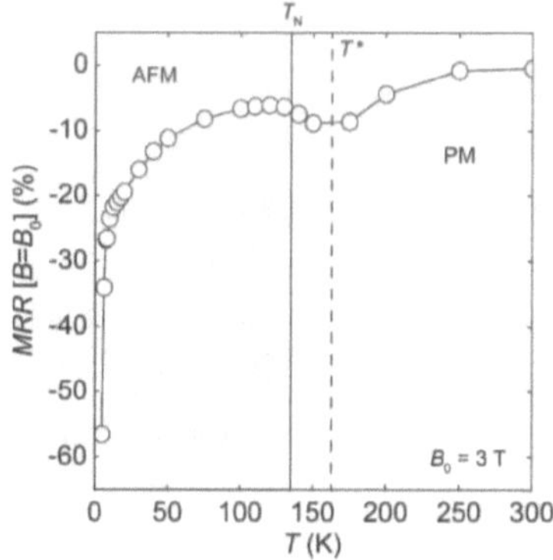

Figure C11: Bilayer CrSBr fixed-field *MRR* versus temperature. *MRR* [*B* = 3 T] versus temperature for the bilayer CrSBr devices presented in the main text. The entire data range is shown to emphasize the size of the n*MRR* at the lowest temperatures measured. The AFM and PM phases are denoted by grey and white regions, respectively. The magnetic transitions T_N and T^* are labelled on the plot as a solid and dashed black line, respectively.

191

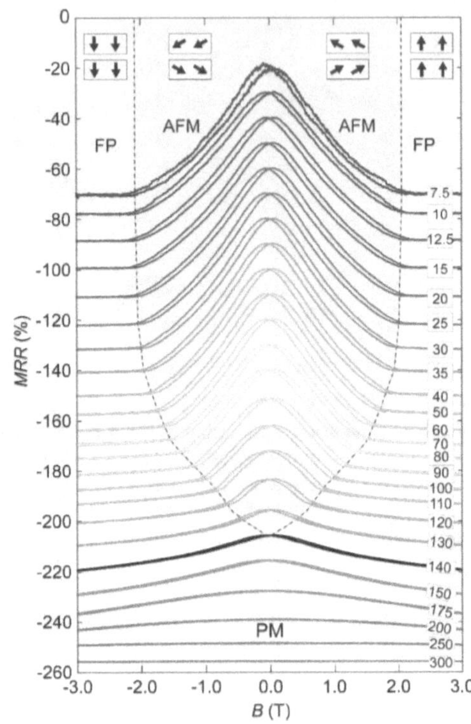

Figure C12: Magnetotransport properties of 9 L CrSBr. Magnetoresistance ratio defined as $MRR(B) = \frac{R(B)-R(B=0)}{R(B=0)} * 100$ versus magnetic field at various temperatures with the field oriented along the c-axis. Both forward and backward magnetic field scans at each temperature are presented. The curves are offset for clarity. The solid black line is the curve taken at a temperature near T_N. The AFM, FP, and PM phases are labeled, and the phase boundary is denoted by a dashed black line. Schematics showing the orientation of the spins in the AFM and FP state are given in the inset.

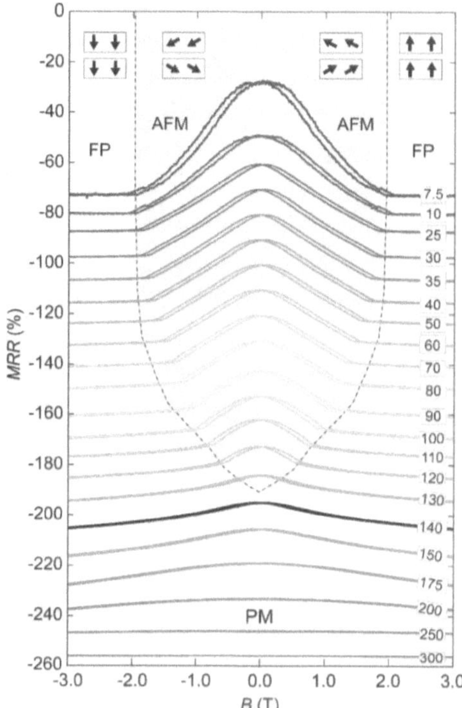

Figure C13: Magnetotransport properties of 5 L CrSBr. Magnetoresistance ratio defined as $MRR(B) = \frac{R(B)-R(B=0)}{R(B=0)} * 100$ versus magnetic field at various temperatures with the field oriented along the c-axis. Both forward and backward magnetic field scans at each temperature are presented. The curves are offset for clarity. The solid black line is the curve taken at a temperature near T_N. The AFM, FP, and PM phases are labeled, and the phase boundary is denoted by a dashed black line. Schematics showing the orientation of the spins in the AFM and FP state are given in the inset.

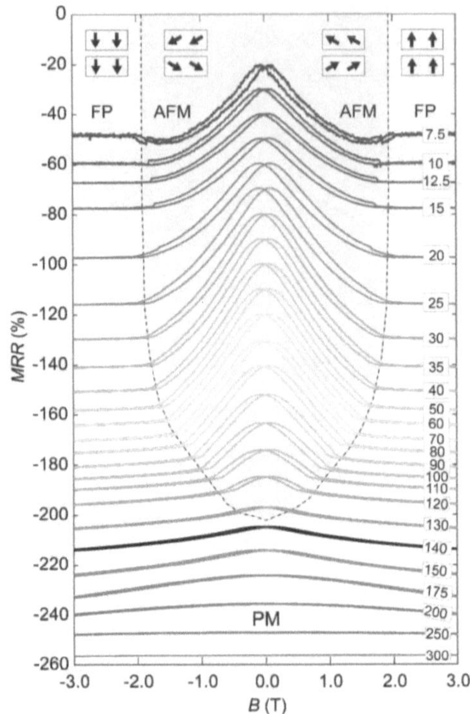

Figure C14: Magnetotransport properties of 4 L CrSBr. Magnetoresistance ratio defined as $MRR(B) = \frac{R(B)-R(B=0)}{R(B=0)} * 100$ versus magnetic field at various temperatures with the field oriented along the c-axis. Both forward and backward magnetic field scans at each temperature are presented. The curves are offset for clarity. The solid black line is the curve taken at a temperature near T_N. The AFM, FP, and PM phases are labeled, and the phase boundary is denoted by a dashed black line. Schematics showing the orientation of the spins in the AFM and FP state are given in the inset.

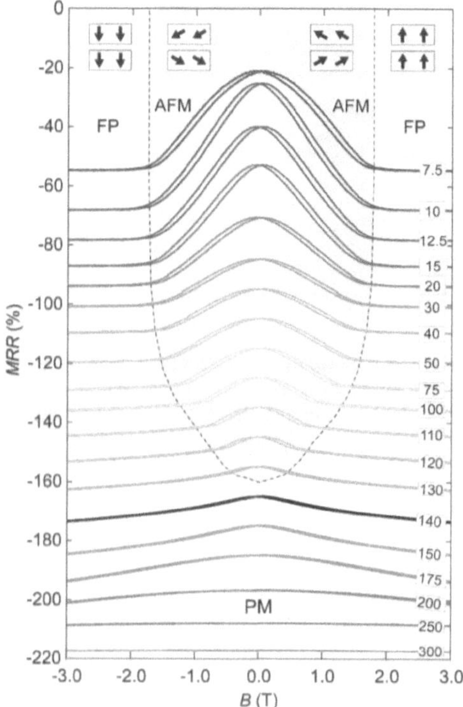

Figure C15: Magnetotransport properties of 3 L CrSBr. Magnetoresistance ratio defined as $MRR(B) = \frac{R(B) - R(B=0)}{R(B=0)} * 100$ versus magnetic field at various temperatures with the field oriented along the c-axis. Both forward and backward magnetic field scans at each temperature are presented. The curves are offset for clarity. The solid black line is the curve taken at a temperature near T_N. The AFM, FP, and PM phases are labeled, and the phase boundary is denoted by a dashed black line. Schematics showing the orientation of the spins in the AFM and FP state are given in the inset.

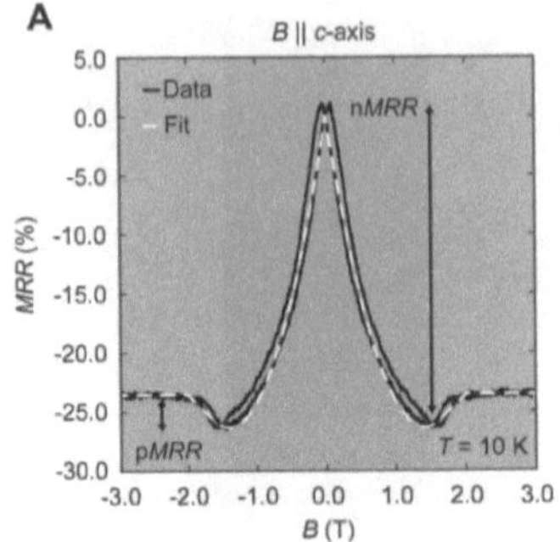

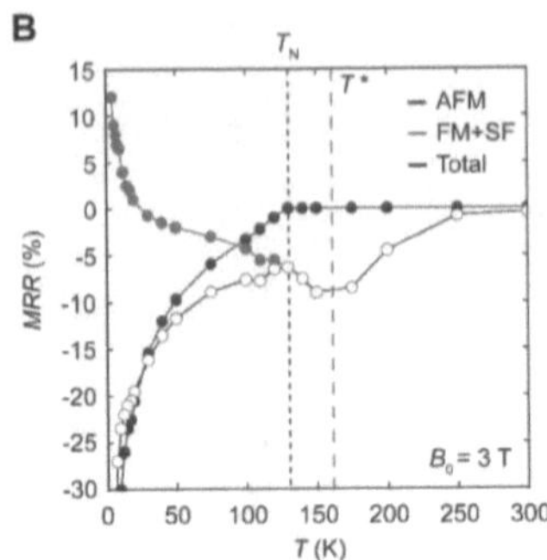

Figure C16: pMRR and nMRR components extracted from bilayer CrSBr MRR. A) *MRR* versus field at 10 K for the bilayer sample presented in the main text. The regions of n*MRR* from the layered AFM ordering and the high-field p*MRR* are denoted by blue and red boxes, respectively. The dashed white line is a fit of the form $MRR \propto A_{\mathrm{NMRR}} \left[\left(1 - \frac{B}{B_{\mathrm{sat}}^{\mathrm{NMRR}}}\right)^2 - 1\right] + A_{\mathrm{PMRR}} \left(\frac{B}{B_{\mathrm{sat}}^{\mathrm{PMRR}}}\right)^2 + O(B)$, where A_{NMRR}, $B_{\mathrm{sat}}^{\mathrm{NMRR}}$ and A_{PMRR}, $B_{\mathrm{sat}}^{\mathrm{PMRR}}$ are the amplitudes and corresponding saturation fields for the n*MRR* and p*MRR* components, respectively. The $O(B)$ term encompasses the high-field linear component observed for higher temperatures. B) Plot of the n*MRR* component A_{NMRR} (solid blue dots and line), the p*MRR* component A_{PMRR} plus the high-field component $O(B)$ (solid red dots and line), and the total *MRR* (solid white dots and black line) versus temperature. The magnetic transition temperatures T_N and T^* are labelled by dashed black lines. The extracted p*MRR* plus high-field component qualitatively reproduces the behavior of monolayer CrSBr, suggesting the p*MRR* in few-layer and bulk CrSBr is related to intraplanar *MRR* effects.

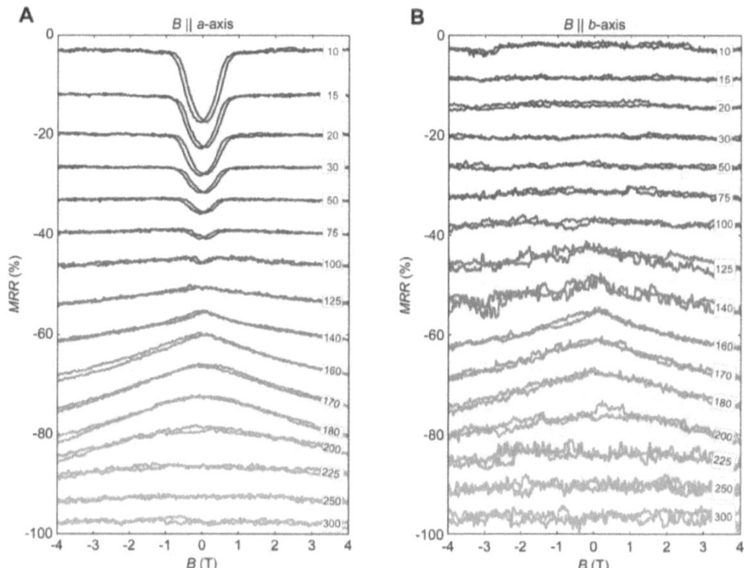

Figure C17: Additional magnetoresistance measurements of monolayer CrSBr. *MRR* versus magnetic field at various temperatures with the field oriented along the *a*-axis (**A**) and *b*-axis(**B**) for the monolayer CrSBr device presented in the main text. Both forward and backward magnetic field scans at each temperature are presented. The curves are offset for clarity.

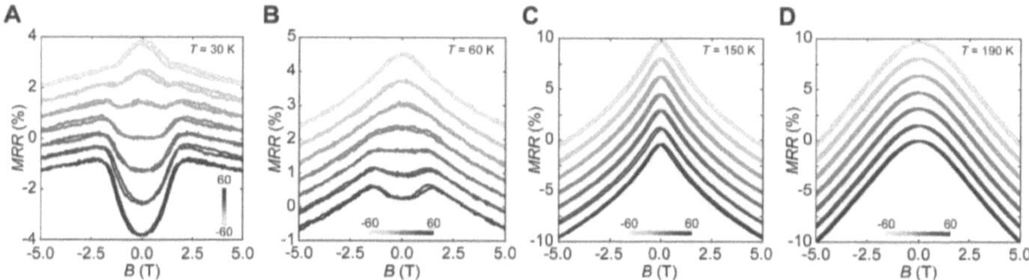

Figure C18: Gate dependence of monolayer CrSBr *MRR* at higher temperatures. A-D) *MRR* versus magnetic field as function of back-gate voltage at $T = 30$ K (**A**), $T = 60$ K (**B**), $T = 150$ K (**C**), and $T = 190$ K (**D**) for the monolayer device presented in the main text. In each plot, both forward and backward magnetic field scans are given. The corresponding range of back-gate values is given in the inset of the plots.

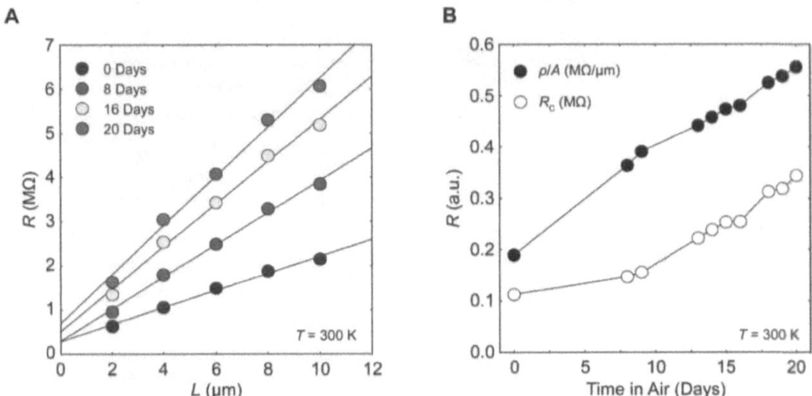

Figure C19: Oxidation dependence of monolayer CrSBr sample and contact resistances. A) Transmission line measurement (TLM) of the monolayer CrSBr sample presented in the main text after removing it from the fridge (solid blue dots) and after sitting under ambient conditions for 8 days (solid green dots), 16 days (solid yellow dots), and 20 days (solid red dots). Linear fits to the data are given by solid black lines. **B)** Extracted sample resistivity per cross-sectional area (solid black dots) and contact resistance (solid white dots) versus time spent under ambient conditions. All measurements were taken at room temperature.

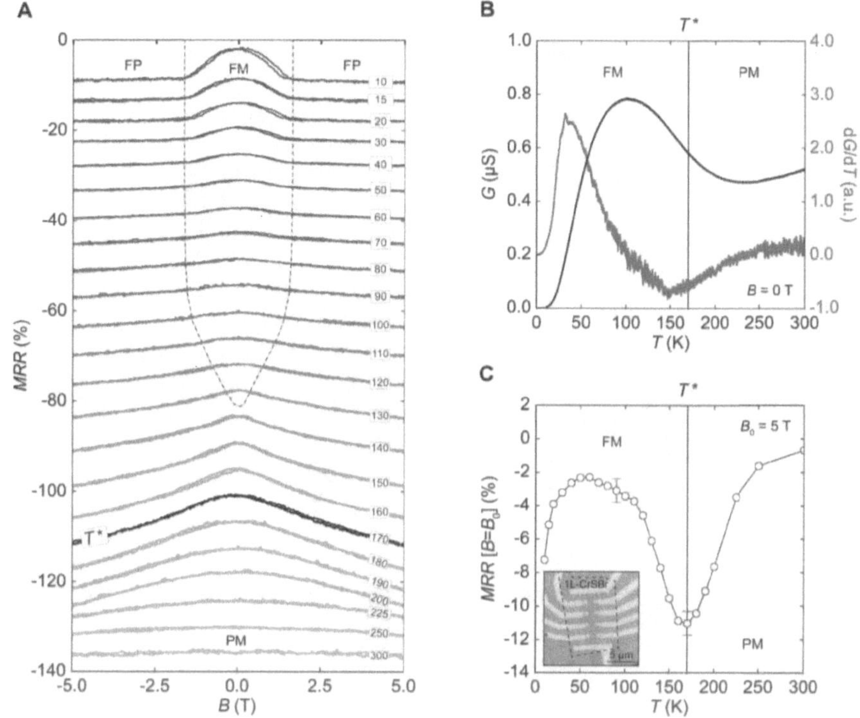

Figure C20: Transport properties of a second monolayer CrSBr device. A) Magnetoresistance ratio $MRR(B) = \frac{R(B)-R(B=0)}{R(B=0)} * 100$ versus magnetic field at various temperatures with the field oriented along the c-axis. Both forward and backward magnetic field scans at each temperature are presented. The curves are offset for clarity. The solid black line is the curve taken at a temperature near T^*. The FM and PM phases are labeled, and the phase boundary is denoted by a dashed black line. **B)** Conductance (solid black line) and derivative of conductance (solid red line) versus temperature at zero magnetic field. The FM and PM phases are denoted by grey and white regions, respectively. **C)** MRR at a fixed magnetic field versus temperature. The magnetic field at which the fixed-field MRR is calculated is $B_0 = 5$ T. A clear minimum in the fixed-field MRR versus temperature at T^* is demarcated. An optical image of the monolayer device is given in the inset. The CrSBr flake is outlined by a dashed black line.

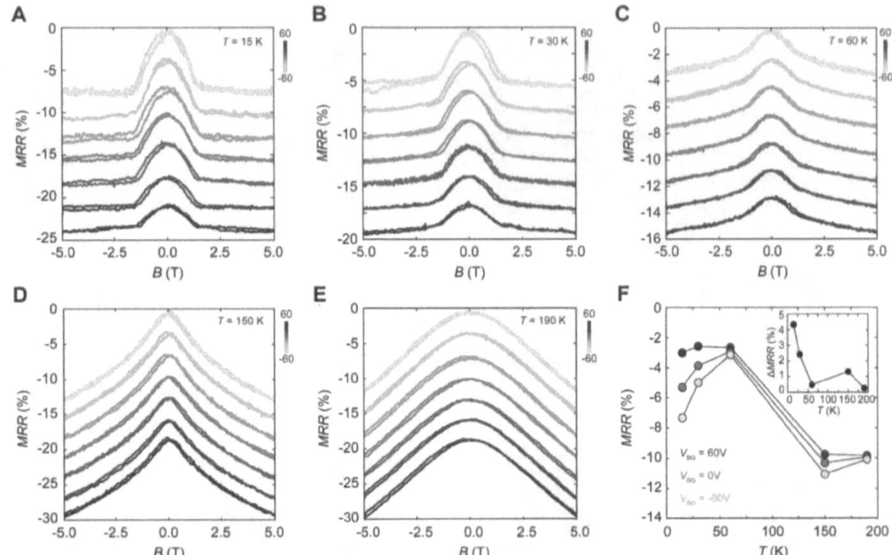

Figure C21: Gate dependence of *MRR* for a second monolayer CrSBr device. A-E) *MRR* versus magnetic field for various back-gate voltages at $T = 15$ K (**A**), $T = 30$ K (**B**), $T = 60$ K (**C**), $T = 150$ K (**D**), and $T = 190$ K (**E**) for a second monolayer CrSBr device. In each plot, both forward and backward magnetic field scans are given. The corresponding back-gate voltage ranges are given on the side of each plot. **F)** Fixed-field *MRR* versus temperature for back-gate voltages of $V_{BG} = 60$ V (blue dots), $V_{BG} = 0$ V (pink dots), and $V_{BG} = -60$ V (yellow dots). The total change in fixed-field *MRR* versus back-gate voltage at each temperature is given in the inset. The fixed-field *MRR* was calculated at $B_0 = 5$ T.

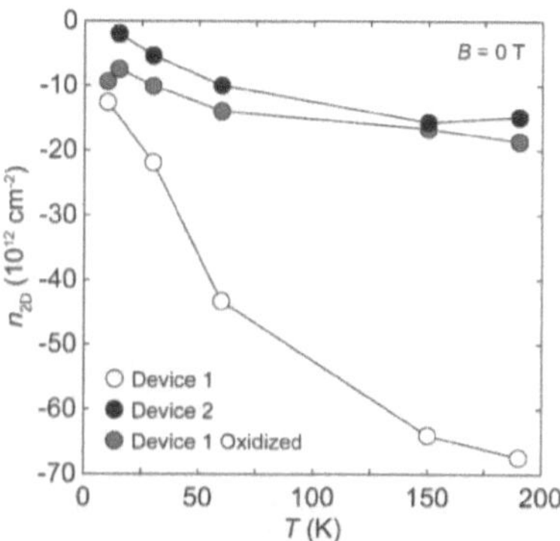

Figure C22: Estimation of electronic carrier density versus temperature for monolayer CrSBr devices. Calculated electronic carrier density versus temperature for device 1 (solid white circles), device 2 (solid black circles), and device 1 after oxidizing (solid red circles). The carrier density was estimated by fitting the conductance versus back-gate voltage to a linear dependence and extrapolating the intrinsic carrier density (see supplemental text for details).

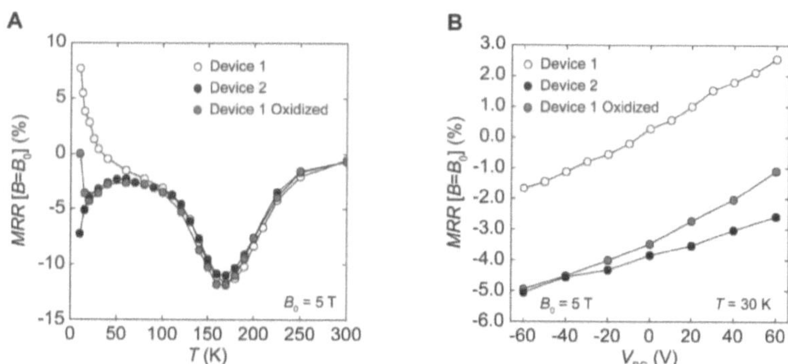

Figure C23: Comparison of *MRR* between monolayer CrSBr devices. A) Fixed-field *MRR* versus temperature for device 1 (solid white dots), device 2 (solid black dots), and device 1 after oxidizing (solid red dots). **B)** Fixed-field *MRR* versus back-gate voltage at 30 K for device 1 (solid white dots), device 2 (solid black dots), and device 1 after oxidizing (solid red dots). For both (**A**) and (**B**), the magnetic field at which the fixed-field *MRR* is determined is $B_0 = 5$ T.

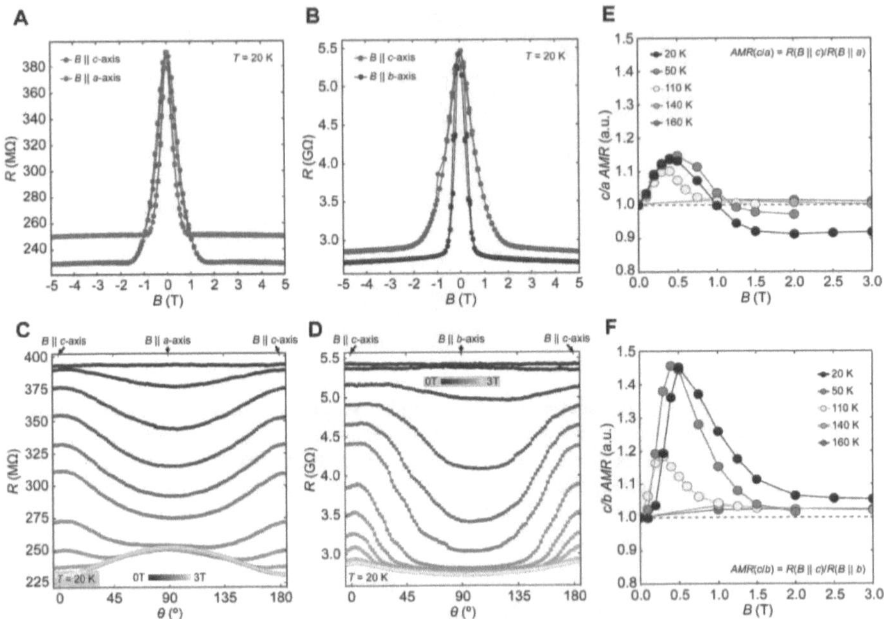

Figure C24: Field-direction dependence of bulk CrSBr *MRR*. A) Resistance versus magnetic field for fields parallel to the *c*-axis (green dots) and *a*-axis (red dots) at 20 K measured in a single bulk CrSBr device. **B)** Resistance versus magnetic field for fields parallel to the *c*-axis (green dots) and *a*-axis (blue dots) at 20 K measured in a second bulk CrSBr device. For (**A**) and (**B**), both devices were fabricated from the same single CrSBr crystal. **C, D)** Resistance versus rotator axis angle for various applied magnetic fields for the device in **A** (**C**) and **B** (**D**) at 20 K. The corresponding crystal axis orientations are given above each plot. The color of each trace corresponds to a different magnetic field value, the range of which is denoted in the inset. **E, F)** Extracted anisotropy versus magnetic field for various temperatures comparing the *c*- and *a*-axes (**E**) and the *c*- and *b*-axes (**F**). Anisotropy is defined as $AMR = R(B \parallel x)/R(B \parallel y)$, where x and y are crystal axes. Above the saturation field at 20 K, $R(B \parallel a) > R(B \parallel c) > R(B \parallel b)$, consistent with measurements on monolayer CrSBr.

Appendix D: Additional Data for Chapter 4

D.1 Synthesis and structural characterization of bulk CrSBr

For this methodology, see **B.1 Methods.**

D.2 Sample preparation

CrSBr is micromechanically exfoliated to substrates using scotch tape. After cleaning with oxygen plasma, substrates are treated with 1-dodecanol to improve homogeneity of dielectric environment of silicon oxide surfaces (*6*). While arbitrary substrates can be chosen, silicon with 90 nm thermal oxide and UVFS are used for studies in this report. Flake thickness is identified with atomic force microscopy, which can be correlated to optical contrast for simplicity.

D.3 Raman Spectroscopy

Raman spectroscopy was performed with a Renishaw inVia confocal Raman microscope. 532 nm laser with ~1mW power was used for excitation. CrSBr flakes were exfoliated on 1-dodecanol passivated fused silica substrates, and samples were placed in a gas-tight cell with nitrogen atmosphere during the measurements. Excitation polarization was controlled with a half wave plate.

D.4 Photoluminescence and Reflectance Spectroscopy

Photoluminescence spectroscopy was performed with a 633 nm HeNe laser with on-sample power of 200 μW. Reflectance spectroscopy was conducted with broadband tungsten-halogen light source. Emission and reflection were collected with a Princeton Instruments PyLoN-IR and SpectraPro HRS-300. Samples were exfoliated on 1-dodecanol passivated UVFS, and were placed in nitrogen gas-tight cell throughout the measurements.

D.5 Second harmonic generation

Second harmonic generation microscopy is performed with Spectra-Physics Tsunami 80 MHz Ti:Sapphire oscillator. 800 nm 420 μJ/cm^2 pulse with ~80 fs pulse-width is used to excite the sample. Achromatic half wave plate is placed between a shortpass dichroic mirror and a microscope objective to control polarizations of both incident pulse and emitting double-frequency radiation. A polarizer is placed before the dichroic to ensure polarization purity of the fundamental. Another half wave plate and a polarizer are placed before photomultiplier tube to choose between parallel and cross polarized configurations. Several filters are used to discriminate residual fundamental.

Sample is placed in an Oxford Instruments Microstat HiRes II with a 0.5 mm thick UVFS window. Base pressure is maintained at high vacuum around 10^{-7}-10^{-8} mbar. Sample is cooled with liquid nitrogen to reproducibly reach 65 K by pulling the cryogen with 0.1 atm. Liquid helium is used for some measurements to reach lower temperature.

Wave equation in a medium is described as

$$\vec{\nabla} \times \left(\vec{\nabla} \times \vec{E}\right) + \frac{1}{c^2}\frac{\partial^2 \vec{E}}{\partial t^2} = -\mu_0 \frac{\partial \vec{J}}{\partial t}$$

where $\vec{J}$ is expanded into multipoles with

$$\vec{J} = \vec{J_0} + \frac{\partial \vec{P}}{\partial t} + \vec{\nabla} \times \vec{M} - \frac{\partial}{\partial t}\vec{\nabla} \cdot \hat{Q} + \cdots.$$

Here we can define the source term

$$\vec{S} = \mu_0 \frac{\partial \vec{J}}{\partial t} = \mu_0 \frac{\partial^2 \vec{P}}{\partial t^2} + \mu_0 \vec{\nabla} \times \frac{\partial \vec{M}}{\partial t} + \cdots$$

where nonlinear electric field follows $\vec{E}(2\omega) \propto \vec{S}^{(2)}$.

Electric dipole SHG is described by $P_i^{(2)} = \sum_{j,k} \varepsilon_0 \chi_{ijk}^{(2)} E_j E_k$ where $\overleftrightarrow{\chi}$ is a rank 3 tensor.

Using permutation symmetry of $\chi_{ijk}^{(2)} = \chi_{ikj}^{(2)}$ induced second harmonic polarization can be written as

$$\begin{pmatrix} P_x(2\omega) \\ P_y(2\omega) \\ P_z(2\omega) \end{pmatrix} = \varepsilon_0 \begin{pmatrix} \chi_{xxx}^{(2)} & \chi_{xyy}^{(2)} & \chi_{xzz}^{(2)} & \chi_{xyz}^{(2)} & \chi_{xzx}^{(2)} & \chi_{xyx}^{(2)} \\ \chi_{yxx}^{(2)} & \chi_{yyy}^{(2)} & \chi_{yzz}^{(2)} & \chi_{yzy}^{(2)} & \chi_{yzx}^{(2)} & \chi_{yxy}^{(2)} \\ \chi_{zxx}^{(2)} & \chi_{yzz}^{(2)} & \chi_{zzz}^{(2)} & \chi_{zyz}^{(2)} & \chi_{zzx}^{(2)} & \chi_{zxy}^{(2)} \end{pmatrix} \begin{pmatrix} E_x(\omega)^2 \\ E_y(\omega)^2 \\ E_z(\omega)^2 \\ 2E_y(\omega)E_z(\omega) \\ 2E_z(\omega)E_x(\omega) \\ 2E_x(\omega)E_y(\omega) \end{pmatrix}.$$

For mm$\underline{m}$ (classical subgroup mm2, or C_{2v}) point group of antiferromagnetic CrSBr bilayer, only c-type tensor is nonzero among the polar tensor. If we define the principal axis of rotation to be in x, the sensor is given as

$$\chi^{(2,c)} = \begin{pmatrix} \chi^{(2)}_{xxx} & \chi^{(2)}_{xyy} & \chi^{(2)}_{xzz} & 0 & 0 & 0 \\ 0 & 0 & 0 & 0 & 0 & \chi^{(2)}_{yxy} \\ 0 & 0 & 0 & 0 & \chi^{(2)}_{zxz} & 0 \end{pmatrix}.$$

SHG microscopy is performed in back-scattering geometry where incident light and emitted light propagate in $-z$ and z directions, respectively. In this configuration we can ignore contributions of $E_z(\omega)$ and $P_z(2\omega)$, which allows us to ignore any tensor element with z component and simplify the tensor to

$$\chi^{(2,c)} = \begin{pmatrix} \chi^{(2)}_{xxx} & \chi^{(2)}_{xyy} & 0 \\ 0 & 0 & \chi^{(2)}_{yxy} \end{pmatrix}.$$

Assuming the incident light is linearly polarized whose polarization is rotated by an angle θ with respect to x axis, parallel and cross polarized components of $\chi^{(2,c)}$ is written as

$$\begin{pmatrix} \chi^{(2)}_{\parallel} \\ \chi^{(2)}_{\perp} \end{pmatrix} = \begin{pmatrix} \cos\theta & \sin\theta \\ -\sin\theta & \cos\theta \end{pmatrix} \begin{pmatrix} \chi^{(2)}_{xxx} & \chi^{(2)}_{xyy} & 0 \\ 0 & 0 & \chi^{(2)}_{yxy} \end{pmatrix} \begin{pmatrix} \cos^2\theta \\ \sin^2\theta \\ 2\cos\theta\sin\theta \end{pmatrix}$$
$$= \begin{pmatrix} \chi^{(2)}_{xxx}\cos^3\theta + \left(\chi^{(2)}_{xyy} + 2\chi^{(2)}_{yxy}\right)\cos\theta\sin^2\theta \\ \left(-\chi^{(2)}_{xxx} + 2\chi^{(2)}_{yxy}\right)\cos^2\theta\sin\theta - \chi^{(2)}_{xyy}\sin^3\theta \end{pmatrix}.$$

Since polar $\chi^{(2)}$ is zero at paramagnetic state with mmm point group, $\chi^{(2)}$ can probe magnetic phase transition of CrSBr bilayer

For magnetic dipole SHG of a centrosymmetric material, we will consider both $\chi^{(2),eem}$ and $\chi^{(2),mee}$, whose SHGs are described with $P_i^{(2)} = \sum_{j,k}\varepsilon_0\chi^{(2),eem}_{ijk}E_jH_k$ and $M_i^{(2)} = \sum_{j,k}\varepsilon_0\chi^{(2),mee}_{ijk}E_jE_k$. For $\chi^{(2),eem}$ we cannot use the permutation symmetry for j and k, and the equation becomes

$$\begin{pmatrix} P_x(2\omega) \\ P_y(2\omega) \\ P_z(2\omega) \end{pmatrix}$$

$$= \varepsilon_0 \begin{pmatrix} \chi^{(2)}_{xxx} & \chi^{(2)}_{xyy} & \chi^{(2)}_{xzz} & \chi^{(2)}_{xyz} & \chi^{(2)}_{xzy} & \chi^{(2)}_{xzx} & \chi^{(2)}_{xxz} & \chi^{(2)}_{xxy} & \chi^{(2)}_{xyx} \\ \chi^{(2)}_{yxx} & \chi^{(2)}_{yyy} & \chi^{(2)}_{yzz} & \chi^{(2)}_{yyz} & \chi^{(2)}_{yzy} & \chi^{(2)}_{yzx} & \chi^{(2)}_{yxz} & \chi^{(2)}_{yxy} & \chi^{(2)}_{yyx} \\ \chi^{(2)}_{zxx} & \chi^{(2)}_{yzz} & \chi^{(2)}_{zzz} & \chi^{(2)}_{zyz} & \chi^{(2)}_{zzy} & \chi^{(2)}_{zzx} & \chi^{(2)}_{zxz} & \chi^{(2)}_{zxy} & \chi^{(2)}_{zyx} \end{pmatrix} \begin{pmatrix} E_x(\omega)^2 \\ E_y(\omega)^2 \\ E_z(\omega)^2 \\ E_y(\omega)H_z(\omega) \\ E_z(\omega)H_y(\omega) \\ E_z(\omega)H_x(\omega) \\ E_x(\omega)H_z(\omega) \\ E_x(\omega)H_y(\omega) \\ E_y(\omega)H_x(\omega) \end{pmatrix},$$

and for $\chi^{(2),mee}$,

$$\begin{pmatrix} M_x(2\omega) \\ M_y(2\omega) \\ M_z(2\omega) \end{pmatrix} = \varepsilon_0 \frac{c}{n_{2\omega}} \begin{pmatrix} \chi^{(2)}_{xxx} & \chi^{(2)}_{xyy} & \chi^{(2)}_{xzz} & \chi^{(2)}_{xyz} & \chi^{(2)}_{xzx} & \chi^{(2)}_{xyx} \\ \chi^{(2)}_{yxx} & \chi^{(2)}_{yyy} & \chi^{(2)}_{yzz} & \chi^{(2)}_{yzy} & \chi^{(2)}_{yzx} & \chi^{(2)}_{yxy} \\ \chi^{(2)}_{zxx} & \chi^{(2)}_{yzz} & \chi^{(2)}_{zzz} & \chi^{(2)}_{zyz} & \chi^{(2)}_{zxz} & \chi^{(2)}_{zxy} \end{pmatrix} \begin{pmatrix} E_x(\omega)^2 \\ E_y(\omega)^2 \\ E_z(\omega)^2 \\ 2E_y(\omega)E_z(\omega) \\ 2E_z(\omega)E_x(\omega) \\ 2E_x(\omega)E_y(\omega) \end{pmatrix}$$

where c is the speed of light and $n_{2\omega}$ is the material index of refraction at frequency ω.

Our material of interest is CrSBr monolayer, whose point group is mmm at its paramagnetic state and <u>mmm</u> at its ferromagnetic state. Since the both point groups are centrosymmetric, all polar tensors are zeros, and terms like $\chi^{(2),eee}$, $\chi^{(2),mem}$, $\chi^{(2),emm}$, and $\chi^{(3),eeem}$ can be ignored. For mmm group, nonzero elements for both i- and c-type axial tensors are $\chi^{(2)}_{xyz}$, $\chi^{(2)}_{xzy}$, $\chi^{(2)}_{yzx}$, $\chi^{(2)}_{yxz}$, $\chi^{(2)}_{zxy}$, and $\chi^{(2)}_{zyx}$. For <u>mmm</u> group, while i-type axial tensor has $\chi^{(2)}_{xyz}$, $\chi^{(2)}_{xzy}$, $\chi^{(2)}_{yzx}$, $\chi^{(2)}_{yxz}$, $\chi^{(2)}_{zxy}$, and $\chi^{(2)}_{zyx}$ as non-zero elements, c-type axial tensor has $\chi^{(2)}_{yyy}$, $\chi^{(2)}_{yxx}$, $\chi^{(2)}_{xyx}$, $\chi^{(2)}_{xxy}$, $\chi^{(2)}_{yzz}$, $\chi^{(2)}_{zyz}$, and $\chi^{(2)}_{zzy}$ as non-zero elements. In back-scattering geometry, ignoring all the elements with z component, only c-type axial tensor of <u>mmm</u> point group has nonzero elements. As a result, MD SHG can probe magnetic transition of CrSBr monolayer. Observing that the magnetic field of electromagnetic wave propagating in free space is perpendicular to the electric field, parallel and cross polarized components of $\chi^{(2,c),eem}$ is written as

$$\begin{pmatrix} \chi^{(2,c),eem}_{\parallel} \\ \chi^{(2,c),eem}_{\perp} \end{pmatrix}$$

$$
= \begin{pmatrix} \cos\theta & \sin\theta \\ -\sin\theta & \cos\theta \end{pmatrix} \begin{pmatrix} 0 & 0 & \chi_{xxy}^{(2,c),eem} & \chi_{xyx}^{(2,c),eem} \\ \chi_{yxx}^{(2,c),eem} & \chi_{yyy}^{(2,c),eem} & 0 & 0 \end{pmatrix} \begin{pmatrix} \cos\theta\cos(\theta+\pi/2) \\ \sin\theta\sin(\theta+\pi/2) \\ \cos\theta\sin(\theta+\pi/2) \\ \sin\theta\cos(\theta+\pi/2) \end{pmatrix}
$$

$$
= \begin{pmatrix} \cos\theta & \sin\theta \\ -\sin\theta & \cos\theta \end{pmatrix} \begin{pmatrix} 0 & 0 & \chi_{xxy}^{(2,c),eem} & \chi_{xyx}^{(2,c),eem} \\ \chi_{yxx}^{(2,c),eem} & \chi_{yyy}^{(2,c),eem} & 0 & 0 \end{pmatrix} \begin{pmatrix} -\cos\theta\sin\theta \\ \cos\theta\sin\theta \\ \cos^2\theta \\ -\sin^2\theta \end{pmatrix}
$$

$$
= \begin{pmatrix} \chi_{xxy}^{(2,c),eem}\cos^3\theta + \left(-\chi_{yxx}^{(2,c),eem} + \chi_{yyy}^{(2,c),eem} - \chi_{xyx}^{(2,c),eem}\right)\cos\theta\sin^2\theta \\ \left(-\chi_{yxx}^{(2,c),eem} + \chi_{yyy}^{(2,c),eem} - \chi_{xxy}^{(2,c),eem}\right)\cos^2\theta\sin\theta + \chi_{xyx}^{(2,c),eem}\sin^3\theta \end{pmatrix}
$$

which has the same functional form as $\chi^{(2),mee}$ of mm2 point group.

For $\chi^{(2,c),mee}$,

$$
\begin{pmatrix} \chi_{\parallel}^{(2,c),mee} \\ \chi_{\perp}^{(2,c),mee} \end{pmatrix} = \begin{pmatrix} \cos\theta & \sin\theta \\ -\sin\theta & \cos\theta \end{pmatrix} \begin{pmatrix} 0 & 0 & \chi_{xyx}^{(2,c),mee} \\ \chi_{yxx}^{(2,c),mee} & \chi_{yyy}^{(2,c),mee} & 0 \end{pmatrix} \begin{pmatrix} \cos^2\theta \\ \sin^2\theta \\ 2\cos\theta\sin\theta \end{pmatrix}
$$

$$
= \begin{pmatrix} \left(\chi_{yxx}^{(2,c),mee} + 2\chi_{xyx}^{(2,c),mee}\right)\cos^2\theta\sin\theta + \chi_{yyy}^{(2,c),mee}\sin^3\theta \\ \chi_{yxx}^{(2,c),mee}\cos^3\theta + \left(\chi_{yyy}^{(2,c),mee} - 2\chi_{xyx}^{(2,c),mee}\right)\cos\theta\sin^2\theta \end{pmatrix}.
$$

These terms govern induced nonlinear magnetization in the material, which translates to the source term by $S \propto \mu_0 \left(\nabla \times \frac{\partial M}{\partial t}\right)$ and can be written as

$$
\begin{pmatrix} S_{\parallel}^{mee}(2\omega) \\ S_{\perp}^{mee}(2\omega) \end{pmatrix} \propto \begin{pmatrix} M_{\perp}^{mee}(2\omega) \\ -M_{\parallel}^{mee}(2\omega) \end{pmatrix} \propto \begin{pmatrix} \chi_{\perp}^{(2,c),mee} \\ -\chi_{\parallel}^{(2,c),mee} \end{pmatrix}
$$

$$
\propto \begin{pmatrix} \chi_{yxx}^{(2,c),mee}\cos^3\theta + \left(\chi_{yyy}^{(2,c),mee} - 2\chi_{xyx}^{(2,c),mee}\right)\cos\theta\sin^2\theta \\ -\left(\chi_{yxx}^{(2,c),mee} + 2\chi_{xyx}^{(2,c),mee}\right)\cos^2\theta\sin\theta - \chi_{yyy}^{(2,c),mee}\sin^3\theta \end{pmatrix}
$$

which now also has the same functional form. The total magnetic dipole second order susceptibility can be written as the sum of $\chi^{(2,c),eem}$ and $\chi^{(2,c),mee}$:

$$
\begin{pmatrix} \chi_{\parallel}^{(2,c),MD} \\ \chi_{\perp}^{(2,c),MD} \end{pmatrix} = \begin{pmatrix} \chi_{\parallel}^{(2,c),eem} + \chi_{\perp}^{(2,c),mee} \\ \chi_{\perp}^{(2,c),eem} - \chi_{\parallel}^{(2,c),mee} \end{pmatrix} = \begin{pmatrix} A\cos^3\theta + (B+C)\cos\theta\sin^2\theta \\ (-A+B)\cos^2\theta\sin\theta - C\sin^3\theta \end{pmatrix}
$$

where

$$
A = \chi_{xxy}^{(2,c),eem} + \chi_{yxx}^{(2,c),mee}
$$

$$
B = -\chi_{yxx}^{(2,c),eem} + \chi_{yyy}^{(2,c),eem} - 2\chi_{xyx}^{(2,c),mee}
$$

$$C = -\chi_{xyx}^{(2,c),eem} + \chi_{yyy}^{(2,c),mee}.$$

As the equations show, polarization resolved measurement alone cannot differentiate between $\chi^{(2),eem}$ and $\chi^{(2),mee}$. Estimating relative orders of $\chi^{(2),eem}$ and $\chi^{(2),mee}$ requires understanding sizes of electric dipole and magnetic dipole transition matrix elements at ω and 2ω.

To achieve amplitude of second harmonic output, the source term must be integrated over the material thickness as the fundamental propagates through the medium. Since the material thickness is much smaller than the wavelengths, we can ignore phase matching conditions and not consider phase differences between second harmonic waves generated at different thicknesses. With these in consideration, second harmonic field amplitude is given as[2]

$$E(2\omega) = \frac{1}{4}\frac{i2\omega d}{2n_{2\omega}c}\chi^{(2)}E(\omega)^2$$

where d is thickness of the material, which is approximated to 0.8 nm $\times$ number of layers. Modifications must be made to reflect gaussian-shaped beam and ultrafast pulse width.[3] However, precisely determining all the relevant parameters on-sample is not very practical. Instead, we compare SHG from samples and a reference, such as α-quartz, to obtain absolute values of $\chi^{(2)}$.[4]

D.6 Temperature dependent SHG

Second order susceptibility is proportional to the order parameters,[5,6] M for odd number of layers and L for even number of layers. Here, we give a justification without proof. Above discussions on magnetic symmetry and second order susceptibilities assume perfect magnetic orderings. In reality, however, magnetic order is disturbed by thermal agitation, or by collective precession of spins called spin waves. Net magnetization is reduced from M_{sat} by the number of magnons in the material. Since those magnons are incoherent, the disturbance in magnetic symmetry experienced by incident electromagnetic wave is averaged out in the directions perpendicular to the easy axis. Effectively, the total magnetic symmetry can be considered as a superposition of the perfectly ferromagnetically ordered symmetry and the paramagnetic symmetry. From Table 2, only the perfect ferromagnetic state has nonzero $\chi_{FM}^{(2)}$, and as a result total $\chi_{tot}^{(2)}$ will be $\chi_{FM}^{(2)}$ multiplied by probability of the perfect FM symmetry. Since net magnetization is M_{sat} multiplied by that probability, $\chi_{tot}^{(2)}$ becomes proportional to magnetization of monolayer.

Similar argument can be extended to antiferromagnetic bilayer to show that $\chi^{(2)}$ is proportional to the size of its antiferromagnetic vector.

In CrSBr, intralayer FM coupling is much stronger than interlayer AFM coupling, and we could approximate that magnetization in isolated monolayer and single layer in bulk show similar temperature dependence. As a result, $\chi^{(2)} \propto (1 - T/T_C)^\beta$ regardless of sample thickness. In the presence of magnetostrictive effect, $\chi^{(2)}$ is proportional to square of the order parameter.[7] We do not observe such effect in our measurements.

D.7 Heat capacity

The measured heat capacity for magnetic materials contains contributions from lattice vibrations/rotations as well as local (dis)order induced by magnetic structure changes. For this reason, heat capacity measurements at temperatures near the magnetic ordering temperature of a material can be a valuable tool towards investigating the mechanism of magnetic ordering events, especially in systems that are highly magnetically anisotropic. The temperature- and magnetic field-dependent adiabatic molar heat capacity of CrSBr were recorded using a Quantum Design Physical Property Measurement System (PPMS) VersaLab between 100 and 200 K. The temperature-dependent heat capacity traces for CrSBr show two main features, a sharp peak at 132 K (zero field curve) and a broad feature around 160 K (zero field curve), both of which show magnetic field dependence. At increasing field strengths, the 132 K peak shifts to lower temperature and flattens into the baseline, while the broad 160 K feature shifts to higher temperature and sharpens. The peak at 132 K is attributed to the antiferromagnetic ordering event given the similarity in temperature between this peak and the reported AFM ordering temperature for CrSBr (T_N = 132 K). However, the disappearance of this feature at magnetic fields above the reported saturation field for CrSBr (H_C ~0.2 T at 120 K) suggests local ferromagnetic ordering takes place at temperatures above the T_N. It has previously been reported that low-dimensional systems show broad features in temperature-dependent heat capacity traces at temperatures above distinct magnetic ordering events due to short-range order induced by local magnetic coupling (15). For this reason, we assign the 160 K feature to the onset of local ferromagnetic ordering, likely within a single or few layer(s) of CrSBr; at applied fields less than H_c, the ferromagnetic domains (layers) couple antiferromagnetically leading to the heat capacity peak ~134 K and at applied fields greater than H_c, the applied field aligns individual domains (layers) ferromagnetically such that the AFM coupling event is absent.

D.8 Scanning tunneling microscopy and spectroscopy

We carried out STM measurements on freshly cleaved CrSBr crystals using our home-made variable temperature STM at 150K in an ultrahigh vacuum (base pressure $< 4.0 \times 10^{-10}$ torr). We obtained the STM topography images in the constant current mode with electrochemically etched tungsten tips. To avoid tip artifacts, each STM tip was prepared on a clean Au(111) surface before all measurements. All tips were verified to be atomically sharp. We obtained the differential conductance (dI/dV) spectra with a lock-in amplifier when keeping the tip fixed above the surface and the feedback loop off.

The statistical analysis of gap information is conducted by averaging the gap parameters obtained by fitting a semiconducting gap function on each individual STS using ordinary least square (OLS) method. This analysis is done via a script in Python.

Table D1. Selected crystallographic data for CrSBr.

T (K)	100
Formula	CrSBr
MW	163.97
Space Group	$Pmmn$
a (Å)	4.7379
b (Å)	3.5043
c (Å)	7.9069
a (°) b	90
(°) g	90
(°)	90
V (Å^3) Z	131.28
ρ_{calc} (g cm^{-3})	2
l (Å)	4.148
$2q_{min}$, $2q_{max}$	0.71073
Nref	10.032, 58.958
R(int), R(s)	1685
μ (mm^{-1})	0.0735, 0.0406
Data	19.976
Restraints	219
Parameters	0
R_1 (obs)	13
wR_2 (all)	0.0674
S	0.1959
	1.486

\

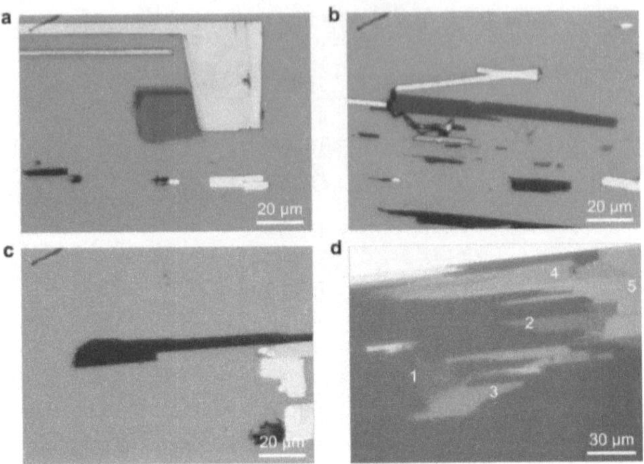

Figure D1. Optical microscope images of exfoliated CrSBr samples. (a) Monolayer (center piece) on a silicon substrate with 90 nm thermal oxide. **(b)** Bilayer (center piece) on a silicon substrate with 90 nm thermal oxide. **(c)** Trilayer on a silicon substrate with 90 nm thermal oxide. **(d)** 1-5 layers on UVFS.

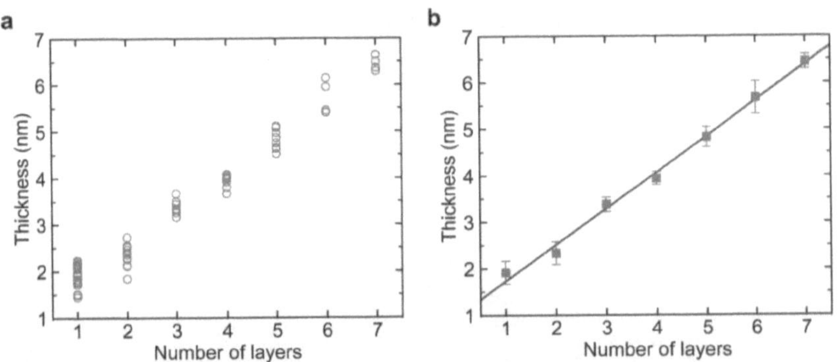

Figure D2. (a) Thicknesses versus the number of layers of various samples of exfoliated CrSBr. **(b)** Linear fit gives 0.78 ± 0.3 nm / layer, which agrees well with 0.791 nm obtained from singlecrystal X-ray diffraction.

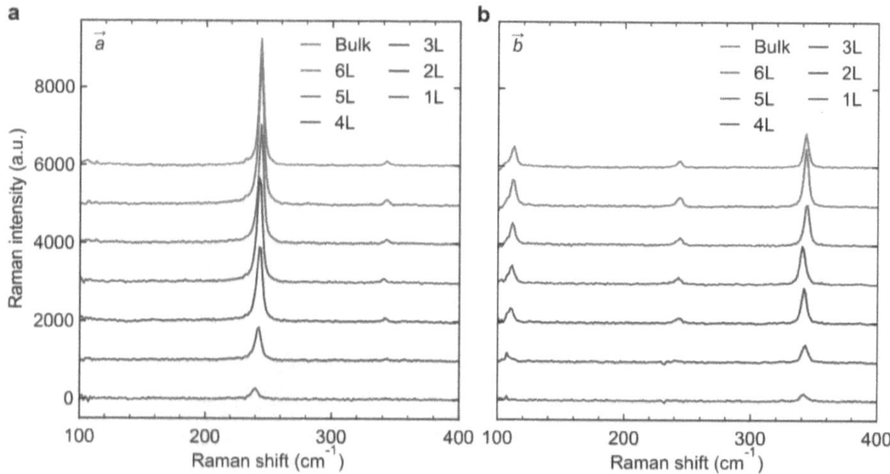

Figure D3. Raman spectra of samples from one to six layers and a thin bulk with excitation laser polarization along (**a**) $\vec{a}$ and (**b**) $b\$^{\rightarrow}$, respectively.

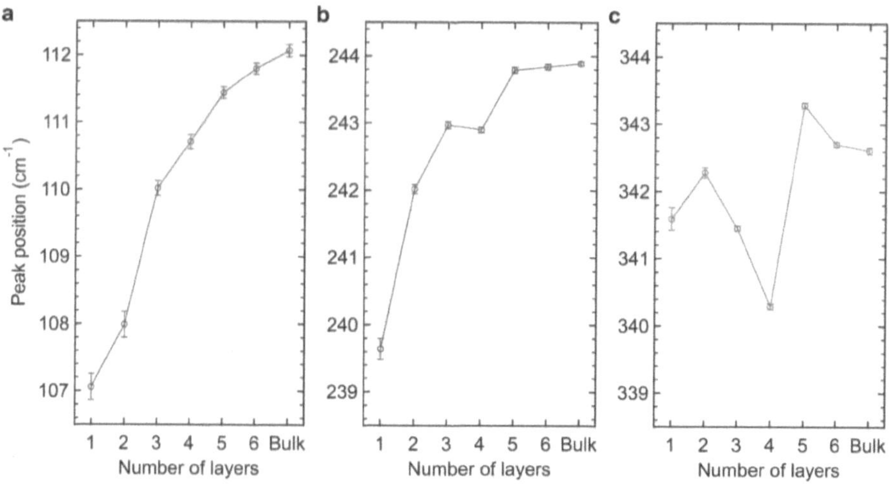

Figure D4. Raman peak positions as a function of layer number.

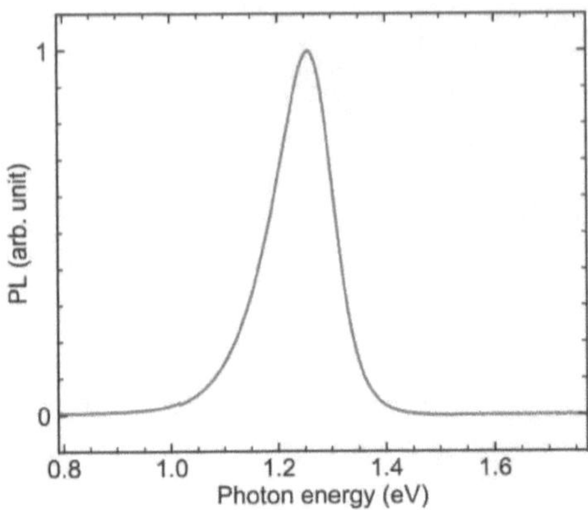

Figure D5. Photoluminescence spectrum of a bulk CrSBr crystal at room temperature.

D.9 Magnetic symmetry of CrSBr bilayer and monolayer

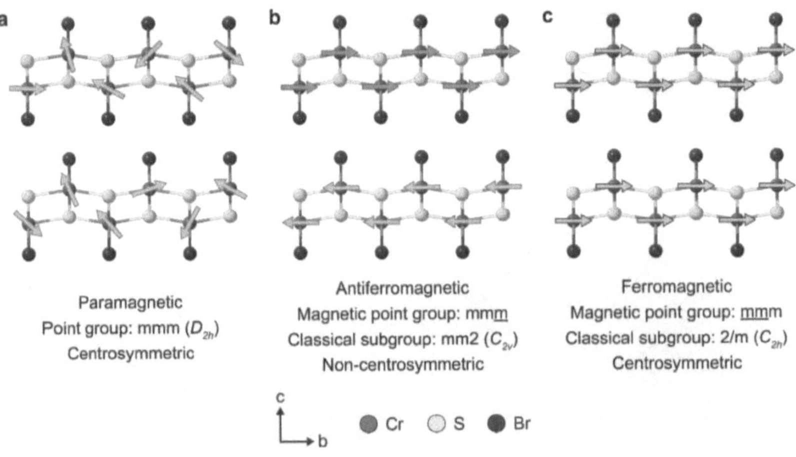

Figure D6. Magnetic point groups of (a) paramagnetic, (b) antiferromagnetic, and (c) ferromagnetic CrSBr bilayer. Only paramagnetic and antiferromagnetic states are experimentally observed.

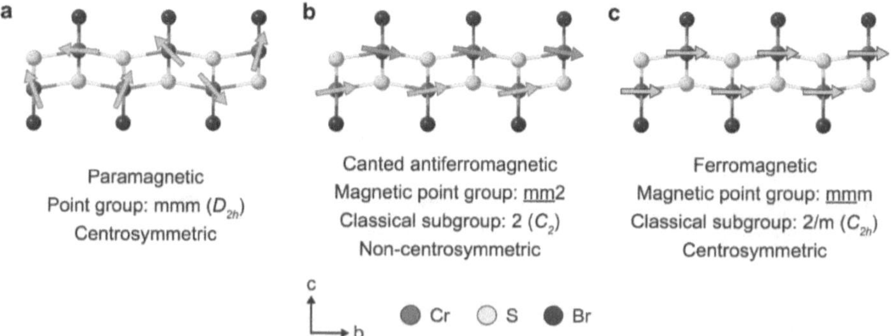

Figure D7. Magnetic point groups of (a) paramagnetic, (b) canted antiferromagnetic, and (c) ferromagnetic CrSBr monolayer. Only paramagnetic and ferromagnetic states are experimentally observed.

D.10 Nonzero elements of second order susceptibilities

Table D2. Nonzero elements of second order susceptibilities of *mmm*, *mmm̲*, and *m̲m̲m* point groups. Classical subgroups are given in parentheses.

Point group	*mmm*, D_{2h}		*mmm̲* (*mm2*, C_{2v})		*m̲m̲m* (*2/m*, C_{2h})	
Principal axis of rotation	x, y, or z		x		y	
Tensor type	Polar	Axial	Polar	Axial	Polar	Axial
Time-invariant (*i*-type)	0	$\chi)^*+(\text{-})$, $\chi)+^*(\text{-})$, $\chi^*+)(\text{-})$, $\chi^*)+(\text{-})$, $\chi+)^*(\text{-})$, $\chi+^*)(\text{-})$	0	$\chi)^*+(\text{-})$, $\chi)+^*(\text{-})$, $\chi^*+)(\text{-})$, $\chi^*)+(\text{-})$, $\chi+)^*(\text{-})$, $\chi+^*)(\text{-})$	0	$\chi)^*+(\text{-})$, $\chi)+^*(\text{-})$, $\chi^*+)(\text{-})$, $\chi^*)+(\text{-})$, $\chi+)^*(\text{-})$, $\chi+^*)(\text{-})$
Timenoninvariant (*c*-type)	0	$\chi)^*+(\text{-})$, $\chi)+^*(\text{-})$, $\chi^*+)(\text{-})$, $\chi^*)+(\text{-})$, $\chi+)^*(\text{-})$, $\chi+^*)(\text{-})$	$\chi))))(\text{-})$, $\chi)^{**}(\text{-})$, $\chi)++(\text{-})$, $\chi^*)^*(\text{-})$, $\chi^{**})(\text{-})$, $\chi+)+(\text{-})$, $\chi++)(\text{-})$	0	0	$\chi^{***}(\text{-})$, $\chi^*))(\text{-})$, $\chi)^*)(\text{-})$, $\chi))^*(\text{-})$, $\chi^*++(\text{-})$, $\chi+^*+(\text{-})$, $\chi++^*(\text{-})$

Table D3. Simplified table of nonzero elements of second order susceptibilities assuming backscattering geometry and ignoring all terms containing z component.

Point group	mmm, D_{2h}		$mm\underline{m}$ ($mm2$, C_{2v})		$\underline{mm}m$ ($2/m$, C_{2h})	
Principal axis of rotation	x, y, or z		x		y	
Tensor type	Polar	Axial	Polar	Axial	Polar	Axial
Time-invariant (i-type)	0	0	0	0	0	0
Time-noninvariant (c-type)	0	0	$\chi_{)))}(\text{-})$, $\chi_{)**}(\text{-})$, $\chi_{*)*}(\text{-})$, $\chi_{**)}(\text{-})$	0	0	$\chi_{***}(\text{-})$, $\chi_{*))}(\text{-})$, $\chi_{)*)}(\text{-})$, $\chi_{))*}(\text{-})$

Table D4. Nonzero elements of second order susceptibilities of _mm_2 point group.

Point group $\qquad$ _mm_2, $(2, C_2)$ $\qquad\qquad\qquad\qquad$ _mm_2, $(2, C_2)$

	y			y	
	Polar	Axial		Polar	Axial
Tensor type					
Time-invariant (_i_-type)	$\chi^{***}(\text{-})$, $\chi^{*))}(\text{-})$, $\chi^{)*)}(\text{-})$, $\chi^{))*}(\text{-})$, $\chi^{*++}(\text{-})$, $\chi^{+*+}(\text{-})$, $\chi^{++*}(\text{-})$	$\chi^{)*+}(\text{-})$, $\chi^{)+*}(\text{-})$, $\chi^{*+)}(\text{-})$, $\chi^{*)+}(\text{-})$, $\chi^{+)*}(\text{-})$, $\chi^{+*)}(\text{-})$	$\rightarrow$ Ignore elements with _z_ component	$\chi^{***}(\text{-})$, $\chi^{*))}(\text{-})$, $\chi^{)*)}(\text{-})$, $\chi^{))*}(\text{-})$	0
Time-noninvariant (_c_-type)	$\chi^{)*+}(\text{-})$, $\chi^{)+*}(\text{-})$, $\chi^{*+)}(\text{-})$, $\chi^{*)+}(\text{-})$, $\chi^{+)*}(\text{-})$, $\chi^{+*)}(\text{-})$	$\chi^{***}(\text{-})$, $\chi^{*))}(\text{-})$, $\chi^{)*)}(\text{-})$, $\chi^{))*}(\text{-})$, $\chi^{*++}(\text{-})$, $\chi^{+*+}(\text{-})$, $\chi^{++*}(\text{-})$		0	$\chi^{***}(\text{-})$, $\chi^{*))}(\text{-})$, $\chi^{)*)}(\text{-})$, $\chi^{))*}(\text{-})$

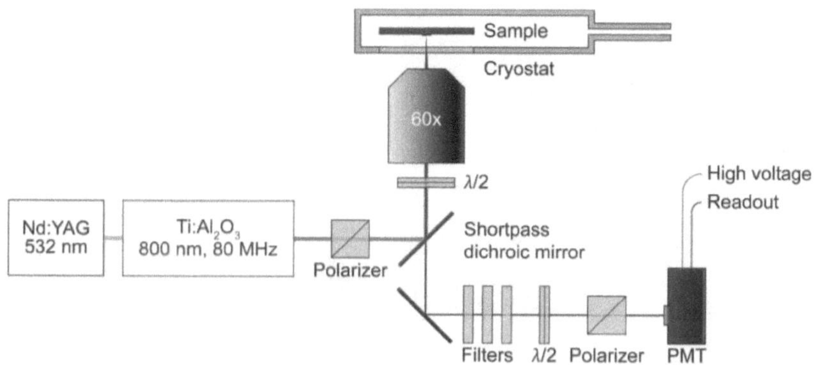

Figure D8. Schematics of SHG microscopy.

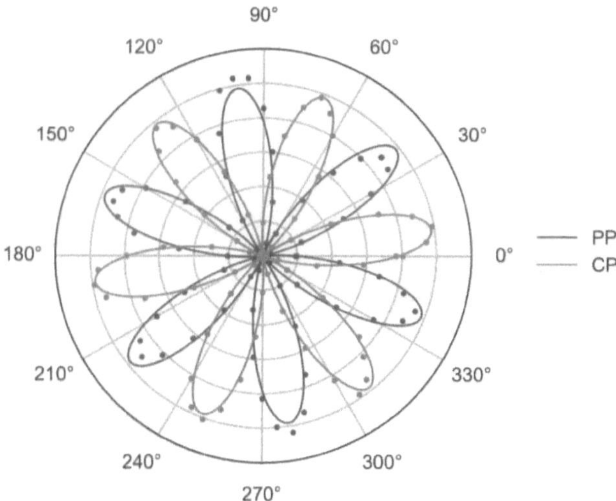

Figure D9. Polarization resolved SHG of MoS$_2$ monolayer.

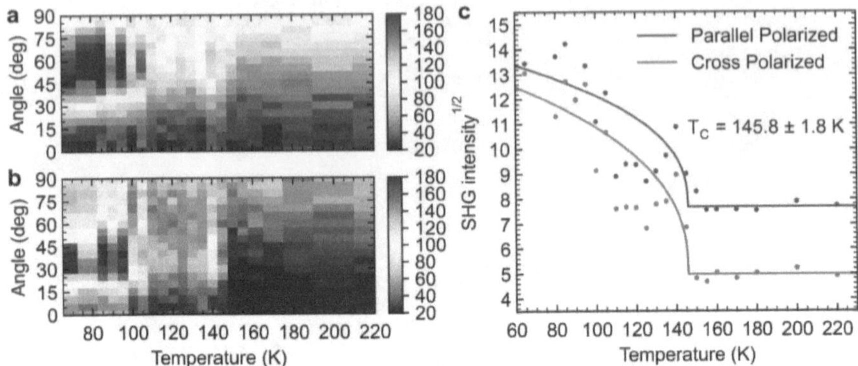

Figure D10. **(a)** Parallel-polarized and **(b)** cross-polarized temperature-dependent SHG for a CrSBr monolayer. Only 0° to 90° range is measured. **(c)** Square root of SHG intensity as a function of temperature. Fitting with $\chi^{(\cdot)} \propto (1 - T/T)$ gives 146.5 K Curie temperature.

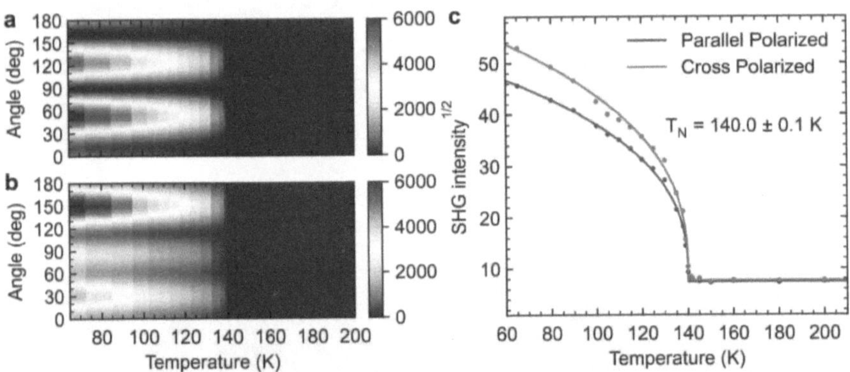

Figure D11. **(a)** Parallel-polarized and **(b)** cross-polarized temperature-dependent SHG for a CrSBr bilayer. **(c)** Square root of SHG intensity as a function of temperature. Fitting with $\chi^{(\cdot)} \propto (1 - T/T)$ gives 140.3 K Néel temperature.

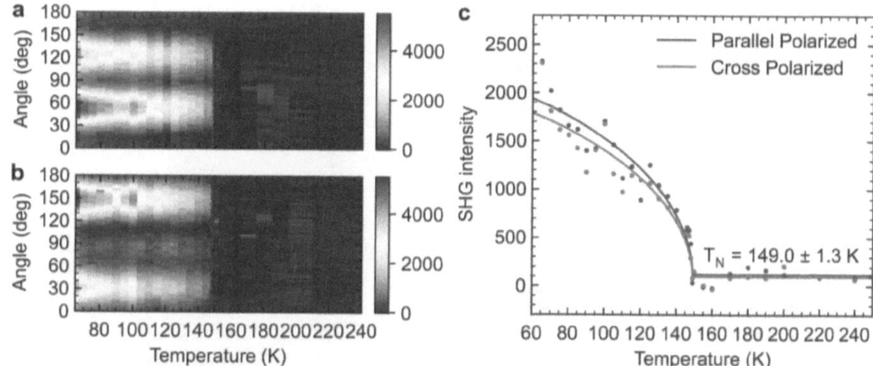

Figure D12. (a) Parallel-polarized and **(b)** cross-polarized temperature-dependent SHG for a different CrSBr bilayer sample. **(c)** Square root of SHG intensity as a function of temperature. Fitting with $\chi^{(\cdot)} \propto (1 - T/T)$ gives 149.0 K Néel temperature.

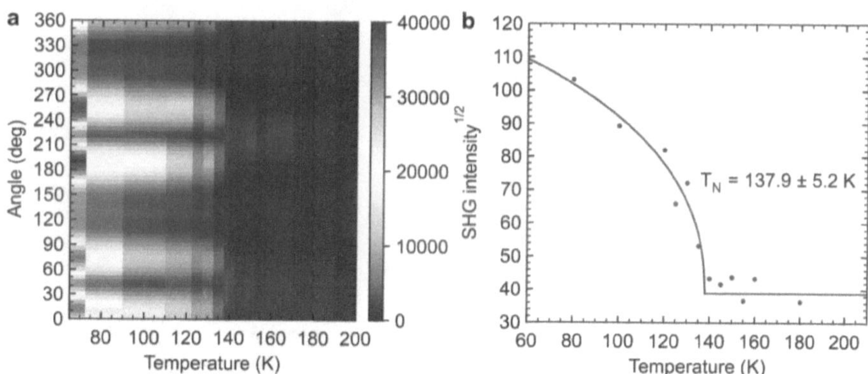

Figure D13. (a) Cross-polarized temperature-dependent SHG for a CrSBr 6 layer sample. **(b)** Square root of SHG intensity as a function of temperature. Fitting with $\chi^{(\cdot)} \propto (1 - T/T)$ gives 137.9 K Néel temperature.

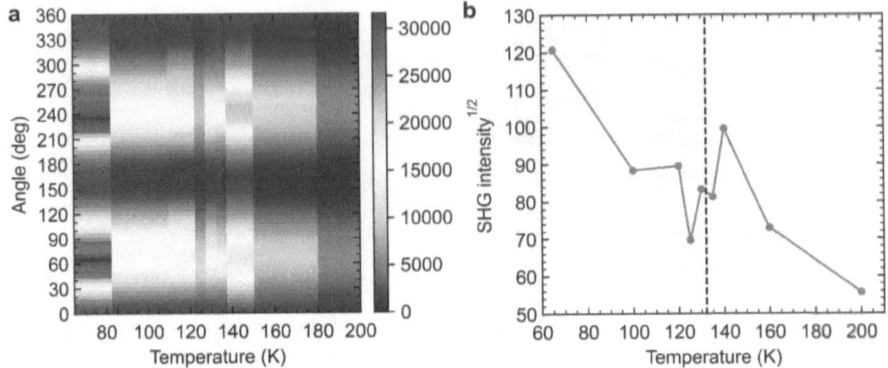

Figure D14. (a) Cross-polarized temperature-dependent SHG for a CrSBr thin bulk sample. **(b)** Square root of SHG intensity as a function of temperature gas a derivative shape across $T_N = 132$ K.

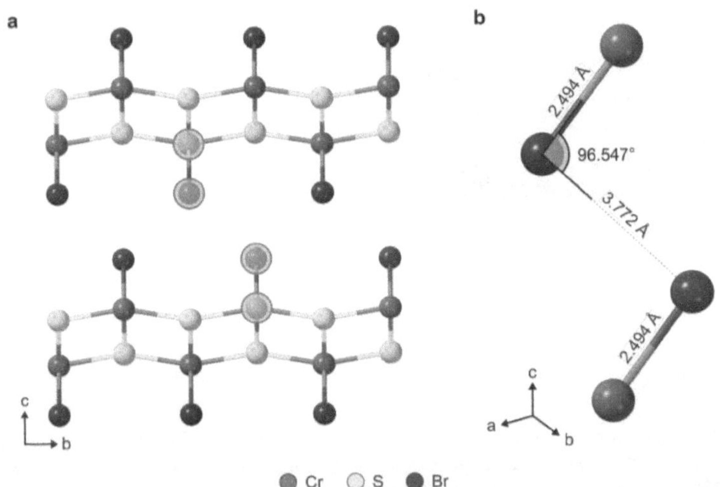

Figure D15. Interlayer geometry and magnetic coupling (a) CrSBr bilayer structure viewed along the crystallographic a-axis. The interlayer magnetic interaction is primarily antiferromagnetic super-superexchange (SSE) of Cr-Br$\cdots$Br-Cr, exemplified by the atoms enclosed within red circles. (b) The four circled atoms from (a) viewed from a direction perpendicular to the plane containing all four atoms. These four atoms are the only symmetrically unique combination that have geometric configuration and close enough distances to host SSE in the intrinsic stacking. Cr-Br-Br angle is 96.547°, suggesting antiferromagnetic interlayer interaction.

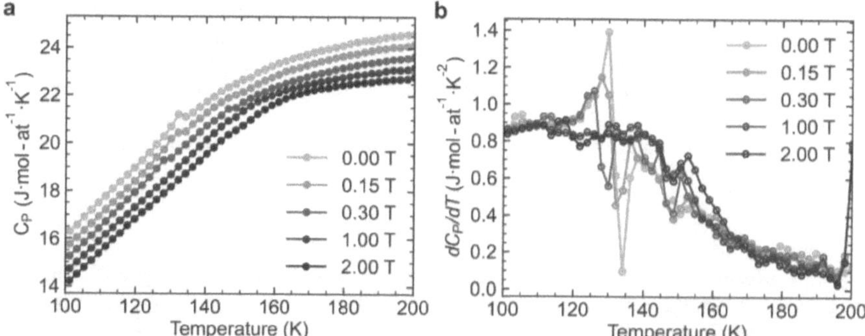

Figure D16. (a) Specific heat capacity of CrSBr at various external magnetic fields. Curves are vertically offset by 0.5 for clarity. At 0 T, a sharp peak at 132 K correspond to the bulk Néel temperature. (b) First derivative of heat capacity to show onset ~160 K indicating local magnetic transition.

D.10 References

1. J. Beck, Über Chalkogenidhalogenide des Chroms Synthese, Kristallstruktur und Magnetismus von Chromsulfidbromid, CrSBr. *Z. Anorg. Allg. Chem.* **585**, 157 (1990).
2. R. C. Clark, J. S. Reid, The analytical calculation of absorption in multifaceted crystals. *Acta Crystallogr., Sect. A: Found. Crystallogr.* **51**, 887 (1995).
3. Rigaku Oxford Diffraction, CrysAlisPro Version 1.171.38.46 (2015).
4. G. M. Sheldrick, Crystal structure refinement with SHELXL. *Acta Crystallogr., Sect. C: Struct. Chem.* **71**, 3 (2015).
5. O. V. Dolomanov, L. J. Bourhis, R. J. Gildea, J. A. K. Howard, H. Puschmann, OLEX2: a complete structure solution, refinement and analysis program. *J. Appl. Crystallogr.* **42**, 339 (2009).
6. O. A. Ajayi, J. V. Ardelean, G. D. Shepard, J. Wang, A. Antony, T. Taniguchi, K. Watanabe, T. F. Heinz, S. Strauf, X. Y. Zhu, J. C. Hone, Approaching the intrinsic photoluminescence linewidth in transition metal dichalcogenide monolayers. *2D Mater.* **4**, 031011 (2017).
7. N. Kumar, S. Najmaei, Q. N. Cui, F. Ceballos, P. M. Ajayan, J. Lou, H. Zhao, Second harmonic microscopy of monolayer MoS2. *Phys. Rev. B* **87**, 161403(R) (2013).
8. Y.-R. Shen, *The principles of nonlinear optics.* (Wiley-Interscience, New York, 1984).
9. Y. Li, Y. Rao, K. F. Mak, Y. You, S. Wang, C. R. Dean, T. F. Heinz, Probing symmetry properties of few-layer MoS2 and h-BN by optical second-harmonic generation. *Nano Lett.* **13**, 3329 (2013).
10. M. Fiebig, D. Frohlich, B. B. Krichevtsov, R. V. Pisarev, Second harmonic generation and magnetic-dipole-electric-dipole interference in antiferromagnetic Cr2O3. *Phys. Rev. Lett.* **73**, 2127 (1994).

11. M. Matsubara, C. Becher, A. Schmehl, J. Mannhart, D. G. Schlom, M. Fiebig, Optical second- and third-harmonic generation on the ferromagnetic semiconductor europium oxide. *J. Appl. Phys.* **109**, 07C309 (2011).

12. D. Sa, R. Valentí, C. Gros, A generalized Ginzburg-Landau approach to second harmonic generation. *Eur. Phys. J. B* **14**, 301 (2000).

13. P. S. Pershan, Nonlinear Optical Properties of Solids: Energy Considerations. *Phys. Rev.* **130**, 919 (1963).

14. M. Fiebig, D. Frohlich, T. Lottermoser, V. V. Pavlov, R. V. Pisarev, H. J. Weber, Second harmonic generation in the centrosymmetric antiferromagnet NiO. *Phys. Rev. Lett.* **87**, 137202 (2001).

15. M. A. McGuire, G. Clark, S. Kc, W. M. Chance, G. E. Jellison, V. R. Cooper, X. Xu, B. C. Sales, Magnetic behavior and spin-lattice coupling in cleavable van der Waals layered CrCl3 crystals. *Phys. Rev. Mater.* **1**, 014001 (2017).

Appendix E: Additional Data for Chapter 6

E.1 Methods

E.1.1 Chromium sulfur halide

See Chapter 2 for synthetic details.

E.1.2 Transport device fabrication

See C.1.5 for methods used here

E.1.3 Magnetrometry

See C.1.6 for methods used here

Table E1: SCXRD comparing the CrSBr and the chloride substituted analogues

Crystal	CrSBr	CrSBr$_{.83}$Cl$_{.17}$	CrSBr$_{.67}$Cl$_{.33}$
Formula mass	163.97	156.91	149.29
Color, habit	Shiny black, needle	Shiny black, needle	Shiny black, needle
Crystal system	orthorhombic	orthorhombic	orthorhombic
Space group	*Pmmn*	*Pmmn*	*Pmmn*
Z	1	1	1
a (Å)	4.7379	4.7498	4.7589
b (Å)	3.5138	3.4882	3.6507(2)
c (Å)	7.9271	7.8623	7.8054
α (°)	90	90	90
β (°)	90	90	90
γ (°)	90	90	90
Temperature (K)	100	100	100
Volume (Å^3)	131.28	130.7	129.57
D_{calc} (g / cm^3)	4.148	4.1664	4.6133
Radiation	Cu Kα = 1.54184	Mo Kα = .71073	Mo Kα = .71073

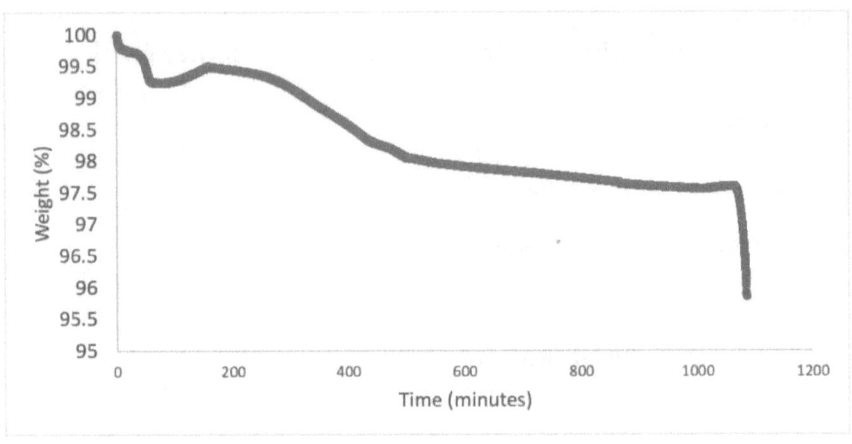

Figure E. 1 TGA of CrSBr under O$_2$ atmosphere

Appendix F: Additional Data for Chapter 7

F.1 Methods

F.1.1 Sample preparation and characterization

We synthesized single crystal the procedure outline in Chapter 2. The long axis of bulk needle crystals of CrSBr has been correlated to the a crystal axis by x-ray diffraction experiments. Bulk crystals were exfoliated by first cleaving them on tape with a fixed crystal orientation, then transferring them mechanically on an Si/SiO_2 substrate passivated by 1-dodecanol[10]. The orientation of the crystals on the tape transfers to the exfoliated crystals, allowing for the crystal orientation of exfoliated samples to be identified. Samples were handled and transported entirely in an oxygen and moisture-free environment (both less than 1 ppm).

F.1.2 Optical spectroscopy

Magnetic field dependence measurements were carried out in a custom closed-cycle cryostat equipped with a 3-axis vector magnet. Sample crystal axes were aligned visually to the vector magnet axes to within 2° along all directions. RMCD measurements were performed using non-resonant 633 nm laser light with quarter-wave modulation from a photoelastic modulator, focused to a spot size of ~ 2 µm on the sample by an aspheric singlet lens. Unless otherwise indicated, PL and reflectance measurements were carried out at a sample temperature of 5±1 K. Excitation for magneto-PL measurements was from a 633 nm laser at a power of 10 µW using a beam spot size of ~ 1 µm. For reflectance spectroscopy, a thermal white light source was employed. Spectra were measured using a CCD array following dispersal by a 500 mm spectrometer. Temperature-dependent PL experiment was performed with a 633 nm HeNe laser as excitation source and on-sample power of 200 µW. Emission was collected with a Princeton Instruments PyLoN-IR and SpectraPro HRS-300.

F.1.3 First-Principles Calculations

The mean-field starting point of the GW calculations uses density functional calculations (DFT) within the spin-polarized generalized gradient approximation (GGA), performed using the Quantum ESPRESSO package[23]. We employed norm-conserving pseudopotentials, with a plane-wave energy cutoff of 85 Ry. In the structural relaxation, we included dispersion corrections within the D2 formalism to account for the van der Waals interactions[24]. The structure was fully relaxed until the force on each atom was smaller than 0.01 eV/Å. The calculated lattice constants along the a and b axes are 3.5 Å and 4.7 Å, respectively, in agreement with experimental results[10]. The calculated interlayer distance is 8.1 Å in bilayer. The scalar-relativistic and full-relativistic band structures show little differences near the VBM or CBM. The GW[25] calculations were carried out using the BerkeleyGW package[26] at the G_0W_0 level. The supercell in the monolayer and bilayer calculations uses out-of-plane lattice constants of 16 Å and 28 Å. A truncated Coulomb interaction is employed along the out-of-plane direction to avoid interactions between the CrSBr layers and its periodic images. In the calculation of the electron self-energy, the dielectric matrix was constructed with a cutoff energy of 35 Ry. The dielectric matrix and the self-energy were calculated on an $8 \times 6 \times 1$ k-grid. 10 subsampling points along the in-plane diagonal of the supercell are included in the calculation of the dielectric function[27]. A static remainder approach is used, together with 1,700 bands in the bilayer calculation[28]. These parameters lead to a converged quasiparticle bandgap within 0.1 eV. The exciton energy levels and wavefunctions are calculated using the GW-BSE methods[29]. The exciton interaction kernel is calculated on a 32 x 24 x 1 k-grid in bilayer, which converges the exciton binding energy to within 0.1 eV, similar to previous report on CrI_3.[30]

F.1.4 Calculations

The exciton wavefunction of a selected excited state $|S\rangle$ can be casted into:

$$\Psi^S(\mathbf{r}_e, \mathbf{r}_h) = \sum_{cv\mathbf{k}} A^S_{cv\mathbf{k}} \psi_{c\mathbf{k}}(\mathbf{r}_e) \psi^*_{v\mathbf{k}}(\mathbf{r}_h)$$

In Fig. 6.3 of the main text, the hole coordinate $\mathbf{r}_l$ is fixed at certain point of the bottom layer, with the electron coordinate $\mathbf{r}_i$ running over a real-space mesh in the supercell. $A^P_{MN\mathbf{k}}$ describes the $k$space exciton envelope function for the exciton state $|S\rangle$ in the quasiparticle state representation. c, v, and $\mathbf{k}$ are the conduction-band, valence-band, and k-point indices, respectively. To characterize the spatial distributions of exciton wavefunction with hole fixed in all possible spots in the bottom layer, the integral of the wavefunction module square $\rho^P(\mathbf{r}_i)$ is evaluated by:

$$\rho^S(\mathbf{r}_e) = \int_{\mathbf{r}_h \in B} \Psi^S(\mathbf{r}_e, \mathbf{r}_h) \Psi^{S*}(\mathbf{r}_e, \mathbf{r}_h) d\mathbf{r}_h$$

where $\mathbf{r}_l$ runs over the bottom layer as the location of the hole may result in different electron wavefunction distributions in the FM bilayer. As $\int_{\mathbf{r}_h \in B} \psi^*_{v\mathbf{k}}(\mathbf{r}_h) \psi_{N\mathbf{z}\mathbf{k}\mathbf{z}}(\mathbf{r}_j) d\mathbf{r}_j = 0,\ \forall \mathbf{k} \neq \mathbf{k}^\wedge$ for two-dimensional materials, $\rho^P(\mathbf{r}_i)$ may be rewritten as:

$$\rho^S(\mathbf{r}_e) = \sum_{cvc'v'\mathbf{k}} A^S_{cv\mathbf{k}} A^{S*}_{cv\mathbf{k}} \psi_{c\mathbf{k}}(\mathbf{r}_e) \psi^*_{c'\mathbf{k}}(\mathbf{r}_e) \int_{\mathbf{r}_h \in B} \psi^*_{v\mathbf{k}}(\mathbf{r}_h) \psi_{v'\mathbf{k}}(\mathbf{r}_h) d\mathbf{r}_h$$

which can be obtained from GW-BSE calculations. Therefore, the ratio η^P of the sum of $\rho^P(\mathbf{r}_l)$ in the top layer to that in the bottom layer is used to characterize the layer-resolved spatial distributions of exciton wavefunction :

$$\eta^S = \frac{\int_{\mathbf{r}_e \in T} \rho^S(\mathbf{r}_e) d\mathbf{r}_e}{\int_{\mathbf{r}_e \in B} \rho^S(\mathbf{r}_e) d\mathbf{r}_e}$$

where $\mathbf{r}_l$ runs over the top and bottom layers, respectively. Here the bottom layer refers to the bottom half of the supercell and the top layer refers to the top half of the supercell. The calculated η^P is $\sim 0.5\%$ in AFM bilayer and $\sim 50\%$ in FM bilayer, which confirms that the electron is localized in the same layer as the hole in AFM bilayer and can delocalize over both layers in FM bilayer.

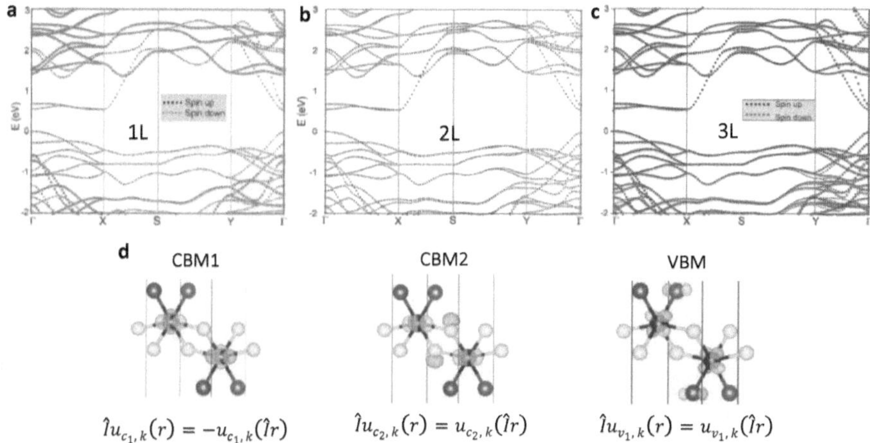

$$\hat{I}u_{c_1,k}(r) = -u_{c_1,k}(\hat{I}r) \qquad \hat{I}u_{c_2,k}(r) = u_{c_2,k}(\hat{I}r) \qquad \hat{I}u_{v_1,k}(r) = u_{v_1,k}(\hat{I}r)$$

Figure F.1 | Electronic properties of layered CrSBr a-c, DFT band structures *without GW correction* for 1-3 layer CrSBr, respectively, in their AFM states. Majority spins are shown in black, and minority spins in red in odd-numbered layers. In the case of the even-numbered layers such as the bilayer, spin-up and spin-down bands are degenerate. Due to this electronic decoupling, there is no significant thickness dependence to the calculated band structure. We note the presence of a second conduction band with a local minimum at Γ (CBM2), which is approximately 40 meV higher in energy than the global conduction band minimum (CBM1) at Γ in the GW calculations depicted in main text fig. 1c. **d,** Diagrams depicting the orbital composition of CBM1, CBM2, and the valence band maximum (VBM). The transformation of the wavefunction $u_{0,1}(r)$ under spatial inversion (I) is noted below each diagram. Based on the parity and spin of the band extrema, the transition between VBM and CBM1 is allowed, but the transition between VBM and CBM2 is dipole forbidden. However, by reduction of symmetry (e.g. by an asymmetric dielectric environment), the VBM to CBM2 transition could be brightened, offering a possible explanation for the presence of multiple exciton resonances near 1.35 eV in the CrSBr photoluminescence and reflectance spectra (as shown in main text figures 3 and 4, and in the supplementary figures that follow).

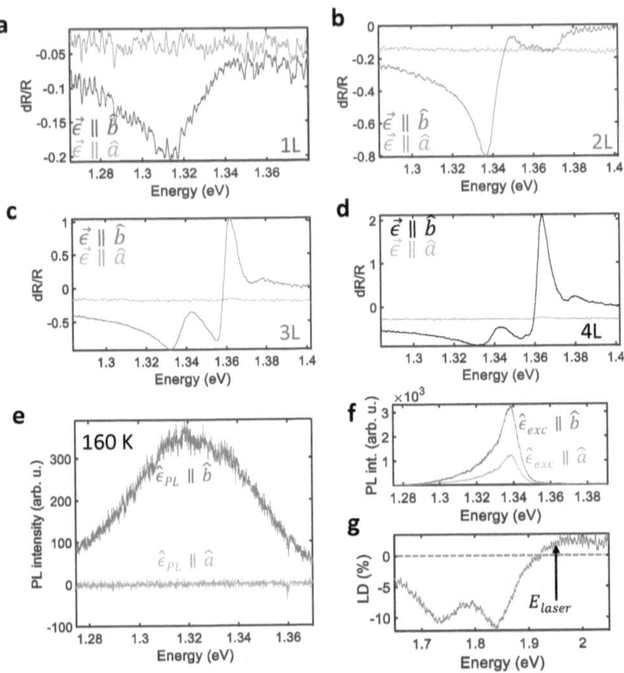

Figure F.2 | Layer-dependent excitons with optical anisotropy
a-d, Polarization-resolved differential reflectance spectra of 1-4 L CrSBr in the vicinity of the lowest energy exciton resonance. All observed resonances are fully polarized along the b direction. **e,** Polarization-resolved PL of bilayer CrSBr above the magnetic transition temperature. The degree of polarization remains near 100%, showing that the polarization is not connected to magnetic order. We note the emergence of multiple strong resonances in multilayer samples and refer to the main text for discussion of these new spectral features. **f,** PL excitation polarization dependence, with PL collected along the b-axis and the excitation polarization along the a- and b-axis, demonstrating the existence of an excitation selection rule. The degree of excitation polarization dependence is around 50%, far greater than the degree of linear dichroism (LD) (**g**) at the laser energy.

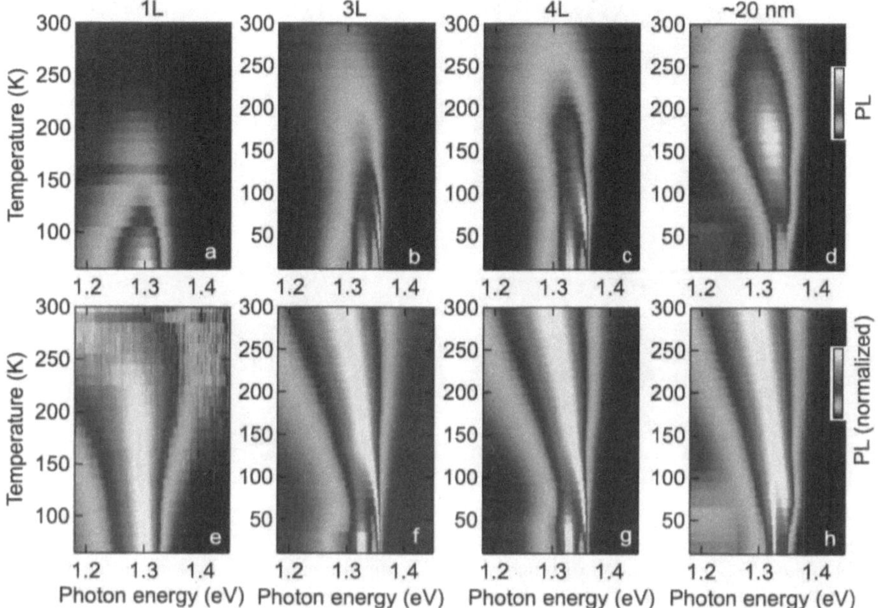

Figure F.3 Temperature dependent PL Temperature-dependent photoluminescence (PL) spectra from a) 1L, b) 3L, c) 4 L, d) thin bulk CrSBr flakes. The bottom panels show corresponding PL spectra with peak intensity normalized at each temperature: e) 1L, f) 3L, g) 4 L, h) thin bulk CrSBr flakes.

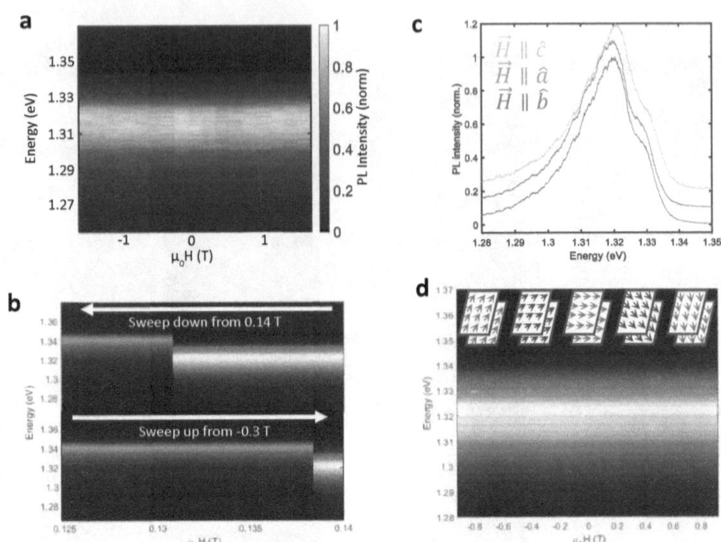

Figure F.4 | Magneto-PL of monolayer and bilayer CrSBr

a, Monolayer PL as a function of magnetic field along the hard axis, showing no response. **b,** Bidirectional magneto-PL sweep of bilayer CrSBr. The spin-flip transition shows hysteretic behavior, with slightly different critical fields for the different sweep directions. **d,** Bilayer PL as a function of magnetic field along the intermediate axis in the presence of a 0.3 T easy-axis field which initializes the bilayer into a field-induced FM state.

234

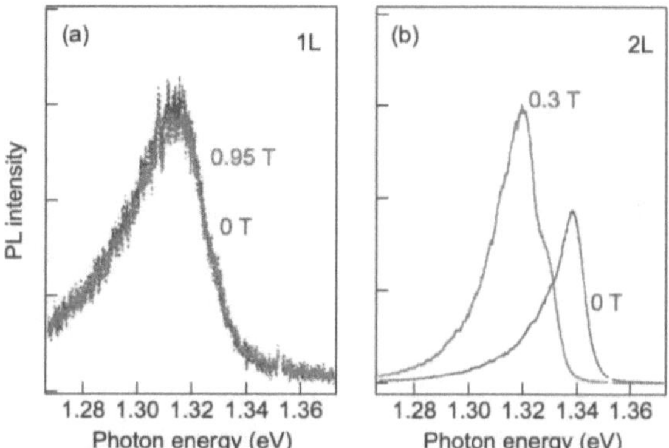

Figure F.5 Magneto-PL spectra of monolayer and bilayer CrSBr at selected B fields Field dependent PL spectra for (a) monolayer and (b) bilayer CrSBr at the indicated magnetic fields along the easy axis. Monolayer: 0.0 T (blue) and 0.95 T (red); Bilayer: 0.0 T (blue) and 0.0.3 T (red). Note that the PL intensities from the monolayer in (a) are one-order of magnitude lower than those from the bilayer in (b). The PL peak widths from the monolayer are also broader than those from the bilayer. We find that the monolayer sample is more susceptible to degradation with time than the bilayer or thicker samples are, especially exposed to the ambient. We attribute the lower PL intensity and broader peak width in the monolayer as compared to the bilayer to higher defect density in the former.

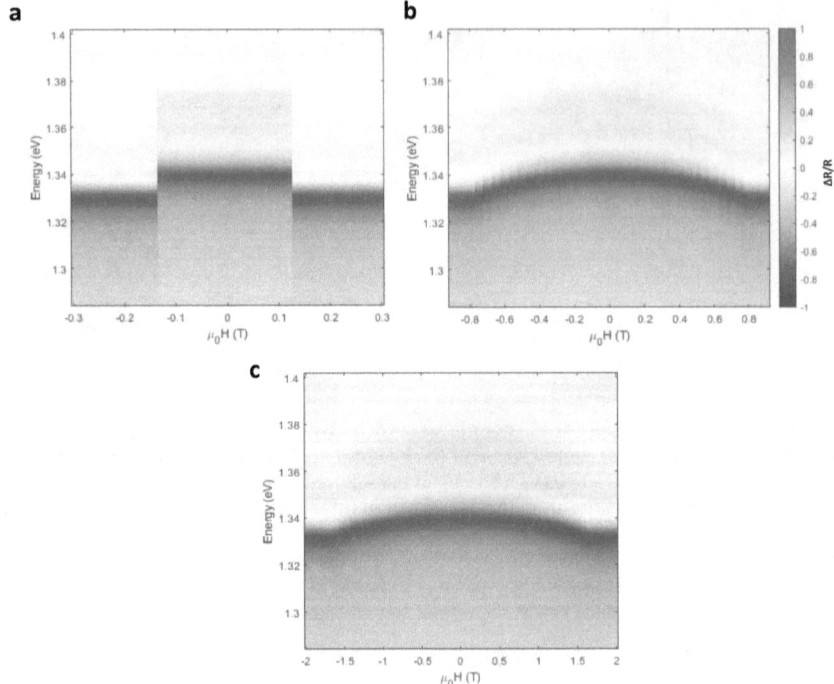

Figure F.6 Bilayer magneto-reflectance spectroscopy
a-c, Differential reflectance of bilayer CrSBr as a function of easy, intermediate, and hard axis magnetic field (respectively).

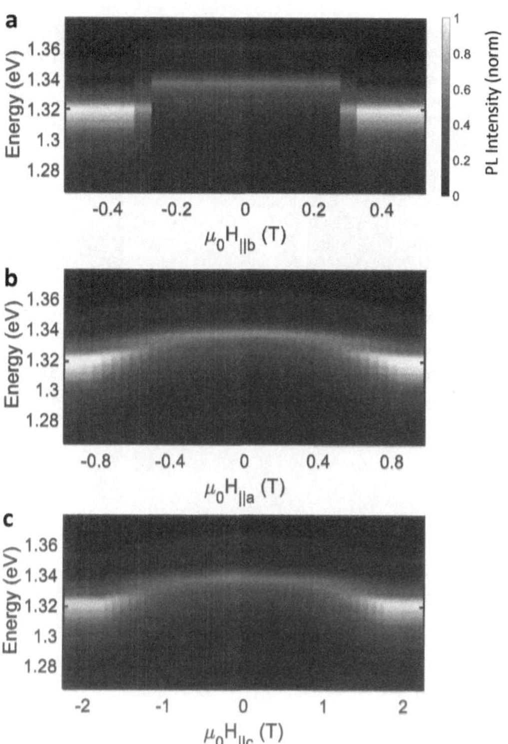

Figure F.7 | Trilayer magneto-PL
a-c, Magneto-PL measurements of trilayer CrSBr with magnetic field along the easy, intermediate, and hard axes, respectively.

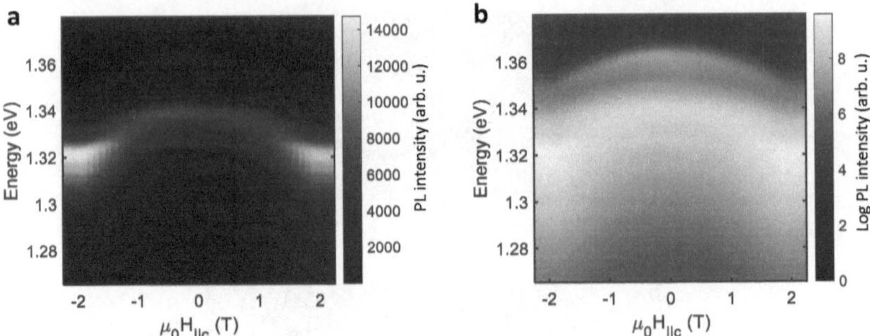

Figure F.8 | Fourlayer hard axis magneto-PL
a-b, Magneto-PL measurement of fourlayer CrSBr with magnetic field along the hard axis. Intensity is plotted in linear and log scales, respectively. The logarithmic scale emphasizes the weaker, higher energy PL features.

F.1.3 References

1. Giannozzi, P. *et al.* QUANTUM ESPRESSO: a modular and open-source software project for quantum simulations of materials. *J. Phys. Condens. Matter* **21**, 395502 (2009).

2. Grimme, S. Semiempirical GGA-type density functional constructed with a long-range dispersion correction. *J. Comput. Chem.* **27**, 1787–1799 (2006).

3. Telford, E. J. *et al.* Layered Antiferromagnetism Induces Large Negative Magnetoresistance in the van der Waals Semiconductor CrSBr. (2020).

4. Hybertsen, M. S. & Louie, S. G. Electron correlation in semiconductors and insulators: Band gaps and quasiparticle energies. *Phys. Rev. B* **34**, 5390 (1986).

5. Deslippe, J. *et al.* BerkeleyGW: A massively parallel computer package for the calculation of the quasiparticle and optical properties of materials and nanostructures. *Comput. Phys. Commun.* **183**, 1269–1289 (2012).

6. Felipe, H., Qiu, D. Y. & Louie, S. G. Nonuniform sampling schemes of the Brillouin zone for many-electron perturbation-theory calculations in reduced dimensionality. *Phys. Rev. B* **95**, 35109 (2017).

7. Deslippe, J., Samsonidze, G., Jain, M., Cohen, M. L. & Louie, S. G. Coulomb-hole summations and energies for G W calculations with limited number of empty orbitals: A modified static remainder approach. *Phys. Rev. B* **87**, 165124 (2013).

8. Rohlfing, M. & Louie, S. G. Electron-hole excitations and optical spectra from first principles. *Phys. Rev. B* **62**, 4927 (2000).

9. Wu, M., Li, Z., Cao, T. & Louie, S. G. Physical origin of giant excitonic and magneto-optical responses in two-dimensional ferromagnetic insulators. *Nat. Commun.* **10**, 1–8 (2019).

Appendix G: Additional Data for Chapter 8

G.1 Methods

G.1.1 Device Fabrication

The bilayer graphene and CrSBr flakes are mechanically cleaved from their bulk crystals on SiO_2/Si substrates, using adhesive tapes [51]. The bilayer graphene flakes are identified by their optical contrast with respect to the substrate [52]. The thicknesses of the flakes are verified by atomic force microscopy (Supplementary, Sec. 1).

Device D1: Using a dry pick-up technique [53], we transfer the bilayer graphene on the bulk CrSBr flake by a Polycarbonate (PC)-PDMS stamp. The PC is removed in chloroform, followed by annealing in Ar/H_2 atmosphere for 6 hours at 350 C. The preparation of the vdW stack is followed by the fabrication of Al_2O_3 (0.9nm)/Co(30 nm)/Ti(5nm)/Au(40nm) electrodes on the vdW stack by e-beam lithography technique (using PMMA as the e-beam resist). The Ti/Au layers are deposited on the Co layer for mechanical strength of the contacts and air-protection. The exfoliation of all the flakes, the atomic-force microscopy characterisations and the device fabrication are performed under exposure to air (ambient condition) for the time scale of about 7 days.

Device D3 (AHE): The large area bilayer graphene flake on the SiO_2 substrate is initially etched into a Hall-bar geometry in O_2 plasma environment, using a pre-patterned PMMA-membrane as the mask. The etching procedure is followed by mechanical removing of the PMMA membrane, leaving the surface of the graphene flake residue free. The bulk CrSBr flake, initially exfoliated on a PDMS stamp is transferred on the etched graphene, partially covering the Hall bar. Device fabrication is completed by the e-beam lithography of the Ti(5 nm)/Au(100 nm) electrodes, deposited by the e-beam evaporation of the metals in ultra-high vacuum.

G.1.2 Electrical Measurements

Low-frequency (< 20 Hz) lock-in technique with AC current source up to 10 μA is used for the charge and spin transport measurements. For the electrical gating, a Keithley source-meter is used as the DC-voltage source. The sample is measured in Helium atmosphere in a cryostat with a variable temperature insert and a superconducting magnet. For applying the magnetic field in all possible directions (in-plane and out-of-plane) rotatable sample holders are used.

G.1.3 SQUID Measurements

The DC magnetic susceptibility is measured in a Cryogenic R-700X SQUID magnetometer. A single crystal of CrSBr is loaded in a determined orientation with respect to the applied magnetic field and the magnetisation was measured as a function of applied magnetic field.

G.1.4 CrSBr Synthesis

For this methodology, see Chapter 2.

G.2 Computational Methods (First Principle Calculations)

The mean-field starting point of the GW calculations uses density functional calculations (DFT) within the spin-polarized generalized gradient approximation (GGA), performed using the Quantum ESPRESSO package[1]. We employed norm-conserving pseudopotentials, with a plane-wave energy cutoff of 85 Ry. In the structural relaxation, we included dispersion corrections within the D2 formalism to account for the van der Waals interactions[2]. The structure was fully relaxed until the force on each atom was smaller than 0.01 eV/Å. The calculated lattice constants along the a and b axes are 3.5 Å and 4.7 Å, respectively, in agreement with experimental results[3]. The calculated interlayer distance is 8.1 Å in bilayer. The scalar-relativistic and full-relativistic band structures show little differences near the VBM or CBM. The GW[4] calculations were carried out using the BerkeleyGW package[5] at the G_0W_0 level. The supercell in the monolayer and bilayer calculations uses out-of-plane lattice constants of 16 Å and 28 Å. A truncated Coulomb interaction is employed along the out-of-plane direction to avoid interactions between the CrSBr layers and its periodic images. In the calculation of the electron self-energy, the dielectric matrix was constructed with a cutoff energy of 35 Ry. The dielectric matrix and the self-energy were calculated on an $8 \times 6 \times 1$ k-grid. 10 subsampling points along the in-plane diagonal of the supercell are included in the calculation of the dielectric function[6]. A static remainder approach is used, together with 1,700 bands in the bilayer calculation[7]. These parameters lead to a converged quasiparticle bandgap within 0.1 eV. The exciton energy levels and wavefunctions are calculated using the GW-BSE methods[8]. The exciton interaction kernel is calculated on a 32 x 24 x 1 k-grid in bilayer, which converges the exciton binding energy to within 0.1 eV, similar to previous report on CrI_3.[9]

G.3 References

1. Giannozzi, P. *et al.* QUANTUM ESPRESSO: a modular and open-source software project for quantum simulations of materials. *J. Phys. Condens. Matter* **21**, 395502 (2009).
2. Grimme, S. Semiempirical GGA-type density functional constructed with a long-range dispersion correction. *J. Comput. Chem.* **27**, 1787–1799 (2006).
3. Telford, E. J. *et al.* Layered Antiferromagnetism Induces Large Negative Magnetoresistance in the van der Waals Semiconductor CrSBr. *arXiv* (2020).
4. Hybertsen, M. S. & Louie, S. G. Electron correlation in semiconductors and insulators: Band gaps and quasiparticle energies. *Phys. Rev. B* **34**, 5390 (1986).
5. Deslippe, J. *et al.* BerkeleyGW: A massively parallel computer package for the calculation of the quasiparticle and optical properties of materials and nanostructures. *Comput. Phys. Commun.* **183**, 1269–1289 (2012).
6. Felipe, H., Qiu, D. Y. & Louie, S. G. Nonuniform sampling schemes of the Brillouin zone for many-electron perturbation-theory calculations in reduced dimensionality. *Phys. Rev. B* **95**, 35109 (2017).
7. Deslippe, J., Samsonidze, G., Jain, M., Cohen, M. L. & Louie, S. G. Coulomb-hole summations and energies for G W calculations with limited number of empty orbitals: A modified static remainder approach. *Phys. Rev. B* **87**, 165124 (2013).
8. Rohlfing, M. & Louie, S. G. Electron-hole excitations and optical spectra from first

principles. *Phys. Rev. B* **62**, 4927 (2000).

9. Wu, M., Li, Z., Cao, T. & Louie, S. G. Physical origin of giant excitonic and magneto-optical responses in two-dimensional ferromagnetic insulators. *Nat. Commun.* **10**, 1–8 (2019).

Appendix H: Additional Data for Chapter 9

H.1 Methods

H.1.1. Strain cell

In order to apply strain to the samples, we constructed homebuilt strain cells consisting of three piezoelectric actuators glued in parallel to a titanium backing plate and a titanium flexure element. The flexure element consists of a W-shaped outer piece and a rectangular inner block, with a 0.5 mm gap formed between them (see Fig. 8.7A). The outer and inner piezostacks are poled oppositely: applying a positive voltage causes the outer piezostacks to expand and the inner one to contract, thereby opening the gap. This configuration also minimizes built-in thermal strain, as the two sides of the gap move together when cooled. The measurements shown in Figure 7E and Figure H.5 were taken using a Razorbill CS100 strain cell, which uses a similar operating principle.

H.1.2 Sample preparation

In our experiments, pieces of 285 nm SiO_2/Si substrate were glued onto 2D flexure sample plates produced by Razorbill instruments using Stycast 2850 FT epoxy. In order to reduce the effective spring constant of the strained silicon, we chose thin (50 μm) silicon wafers, and cut them into narrow ($\sim$ 300 μm) pillars. The distance between the epoxied ends is $\sim$ 400 μm, giving an effective spring constant of $k = Y\frac{A}{L} \sim 5\frac{N}{\mu m}$, where we used a value of 140 GPa for the Young's modulus of silicon. This value is much lower than the blocking force of the piezostacks, enabling the application of strain.

After the pillar is glued in place, we transferred the strain gauge heterostructure on top of it through a dry-transfer technique using a stamp consisting of a polypropylene carbonate (PPC) film spin coated on top of a polydimethylsiloxane (PDMS) cylinder. Flakes were picked up in the following order: 20-30 nm top hBN, graphene, and > 20 nm CrSBr. The pillar was then aligned with the long axis of the CrSBr flake, which is the crystal a-axis, and then the stack was deposited on top of it.

For suspended samples, large rectangular pieces of the same substrate were glued to the titanium plate and then fractured with a diamond scribe. The fracture produces a gap around ~ 3-5 μm, with near height uniformity on both sides. The sample plate is then screwed down to the strainer, and the thin CrSBr transferred over the gap using the same dry-transfer method. The entire strain apparatus is then loaded into the cryostat for measurement.

H.1.2 Optical Measurements

Optical measurements of the strain gauge heterostructure were performed using the backscattering geometry in a closed-cycle helium cryostat (Opticool by Quantum Design) with a nominal sample temperature of 2.2 K. An objective lens focused 632.8 nm light from a He/Ne laser to a spot size of ~ 1.5 μm. Collected light was then dispersed by a 1200 mm^{-1} groove-density grating and detected with a cooled charge-coupled device (CCD). A laser power of 300 μW was used for the Raman measurements, with integration times of 120 seconds for the graphene and 30 seconds for both the CrSBr and silicon spectra. BragGrate notch filters were utilized to reject Rayleigh scattering down to 5 cm^{-1}. Measurements of the suspended sample presented in Figure 1 were taken in a coldfinger cryostat from Montana Instruments at a sample temperature of ~ 15 K. The data in Figures 2-4 were taken using a vector magnet cryostat from Montana Instruments at a nominal sample temperature of about 5 K with 4 μW of power and dispersed by a 600 mm^{-1}

groove-density grating. To increase the spatial sensitivity of the experiment, a confocal setup with a 50 μW pinhole was used for the PL measurements.

H.1.3 Finite Element Analysis

We used the ANSYS Mechanical 2021 R1 finite element analysis software to calculate and visualize the strain distribution on the top surface of a strained silicon pillar. The model geometry and dimensions match our experimental conditions: the pillar is 50 μm thick, 1 mm long and 300 μm wide. On top of the silicon is a 285nm layer of SiO_2, and underneath are two 10 μm thick pads of Stycast 2850FT epoxy which form a 400μm gap. The contact between materials is modeled via shared topology between each solid. The boundary conditions are set to apply a 5μm displacement to the bottom face of each epoxy pad directed parallel to the pillar's long axis. We use the elastic constants reported in Ref. [27] for the <110> directions of a (100) wafer. To account for the orthotropic elasticity in silicon, we made an additional model which was rotated by 45 degrees such that strain is applied along the [100] axis. The SiO_2 and Stycast layers are modeled with isotropic elasticity with Young's modulus and Poisson's ratio provided by Ref. and Ref. [23] , respectively.

H.1.3 First-Principles Calculations

First-principles calculations of few-layer and bulk CrSBr were performed using density functional theory (DFT) implemented in the Quantum ESPRESSO package[28]. We employed norm-conserving pseudopotentials, with a plane-wave energy cutoff of 85 Ry. In the structural relaxation, we used spin-polarized Perdew–Burke–Ernzerhof exchange-correlation functional (PBE) that included dispersion corrections within the D2 formalism[29] to account for the van der Waals interactions. The structure was fully relaxed until the force on each atom was smaller than

0.002 eV/Å. The calculated equilibrium lattice constants along the a and b axes were 3.5 Å and 4.7 Å, respectively. The calculated interlayer distance was 8.0 Å in the bulk. These results were in excellent agreement with experiments[21]. Applied strain along the intermediate axis was calculated in percentile relative to the equilibrium structure. For each strain, the energy differences between interlayer AFM and FM phases were calculated within the local spin density approximation (LSDA). We note that the calculated value of critical strain can be affected by factors such as the choice pseudopotential used in the calculations. Calculation of the Raman-active phonon modes used the frozen-phonon method.

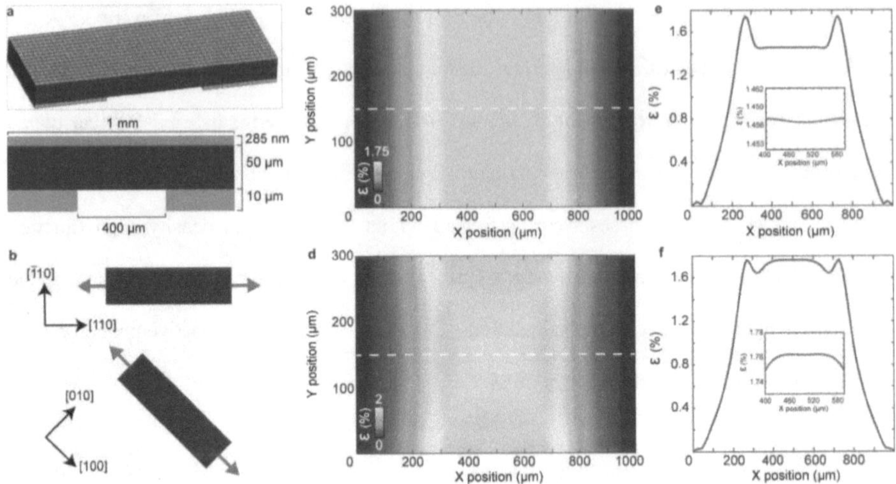

Figure H1 | Finite element analysis of strained silicon pillar. a, Render of silicon pillar geometry with dimensions and mesh used for the model. We use a 1 mm x .3 mm x .05 mm thick silicon pillar (purple), similar to the pillars used in our experiments. A 285 nm layer of SiO_2 is deposited on top of the silicon, and underneath are two 10 μm thick pads of epoxy which form a 400 μm gap. A 5 μm displacement was applied to each side to model the displacement from the piezostacks. **b,** To account for the orthotropic elasticity of silicon, we model the strain in two cases: with the strain applied along the [110] crystal axis (top) and [100] axis (bottom). **c-d,** FEM strain distribution for strain applied along [110] (**c**) and [100] (**d**) crystal axes. **e-f,** Line cut of strain at the center (white dashed line) of **c** and **d**, respectively. Zoom in of the strain distribution at the center of the pillar is inset. The total strain variation is < 0.1% in both cases.

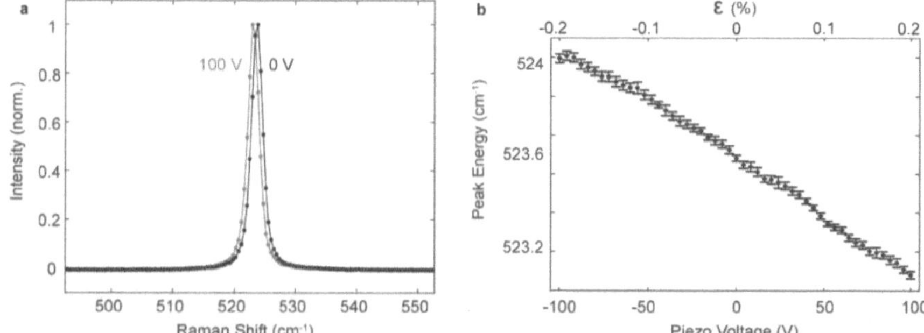

Figure H2 | Strain calibration using silicon Raman scattering. a, Raman spectra of the silicon optical phonon mode with 0 V (black) and 100 V (red) applied to the piezostacks. **b,** Energy of the phonon mode as a function of piezo voltage. The energies are determined by Lorentzian fits with the error bars representing the uncertainty of the fit. The difference of the peak energy with the zero-strain value is multiplied by a previously reported Raman strain shift rate [Ref.] to determine the applied strain (top axis). In order to determine the amount of built-in thermal strain due to sample fabrication and differences in thermal expansion coefficients, we also measured a freestanding silicon chip glued next to the strained chip. Comparing the strained silicon pillar at zero volts to the freestanding chip right next to it, we found that the built-in strain on this particular sample was negligible.

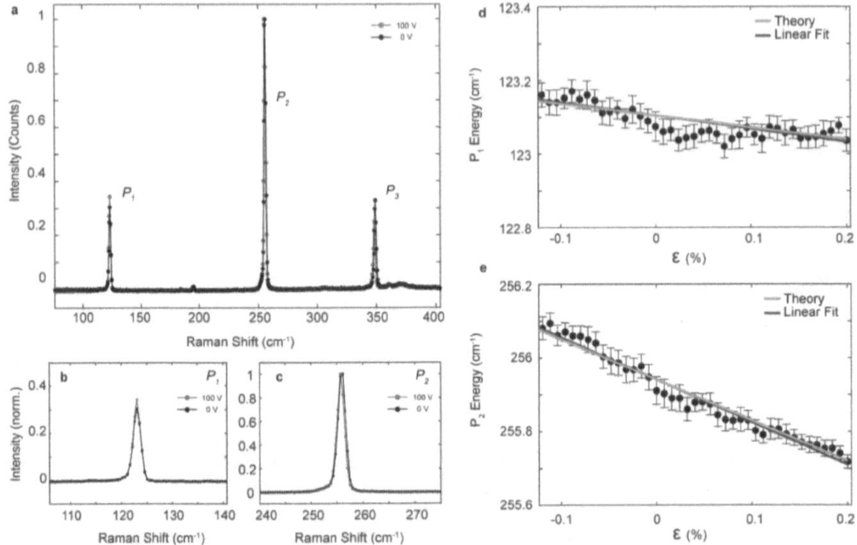

Figure H3: Strain dependent Raman scattering of *P₁* and *P₂*. a, Raman spectrum of the CrSBr flake in the strain gauge heterostructure with 0 V (black) and 100 V (red) applied to the piezostacks. **b-c,** Zoomed in Raman spectra of *P₁* (**b**) and *P₂* (**c**). *P₁* has a barely detectable redshift with the applied voltage, while *P₂* has a larger one. **d-e,** Strain dependence of the energy of peaks *P₁* and *P₂*, respectively. The blue line corresponds to a linear fit of the data while the green line corresponds to the calculated Raman shift rate. The calculated phonon frequency has been shifted vertically to match experimental results at V = 0. The fit and the calculation match each other well.

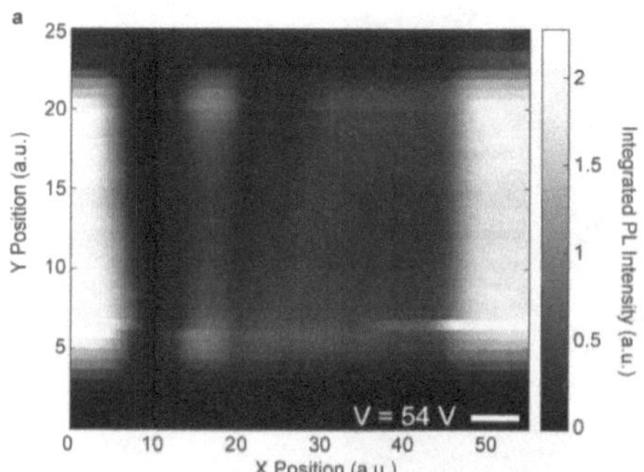

Figure H4: Spatial photoluminescence intensity map of sample S2. a, Spatial map of PL intensity integrated from 1.363 eV to 1.39 eV with 54 V applied to the piezo stacks. This spectral range captures PL from the highest energy exciton in the AFM state, but not in the FM state. That is, the dark regions in the PL map are the highest strained since they are in the FM state, while the brightest regions have the strongest AFM state and thus lowest strain. Scalebar: 10 μm. The data presented in the paper were taken in the center of the high strain region.

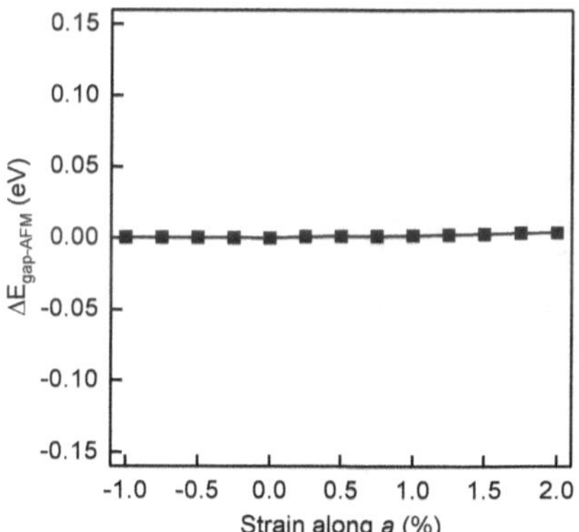

Figure H5 | Strain-dependent band gap. Plot shows the change of the DFT-LDA band gap of bulk CrSBr in the interlayer AFM phase as the strain is applied along a-axis, while b- and c-axes are free to relax. The change of band gap is < 5 meV for < 1% strain.

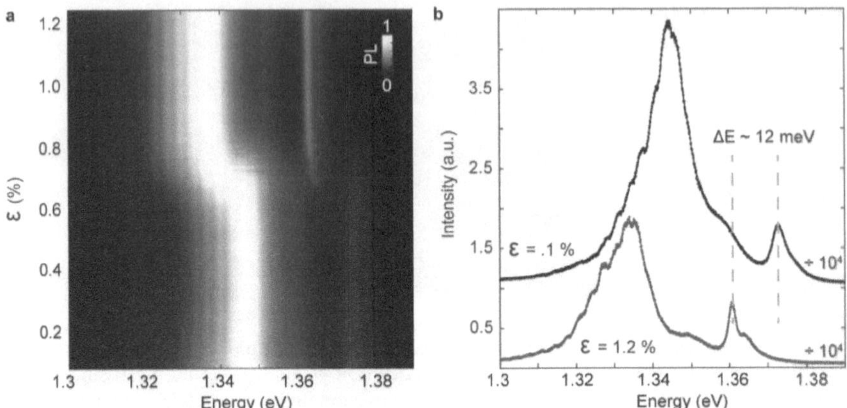

Figure H6 | Strain-induced phase transition in a second suspended sample. a, Strain dependent photoluminescence measurements of a second exfoliated CrSBr sample. The spectra are normalized at each strain. The nominal sample temperature is 15 K. **b,** PL spectra at strain below and above the phase transition reveals a ~ 12 meV redshift between the two.

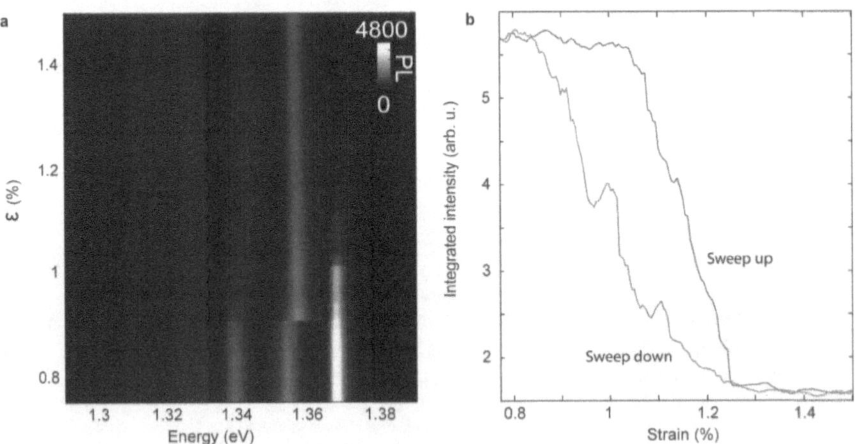

Figure H7 | Hysteresis in the strain-induced magnetic phase transition. a, Intensity plot of photoluminescence as a function of strain as the piezo voltage is swept down from a high strain state. **b,** Integrated intensity of the entire spectral range as the strain is swept up (blue) and down (orange). To account for hysteresis in the piezostacks, we calibrated the strain using Raman sweeps in the same direction.

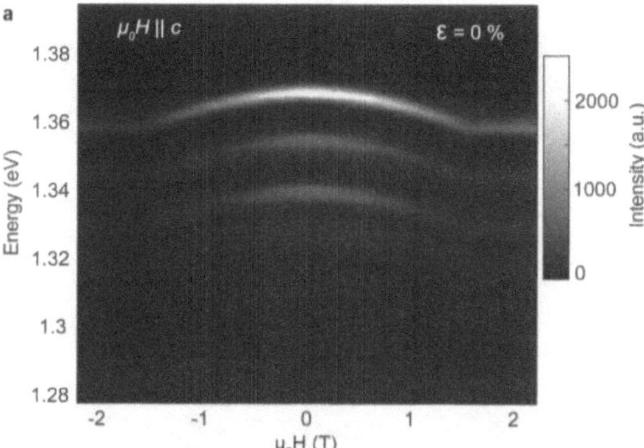

Figure H8 | Magneto-photoluminescence measurements with the field swept along the hard (*c*) axis. a, Magnetic field dependent photoluminescence measurement of unstrained CrSBr as the field is swept along the *c* crystal axis (magnetic hard axis).

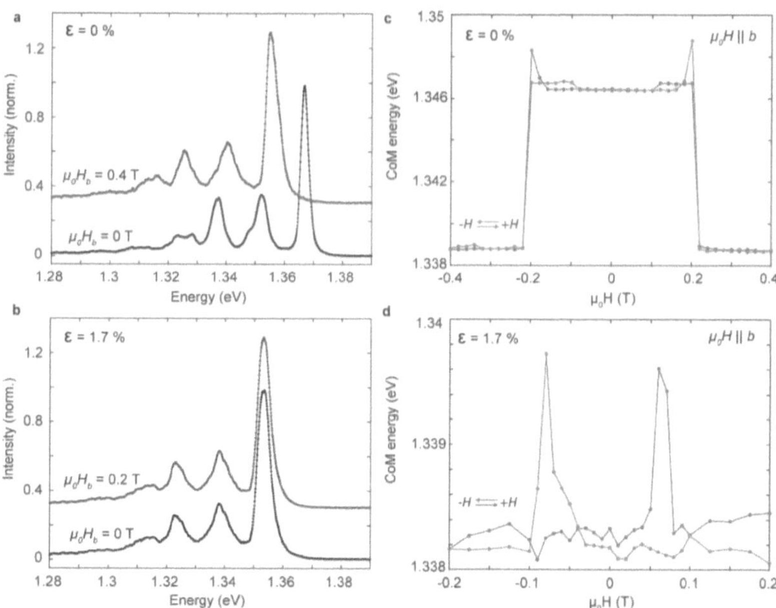

Figure H9 | Comparison of photoluminescence at select magnetic fields and integrated intensity of unstrained and highly strained CrSBr. a-b, Photoluminescence spectrum of the unstrained (**a**) and highly strained (**b**) CrSBr at zero magnetic field $\mu_0 H$ (black) and with a saturating $\mu_0 H$ (blue) applied along the easy *b*-axis. **c-d,** Extracted center of mass (COM) of the entire spectra range as a function of $\mu_0 H \parallel b$-axis in the unstrained (**c**) and highly strained (**d**) samples.

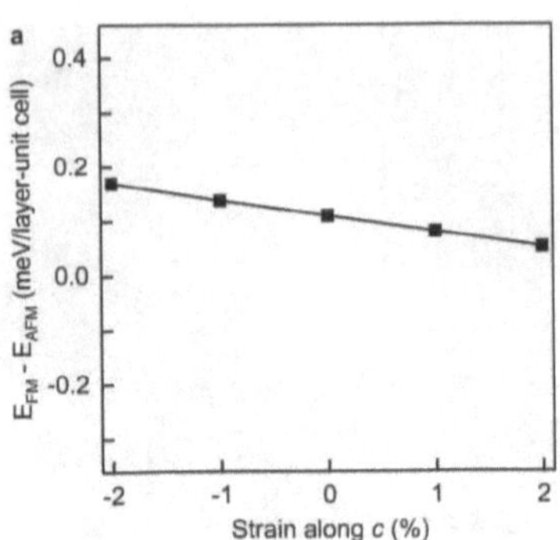

Figure H10: Calculated stacking arrangements of CrSBr and dependence of interlayer exchange on interlayer spacing.

Appendix I: Additional Data for Chapter 10

I.1 Methods

I.1.1 Synthetic details

See Chapter 2 for more details.

I.1.2 SCXRD

See Chapter 2 for more general methods.

Single crystals of $Mo_6S_3Br_6$ grow in needle-like shapes and have anisotropic lengths in three directions. By taking SCXRD on the crystal and comparing the resolved crystal structure to the orientation of the mounted crystal, we were able to identify that c-axis corresponds to the elongated direction of the crystals (Figure I.1). Temperature dependent SC-XRD measurements were carried out in temperature range of 100-300 K with every 10 K interval. To reduce the thermal fluctuations, the sample was stabilized for 15 min after reaching each target temperature. The structure of $Mo_6S_3Br_6$ maintains the orthorhombic phase (*Cmcm* space group) within this temperature range, as demonstrated by the nearly identical diffraction patterns (Figure I.2a-d) along the principal directions at T = 297 K and T = 100 K, respectively. Figure I.2e shows a monotonic increase of the lattice due to thermal expansion. Details of crystallographic data are listed in Table I1.

I.1.3 STM/STS

Experiments were carried out on the freshly cleaved Mo6S3Br6 crystal on the Omicron scanning tunneling microscope at room temperature (292 K) in ultrahigh vacuum (base pressure <

4.0 x 10-10 Torr). Images were obtained in the constant-current mode with an electrochemically etched tungsten tip. To avoid tip artifacts, the STM tip was calibrated on a clean Au (111) surface before all measurements. The differential conductance (dI/dV-V) spectra were performed with a lock-in amplifier at an AC modulation of 10 mV and at a frequency of 861.1 Hz. The corresponding current change was acquired by keeping the tip fixed above the surface with the feedback loop off. dI/dV-V spectra are consistent at various spots on the surface with different tips at the same tunneling conditions.

I1.4. Polarization dependent Raman

Polarization dependent Raman spectroscopy was performed with a Renishaw microscopic Raman spectrometer. Spectra were taken in a backscattering geometry, where the incident and scattered light are both perpendicular to the sample. A 1mW 633 nm He-Ne laser was focused on the $Mo_6S_3Br_6$ surface with ~1 μm spot size. A linear polarizing filter was used in the laser path before the sample for polarization purity, and an additional polarizer was placed between sample and detector to reject cross-polarized light at parallel polarizing configuration. After the polarizing filter within the incident path, a removable half waveplate was placed at a 45° angle between the fast axis and laser polarization, so that the parallel and cross polarizing configurations could be switched with ease. The sample was manually rotated by 15° for each measurement.

I.1.5 Computational details

DFT calculations were performed on the 3D-bulk and 2D phases of $Mo_6S_3Br_6$. The Bravais lattice of the bulk system is orthorhombic with room temperature cell parameter a=17.250 Å, b=6.600 Å, c=11.929 Å, $\alpha = \beta = \gamma = 90$ ° and has 4 formula units (space group 63 – *Cmcm*). Both geometry relaxations and electronic structure calculations were carried out in the primitive cell of $Mo_6S_3Br_6$ (a = b = 9.235 Å, c = 11.929 Å, $\alpha = \beta = 90°$, $\gamma = 41.87°$, 2 formula units). The 2D sheet of $Mo_6S_3Br_6$ was modelled in the supercell approach starting from the primitive cell and by introducing 10 Å of vacuum between in-plane layers.

All calculations were carried out in periodic boundary conditions by using plane waves basis set and pseudopotentials. Converged grid of k-points in the Brillouin zone was adopted throughout calculations. Equilibrium structures was found by using Ultrasoft pseudopotentials and the Perdew-Burke-Ernzherof (PBE) exchange correlation functional[27] by relaxing ions positions until a threshold on forces of 0.001 Ryd/a.u was reached. A cutoff on the plane waves of 40 Ryd (320 Ryd on the charge density) was used. The electronic structure of 3D and 2D systems was further refined by performing single point calculations by using the hybrid HSE06 functional[28] at the PBE relaxed geometries. Hybrid calculations was carried out by using Norm-conserving pseudopotentials with a cutoff on the wavefunction of 70 Ryd (140 Ryd on the Fock grid). All calculations were performed by using the Quantum-Espresso package.[47]

I.2 Effects of Nb on synthesized crystals

In the synthesis, a small amount of Nb leads to the production of large single crystals, which allows us to exfoliate the material and obtain macroscopic flakes that can be manipulated and electrically contacted. $NbBr_5$, formed as orange crystals at the cold end of the tube during the reaction, serves as a chemical vapor transport agent to facilitate the crystal growth.

To investigate the effects of Nb on synthesized crystals, we have characterized the $Mo_6S_3Br_6$ single crystals using a combination of techniques. SC-XRD was used to determine the atomic structure of the material, which is consistent with previous reports (shown in **S1**). The $Mo_6S_3Br_6$

composition obtained from SC-XRD is confirmed by energy dispersive x-ray spectroscopy (EDX; Table I2). Within experimental error, the Mo:S:Br 6.0:2.6:5.6 atomic ratio agrees well with the 6:3:6 composition determined by SC-XRD. X-ray photoelectron spectroscopy (XPS) was used to determine whether any Nb was incorporated into the lattice. Within the detection limit of the instrument, we observe no trace of Nb impurity in the crystals (Figure I.3).

I.3 STM characterized defects

In addition to the surface structure revealed in the high-resolution STM image, we also characterize several types of defects in Figure I.4a, including missing Br atoms or incomplete clusters. Filtered image of Figure I.4a from fast Fourier transform (FFT) is shown in Figure I.4b for better identifying these defects. Three typical defects are highlighted with rectangular boxes in different colors in Figure I.4a & 4b. The most obvious ones are missing clusters, appeared as dark holes with lateral dimension comparable to the size of clusters in the STM image (marked by the dark blue box in Figure I.4a & S4b and in Figure I.4c).The striking height drop (~ 1 nm) across the defects in the line profile agrees well with the size of clusters as well.(Figure I.4e). We also found several Br atoms sitting on the right lateral positions with apparent height lower than their neighboring atoms (marked in a sky-blue box in Figure I.4a & S4b and in Figure I.4f), as illustrated in the line profile (Figure I.4i) along the white line in Figure I.4f. It may result from electronic density of state change or the topological change induced by the defects underneath the top layer as well as the incomplete cluster linked to the Br atoms. Besides, a shadow dark hole highlighted in the STM image (in the light blue box in Figure I.4a & S4b) corresponds to the incomplete clusters with breaking Mo-S linkages or missing Br atoms at the vertex of the $[Mo_6S_4Br_4]$ by comparing to the atomic structure of $Mo_6S_3Br_6$, shown in Figure I.4g. Point defects of missing Br atoms are found as well in other STM images shown in Figure I.4d (not in Figure I.4a) with the structure model laying on top of it. These defects can be introduced into the crystals intrinsically during the synthetic process or on the surface induced by the stress during exfoliation. Defects types could be even more complex and their effects on the electronic structure are reflected on the broad peak appeared in the band gap.

I.4 Raman tensor determination

Since $Mo_6S_3Br_6$ belongs to the orthorhombic crystal system with *Cmcm* space group (No.63), there are 45 Raman active modes ($13A_g + 11\,B_g + 9\,B_{2g} + 12\,B_{3g}$), among which 25 modes ($13A_g + 12\,B_{3g}$) are detectable in the backscattering geometry we used. 15 out of 25 Raman modes are resolved and assigned to A_g or B_{3g} mode based on DFT calculations (Table I3) The simulated nonresonant Raman spectrum is shown in Figure I.5 as a reference.

The Raman tensor of each mode can be written as:

$$\overleftrightarrow{R}_{A_g} = \begin{bmatrix} a & 0 & 0 \\ 0 & b & 0 \\ 0 & 0 & c \end{bmatrix}, \qquad \overleftrightarrow{R}_{B_{3g}} = \begin{bmatrix} 0 & 0 & 0 \\ 0 & 0 & f \\ 0 & f^* & 0 \end{bmatrix}.$$

Where a,b,c,f are the complex Raman tensors. Experiments are performed in a backscattering geometry where the incident light is aligned with the normal of the sample, i.e, *a*-axis, and the angle θ is the angle between the polarization of the light and the *c*-axis of the sample. The incident light vector is $\hat{e}_i = (0, sin\theta, cos\theta)$ and the scattering light vector is $\hat{e}_s = (0, sin\theta, cos\theta)$ for parallel-polarized configuration and $\hat{e}_s = (0, cos\theta, -sin\theta)$ for cross-polarized configuration. Raman cross-section is determined by:

$$S_k = \left| \hat{e}_i \cdot \overleftrightarrow{R}_k \cdot \hat{e}_s \right|^2 \tag{1}$$

As a result, Raman cross-sections of A_g and B_{3g} modes follow

$$S_{A_g,\parallel} = (|b|\sin^2\theta + |c|\cos\phi\cos^2\theta)^2 + |c|^2\sin^2\phi\cos^4\theta \tag{2}$$

$$S_{A_g,\perp} = ((|b| - |c|\cos\phi)^2 + |c|^2\sin^2\phi)\,sin^2\theta\cos^2\theta \tag{3}$$

$$S_{B_{3g},\parallel} = (|f|\,sin\,2\theta)^2 \tag{4}$$

$$S_{B_{3g},\perp} = (|f|\,cos\,2\theta)^2 \tag{5}$$

where $\phi = Arg(c) - Arg(a) - \phi_{cyrstal}$. It gives A_g mode two-fold symmetry for parallel polarization and four-fold symmetry for cross polarization, while B_{3g} mode four-fold symmetry in both configurations. There are additional tensors for Raman active modes of B_{1g} and B_{2g}, given as:

$$\overset{\leftrightarrow}{R}_{B_{1g}} = \begin{bmatrix} 0 & d & 0 \\ d^* & 0 & 0 \\ 0 & 0 & 0 \end{bmatrix}, \qquad \overset{\leftrightarrow}{R}_{B_{2g}} = \begin{bmatrix} 0 & 0 & e \\ 0 & 0 & 0 \\ e^* & 0 & 0 \end{bmatrix}.$$

However, they are not experimentally detectable as $S_{B_{1g},\parallel} = S_{B_{1g},\perp} = S_{B_{2g},\parallel} = S_{B_{2g},\perp} = 0$.

By fitting both parallel and cross polarized Raman spectra simultaneously, we obtained Raman tensor elements and the phase factor. The fitting agrees well with the experimental results, as shown in Figure I.6 with their corresponding nuclear motions. $|c|^2/|b|^2$ reflects the Raman anisotropy in the bc-plane and the fitted values of $|c|/|b|$ for A_g modes are listed in Table I4.

Figure I.1. Optical image of a $Mo_6S_3Br_6$ single crystal (marked by the white margin) on the SC-XRD mount. The different lattice axes are shown in red.

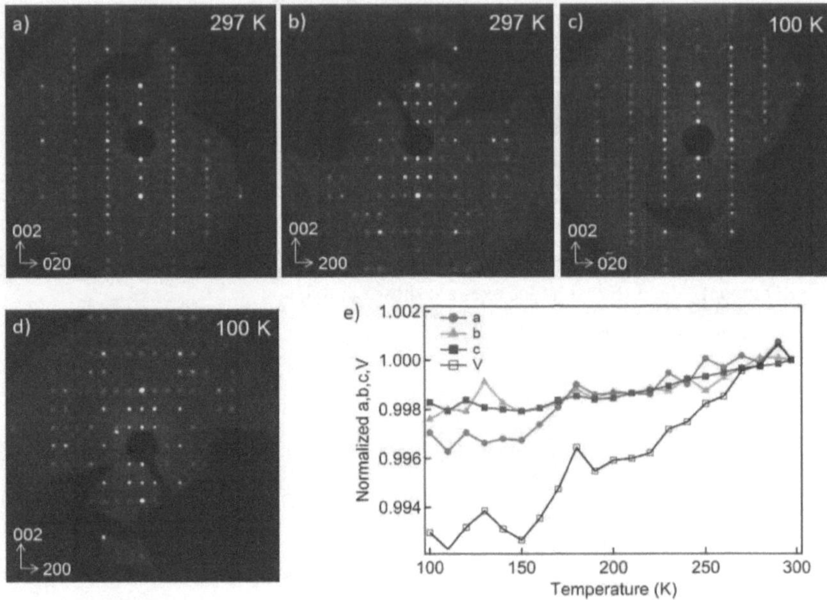

Figure I.2 single crystal X-ray diffraction patterns of crystal Mo$_6$S$_3$Br$_6$. a) b) Room temperature (297 K) patterns on the (100) plane and (010) plane, respectively. It confirms the orthorhombic structure with space group *Cmcm* of this crystal, in agreement with previous results. c) d) Low temperature (100 K) patterns on the (100) plane and (010) plane, respectively. It indicates that the crystal maintains the orthorhombic phase in the temperature range of 100 – 297 K. e) Temperature-dependent lattice parameters (normalized a, b, c and unit volume) of the orthorhombic Mo$_6$S$_3$Br$_6$. Lattice shrinking (~ 0.4%) at lower temperature is due to thermal effects.

Table I1. Selected crystallographic data

Formula	$Mo_6S_3Br_6$	
MW	1151.3	
Space group	*Cmcm*	
Z	4	
T (K)	297	100
a (Å)	17.267	17.217
b (Å)	6.5823	6.5666
c (Å)	11.899	11.8784
α (°)	89.991	89.983
β (°)	90.172	90.15
γ (°)	90.244	89.909
V (Å^3)	1352.4	1342.9
ρ_{calc} (g cm^{-3})	5.656	5.700

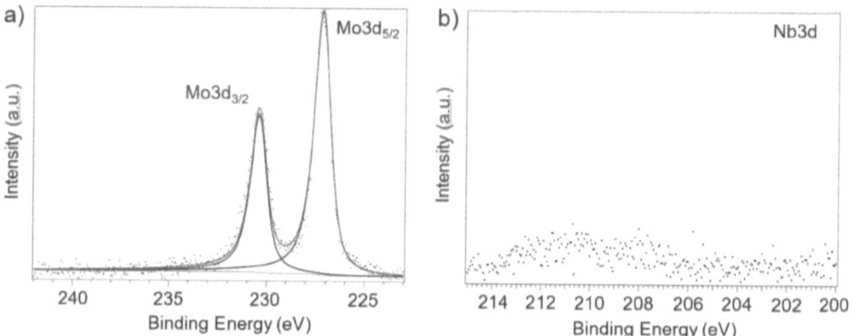

Figure I.3. XPS spectra in (a) Mo3d and (b) Nb3d regions for $Mo_6S_3Br_6$ single crystals

Table I2. Elemental composition as determined from EDX spectroscopy

Element	Atomic Ratio
Mo	6.0
S	2.6
Br	5.6

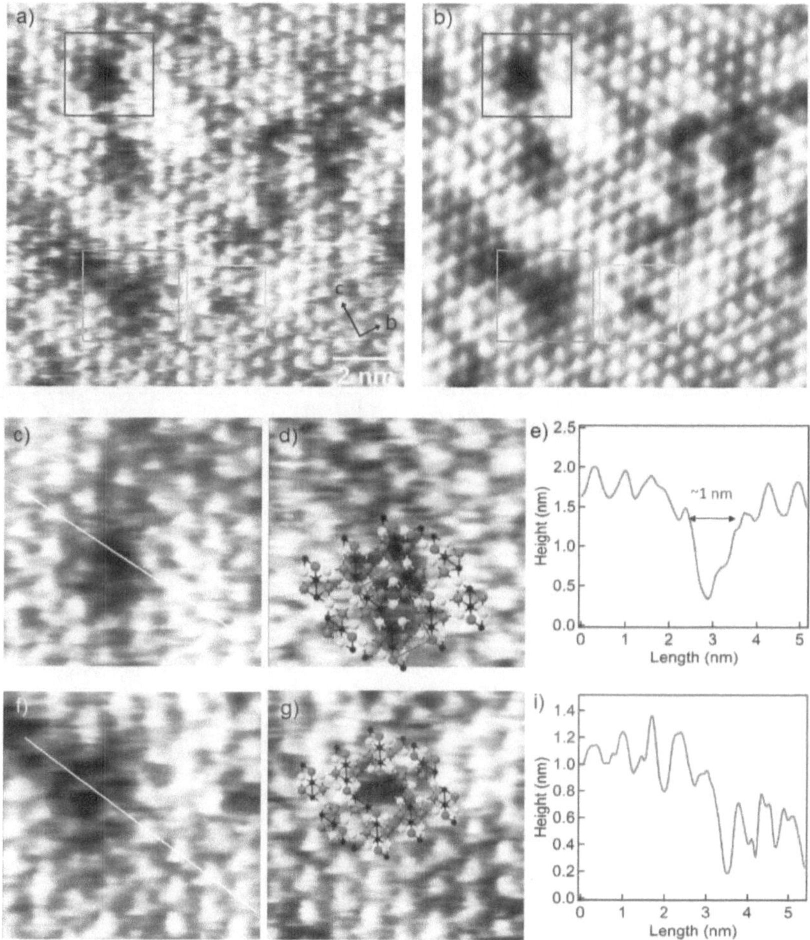

Figure I.4 surface defects characterized by STM. a) STM image of $Mo_6S_3Br_6$ at 298 K on a defective surface (12 x 12 nm, U = 1.6 V, I = 60 pA). b) Filtered image of a) from fast Fourier transform. Three types of defects are marked with rectangular boxes. c) missing entire clusters on the top layer. d) missing bridging Br atoms on the top layer with atomic structure sitting on top of it. e) line profile along the white line in a) showing a striking height drop. f) defects underneath the bridging Br atoms with lower apparent height compared to their neighboring atoms. g) incomplete clusters with no Mo-S linkages or Br atoms at the at the vertex of the $[Mo_6S_4Br_4]$. i) line profile along the white line in f).

Table I3. Calculated (Cal.) frequencies and phonon modes at Γ point of the 3D bulk by using the LDA functional and their assignments with experimental (Exp.) detected Raman peaks. Red color highlights the peaks resolved in the calculated nonresonant Raman spectrum.

	Exp. (cm^{-1})	Cal. (cm^{-1})	Symmetry			Exp. (cm^{-1})	Cal. (cm^{-1})	Symmetry
1	104.9	108.7	B$_{3g}$		8	234.1	230.5	A$_g$
2	119.7	122.0	B$_{3g}$		9	253.4	253.0	A$_g$
3	126.1	132.3	A$_g$		10	285.7	282.1	A$_g$
4	139.3	138.4	A$_g$		11	301.7	299.0	A$_g$
5	169.7	170.8	A$_g$		12	314.0	313.0	A$_g$
6	181.3	179.5	A$_g$		13	323.5	328.4	A$_g$
		221.3	A$_g$		14	345.6	345.7	A$_g$
7	219.3	221.4	B$_{3g}$		15	421.2	424.1	A$_g$

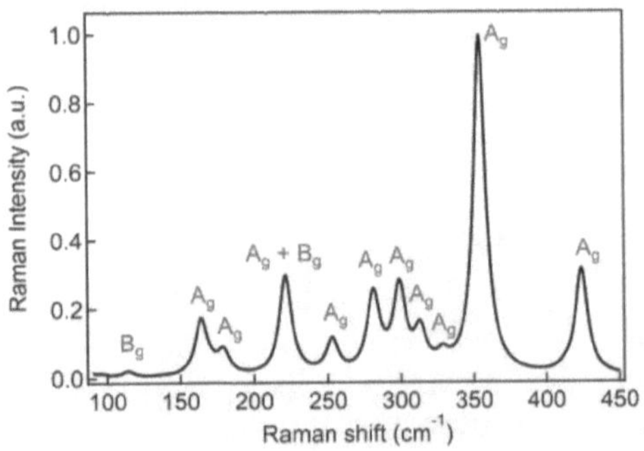

Figure I.5. DFT calculated nonresonant Raman spectrum of bulk Mo$_6$S$_3$Br$_6$.

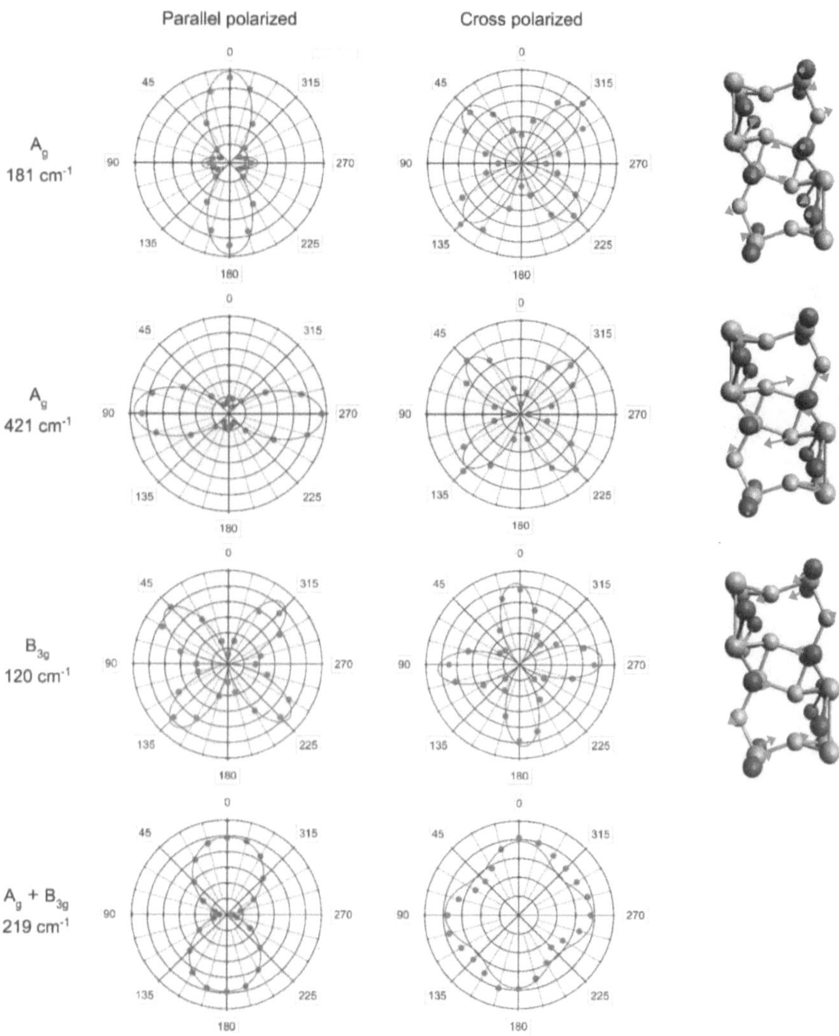

Figure I6. Representative angle-resolved Raman spectra in parallel polarized (left) and cross polarized (middle) configurations with their corresponding nuclear motions (right).

Table I4. Fitted values of $|c|/|b|$ for A_g modes

Wave number (cm^{-1})	$|c|/|b|$
126.1	2.76
181.3	2.05
219.3	3.62
301.7	0.36
323.5	0.71
345.6	0.66
421.2	0.41

Appendix J: Additional Data for Chapter 11

J.1 Methods

J.1.1 Sample preparation

See Chapter 2 for more details $Mo_6S_3Br_6$ was prepared using the same methods as described in
Appendix I.1.1.

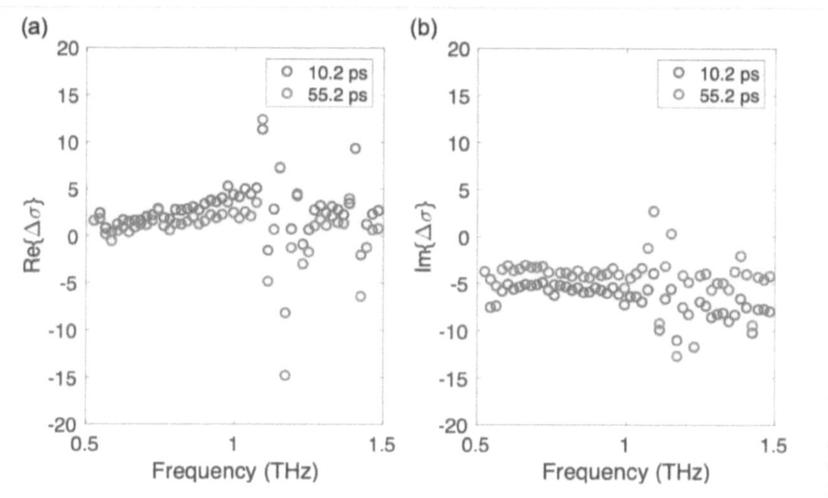

Figure J1. The real **(A)** and the imaginary **(B)** parts of the complex photoconductivity spectra of
$Re_2Se_8Cl_2$ obtained at the time delay of t = 10 ps (blue) and 55 ps (orange) after 800 nm
excitation at 84 K. The amplitudes decrease without changing the lineshape.

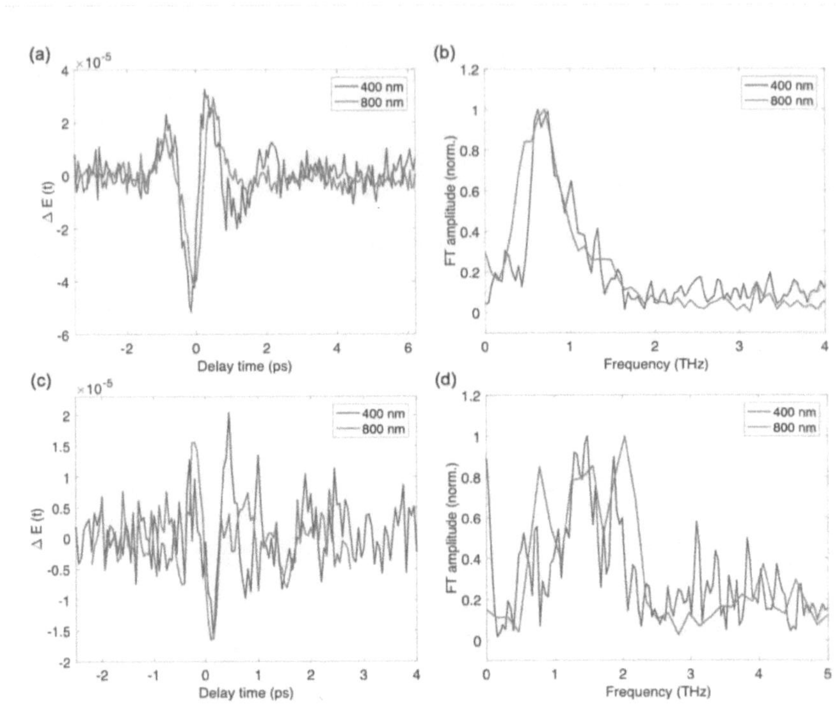

Figure J2. The pump-induced THz generation/emission observed in Re₆Se₈Cl₂ (a, b) and Mo₆S₃Br₆ (c, d) after both 400 and 800 nm pump pulses. These THz responses were detected in time domain (a, c) without the incident probe THz pulses and were Fourier transformed (b, d). The spectra of the emitted THz pulses after excitation of 800 nm and 400 nm are identical.

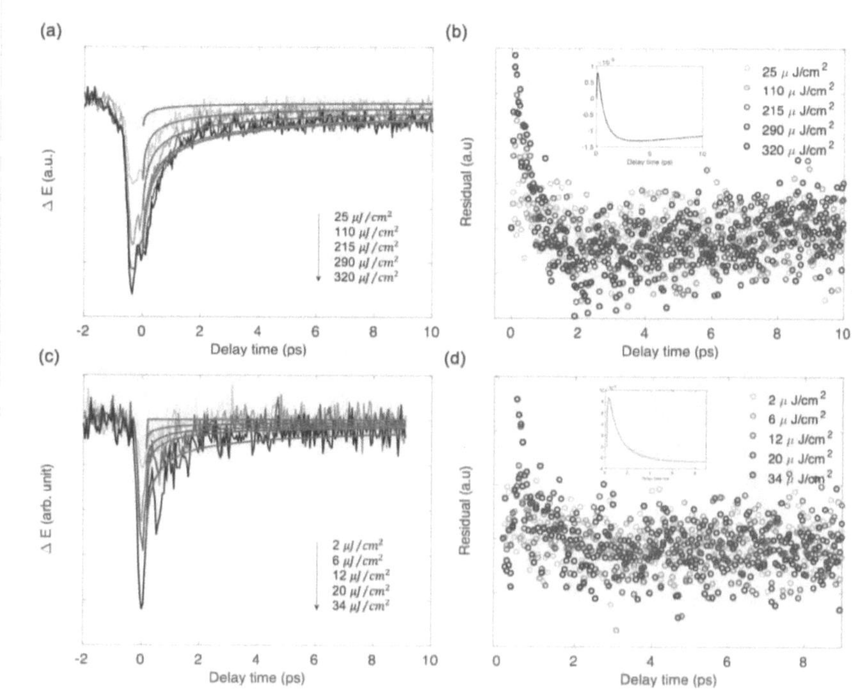

Figure J3. The cubic dependence model fits with one-dimensional pump scans acquired from $Mo_6S_3Br_6$ for 800 nm (a) and the residua (b). Inset of (b) depicts the difference a cubic and a quadratic dependence model with parameters: $k_3 = 1.4 \times 10^{-27}$ for a cubic dependence and $k_2 = 4.6 \times 10^{-8}$ for a quadratic dependence. The cubic dependence model fits with one-dimensional pump scans acquired from $Mo_6S_3Br_6$ for 400 nm (c) and the residua (d). Inset of (d) depicts the difference a cubic and a quadratic dependence model with parameters: $k_3 = 3.5 \times 10^{-26}$ for a cubic dependence and $k_2 = 1.5 \times 10^{-7}$ for a quadratic dependence.

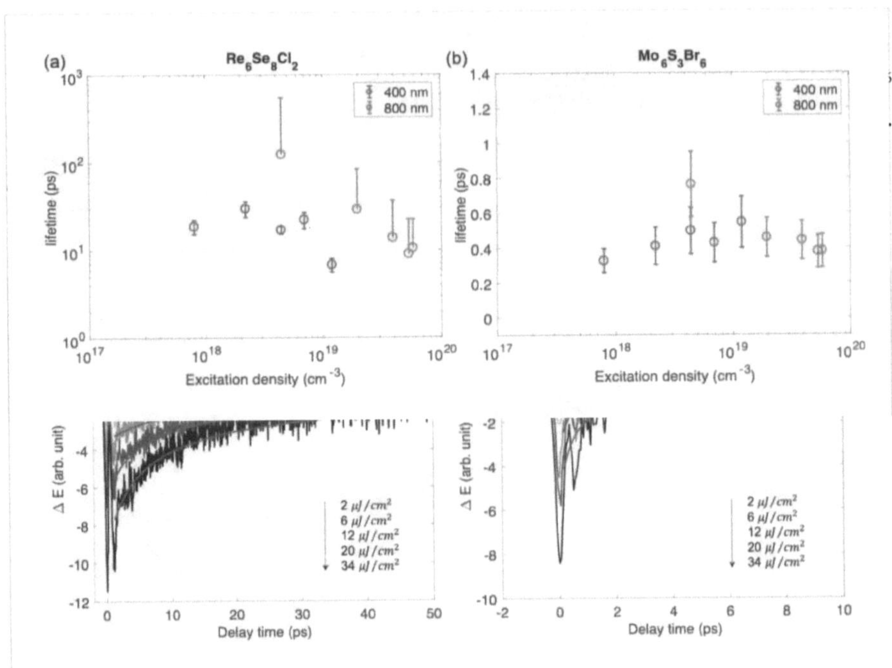

Figure J4. One-dimensional pump scans acquired from Re$_6$Se$_8$Cl$_2$ (a) and Mo$_6$S$_3$Br$_6$ (b) for 400 nm excitation with different pump-fluences. The red curves are the fitted model of cubic (a) and quadratic (b) dependences on the carrier density.

J.2 References

1. X. Zhong, K. Lee, B. Choi, D. Meggiolaro, F. Liu, C. Nuckolls, A. Pasupathy, F. De Angelis, P. Batail, X. Roy, and X. Zhu, Nano Lett. **18**, 1483 (2018).
2. X. Zhong, K. Lee, D. Meggiolaro, A. H. Dismukes, B. Choi, F. Wang, C. Nuckolls, D. W. Paley, P. Batail, F. De Angelis, X. Roy, and X. Y. Zhu, Adv. Funct. Mater. **1902951**, 1 (2019).
3. A. McAllister, D. Bayerl, and E. Kioupakis, Appl. Phys. Lett. **112**, 1 (2018).

Appendix K: Additional Data for Chapter 12

K.1 Experimental Methods

K.1.1 Synthesis of α-TaFeTe$_4$

See Chapter 2 for more details.

K.1.2 Conversion of α-TaFeTe$_4$ into β-TaFeTe$_4$

See Chapter 2 for more details. The conversion of α-TaFeTe$_4$ to β-TaFeTe$_4$ does not occur to completion but single-crystal X-ray diffraction confirms partial conversion (see **Table K2** and **K3**).

K.1.3 α-TaFeTe$_4$ Exfoliation

Crystals of α-TaFeTe$_4$ were mechanically exfoliated using Scotch brand Magic tape. Single crystals of α-TaFeTe$_4$ were cleaved along the stacking axis 5-6 times using Magic tape before flakes were transferred using Magic tape to Si/SiO$_2$ chips that had been pre-cleaned under O$_2$ plasma for 5 minutes prior to transfer. The flake exfoliation and transfer processes were performed under ambient conditions without heating.

K.1.4 SCXRD

Single-crystal X-ray diffraction data were collected using an Agilent SuperNova X-ray diffractometer configured in a four-circle kappa goniometer geometry. The diffractometer is equipped with a low-temperature device and a mirror-monochromated microfocus Cu source (λ = 1.54187 Å). X-ray intensities were measured at 85 K, 95 K, or room temperature with the Titan

CCD detector placed ~34-42 mm from the sample. The data were processed with CrysAlisPro (Oxford) and corrected for absorption. The structures were determined in OLEX2[1] using SHELXT[2] and refined using SHELXL[3]. All atoms in the structures collected before heating the sample were refined anisotropically. Single crystals were mounted on a 150 μm MiTeGen MicroMount using Paratone oil.

K.1.5 Atomic Force Microscopy

AFM images were acquired in PeakForce QNM in scanning mode using a Bruker Dimension FastScan AFM under ambient conditions and at room temperature. Height profiles were analyzed and extracted from the AFM images using Gwyddion.

K.1.6 SQUID Magnetometry

DC magnetic susceptibility was measured in a Cryogenic R-700 X SQUID magnetometer. The sample mass was on the order of 8 mg and was prepared in ambient conditions by encapsulation in Scotch Magic Tape with care taken to ensure air could escape from the sample space and mounted to the inside of a gel capsule with an additional piece of tape. This set-up allowed alignment of the sample for orientation-dependent measurements. Once loaded inside of the gel capsule, the capsule was punctured to ensure no air would remain in the sample upon evacuation. Temperature and magnetic field were monitored for stability at each data point.

K.1.7 X-ray Photoelectron Spectroscopy

XPS spectra were measured using a PHI Versaprobe II X-ray photoelectron spectroscope with a Mg or Al source and controlled by the PHI SmartSoft user interface. Single crystals of α-

TaFeTe$_4$ were adhered to the XPS sample holder using double-sided Scotch tape and the surface exfoliated immediately before loading the sample into the XPS. A survey scan was measured from 0 eV to 1100 eV with a 1 eV step width. The Ta4f (4 scans of 17 eV to 37 eV with a 0.1250 eV step width), Te3d5 (1 scan of 567 eV to 587 eV with a 0.1250 eV step width), Fe 2p3 (10 scans of 702 eV to 727 eV with a 0.1250 eV step width), and C1s (1 scan of 278 eV to 298 eV with a 0.250 eV step width) regions were also collected. Background subtraction, shift calibration, peak fitting, and integration were performed using the MultiPak Spectrum software package offered by PHI.

K.1.8 Transport Device Fabrication

Exfoliated α-TaFeTe$_4$ single crystals were bonded to a glass cover slide using low-temperature non-conducting epoxy (Loctite EA 1C). Direct electrical connections to the sample were made by hand with Ga-In eutectic and 25 µm diameter 99.99% gold wire. This sample set-up was then loaded into a 16-pin DIP socket and the 25 µm gold wire connected to the gold contact pads with silver paint (Dupont 4929N). Large enough crystals were selected to paint four parallel contact pads each for both orientations of the in-plane transport measurements.

K.1.9 Transport Measurements

Resistance was measured as the voltage between two inner contacts using a nanovoltmeter while sourcing 1 mA of current using a current amplifier from the two outer contacts in a four-parallel contact configuration. Variable temperatures between 15 K and 300 K were achieved in a Janis continuous-flow He low-temperature system. All transport measurements were performed at zero magnetic field.

K.1.10 Variable-Temperature Heat Capacity Measurements

Heat capacity was measured using the Heat Capacity module of the Quantum Design PPMS VersaLab. Multiple single crystals of α-TaFeTe$_4$ were adhered to the heat capacity measurement puck using low temperature grease. The sample heat capacity was calculated from the difference in heat capacity between the C_P measurement of the sample and grease and the C_P measurement of the grease. Variable temperatures between 80 and 100 K were achieved by the Quantum Design cryogen free cryocooler and controlled using the Quantum Design Multi-VU software. All heat capacity measurements were performed at zero magnetic field.

K.2 Table of Crystallographic Parameters

Table K1. Crystallographic data tables for α-TaFeTe$_4$

Crystal	α-TaFeTe4 – 85 K	α-TaFeTe$_4$ – 95 K	α-TaFeTe$_4$ – 295 K
CCDC Code			
Formula mass	593.79(8)	593.79(8)	593.79(8)
Color, habit	Metallic grey	Metallic grey	Metallic grey
Crystal system	Monoclinic	Monoclinic	Monoclinic
Space group	*I2/m*	*I2/m*	*I2/m*
Z	4	4	4
a (Å)	12.4196(12)	12.4128(10)	12.4547(10)
b (Å)	3.6348(3)	3.6295(2)	3.6507(2)
c (Å)	13.9435(16)	13.9234(12)	13.9661(10)
α (°)	90	90	90
β (°)	110.670(12)	110.758(9)	110.756(8)
γ (°)	90	90	90
Temperature (K)	85(1)	95(1)	295(1)
Volume (Å^3)	588.93(11)	586.561	593.802
D_{calc} (g / cm^3)	8.427	8.461	8.358
Radiation	Cu Kα = 1.54184	Cu Kα = 1.54184	Cu Kα = 1.54184
R_1/wR_2	5.46/15.29	3.84/7.46	2.91/6.22
Goodness-of-fit	1.165	1.040	1.033
Shortest Fe-Te (Å)	2.609	2.613	2.618
Shortest Fe-Fe (Å)	3.635	3.630	3.651
Shortest Te-Te (Å)*	3.253	3.256	3.272

*interplanar Te-Te interaction

Table K2. Full crystallographic data for a TaFeTe$_4$ crystal after heating to 450 °C solved in $I2/m$ and $Pmn2_1$

Crystal	α-TaFeTe4 – 295 K	β-TaFeTe4 – 295 K
Formula mass	593.79(8)	593.79(8)
Color, habit	Metallic grey	Metallic grey
Spots Indexed (%)	17.17	35.65
R_{int} (%)	12.64	10.09
Crystal system	Monoclinic	Orthorhombic
Space group	$I2/m$	$Pmn2_1$
Z	4	4
a (Å)	12.424(11)	3.6460(10)
b (Å)	3.636(2)	12.405(3)
c (Å)	13.992(15)	13.143(3)
α (°)	90	90
β (°)	111.55(11)	90
γ (°)	90	90
Temperature (K)	295(1)	295(1)
Volume (Å^3)	587.9(10)	594.5(3)
D_{calc} (g / cm^3)	8.442	8.350
Radiation	Cu Kα = 1.54184	Cu Kα = 1.54184
R_1/wR_2	50.50/82.57	30.00/63.74
Goodness-of-fit	5.107	2.639
Shortest Fe-Te (Å)	2.864	2.952
Shortest Fe-Fe (Å)	3.636	3.646
Shortest Te-Te (Å)*	3.748	3.717

*interplanar Te-Te interaction

Table K3. Crystallographic data for a TaFeTe$_4$ crystal after heating to 450 °C solved in $I2/m$ and

$$Pmn2_1$$

Crystal	Sample 1	Sample 2	Sample 3
Before Annealing			
Laue Class	$2/m$	$2/m$	$2/m$
a (Å)	12.43(3)	12.429(11)	12.38(3)
b (Å)	3.261(7)	3.6443(16)	3.665(3)
c (Å)	14.08(3)	13.996(15)	14.08(3)
β (°)	111.2(9)	110.59(12)	111.2(3)
Volume (Å^3)	591(2)	593.5(9)	596(2)
After Annealing			
Percent Fitted Peaks	36.3%	35.3%	42.0%
Laue Class	$2/m$	$2/m$	$2/m$
a (Å)	12.4439	12.4425	12.4127
b (Å)	3.6356	3.6394	3.6714
c (Å)	14.1701	13.9954	13.8521
β (°)	111.535	110.369	110.827
Volume (Å^3)	596.2	594.1	589.7
Percent Fitted Peaks	63.7%	64.7%	58.0%
Laue Class	$mm2$	$mm2$	$mm2$
a (Å)	3.6464	3.6397	3.6945
b (Å)	12.4366	12.4460	12.4286
c (Å)	13.1486	13.1251	13.2202
β (°)	90	90	90
Volume (Å^3)	596.2	594.4	606.8

K.3 ORTEP for α-TaFeTe₄

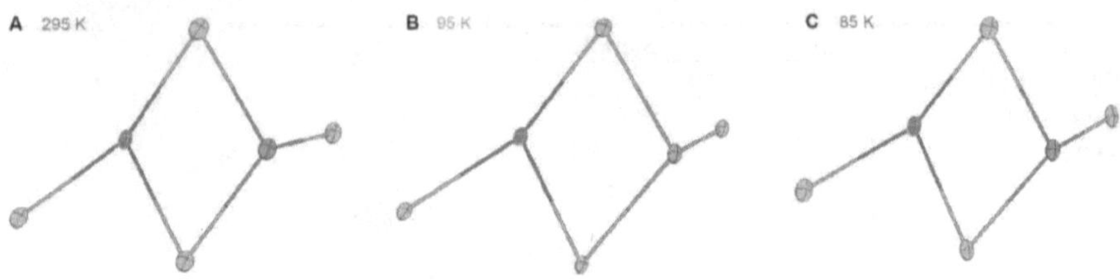

Figure K1 ORTEP Diagrams for α-TaFeTe₄. ORTEP diagram for α-TaFeTe₄ collected at (**A**) 295 K, (**B**) 95 K, and (**C**) 85 K with thermal ellipsoids of 50% probability.

K.4. Crystal Packing Comparison for α-TaFeTe₄ and β-TaFeTe₄ After Heating to 450 °C

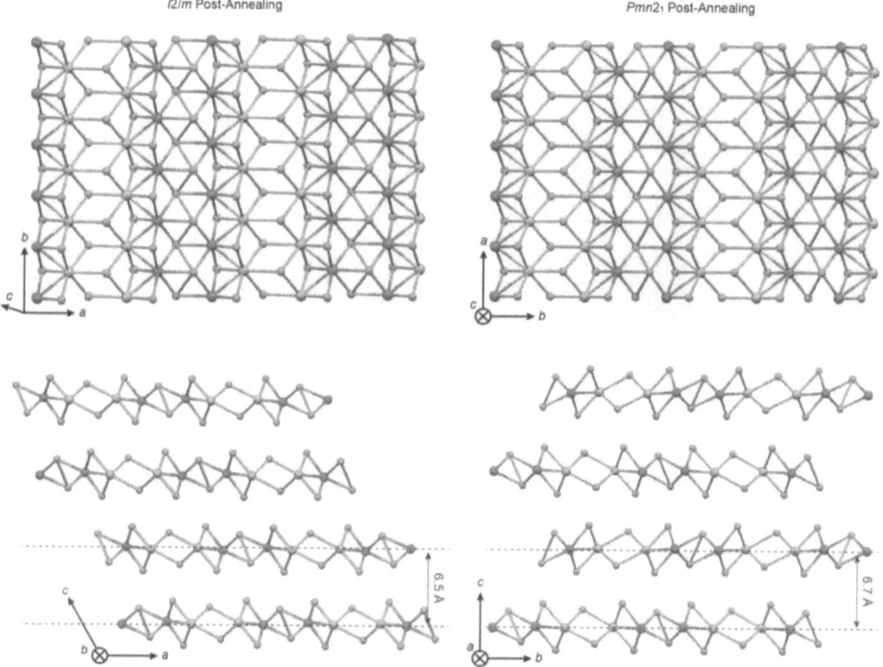

Figure K2. Crystal Packing Diagrams for α-TaFeTe₄ and β-TaFeTe₄. (Left) Views parallel and perpendicular to the stacking axis of the crystal structure solved at room temperature for α-TaFeTe₄ (*I2/m*) following thermal annealing. **(Right)** Views parallel and perpendicular to the stacking axis of the crystal structure solved at room temperature for β-TaFeTe₄ (*Pmn2₁*) following thermal annealing. For both structures, red spheres indicate Fe atoms, blue spheres represent Ta atoms, and gold spheres are Te atoms. The dashed lines indicate mean planes calculated for a sheet of metal atoms and the interplanar spacing is calculated as the distance between the mean plane and the average centroid calculated for the plane of atoms on the neighboring sheets.

K.5 Crystal Packing Comparison for α-TaFeTe₄ measured at 85 K and 95 K

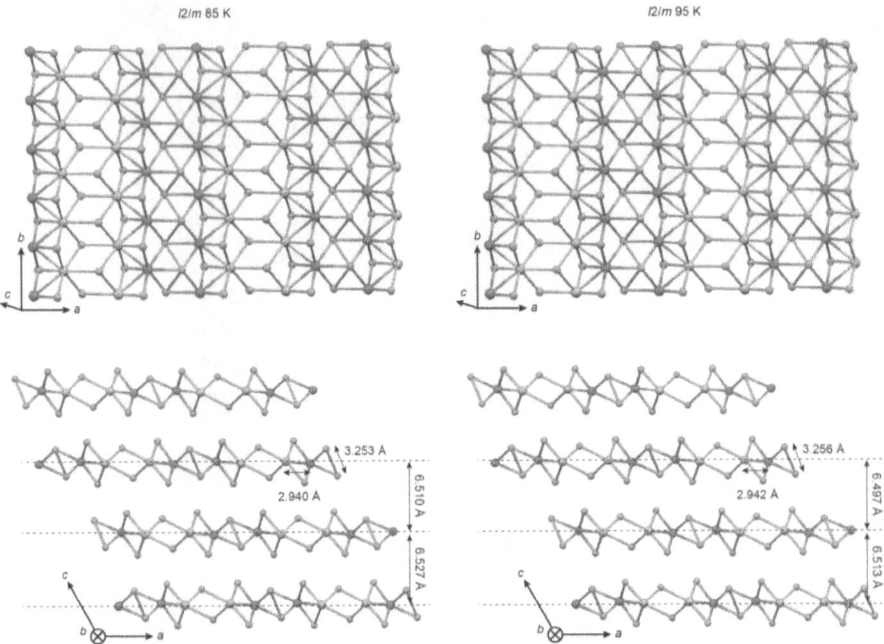

Figure K3. Crystal Packing Diagrams for α-TaFeTe₄. (Left) Views parallel and perpendicular to the stacking axis of the crystal structure solved at 95 K for α-TaFeTe₄ (*I2/m*). **(Right)** Views parallel and perpendicular to the stacking axis of the crystal structure solved at 85 K for β-TaFeTe₄ (*Pmn2₁*). For both structures, red spheres indicate Fe atoms, blue spheres represent Ta atoms, and gold spheres are Te atoms. The dashed lines indicate mean planes calculated for a sheet of metal atoms and the interplanar spacing is calculated as the distance between the mean plane and the average centroid calculated for the plane of atoms on the neighboring sheets.

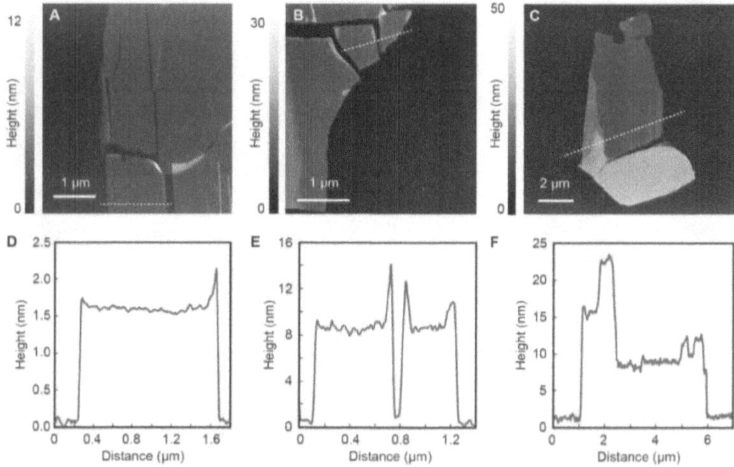

Figure K4. AFM Images of Exfoliated α-TaFeTe₄ Flakes. (A-C) AFM images of exfoliated α-TaFeTe₄ flakes of various thicknesses on Si/SiO₂; (**D-E**) height profile measurements for line cuts through the AFM images indicated by a white dotted line. A single layer of α-TaFeTe₄ is about ~8 Å as measured from the SCXRD crystal structure, indicating that image **A** and profile **D** is an α-TaFeTe₄ bilayer, image **B** and profile **E** is ten layers, and image **C** and profile **F** contains 10-28 layers.

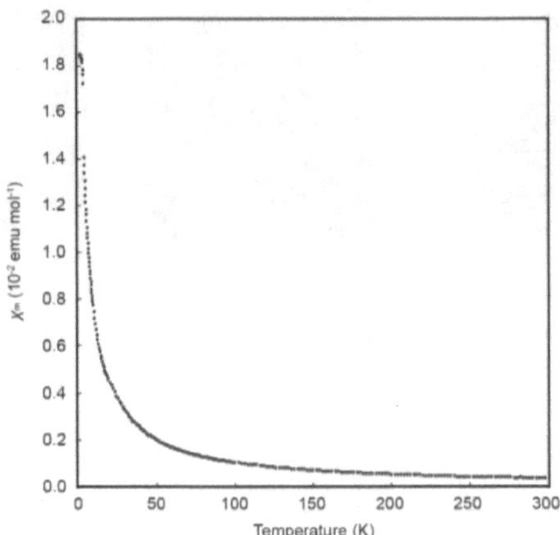

Figure K5. Zero-Field- and Field-Cooled χ-T Traces for α-TaFeTe₄. DC zero-fieldχ-T trace for α-TaFeTe₄ collected at 0.3 T with the magnetic field aligned in-plane. No features are present in the χ-T trace at 93 K that would indicate a change in magnetic ordering associated with the feature present in the transport curve.

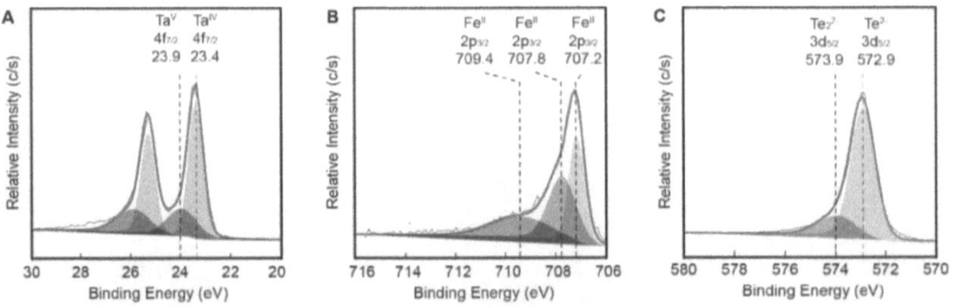

Figure K6. XPS Spectra for α-TaFeTe₄. XPS spectra for α-TaFeTe₄ focused on the (**A**) Ta4f, (**B**) Te3d5, and (**C**) Fe 2p3 regions. The black line indicates the data trace, while the red line indicates the sum of the fitted peaks. The characteristic peak in the C1s spectrum was used as a shift standard and the peaks in the Ta4f (doublet), Te3d5, and Fe 2p3 regions were assigned using NIST standards. The presence of Ta^V is consistent with surface oxidation of the material. The Fe^{II} peak at 709.4 eV is consistent with a change in coordination environment from octahedral to tetrahedral.

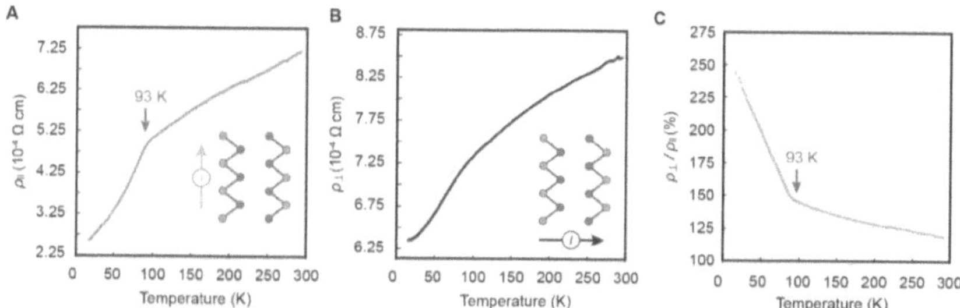

Figure K7. In-plane ρ-T Plots for α-TaFeTe₄. In-plane ρ-T plots measured for the same crystal of α-TaFeTe₄ both (**A**) parallel and (**B**) perpendicular to the Ta-Fe zigzag chains using a four-parallel contact method; (**C**) the in-plane ρ anisotropy ratio calculated as $\rho_\perp/\rho_\parallel$ measured as a function of temperature.

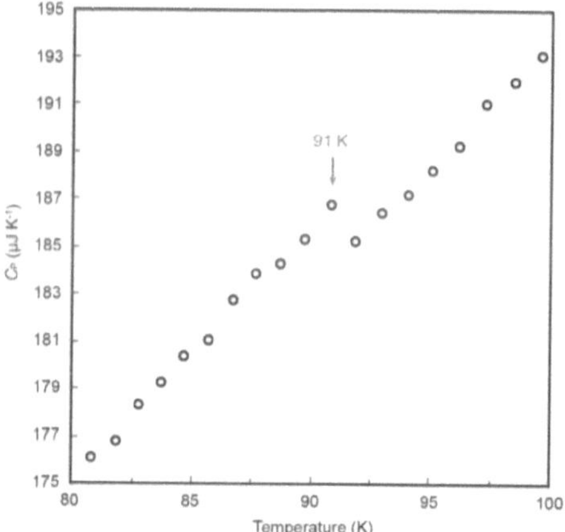

Figure K8. Heat Capacity Measurements for α-TaFeTe₄. Heat capacity (C_P) measured as a function of temperature for α-TaFeTe₄, confirming that the feature present in the transport measurement is associated with a change in heat capacity for the sample, consistent with a charge-transfer event.

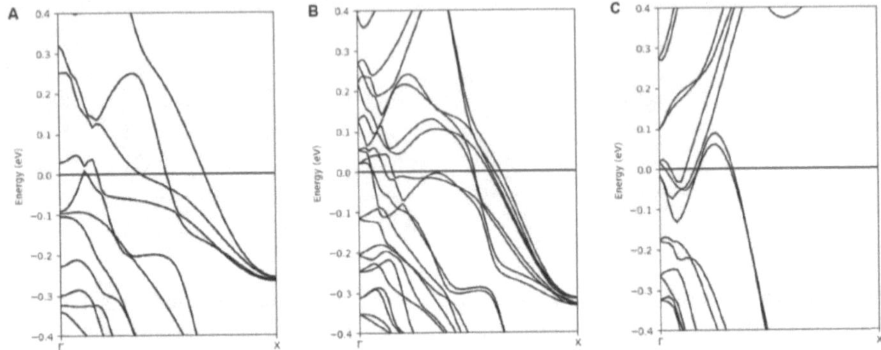

Figure K9. Electronic Band Structure Calculations for α-TaFeTe₄, β-TaFeTe₄, and TaIrTe₄.
Electronic band structures calculated for (**A**) α-TaFeTe₄, (**B**) β-TaFeTe₄, and (**C**) TaIrTe₄ based on X-ray crystal structures measured at room temperature. The electronic band structures are projected along the high-symmetry lines along which the Weyl nodes are observed (Γ-X).

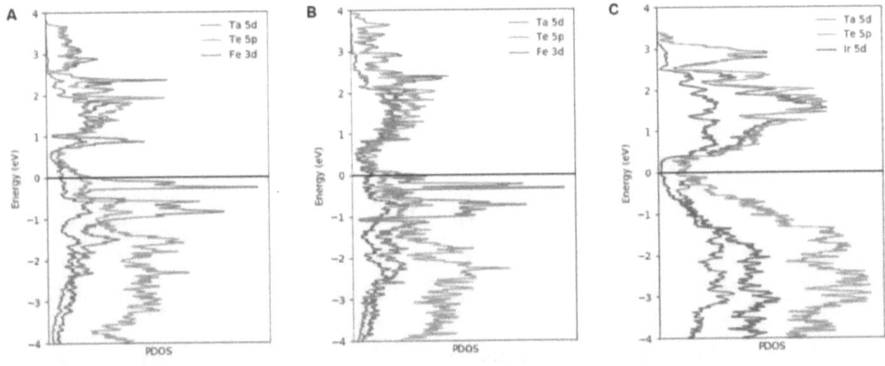

Figure K10. Projected Density of States for α-TaFeTe₄, β-TaFeTe₄, and TaIrTe₄. The projected density of states (PDOS) for (**A**) α-TaFeTe₄, (**B**) β-TaFeTe₄, and (**C**) TaIrTe₄ based on X-ray crystal structures measured at room temperature. The PDOS highlight the states introduced at/near the Fermi energy by the Fe 3d orbitals.

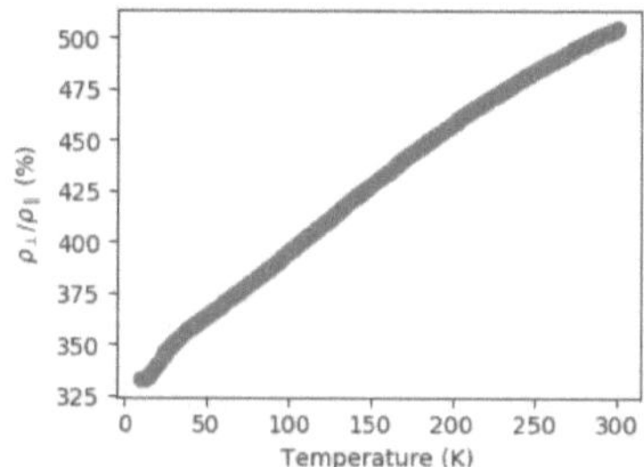

Figure K11 Calculated resistivity anisotropy. Qualitative approximation of the resistivity anisotropy for α-TaFeTe₄ as it evolves with temperature, predicting strong transport anisotropy at room temperature. The calculations were carried out using BoltzTrap[4] with the relaxation time assumed to be constant.

K.6 References

1. Dolomanov, O. V.; Bourhis, L. J.; Gildea, R. J.; Howard, J. K.; Puschmann, H. *J. Appl. Cryst.* **2009**, *42*, 339-341.
2. Sheldrick, G. M. *Acta Cryst.* **2015**, *C71*, 3-8.
3. Sheldrick, G. M. *Acta Cryst.* **2015**, *A71*, 3-8.
4. Madsen, G. K. H; Singh, D. J. *Comut. Phys. Commun.* **2006**, *175*, 67-71.